AF600260

The First Chief Justice

SUNY series in American Constitutionalism

Robert J. Spitzer, editor

The First Chief Justice

John Jay and the Struggle of a New Nation

MARK C. DILLON

Cover: *Portrait of John Jay* (1794) by artist Gilbert Stuart

Published by State University of New York Press, Albany

© 2022 State University of New York

All rights reserved

Printed in the United States of America

No part of this book may be used or reproduced in any manner whatsoever without written permission. No part of this book may be stored in a retrieval system or transmitted in any form or by any means including electronic, electrostatic, magnetic tape, mechanical, photocopying, recording, or otherwise without the prior permission in writing of the publisher.

For information, contact State University of New York Press, Albany, NY
www.sunypress.edu

Library of Congress Cataloging-in-Publication Data

Name: Dillon, Mark C., author.
Title: The first Chief Justice : John Jay and the struggle of a new nation / Mark C. Dillon.
Description: Albany : State University of New York Press, 2022. | Series: SUNY series in American constitutionalism | Includes bibliographical references and index.
Identifiers: LCCN 2021049679 (print) | LCCN 2021049680 (ebook) | ISBN 9781438487854 (hardcover : alk. paper) | ISBN 9781438487878 (ebook)
Subjects: LCSH: United States. Supreme Court—History. | United States. Supreme Court—Cases—History. | Jay, John, 1745–1829. | Judges—United States—Biography. | United States. Supreme Court—Officials and employees—Biography. | United States—Politics and government—1775–1783. | United States—Politics and government—1783–1809. | New York (State)—Politics and government—To 1775.
Classification: LCC KF8742 .D55 2022 (print) | LCC KF8742 (ebook) | DDC 347.73/2634—dc23/eng/20211220
LC record available at https://lccn.loc.gov/2021049679
LC ebook record available at https://lccn.loc.gov/2021049680

10 9 8 7 6 5 4 3 2 1

This book is inscribed to my father, attorney William V. Dillon,
and my grandfather, Justice John J. Dillon.
Both men were the salutatorians of their classes at
Fordham University School of Law,
both were assets to the courts of the State of New York,
and both made their careers in
John Jay's home county of Westchester.
They would enjoy this book were they still with us today.

Contents

Illustrations

Preface

I visited the John Jay Homestead in Bedford, New York, when I was approximately nine years old, with my mother, brother, and sister. I remember few of the details of the time spent there, other than there was a large white house with expansive lawns, and it was a hot sunny day. Little did I know that five decades later, I would select the judicial career and cases of John Jay as a topic for a book of legal history.

This is my second book exploring the intersection of history and law. The first book was *Montana Vigilantes 1863–1870: Gold, Guns & Gallows*. The challenges in selecting a topic for any history book are threefold. First, the topic should be of interest to potential readers. Second, the author must present a new insight or approach to the topic that has not been done before; otherwise, there is no point to the project in the first instance. And third, the topic must be one that the author finds fascinating, as the undertaking of any serious book project requires considerable time, expense, attention to detail, patience, and commitment by its author. Fortunately for me, the Supreme Court career of Chief Justice John Jay fit neatly into my self-imposed criteria. I returned to the John Jay Homestead on February 17, 2018, with my wife, Michele, approximately fifty years after my childhood visit there, to confirm in my mind the underpinnings of this book.

The concept and structure of this book are unique. This is not intended as a biography of John Jay's life. Other books have already covered that topic and have done so very capably, particularly Walter Stahr's *John Jay: Founding Father*, for its completeness and detail. This is not a book intended to generally recount American history at the time when John Jay was on the national stage. Other books have exhausted that general topic as well. It is not a law book, as it intended for any interested reader who browses the aisles of Barnes & Noble. Nor does this book discuss any new discoveries about people, places, or things more than two centuries after the fact.

Rather, this book is primarily focused on the cases that were handled by the United States Supreme Court during the time that John Jay was our nation's first chief justice, and the manner in which those cases reflect the broader domestic, legal, and international issues that were facing our young country during the earliest years of its founding. Aspects of Jay's personal life and career influenced how he viewed some of the cases that he heard at the Supreme Court, so a biography of Jay is wrapped around his years at the court. Each case Jay handled presents its own fascinating story involving events before, during, and after they were heard. No prior book has ever been crafted in this fashion, either with Chief Justice John Jay as the crucial unifying character or the Supreme Court as the central institutional focus during Jay's time there. This book analyzes not just the cases themselves, but how John Jay presided over them, and the effect those cases had on the early development of the country's history, judiciary, and laws. Because our government, its judiciary, and the cases handled by the judiciary are all products of human interactions, competing interests, and civil disagreements, the analysis of the cases adjudicated by the Jay Court are best approached through the personification of their principal actors. And no actor is more central to this subject than John Jay himself.

Court systems reflect the states and nations of which they are a part. Today, federal courts hear a variety of case subjects that were unheard-of in the late 1700s, such as securities regulation, antitrust, and federal regulatory laws. In the parallel state courts, dockets are today filled with disputes over personal injuries, divorce, defamation, wills, property, and contracts. There are also matters in the state courts not known in the late 1700s, including medical malpractice, real property regulations, and extensive sets of state administrative laws. Federal and state court systems each handle criminal matters, with some, such as assault or murder, as known today as they were during the early American period, and others, such as internet stalking and credit card fraud, new to our time. The cases overseen by John Jay reflect the societal, economic, and international issues, questions, and challenges that the United States uniquely faced during Jay's tenure as chief justice, which were different from what we see today.

A separate chapter is devoted to each of the major cases handled by John Jay between the time George Washington appointed the initial members of the court in 1789 and Jay's resignation as the nation's first chief justice on June 29, 1795. Understandably, no book on this subject should jump cold into Jay's first case at the Supreme Court. History and law have broader contexts that must be taken into account by both the writer and the readers. To best understand the significance of Jay's tenure as chief judge during the court's inaugural years, there necessarily must be an acknowledgment of Jay's life, upbringing, education, politics, loyalties, career advancement, national service, and an understanding of what proverbially "made him tick." There must also be an acknowledgment of relevant historical events that provide the backdrop for the cases argued at the Supreme Court and the decisions that were rendered by its justices. Therefore, to the extent that this book contains biographical and historical descriptions, analyses, and insights beyond the docketed cases themselves, they are included for establishing the broader contexts within which the Jay Court fielded our nation's earliest appellate cases, rendered decisions for or against litigants, and developed procedural and substantive forms of American jurisprudence for a newly created nation. As the reader will see, many of those court decisions, though rendered more than two centuries ago, continue to define our national jurisprudence today.

Chapter 1

Formative Days in Colonial New York

> "You have now a call to go forth unto my vineyard; and this you must do, too, upon an evangelical principle—that the master may receive the fruits of it."
>
> —Letter from Benjamin Kissam to John Jay
> November 6, 1769

On the morning of May 12, 1794, the first chief justice of the United States, John Jay, prepared to set sail for England on a ship named the *Ohio*. His mission was to negotiate a treaty between the United States and Great Britain that would keep the two nations from engaging in yet another destructive war. Internationally, the times were dire. A throng of well-wishers gathered in lower Manhattan near where the ship was moored to send John Jay off with their encouragement and well-wishes. As Jay boarded the ship, he turned to the crowd, expressed his "sensibility and gratitude for their intentions," and promised them that he was determined "to do everything in his power to effect the object of his mission and secure the blessings of peace." The crowd responded to the remarks with enthusiastic chants of "huzzah!" and then followed the ship on foot as it sailed toward the Battery at the southernmost tip of Manhattan island. There, the occasion was saluted with commemorative bursts of cannon fire as the *Ohio* began its voyage toward Staten Island and across the Atlantic Ocean.[1]

On that morning, John Jay—a New Yorker, a lawyer, a founder of the nation, a covert intelligence operative during the Revolutionary War, a coauthor of the infamous *Federalist Papers*, a former diplomat, a former chief judge of the New York State Supreme Court of Judicature, and current chief justice of the US Supreme Court—embarked on what some believed could be the greatest mission, or the greatest challenge, of his days in public life. The trans-Atlantic peace was at stake. George Washington was nearing the second half of his final term as president of the United States, and three persons stood out as among Washington's most probable successors. If a Democratic-Republican were to win the presidency in 1796, former Secretary of State Thomas Jefferson was Washington's likely successor. If the Federalist Party retained control of the presidency, Washington's successor was expected to be either Vice President John Adams of Massachusetts or the current chief justice of the United States, John Jay. Jay's political fate in the 1796 election and beyond, if he were to have any interest in being a candidate, would be affected by whether he could successfully negotiate a peace treaty with Great Britain, and if so, whether the terms of any such a treaty would merit the approval of the American people.

John Jay's extraordinary life began on December 12, 1745, in lower Manhattan, not far from where he would sail on the *Ohio* almost fifty years later. He was born into an exclusive circle of New York wealth. Jay's maternal grandfather was Jacobus Van Cortlandt of the prominent Van Cortlandt family, who served as a member of the New York Assembly and as a mayor of New York City. His maternal grandmother, Eva Philipse, was also from a prominent family of landowning wealth. On the paternal side, John Jay's grandparents were Augustus Jay and Anna Maria Bayard (Jay), both of merchant families. Jay was mostly of Dutch descent, but his paternal grandfather had been a French Huguenot. The Dutch comprised a significant portion of the population of New York City at the time.[2]

The daughter of Jacobus and Eva was Mary, and the son of Augustus and Anna was Peter. Peter Jay became a successful merchant, trading cloth and clothing from England and Holland, flax seed from Ireland, and timber, furs, and wheat from the American colonies. Peter Jay and Mary Van Cortlandt married one another in 1728 and had ten children, three daughters and seven sons. The third child, Jacobus, and the seventh child, Frederick, each survived for only several weeks, and the tenth child, Mary, died at age three. The eighth child was John Jay. Jay likely was born at 66 Pearl Street in Manhattan.[3]

The family bore other personal tragedies. Jay's brother Peter and sister Anna were both permanently blinded by smallpox in 1739. The oldest sister, Eve, suffered from fits of hysterics. The eldest brother, Augustus, was so mentally slow that he never learned to read. Reverend Samuel Johnson, who was among those who failed to teach Augustus how to read, diagnosed the boy to Peter Jay as "bird-witted," a condition that did not improve with age. The Jay children who did not suffer from ongoing physical or mental maladies were James, John, and the youngest brother, also named Frederick.[4]

The family threw off its earlier French Calvinism before John Jay was born in favor of membership in the Church of England. John was baptized at the historic Trinity Church in lower Manhattan within days of his birth, and he remained a devout Anglican/Episcopalian for the entirety of his life.[5]

At about the time that John Jay was born, his father, Peter, purchased a 400-acre farm and farmhouse in Rye, New York, in the southeast quadrant of Westchester County north of New York City. The move to Rye allowed for Peter Jay's retirement from active commercial life and kept the family safe from a potential war that was feared in 1745. Black slaves worked at the Jay family farm during John's childhood but were treated "humanely" for the times, and this influenced John's own views of slavery that would emerge during his adulthood in a way that would prove consequential.[6]

Figure 1.1. Drawing of John Jay's boyhood home in Rye, New York.

Although Peter Jay retired from trading in 1745, he was still owed money from British merchants and spent considerable time and energy collecting on those debts. The various debts owed to him originally totaled 4,000 British pounds, with only one-eighth of it still outstanding by 1748. The conversion of British pounds into current dollars can be estimated through different methodologies, but by comparing the cost of consumer goods then and now, 4,000 British pounds in 1745 is worth approximately $1.1 million today. John Jay, later in his childhood, knew of his father's debt collection efforts, and, as will be shown, it appears to have influenced his views as an adult about enabling creditors from different countries to collect upon debts from others.[7]

John Jay received his earliest formal education at the family home in Rye and demonstrated an ability for learning. At age eight, he was sent to a boarding school in New Rochelle, New York, that was operated by Reverend Peter Stroupe approximately eight miles from the family farm. In 1756, John returned home for further education provided by a private tutor, George Murray. He entered Kings College in New York City in 1760 at the tender age of fourteen. To be admitted to the college, Jay needed to establish that he was fluent in Latin and Greek by translating chapters of the Bible from one to the other and translating Virgil's *Aeneid* from Latin to English, and proficient in mathematics to the Rule of Reduction.[8] Enrollment at Kings College must have been an easy choice for the Jay family. John's older brother, James, had attended the same college before beginning his medical studies at the University of Edinburgh and becoming a physician. The college was Anglican, which neatly fit the family's religious preferences. The college was run by a family friend, Reverend Samuel Johnson, who, years earlier, had been among those who unsuccessfully tried to teach Augustus Jay to read. And Kings College was located closer to the family home in Rye than other notable institutions of higher learning on the East Coast. There, Jay was exposed to a classical education rich with Greek, Latin, English, philosophy, law, math, and science.[9]

A few weeks before graduation, some assembled students broke a table either as a result of teenage mischief or as an act of defiance, and each student who was present was questioned by Samuel Johnson's successor, Dr. Myles Cooper, about who was responsible. None of the students professed any knowledge of the culprits until Cooper reached Jay, who was second from last in the line. Jay apparently knew who was responsible but said to Cooper, "I do not choose to tell you, sir." The youthful defiance earned Jay a suspension and jeopardized his graduation, as the school had required all students to sign an oath of obedience to the college statutes. In a lawyerly fashion, Jay maintained that there was no school statute that required him to inform on his companions or disgorge information against his will. According to Jay's son William, Jay "retained among his papers to the day of his death a copy of the [college] statutes, from which it appears that the conduct for which he was suspended was not even indirectly forbidden by them." The incident demonstrates that even in his teens Jay was a stickler for detail and procedure, as would prove to be the case in his adulthood as well. The incident also demonstrates that Jay may have been more honest than his classmates, almost all of whom denied knowing how the table was damaged. Notwithstanding the incident, Jay was permitted to graduate from Kings College with his class on May 15, 1764.[10]

Jay made valuable friends while at Kings College, some of whom would become prominent attorneys and government leaders. Those included Robert R. Livingston Jr., a member of an established and wealthy New York family and son of a justice of the New York State Supreme Court. Of the two friends, Jay was the more reserved, quiet academic, while Livingston was outgoing, confident, and brash. A year after Jay's college graduation, Jay wrote to Livingston, whom he addressed as "Dear Rob," that their friendship was a "tie [that was] firm and indissoluable, which, once entered into, ought ever to be preserved as inviolable." Later in life, events would cause the inviolable friendship to decay. Jay was also a classmate of Peter Van Schaack, who would later be involved in revolutionary activities and become Jay's personal attorney; Egbert Benson, who would become a leading revolutionary in New York, a member of the First and Second Continental Congresses, the first attorney general of the state of New York, a US congressman, and a federal circuit court judge; Gouverneur Morris, who would become a member of the New York legislature, a member of the Second Continental Congress, the author of the preamble to the US Constitution, minister plenipotentiary to France, and a US senator of New York; and Richard Harison, a future law partner of Alexander Hamilton and US attorney for the District of New York. The Kings College Class of 1764 was, with limited exceptions, an impressive group of young men who would put their educations and privileges to good use in their years ahead.[11]

There was a seedier side to New York City in the 1760s. The city teemed with British troops away from home, merchant sailors, privateers, rowdies, thieves, an abundance of taverns, and brothels. John Jay assiduously avoided those aspects of society, as it was not in his reserved nature, and instead attended daily services at Trinity Church in the family pew. He also spent a recurring portion of his free time with his godfather, former New York Supreme Court Justice John Chambers. Chambers resigned his position at the state's Supreme Court as a matter of principle, rather than accepting a new appointment that would have required him to serve at the pleasure of the British Crown. Upon Chambers's death in 1764, he bequeathed to Jay half of the books in his extensive law library. It was an appropriate bequest, as Jay was intent on becoming an attorney after his graduation from college.[12]

The number of attorneys comprising the New York bar during much of the 1700s was small. Between 1709 to and 1776, only 136 attorneys were licensed to practice law in the colony of New York, and from roughly those, only 41 practiced in New York City between 1695 and 1769. Some of those attorneys were no doubt "sharpers and pettifoggers," while others were capable "learned and accomplished men." In the 1760s, attorneys did not receive their legal educations from law schools, as no such thing yet existed on the continent. William & Mary would be the first college to offer a dedicated degree in law, but that did not occur until 1779, followed by the Litchfield Law School in 1784 (no longer in existence), Harvard in 1817, Dickinson College in 1834, Yale in 1843, and Albany Law School in 1851. In the first half of the 1800s, only a handful of schools offered degrees in law so that even then, the vast majority of attorneys still received their legal training through the method of clerking for an attorney at an established law office.[13]

Good or bad timing is sometimes a serendipitous factor in life. Since 1756, including much of the time that John Jay was in college, New York's legal profession was closed to new members, as there were too many lawyers and not enough work to sustain them all. For that reason, Jay's father, Peter, preferred that his son become a religious minister. But in January 1764, a mere four months before John Jay's graduation from college, the New York bar changed its policy to reopen the profession. The rule in New York was that individuals wishing to become attorneys were required to clerk for a member of the bar for five years to then be considered for membership in the bar. The timing was fortuitous for Jay, who graduated from Kings College in May 1764 and began his clerkship in the law later that same year.[14]

John Jay clerked for an established, successful attorney named Benjamin Kissam. Kissam's clients included members of some of New York's most illustrious families, including DeLancey, DePeyster, Livingston, Van Cortlandt, and Van Rensselaer. Kissam was married to Catherine Rutgers, whose family owned considerable tracts of land in New York and who had a brother, Daniel, who was a judge in the Court of Common Pleas in Jamaica, New York. The Jay family paid Kissam 200 British pounds for the privilege for five years, with the understanding that during the final two years, John would have the freedom to read law on his own. Peter Jay advised his son John on August 23, 1763, that "[A]s its [sic] your inclination to be of that Profession, I hope you'll closely attend to it with a firm Resolution that no difficulties in prosecuting that Study shall discourage you from applying very close to it, and if possible, from taking delight in it." The son would not disappoint the father. Benjamin Kissam was certainly among the "best" attorneys to clerk for, as he and Jay forged a true collegial friendship with each other, and Jay was able to learn much about the substantive, procedural, and practical aspects of law at Kissam's elbow.[15]

Figure 1.2. John Jay's father, Peter Jay.

The positive relationship between Kissam and Jay must have made the portions of the law clerkship that were sheer drudgery easier for Jay. Printed fill-in-the-blank legal forms were unknown at the time. All law clerks were expected to perform the most mundane of office tasks for their employers—hand copying dense legal contracts, wills, deeds, pleadings, and judgments; hunting for obscure law books and research; and performing whatever other menial work the attorney in charge directed. Sixteen of the seventeen judgments filed by Kissam between June 1764 and November 1765 were written in Jay's handwriting. Certainly some of Jay's work was mundane, but Jay emerged from the experience with a grasp of the law that would suit him well in the years ahead. John's father, Peter, wrote that his son was "very happily placed, with a gentleman who is extremely fond of him and who spares no pains in instructing of him."[16]

Initially Jay's work was also overseen by a more senior clerk at Kissam's office, Lindley Murray. Jay and Murray would stay in touch with each other for several decades. Jay's non-mundane work included the preparation anew of legal documents, the drafting of deeds, and the drafting of wills. When the day's work was done, Jay had the right to read law from the stacks in Kissam's library. Elementary treatises on law were not plentiful at the time, but they included Finch's Law, Wood's Institutes, Coke Upon Littleton, and, for the truly fortunate, Blackstone's Commentaries.[17]

Early in John Jay's clerkship, Benjamin Kissam was hired to act as the notary at a high-profile civil jury trial where a plaintiff named Thomas Forsey sought money damages for personal injuries caused to him by defendant Waddell Cunningham as a result of a waterfront stabbing where Forsey was almost killed. Jay likely attended at least portions of the trial. The jury returned a verdict in favor of Forsey, and Cunningham sought to appeal the verdict to the colonial acting governor, Cadwallader Colden. While Colden was eager to gain control over the courts by hearing the appeal, and to perhaps then hear others, there was a public outcry against it. Opponents refused to recognize Colden's authority to review Forsey's verdict, as his doing so would divest the citizens of the right to have cases ultimately determined by juries of their peers. New York's Supreme Court of Judicature refused to allow the appeal to go to the governor. Governor Colden eventually backed down, and the controversy underscored for Jay the need of separating judicial powers from the other arms of government.[18]

In May 1765, during the first year of John Jay's clerkship, the British Parliament enacted the Stamp Act. It required the purchase of special stamps to be used on all legal papers, shipping papers, newspapers, almanacs, playing cards, and even dice, even if exchanged solely within the American colonies. It was to become effective on November 1, 1765. The Stamp Act was particularly controversial because it was a form of tax that was "internal" to the colonies, and not a tax on any transactions between the colonies and Europe. The Stamp Act undermined the colonies' right to govern themselves through elected assemblies, as it was a form of taxation without representation.[19]

On August 14, 1765, a mob in Boston stormed the house of the local stamp distributor, Andrew Oliver, calling for his death. Oliver, who fortunately was not present at the time, resigned from his office the next day. By October 1765, as the first year of Jay's clerkship with Benjamin Kissam came to a close, the merchants boycotted British goods, citizens participated in riots, and many attorneys announced their refusal to use stamped paper in the courts. The Stamp Act Congress, which convened in October 1765 and was attended by representatives of nine colonies, passed a resolution urging the British Parliament not to impose taxes without the colonies' consent. On October 31, 1765, there were incidences in New York City of rioting, property damage, and a confrontation between a large crowd and British troops, though no one was injured. A mob carrying an effigy of New York Governor Colden forcibly took his coach, smashed its wood, and used the wood to fuel a large bonfire at Bowling Green. As a result of threats to the life of Governor Colden and other citizen outrages, the stamps were not distributed throughout the New York colony. Within days, courts closed, and without their legally stamped papers, law offices closed as well, including the law office of Benjamin Kissam.[20]

Jay and his college friend Livingston, whose own legal clerkship had also been placed on hiatus, decided to use the once-in-a-lifetime opportunity to enjoy some leisure, ride horses, and read law books. Livingston apparently used more of that time frolicking and carousing while Jay studied books, prompting Jay to write to his friend on May 1, 1765, that he [Livingston] was gaining a reputation as a "man of pleasure," wisely suggesting that he not neglect the opportunity for study and self-improvement.[21]

The Stamp Act was repealed in March 1766, and attorneys' law offices then reopened with months of overdue work. Soon after Jay returned to his clerkship work, Kissam was away from the office for a considerable time representing certain tenant rioters in a high-profile trial at the original Dutchess County Courthouse in Poughkeepsie. Tenant farmers in the county had been leasing land from the Wappinger Indians, but the Philipse family claimed the land as part of its large royal land grant. John Jay was related to the Philipse family through his maternal grandmother. In 1765, before the controversy over the Stamp Court closed the law offices, the Philipse family had successfully enforced its claim against the Wappinger in court, became the landlord of the tenant farmers, and promptly raised the tenants' rent, which was to become payable by them in perpetuity. Many tenants defaulted on their new leases under the higher rents, including some who were sent to debtors' prison, and 1,700 tenant farmers organized themselves for resistance. Tied as he was to the landed gentry, it is unlikely that Jay could have considered bloody riots against property owners as a legitimate form of protest, as he preferred legal processes over lawlessness.[22]

The reopening of the courts after the repeal of the Stamp Act prompted a spate of pent-up ejectment proceedings against the tenants who had defaulted in paying their rents, which in turn inspired large-scale rent riots and violence. The new governor, Henry Moore, responded to a rent riot in May of 1766 by sending a regiment of troops from New York City to Dutchess County to confront the rebellious tenants. Several militiamen who supported the troops were killed in the skirmish that followed. Many rioters were captured, and forty-seven were indicted for crimes including treason, "constructive murder," unlawful assembly, and making war against the peace. The charges of treason and "constructive murder" meant that the rioters could be held accountable for the killing of the militiamen even if individual rioters did not fire any shots or cause any particular deaths. The trials began on August 6, 1766. Kissam argued that the rioters he represented had been asserting private grievances rather than engaging in public demonstrations, and that private grievances were not subject to charges of treason or sentences of death. The trial must have weighed heavily on Kissam, as he wrote Jay, "it is terrible to think that so many lives could be at stake upon the principles of constructive murder."[23]

The Dutchess County rent trials illustrate the harsh state of criminal justice that existed under the Crown's courts. The results of the trials were likely foregone conclusions before they even began. The leaders of the riots were found guilty, including their titular head, William Prendergast, whose sentence was to be disemboweled, drawn, and quartered;

and then, for extra good measure, beheaded. Prendergast's wife, Mehitabel Wing, undertook a desperate, eighty-five–mile nonstop ride on horseback to lower Manhattan to make a personal plea to Governor Moore for a stay of the death sentence upon her husband pending its appeal to King George III. The stay was granted, and ultimately Prendergast was pardoned by King George III. During the time of the notorious Dutchess rent riot trials, John Jay and Lindley Murray were busy in the office preparing Kissam's next round of trials scheduled for the upcoming court terms in New York City.[24]

When Lindley Murray's clerkship with Kissam ended during the fall 1866, Jay was essentially in charge of the law office for the next two years. Additional clerks and scriveners worked in the office under Jay's direction. While thirteen of Kissam's judgments were in Jay's handwriting between May 1866 and October 1868, another twenty-one were not, although Jay's endorsements were signed to most of them. Jay's signature on the documents suggests that he was acting at those times in a supervisory capacity. Jay managed Kissam's dockets and maintained

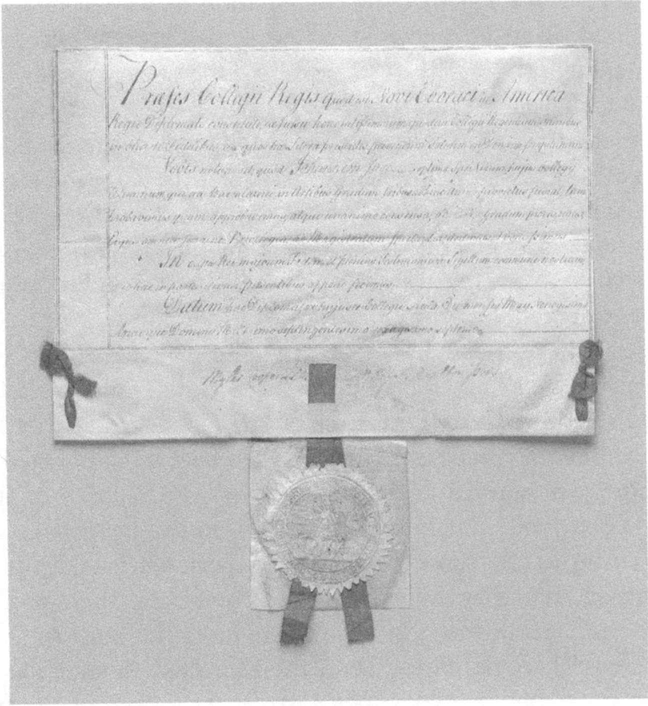

Figure 1.3. John Jay's Master's Degree from Kings College.

the disbursements and fee registers of the office. Jay also managed to find time to undertake further studies at Kings College, where he was awarded a master of arts degree on May 19, 1767.[25]

During Jay's apprenticeship with Kissam, the bar changed the rules so that clerks with college degrees, such as Jay, became eligible for admission to the bar after only three years of work instead of five. Jay, of course, had already committed to Benjamin Kissam for a clerkship that was to be for five years. While Jay likely was eager to conclude his clerkship under the newer rule, he had lost six months of work experience while Kissam's law office was closed because of the Stamp Act. The men split the difference by amicably amending Jay's commitment to Kissam from five years to four.[26]

In those days, clerks working toward a career in the law often did not have to take and pass a bar examination to attain a professional license. A bar examination procedure was created in 1764, but not all aspiring attorneys were required to take it. Instead, the attorneys who sponsored clerks could, at the conclusion of the clerk's apprenticeship, merely vouch for the clerk's training and abilities and recommend to all colleagues in the bar that the examination be waived and the clerk be recognized as an attorney. The New York City bar was small and parochial enough that many of its members knew one another, and they were willing to accept each other's word that a clerk was a worthwhile addition to the profession. The clerk would then become a member of the bar of New York, subject only to the taking of an oath and signing the official membership roll. Attorneys' licenses were issued by the colonial governor, unlike the practice today where law licensure is overseen and administered by New York State's appellate judiciary. John Jay received his license to practice law from Governor Moore on October 26, 1768. Jay and his college friend Robert R. Livingston Jr. were then sworn in together at the Supreme Court by Hon. David Jones and were the only two persons admitted to the practice of law in New York that year.[27]

Jay and Livingston decided to open their own law firm together. Law partnerships were unusual at the time, as the vast majority of attorneys engaged in the profession as solo practitioners. For Jay and Livingston, the partnership made sense beyond their personal friendship. Likely, they surmised that they were better off combining their professional and family connections as a means of generating business so that their law firm would become greater than the sum of their individual parts. The location of their joint law office might have been at the home of Livingston's father, Supreme Court Justice Robert R. Livingston Sr. The rent there would have been reasonable, if not entirely free. New York City was wide open to both Jay and Livingston. With a population of 18,000 persons, New York was the second-largest city in all of the colonies at the time, behind only Philadelphia. During their first year together the pair was not particularly busy, but the establishment of any business usually requires time, effort, and patience. The lack of work early in the two men's partnership afforded Livingston the opportunity to travel to his ancestral home.[28]

One good piece of substantive legal work that Jay did procure was the position of clerk to a seven-member commission that was established to settle border disputes between the colonial provinces of New York and New Jersey. The members of the Boundary Commission

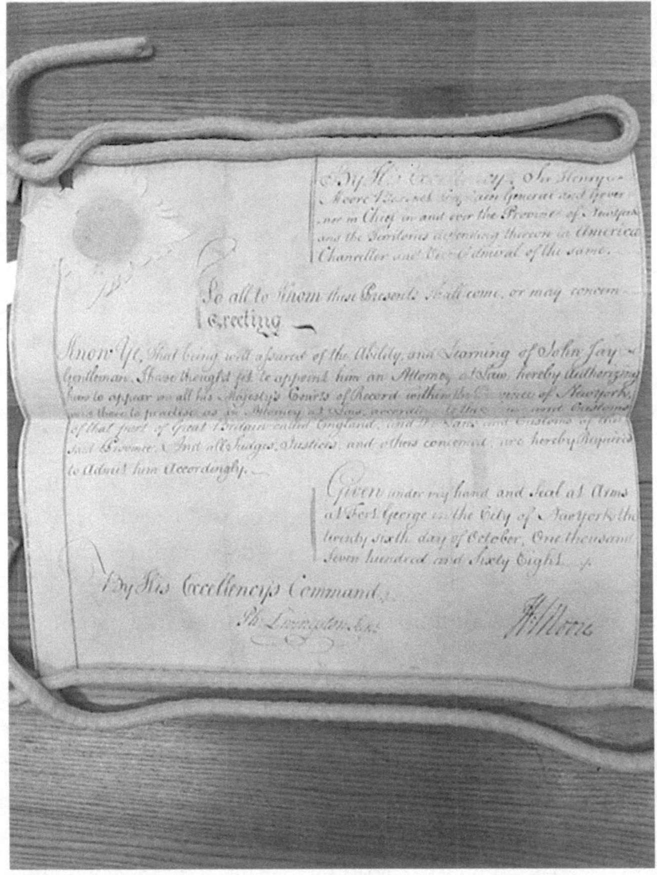
By His [illegible] Sir Henry Moore [illegible] General and Governor in Chief in and over the Province of New York and the Territories [illegible] thereon in America Chancellor and Vice Admiral of the same.

To all to whom these Presents shall come, or may concern Greeting —

Know Ye, That being well assured of the Ability, and Learning of John Jay Gentleman, I have thought fit to appoint him an Attorney at Law, hereby Authorizing him to appear in all his Majesty's Courts of Record within the [illegible] of Newyork, [illegible] there to practise as an Attorney at Law, [illegible] Customs of that part of Great Britain called England, and the Laws and Customs of the said Province. And all Judges, Justices, and others concerned, are hereby Required to Admit him Accordingly.

Given under my hand and Seal at Arms at Fort George in the City of Newyork the twenty sixth day of October, One thousand Seven hundred and Sixty Eight.

By His Excellency's Command,
[illegible] Livingston [illegible]

H Moore

Figure 1.4. A copy of John Jay's law license issued on October 26, 1768.

were all well-connected men of national repute, including attorney Jared Ingersoll, who would become a Pennsylvania delegate at the Second Continental Congress, an attorney arguing cases before John Jay at the US Supreme Court, a Pennsylvania attorney general, and the Federalist candidate for the US vice presidency in 1812; Peyton Randolph, the speaker of Virginia's House of Burgesses; and James Duane, who would also be a delegate to the First and Second Continental Congresses and later become the first judge appointed to the federal District Court for the District of New York.[29]

New York claimed parts of what is today northern New Jersey, while New Jersey claimed the land that today comprises Rockland and Orange counties in New York. Jay's appointment as clerk of the Boundary Commission was likely a product of having the right professional connections, perhaps through Kissam. The commission met and held hearings from July through September 1769, which included the taking of witness testimonies, reviewing land surveys, and examining ancient Dutch land grants. Commission meetings scheduled for December 1869 and July 1770 failed to meet quorum requirements, suggesting that both colonies would accept the border line that the surveyors had recommended the previous September, which, on balance, was somewhat favorable to the arguments of New Jersey. Each colony also wished to appeal the commission's anticipated findings to the British Privy Council, but to do so, they needed to obtain a final and official record of the proceedings from the commission's clerk, John Jay. When Jay was asked by the attorneys for New York and New Jersey to provide a transcript of the work conducted so far, Jay refused to do so in the absence of an order from either the Boundary Commission or the British Privy Council. Jay's refusal to provide the record is a further indication early in his career that he was a stickler for detail and procedure, which, as will be seen, would arise again while Jay was chief justice handling cases at the US Supreme Court.[30]

The Boundary Commission suffered from its inability to obtain a quorum for further meetings. To deal with the problem, the quorum rules were changed to enable the commission to conclude its work. Unfortunately, when only one commissioner attended the session that had been scheduled for a date in May 1771, a question naturally arose of whether the presence of only one man qualified as a "meeting." Eventually, a second member of the commission was located, and a final report was issued. By the time the Boundary Commission issued its ultimate findings and recommendations, the New York and New Jersey provinces were agreeable to its results. In early 1772, the governors and legislatures of both colonies formally accepted the Boundary Commission's recommendations, subject to their approval by British authorities in London. However, by then, the order that had allowed for less than a quorum to act had expired, and the final recommendations had been issued by only two commissioners. Once again, Jay refused to release a certified copy of the commission's records without a directive from the commission itself or the Privy Council. The official records of the Boundary Commission remained with Jay until 1773, when the New York Assembly voted to direct that the records be surrendered to then-Governor William Tryon for their later submission to the Privy Council. The Assembly vote was aimed directly at John Jay.[31]

Much of John Jay's law practice involved trial work. One case, *Budd v Tompkins*, handled in Westchester County, involved a plaintiff schoolteacher who sued certain White Plains defendants for wages that were allegedly owed for the teaching of the defendants' children. John Jay represented the parents and won the trial by turning the jury against the plaintiff. He did so by presenting evidence that the defendants were deceived into hiring the plaintiff and that the plaintiff had stolen a bag of corn from his clients.[32]

In another matter, Jay was co-counsel in a high-profile litigation at the provincial High Court of Chancery on behalf of a religious minister, Reverend Joshua Bloomer. In *Bloomer v Hinchman*, the minister, who was appointed by the provincial governor to a parish in Jamaica, New York, sued for wages that had not been paid by the Presbyterian vestrymen of the parish, who had preferred a competing minister. The governor upheld his own authority to appoint the minister, which presumably entitled Jay's client to his overdue wages, and any appeal to the Privy Council was interrupted by the Revolutionary War.[33]

Another matter involved Jay's representation of the defendant in *King v Nathaniel Underhill*, where the British Crown, as plaintiff, challenged the propriety of the defendant's election as mayor of the now-nonexistent Town of Westchester. The Town of Westchester was subsumed into Bronx County in 1895. Jay successfully delayed the progress of the case from 1772 to the latter part of 1774, when the Crown lost interest in further prosecuting the matter and Underhill was able to serve out the remainder of his elective term without further complication.[34]

Yet another case was *Leadbetter v Harison*, which was tried before a jury at the New York State Supreme Court. It involved a claim of slander by plaintiff Leadbetter against George Harison, a relative of Jay's college classmate Richard Harison. The plaintiff and defendant owned a brewery business together. Jay called a total of ten witnesses to testify, while Richard Harison called three more on behalf of the defense. No doubt, the volume of witnesses and the nature of the claim suggest that the trial was hotly contested. The judgment roll reflecting the verdict has not survived to inform us of the trial's outcome.[35]

Other cases handled by Jay, which reflect the variety of legal matters he dealt with in his practice, included *Canfield v Dickerson* (breach of contract), *Deane v Vernon* (slander), *Anthony v Franklin* (assault), *Rapalje v Brower* (property damage), and *John Doe* ex dem. *Philip Verplanck v Griffin* and *Peter Quiet* ex dem. *Susannah Warren v Van Cortlandt* (ejectments).[36]

Jurors at the time needed to be white males between the ages of twenty-one and seventy and listed on county assessment rolls as owning real property worth at least sixty British pounds. If a citizen performed jury service one year, he would be excused from service during the next. If a trial involved a specialized dispute such as a commercial matter, a "special jury" could be requested by the attorneys that would be composed of jurors familiar with the general nature of the parties' dealings. Later in John Jay's life, his familiarity with the role of special juries would influence the handling of a case at the US Supreme Court.[37]

The trials that John Jay handled as an attorney necessarily formed some of the experiences that would relate to his later career as a jurist. There are problems and pressures associated with the private practice of law that jurists are best off knowing and understanding. Judges with prior experience as trial attorneys bring to the bench insights that help shape their understanding of claims, defenses, legal paperwork, courtroom strategies, arguments, rules of evidence, and proper courtroom procedure. Jay's years as a trial attorney undoubtedly helped prepare him for his later responsibilities at the US Supreme Court, though no one could have known or foreseen that at the time.

Jay's law practice boomed. He and Livingston dissolved their business partnership in October 1771 but remained good friends until political disagreements strained their personal relationship in later years. Jay moved his office to a location in Manhattan that is no longer precisely known.

Jay was necessarily a hard worker. His law practice focused on civil litigation in the New York Supreme Court, the New York Court of Chancery, the New York City Mayor's Court, and the Westchester and Dutchess County Courts of Common Pleas. At that time, Westchester and Dutchess counties were contiguous to one another, with Westchester

County's northern boundary being the same as Dutchess County's southern boundary. Another county in between, Putnam County, would not come into existence in its own right until 1812. Jay's practice stretched from New York City, north through Westchester County, into Dutchess County, all on the east side of the Hudson River. Jay does not appear to have ventured much into counties west of the Hudson River, perhaps because of the existence of the river itself. Some of his caseload was referred to him by his former mentor, Benjamin Kissam, who had become lame by late 1769. In a letter dated November 6, 1769, Kissam referred his cases to Jay and instructed, "You have now a call to go forth unto my vineyard; and this you must do, too, upon an evangelical principle—that the master may receive the fruits of it." Kissam described some of the cases as one involving a horse race "in which I suppose there is some cheat," a second involving an eloped wife and the loss of affections, and a third regarding "horseflesh." The cases Jay handled were as varied as were the human interactions of his clients.[38]

Jay rode horseback six miles most days from his home to his office, which he considered good for his health. Cases in Westchester and Dutchess Counties required much greater travel. He hired law clerks to assist his efforts at various and overlapping times. Those clerks included Thomas H. Barclay, John Strang, and Robert Troup, the last of whom was a former roommate at Kings College of Alexander Hamilton. Troup was another person in Jay's early professional life who remained a friend and confidante for several decades.[39]

The cases Jay handled, which he acquired either directly or from Kissam, appear to represent a broad spectrum of pedestrian disputes among commoners and merchants, which had the effect of merging his aristocratic surroundings with the real-life problems of the common folk. Jay, like his colleagues in the bar, did not turn away good clients or good cases. Attorneys in the latter 1700s were mostly general practitioners who took whatever meritorious matters came through the door, rather than concentrating in one or two narrow areas of the law that would be insufficient for sustaining a livelihood. By late 1773, Jay was counsel on 136 cases pending in the Supreme Court of Judicature and 118 in the Westchester County Court of Common Pleas. By 1774, Jay's law practice was perhaps the most prosperous in the colony, earning him roughly 1,000 British pounds a year, which is equivalent in today's value to roughly $257,000. He used a portion of his earnings to purchase additional books for his personal law library.[40]

Jay handed over his Dutchess County cases to his former partner, Livingston. This development demonstrates that as between the two men, Jay's practice was the more robust, as Jay had cases he could surrender, and Livingston had room to take them on. By referring to Livingston the Dutchess County cases, rather than cases pending in New York or Westchester, Jay shed the portion of his workload that was most geographically inconvenient for him to handle. Today, it is common for civil litigators in the greater New York City area to travel to various law offices, county clerk's offices, courthouses, and other locations for the conduct of case-related business. Contemporary New York litigators have the benefit of heated and air-conditioned automobiles, trains, subways, and even public trams and motorized ferries. During Jay's time, attorneys rode horses to conduct their business, which necessarily included doing so on days of heat, rain, biting cold, high wind, and snow. The public then did not have the benefit of modern-day transportation or weather forecasting. Nor were there telephones, email, fax machines, telecommuting, or Zoom or Teams conferences that render the practice of law more efficient today. Jay's Dutchess County cases were the most distant from his home and office at a time when there were no modern conveniences and were the logical cases for him to surrender to his trustworthy friend and colleague.[41]

In late 1772, Jay and Livingston made an offer to the colony of New York that it might have thought better not to refuse. Both men had observed that in the counties outside New York City, judges in the Courts of Common Pleas tended to be non-lawyers. Jay and Livingston proposed that they and other legally trained attorneys be organized to travel from county to county to act as uncompensated advisors to the common pleas judges. Opposition arose to the proposal from within the counties themselves that a team of advisors was an affront to the capabilities and autonomy of the county judges who were serving there. The plan died on Governor William Tyron's desk. Jay's proposal is noteworthy for three reasons. First, it reflects a true commitment on his part to elevating the standards of the New York judiciary, which was laudable. Second, because the part-time advisor role would have been without financial compensation, the offer by Jay and Livingston was selfless and would have taken each of them away from their paying clients at least some of the time. And third, the proposal is the first indication that John Jay held any interest in decision-making from the judges' side of the bench. If the role had been approved by New York, it would have burnished his resume for a possible future appointment to a provincial judgeship.[42]

Jay involved himself in various aspects of New York society during the time of his legal apprenticeship and law practice. During his clerkship, he joined a debating society to hone his speaking abilities. As an attorney, he belonged to a loose association of lawyers called "the Moot," which included his former college classmates Egbert Benson, Peter Van Schaack, Robert R. Livingston Jr., Gouverneur Morris, and James Duane, and which, like modern-day bar associations, fostered discussions on thorny issues of substantive and procedural law. He was also a member of the "Social Club," which met frequently at Samuel Fraunces's Tavern and at Kip's Bay in Manhattan. And he managed a dancing assembly where eligible men and women could meet one another in an entirely respectable fashion.[43]

What is notable about John Jay's years as a law clerk and attorney was that he displayed little if any outward involvement in politics. His main focus was on the law and his law practice. To the extent that he was politically aligned at all, he was close to the "Livingston faction" of provincial politics as related to Jay's college friend and onetime law

Figure 1.5. Drawing of historic Fraunces Tavern, New York City.

partner, Robert R. Livingston Jr. For the most part, Jay either had not yet experienced a political awakening, or if he had, he kept it to himself.

Jay's relationship with the Livingstons took a step closer with his courtship of Sarah Livingston, whom he met in late 1772 or early 1773. He called her "Sally." Sarah was the sixteen-year-old daughter of William and Susannah Livingston. They married on April 28, 1774, at the Livingston home, four months short of Sarah's eighteenth birthday. Although Jay was twenty-eight years old, the age difference between them was not unusual for the time, nor was it unusual for women to marry in their latter teens. Jay's father-in-law, William Livingston, would become the first governor of the state of New Jersey and served in that capacity for fourteen years, from 1776 to 1790. The happy couple traveled to Rye to meet the Jay family, and from there took a honeymoon touring the northern counties of the Hudson Valley.[44]

Jay was not yet thirty years old, but his future was bright. He was young and educated, lean of build, and close to six feet tall. His law practice was financially successful and secure. He had married into a wealthy family. He was professionally and socially connected to the movers and shakers of colonial New York. And there were no visible impediments to whatever his future might hold.

Although John Jay's future looked bright in 1774, events in colonial America would hurdle the provinces toward revolution later that same decade. By the time of his marriage, John Jay's worldview was formed and influenced by the people, education, events, issues, and experiences that he had encountered in his childhood, teens, and twenties. Jay, who was quiet, reserved, and academically inclined, was not by nature a revolutionary. He knew that years earlier, his father, Peter, successfully collected the bulk of the debt that was owed to him upon retirement through normal adjudicative channels. He had watched Governor Colton back down in the face of public opposition to his executive review of the jury's verdict in *Forsey v Cunningham*. He had observed the mercy of King George III's pardon of William Prendergast after Prendergast's death sentence was rendered in Dutchess County. He had witnessed the British Parliament's repeal of the Stamp Act on account of strong public opposition. He had been engaged in a process where border disputes between the New York and New Jersey provinces were cordially and peacefully resolved. The workings of democratic processes and opinion had operated in many instances and contexts as a powerful check on the potential abuses of government in ways that Jay saw and absorbed firsthand. To the extent that the relationship between the American colonies and Great Britain was becoming increasingly strained, issues could be resolved through democratic processes short of a bold or reckless declaration of independence from the Mother Country. At least, that is what Jay believed at that time.

JAY'S DAYS

Kings College, founded in 1754, is the oldest institution of higher learning in the state of New York and the fifth oldest in the United States. Its original location was in a schoolhouse near Trinity Church in lower Manhattan. Classes were suspended for eight years during the Revolutionary War, but the school reopened in 1784 under the name of Columbia College, now Columbia University. The school moved to Madison Avenue and 49th Street, where it was located from 1857 to 1897, until it moved to its current location on the Upper West Side of Manhattan. Besides John Jay, Columbia Law School produced two other chief justices of the US Supreme Court, Charles Evans Hughes (1930 to 1941) and Harlan Fiske Stone (1941 to 1946). Fittingly, the extensive collection of John Jay's original papers is kept at the Rare Book and Manuscript Room of the Butler Library of Columbia University.[45]

Benjamin Kissam was a member of New York's Committee of 100 and the First and Second New York Provincial Congresses. He died in 1782 at the age of fifty-four.[46]

Lindley Murray, who clerked with John Jay at Kissam's law office, was the son of a successful merchant, and the Murray Hill section of Manhattan is named after his family. Murray was a Loyalist opposed to the Revolutionary War, left the practice of law, and moved in 1784 to Holgate, a Quaker community on the outskirts of York, England. There, he became an author of books on literacy and grammar, which sold an astounding and estimated 15.5 million copies in Great Britain and the United States between 1800 and 1840. He was both the Noah Webster, and Strunk & White, of his time. His success as a grammarian earned him the title "the Father of English Grammar." He and Jay stayed in touch over the decades. During the last sixteen years of his life, Murray was confined to his home because of the effects of late-life polio. Murray died on February 16, 1826, at the age of eighty.[47]

Chapter 2

Passing the Rubicon

A Key Man in the Birth of a Nation

> "Sir we have passed the Rubicon and it is now necessary every man Take his part, Cast off allegiance to the King of Great Britain and take an oath of Allegiance to the States of America or Go over to the Enemy for we have Declared our Selves Independent."
>
> —John Jay to Beverly Robinson
> February 22, 1777

Word of a new tax on tea reached the American colonies in October 1773. The infamous Boston Tea Party occurred on December 16, 1773, where 150 Bostonians poured 342 chests of tea into the harbor, followed by a similar but less notorious event in New York City in late April 1774. The British prime minister and chancellor of the Exchequer, Frederick "Lord" North, responded to the Boston incident by drafting the Boston Port Act, which was passed by the British Parliament, and which ordered the closure of the port until restitution was made for the destroyed tea. It was followed by the Massachusetts Government Act, the Administration of Justice Act, and the Quartering Act, known in the collective as the "Intolerable Acts." Under the Intolerable Acts, the British Parliament asserted its control over the Massachusetts government as backed up by the British Army, and in the process erased many of the rights that colonists held dear, including the all-important and highly popular right to trials by jury.[1]

John Jay returned from his honeymoon with Sarah to learn that he had been appointed to a committee that was formed in New York City to consider the events that had occurred in Massachusetts. Jay was appointed to a subcommittee that was assembled to draft a response to a letter received from Boston. The subcommittee's letter, drafted by James Duane from John Jay's notes, called for a general continental congress for the purpose of coordinating the various colonies' responses to the Intolerable Acts.[2]

The First Continental Congress met at Carpenter's Hall in Philadelphia on September 5, 1774, and continued during the seven weeks that followed. It was attended by fifty-one delegates from all of the colonies except Georgia. Jay traveled to Philadelphia with his father-in-law, William Livingston. At age twenty-eight, Jay was the second-youngest member of the Congress. Other delegates included persons whose names had already become, or would later become, well-known to history, including George Washington, Patrick Henry, and Richard Henry Lee of Virginia; John and Samuel Adams of Massachusetts; Roger Sherman of Connecticut; Samuel Chase of Maryland; Caesar Rodney of Delaware; John Dickinson of Pennsylvania; Stephen Hopkins of Rhode Island; and John and Edward Rutledge of South Carolina.[3]

The mood of the First Continental Congress was not to break from Great Britain, but to have the colonies' grievances heard and addressed by the British Parliament. Naturally, there were differences of opinion, with Samuel Adams and Patrick Henry urging a more aggressive stance toward Great Britain, and Joseph Galloway of Pennsylvania perhaps representing the most conservative of views. John Jay aligned himself with neither of the extremes. One of Jay's specific roles was as a key member of a committee with Richard Henry Lee and William Livingston that authored the "Address to the People of Great Britain." The address summarized American grievances with the mother country, but in a way that was lawyerly and respectful to British authorities. It explained that the inhabitants of the colonies had risked disease and death to travel to the American continent and promote the interests and success of the British Crown, only to see Britain drain the colonies of their money and deprive individuals of their rights.[4]

As for the First Continental Congress as a whole, a middle consensus prevailed in the form of a resolution that denied the Parliament authority over the colonies, but submitted the colonies to Great Britain's regulation of colonial trade. According to notes of John Adams, Jay observed that "negotiation, suspension of commerce, and war are the only three things. War is by general consent to be waived at present. I am for negotiation and suspension of commerce." The colonies agreed at the First Continental Congress to boycott British imports commencing December 1, 1774, and to cease exports to Britain as of September 10, 1775. The schedule allowed for the exportation in the interim of the year's tobacco crop that was of particular importance to Virginia. The trade boycotts were intended to put pressure on the British Parliament to rescind the Intolerable Acts. Additionally, the delegates called for a Second Continental Congress to convene on May 10, 1775. Jay returned to New York having worked with some of the most illustrious and influential political leaders on the continent.[5]

Jay was not particularly active in politics in early 1775. In a letter to Robert R. Livingston Jr. at the beginning of the new year, he wrote, "I ought to say something to you about politicks [sic], but am sick of the subject." Nevertheless, during the spring of that year, he became a member of the Committee of Sixty, which, among other things, would select the delegates to represent New York at the anticipated Second Continental Congress. The battles at Lexington and Concord were fought on April 19, 1775, but word of those conflicts did not reach New York City until four days later. The Committee of Sixty convened on April 20 without any knowledge of the violence in Massachusetts. On April 21, 1775, Jay was selected to be among New York's delegates to the Second Continental Congress. When news of the battles at Lexington and Concord then reached New York, all business in the city came to a halt for several days as New Yorkers anticipated that they might be attacked by the British next. Armed mobs roamed the city threatening loyalists. On April 26, 1775, a Committee of One Hundred was formed to hold a Provincial Congress. John Jay helped draft the role of the new committee, which was quickly signed and endorsed by more than 1,000 persons, and which met for several days in May.[6]

Jay could play no significant role with the Committee of One Hundred, as the Second Continental Congress convened on May 10, 1775, and he needed to return to Philadelphia. The Second Continental Congress met at what is now known as Independence Hall. It met on various dates, at various locations, for years. Its original members included many of the prominent participants of the first congress, plus Benjamin

Franklin, Thomas Jefferson, and other notables. Jay, arriving at the Second Continental Congress at the age of twenty-nine, distinguished himself even more so than he had at the first congress.

Initial sentiment within the Second Continental Congress was not to seek independence from Great Britain. Taking issue with the policies of the Parliament in London did not mean that there needed to be a repudiation of loyalty to the King. In late June, the Congress appointed a committee that included John Dickinson and Benjamin Franklin of Pennsylvania, John Rutledge of South Carolina, Thomas Johnson of Maryland, and John Jay of New York to draft another Petition to the King. The Petition from the First Continental Congress had not yet been answered, at least not officially, so there was debate over whether to send any new Petition at all. Jay created an early draft of the new Petition, which acknowledged Britain's right to regulate trans-Atlantic commerce, and which proposed the formation of a commission to resolve the contentious issues that were dividing Great Britain and the colonies. Jay's draft was found in the papers of John Dickinson. The final draft, written in Dickinson's hand, which was adopted by Congress, became known as the "Olive Branch Petition." The Olive Branch Petition asked for King George III to personally involve himself in efforts to have Parliament repeal the measures that were oppressing the colonies and for the appointment of a commission, including American participants appointed by the colonial legislatures, to iron out the divisive issues. It distinguished between loyalty to the king and disagreements with ministerial policies. The Olive Branch Petition did not go as far as Jay had proposed in his earlier draft and acknowledge Great Britain's supremacy on matters involving commerce. This suggests that Jay was more of a conciliator than his other committee members, and more of a conciliator than Congress as a whole.[7]

While Congress extended a hand of negotiation to the king, it simultaneously undertook efforts to protect the colonies militarily. Congress transformed the provincial militias into a continental army that was to be under the command of George Washington as its general. The Congress made plans for recapturing Fort Ticonderoga from Ethan Allen and Crown Point from Benedict Arnold and to build forts along the Hudson River to block British ships from accessing the northeast continental interior. The Congress issued paper money to support the troops and appointed a diplomatic committee to reach out to other nations, with Jay as one of its members.[8]

Unbeknownst to the congressional delegates at the time, King George III had issued a Proclamation on August 23, 1775, declaring the colonies to be in a state of rebellion, and in the December that followed, Parliament enacted a law outlawing all trade with the colonies and authorizing the confiscation of American ships and goods. The King never considered the Olive Branch Petition, as a letter by John Adams that had been intercepted by the British predicted that war was inevitable, and persons close to the King viewed the petition to be insincere. The well-intentioned Olive Branch Petition accomplished nothing. The wording of the petition, whether penned with Jay's language or Dickinson's, would have made no difference to any developments that would be forthcoming.[9]

In late 1775 and early 1776, Jay involved himself in diplomatic endeavors with both France and Britain. Jay, as a member of the diplomatic committee of the Second Continental Congress, discussed with a French representative, Achard de Bonvouloir, whether France might assist the colonies. De Bonvouloir suggested that assistance might be possible but did not specify its form. In early 1776, Jay was among the members of Congress who entered into private negotiations with Lord Drummond of Great Britain. Drummond, who claimed to speak on behalf of other high-ranking British ministers, suggested a conciliatory resolution that the colonies guarantee a perpetual revenue stream to the king with the understanding that the colonies, rather than Parliament, would devise how the taxes for that revenue would be raised. There was nothing inherently wrong with Jay negotiating with both France and Great Britain at roughly the same time, as he was merely seeking the best possible deal for the colonies under circumstances that were still evolving.[10]

Meanwhile, Jay's law practice was floundering, as would be expected from Jay's lack of attention to it. Jay's clerk, Robert Troup, wrote on October 30, 1775, that "[w]hen I reflect upon the present Business of the office, I am filled with the deepest Sorrow. Formerly it was extensive, and attended with much Profit. Now it is confined within very narrow Bounds, and of Course accompanied with little Gain." The $4.00 per day compensation that Jay received as a member of Congress was a small fraction of the compensation that he could have expected to derive from his practice of law were he tending it.[11]

Also in early 1776, on January 24, Jay's wife, Sarah, gave birth to the Jays' first child, Peter Augustus. Early that same year, Jay was elected to the New York Assembly, but the provincial Assembly was never called into session by the colonial governor, William Tryon.[12]

The relationship between Great Britain and the colonies went from bad to worse during the remainder of 1776. King George III did not respond to the Olive Branch Petition, but the Parliament did by ordering 25,000 fresh British troops to the colonies, in addition to the 15,000 troops who were already there. Thomas Paine's pamphlet *Common Sense* was published on January 10, 1776, and widely circulated, and its impact was keenly seen in the colonies during the course of the year. The Battle of Bunker Hill was fought in Charlestown, Massachusetts on June 16, 1775. Public opinion in the colonies shifted in favor of independence from Great Britain. The Declaration of Independence was adopted by the Second Continental Congress by July 4, 1776. The Battle of Brooklyn Heights was fought on August 27, 1776, followed by the battles at White Plains on October 28, Washington Heights on November 16, and Trenton on December 26, 1776.[13]

John Jay was not in Philadelphia in July 1776, and he therefore did not vote on the Declaration of Independence and never added his signature to the document. At New York's Provincial Congress, Jay proposed a resolution that was supported by all members of that assembly, by which New York joined the other colonies in adopting the Declaration of Independence. Jay wrote the resolution approving the Declaration of Independence after the fact, which stated that its supporters "will, at the risk of our lives and fortunes, join with the other Colonies in supporting it." By that action, Jay made the pivotal transition from being a loyalist hopeful for a reconciliation with Great Britain to that of a revolutionary in favor of outright independence. He attributed his support of independence to the "cruel necessity" that made the need for independence "unavoidable."[14]

In May 1776, Jay, Gouverneur Morris, and Philip Livingston were appointed by New York's provincial congress to a secret intelligence committee formed to investigate the enemies of American independence. By June, information was uncovered of an ongoing plot to kill or capture General Washington. Jay's secret committee spoke with witnesses, conducted interrogations, and ultimately questioned and arrested New York Mayor David Matthews for plotting with others to bribe provincial soldiers and members of General Washington's guard to join the British. The group interrogated approximately twenty suspects. There was concern, perhaps exaggerated at the time, that the plot was designed to kill or capture General Washington. Mayor Matthews was found guilty by the inquisitors of "treasonable practices" and was sent to a jail in Litchfield,

Connecticut. One soldier who Jay questioned, Thomas Hickey, was given over to the military, court-martialed on June 26, and publicly executed at 11:00 a.m. on June 28 for his participation in whatever conspiracy was afoot to undermine the continental Army. Jay's role in helping protect Washington from potential insurrection was the type of bonding activity that Washington likely long remembered.[15]

The circumstances involving Matthews, Hickey, and other suspects underscored the need for the provinces to gather military intelligence as part of the war effort. Jay was one of six active members of a standing Committee for Detecting and Defeating Conspiracies that was formed by the New York provincial congress on September 21, and which met for the first time on September 28. Its other members were William Duer of Charlotte County, Charles DeWitt of Ulster County, Leonard Gansevoort of Albany County, and Zephaniah Platt and Nathaniel Dackett of Dutchess County. The purpose of the committee was to help determine who was loyal to the British Crown in ways that could pose dangers to the New Yorkers working toward independence. The committee operated as an intelligence agency within the New York province. It developed information from secret agents and other sources, pursued reports, examined witnesses, jailed suspects, and considered the deportation of prisoners in its custody. Its work was cloak-and-dagger, and committee members used invisible ink for their written communications.[16]

For reasons of safety, Jay moved his family and parents to a rented farm in Fishkill, New York, near the Hudson River in Dutchess County. Fishkill, while a sleepy town today, was a prominent crossroad in the 1770s. North-south travelers between New York City and upstate New York typically passed through Fishkill on the Albany Post Road, which paralleled the Hudson River. The east-west route between Philadelphia and New England likewise went through Fishkill. During the Revolutionary War, Fishkill saw its share of continental soldiers passing through the same routes to and from battles. And nearby Fishkill Landing, in the present-day city of Beacon, was an active drop-off point for commercial goods delivered via the Hudson River to the middle Hudson Valley and a point of departure for Hudson Valley goods destined for markets downriver. Jay's move to Fishkill, while enhancing his family's safety, kept him in a center of activity.[17]

At Fishkill, John Jay became the personal spymaster of a shoemaker named Enoch Crosby, who on multiple occasions posed as a Tory and provided valuable information about British activities obtained from both sides of the Hudson River. If caught, Crosby would certainly have been executed by the British like most spies during wartime, and Jay might have faced execution as well. Years later, Jay provided information about Crosby to author James Fenimore Cooper, which Cooper appears to have used to create the character of Harvey Birch in the 1821 book *The Spy: A Tale of the Neutral Ground.*[18]

Jay's role on the Committee for Detecting Conspiracies steeled his commitment to the cause of American independence. The committee's records have been preserved by the New York State Historical Society. One record, reflecting the questioning on February 22, 1777, of a man named Beverly Robinson in Fishkill, quotes Jay as saying to Robinson,

Figure 2.1. Enoch Crosby.

"Sir we have passed the Rubicon and it is now necessary every man Take his part, Cast off allegiance to the King of Great Britain and take an oath of Allegiance to the States of America or Go over to the Enemy for we have Declared our Selves Independent." In other words, in Jay's view, the residents of New York were expected to declare allegiance to either King George III or to New York, with no room for indecisiveness or neutrality in between. Robinson was a man of means, having married into the Philipse family with an estate on the Hudson River across from West Point. Jay's conspiracies committee had no hard evidence of treason against Robinson at that time, though later, Robinson served as a colonel in the Loyal American Regiment of New York City and relocated with his wife to England in 1783.[19]

New York declared itself independent from Great Britain on July 9, 1776. The war forced the delegates to move New York's provincial congress steadily northward from New York City to White Plains, to Philipse Manor, to Fishkill, to Poughkeepsie, and to Kingston within the span of a year. Efforts at drafting a state constitution during the latter half of that year suffered from fits and false starts because of other pressing business being performed by the members of the state's legislature. Jay was named to a committee that was tasked with drafting a state constitution, and he appears to have been its principal drafter during the early part of 1777. He had assistance from his college friends Robert R. Livingston Jr. and Gouverneur Morris.[20]

The concept of a governmental entity having a written constitution defining municipal functions and guaranteeing individual liberties was fairly new and unconventional at the time. The draft debated at the New York constitutional convention in March and April 1777 proposed a bicameral legislature consisting of assemblymen elected locally by taxpaying landowners to four-year terms and landowner senators elected from four districts for four-year terms; a landowner governor with limited executive powers chosen by the Senate; and a judicial system composed of a state Supreme Court of Judicature and local Courts of Chancery. The draft, reflecting the norms of the time, did not provide rights for women such as voting or serving on juries. Jay's draft contained a clause guaranteeing the free toleration of religious worship, but during convention debate, he sought to amend his own language with what today might be viewed as an unusual condition upon Roman Catholics—that for Catholics to own real property or vote in elections, they first be required to take an oath of allegiance to the state and renounce any higher loyalty to the Pope.

That proposal, which was made by Jay three times in three different ways, was rejected by the convention by solid majorities each time. Jay also supported a forward-thinking amendment by Gouverneur Morris, not adopted by the convention, that would have phased out slavery in New York gradually over time. It would not be the last time that Jay would be associated with statewide efforts to abolish slavery. The draft of the state constitution of 1777 included Article XXXV, which adopted the common law and statutes of Great Britain except as modified or overridden by statutes enacted by New York.[21]

Convention delegates made various tweaks and modifications to the draft constitution at the courthouse in Kingston, including a reduction of Assembly terms in office from four years to one, changes to the amount of property that men needed to own to be eligible to vote, and a mechanism for vetoing legislation and for overriding vetoes. They did so at a time when British troops were advancing up the Hudson River, with several hundred debarked at Peekskill a mere fifty miles south of Kingston. Jay missed the final days of the convention when he was called to Fishkill on April 17 because of the death of his mother. The state constitution was approved by the convention on April 20, 1777, years before a federal version that would be adopted in 1789 forming a government of the United States. Jay believed that the state constitution had been debated and adopted too hastily. He was not pleased with some aspects of the final version that was enacted, including the absence of oaths of allegiance and abolitionist provisions. But he supported New York's constitution publicly overall and accepted appointment to a committee responsible for organizing and establishing a government consistent with its terms.[22]

There was serious discussion that John Jay be drafted as a candidate for the first gubernatorial term of the newly formed state of New York. Jay actively discouraged any talk of his becoming governor and instead actively promoted one of his many friends, General Philip Schuyler. With great modesty, Jay wrote to Abraham Yates that while being governor would be "more respectable, as well as more lucrative, and consequently more desirable than the place I now fill, . . . [my] object in the course of the present great contest has neither been, nor will be, either rank or money. I am persuaded that I can be more useful to the State in the office I now hold than in the one alluded to, and therefore think it my duty to continue in it." Schuyler ran for the office but was defeated by General George Clinton by a margin of more than 60 percent to 40 percent. Clinton won by relying not so much on aristocratic family connections but by forming a bond with common people who were eligible to vote, particularly the farmers and soldiers from Dutchess, Orange, and Ulster Counties.[23]

On May 7, 1777, several weeks ahead of the gubernatorial election, New York's provincial congress elected thirty-one-year-old John Jay to be the state's first chief judge of the State Supreme Court of Judicature, subject to confirmation by a Council of Appointment to be composed of a future governor and four future state senators. The state's 1777 Constitution continued the form and substance of the court system that had been established by the New York provincial Assembly in 1691. Jay's selection as chief judge was the primary reason he identified for not wishing to be governor. Given George Clinton's popularity with the state's voters and Clinton's margin of election, Jay was wise to not run for governor in 1777, as he very well may have lost the contest.[24]

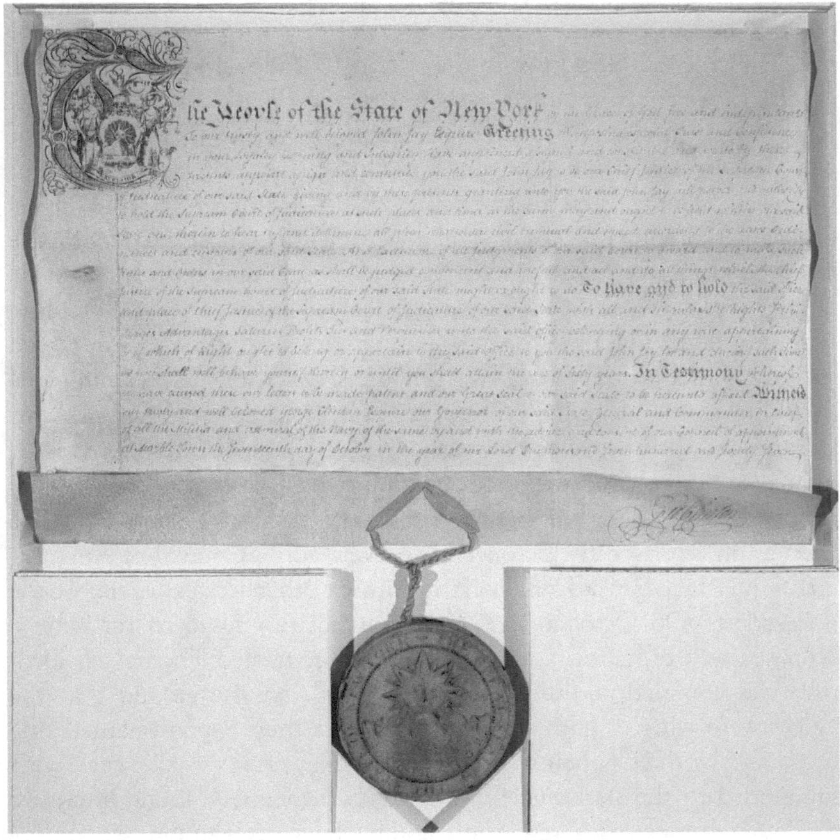
The People of the State of New York
Greeting
To Have and to Hold
In Testimony
Witness

Figure 2.2. Appointment as Chief Judge to the NYC Supreme Court of Judicature.

As chief judge, Jay became responsible for overseeing the creation of a statewide court system. No one could have foreseen that he would later have a similar responsibility overseeing the implementation of a federal court system when he would become the nation's first chief justice after ratification of the future federal constitution. Jay opened his first session of court as the state's chief judge in Kingston on September 9, 1777. In his opening instructions to the assembled Grand Jury, he likened New York's independence from Great Britain to the emancipation of the Jews from Egyptian servitude. In addition to courtroom duties, Jay, as chief judge, was a member of a Council of Review that evaluated all bills pending in the legislature before being signed into law and that required him to attend legislative sessions as well.[25]

One of Jay's earliest trials was that of a slave named Jack who was accused of assaulting and attempting to rape complainant Catherine Helme. There were four witnesses for the prosecution and six for the defense, and in the end the defendant was convicted and sentenced to jail. The case is noteworthy to the extent that Jay afforded the full due process of a trial to a Negro slave.[26]

Within the month, Jay and the state's government needed to flee Kingston because of the proximity of British General John Burgoyne's troops in Saratoga and reestablish itself at Poughkeepsie. Had Jay or other high-ranking officials of state government been captured by British troops at Kingston, they would have at a minimum been arrested on charges of treason and perhaps executed as enemies of the Crown either sooner or later. The British Army then overtook Kingston and burned it to the ground, not leaving a single house. American fortunes improved the following month, on October 17, 1777, when the continental Army won a significant battle at Saratoga, which had the effect of convincing France to tangibly aid the states in their fight against the British.[27]

Jay proved he was as much a stickler for detail as a judge as he had been as an attorney. By October 1777, New York's Council of Appointments had met but did not confirm him or other judges to any of the state courts. On October 1, 1777, the judiciary refused to act upon a proposed writ of habeas corpus by a petitioner named Thomas Hadden, who was confined at the Ulster County jail, on the ground that the judges were without authority to act without their appointments being confirmed by the Council of Appointments. Jay and two colleagues were summoned to the state Assembly to explain themselves, and afterward the Assembly passed a resolution finding Jay's explanation satisfactory and urged the Council on Appointments to approve the original judicial appointments. It took the Council at least another two weeks to confirm the appointments, on October 17 of that year, as its members were still scattered as a result of their flight from Kingston.[28]

Meanwhile, in Philadelphia, the Second Continental Congress approved the Articles of Confederation on November 15, 1777.

Jay spent most of 1778 focused on his judicial duties. He heard a wide variety of pedestrian civil and criminal matters and gained some limited but meaningful experience as a jurist. Many of the cases Jay heard were criminal, particularly robberies and assaults. Most of the records for the cases that year no longer exist. The absence of records is explained by the fact that Jay presided over sessions of court in various counties, when and where he was needed, and the minutes of those proceedings were kept not by the state judiciary but by the individual counties. That year, from the fragmented records that have survived, he and other New York judges sentenced a total of eleven men to death, but Jay recommended that the governor pardon three of them. Governor Clinton, in granting each of the three pardons, wrote from Poughkeepsie that Jay "fills the bench with great dignity and pronounces the sentences of the court with becoming grace."[29]

By October 1778, Jay was asked by Governor Clinton to be one of the state's delegates to the Continental Congress in Philadelphia, for the primary purpose of seeking Congress' assistance in suppressing "rebels" from present-day Vermont who were attempting to secede from the state of New York. Delegates from twenty-eight New England towns had met at a convention in January of 1777 and declared themselves an independent state, which conflicted with the land claims of the British colony of Quebec and of the states of New York and New Hampshire. New York's Constitution provided that its chief judge could hold no other public office except as a delegate to the Continental Congress on a "special occasion." By vote, the state legislature determined that the Vermont controversy qualified as a special occasion, resulting in Governor Clinton's request that Jay travel to Philadelphia. Jay dutifully accepted the assignment.[30]

One day after Jay's arrival in Philadelphia, on December 9, 1778, the president of the Second Continental Congress, Henry Laurens, unexpectedly resigned. The following day, John Jay was elected as the new president of the Congress by a vote of eight states to four. He agreed to accept the presidency only if arrangements could be made with family to care for his father, which were arranged through Jay's younger brother, Frederick. As president, Jay presided over congressional debates, wrote and received correspondence on behalf of the Congress, met and corresponded with military leaders, and negotiated with foreign diplomats stationed in the American states, such as Conrad Alexandre Gerard of France and Don Juan de Miralles of Spain.[31]

Jay's election to the presidency of the Congress meant as a practical matter that his days as chief judge in New York were over, and he resigned from his judicial position on August 10, 1779. The event marked a career transition away from the judiciary, which Jay would not resume until the time he would assume the role as chief justice of the future United States. The presidency of the Congress also meant that Jay would be away from his family for an extended time, a problem Jay eventually solved by bringing his family to a house he rented near the Philadelphia waterfront.[32]

A vexing issue facing the Second Continental Congress was the devaluation of the continental dollar caused by the liberal printing of money to help finance the cost of the Revolutionary War and the inability of the Congress to impose direct taxes on the American people. Between January 1778 and January 1779, the purchasing power of the continental dollars dropped by half against the equivalent amount of gold or silver, and by January 1780, its purchasing power dropped roughly 650 percent from the January 1778 level. Congress passed resolutions urging the states to raise greater tax revenues from their citizens, which then could be applied to the costs of the continental war, and "called in" two series of continental paper currency that were frequently counterfeited. The efforts of the delegates did little to stem the hemorrhage of the continental currency, and, as will be seen, currency problems continued to plague the states, and nation, for several years.[33]

Ironically, the reason that Jay was sent to the Second Continental Congress as a delegate of New York—to seek assistance in resolving the Vermont issue—failed. Jay constructively suggested that New York, New Hampshire, and Massachusetts each pass laws authorizing the Vermont boundary dispute to be resolved by the Congress. While New York passed the enabling legislation in October 1779, the other two states that were necessary parts of the equation did not, and the issue festered for several more years.[34]

The Congress named Jay its minister plenipotentiary to Spain in late September 1779, and he sailed for that country the following month.

Great Britain and Spain were at war with each other at that time. John and Sarah Jay calculated that the assignment abroad could run years, and for that reason the couple traveled to Spain together. However, they chose to leave their three-year-old son, Peter Augustus, with Sarah's parents in New Jersey rather than subject him to the risk of a wartime voyage across the Atlantic. The decision represented family sacrifice in service of the American states. The Jays traveled with Conrad Alexandre Gerard aboard a frigate, the *Confederacy*, captained by Seth Harding.[35]

Seasickness was a problem for Jay. It also was a difficult voyage because of problems with the ship's masts and rudder that caused them to change ships in Martinique and to take a French warship, the *Aurora*, across the Atlantic from there. The masts were damaged during a fierce storm, which broke the arm of one crew member and required the amputation of the arm of another. At Martinique, the *Confederacy* fortuitously docked at the Port of St. Pierre on the north side of the island. Had it instead docked at Port Royal on the south side of the island, as had been strongly considered, it likely would have been captured by the British with other French ships that were seized there, and Jay would have been identified, arrested, and, at minimum, imprisoned. During the layover in Martinique, Jay observed slavery in its most raw form, with men at sugar plantations wearing collars on their necks and chains on their ankles. The images there may have influenced future actions he would take with regard to the abolition of slavery. The *Aurora* left Martinique on December 28, 1779, and arrived safely at Cadiz, Spain, on January 22, 1780.[36]

Jay served as minister to Spain from September 27, 1779, to May 20, 1782. He had three goals while there. The first was to obtain Spanish recognition of the independent states. The second was to obtain money from the Spanish government. The third was to enter into commercial trade treaties to help offset the states' substantial loss of trade with Great Britain. The Spanish Royal Court refused to officially receive Jay, fearing that the recognition of independent states in North America might incite independence movements against Spanish possessions elsewhere. Spain's primary American interest was in obtaining control of the southern Mississippi River. Jay engaged in "unofficial" discussions as a private citizen with the Spanish foreign minister, the Conde de Floridablanca. Absent an official recognition of the states, there could be no commercial treaties. Jay ultimately came to doubt Spain's goodwill. His only success was in securing from Spain relatively small advances of money, which failed to even cover the bills Jay incurred during his mission to the country. From the beginning, Jay's diplomatic mission to Spain was destined to fail. In the end, overall, it accomplished little.[37]

Across the Atlantic, General Washington and his Army defeated the troops of British Lt. General Charles Cornwallis at the Battle of Yorktown, which concluded on October 19, 1781. It was not initially known whether Cornwallis's defeat at Yorktown would mark the end of the Revolutionary War or whether the British government would respond by sending even more troops to North America to beat the American rebels into submission. Nevertheless, the British defeat at Yorktown rendered Jay's further service in Madrid far less important. Jay's time in Madrid, while unsuccessful, further honed his diplomatic skills in ways that would prove helpful during later diplomatic missions and affected his future views of Spanish-American relations. And as events would unfold, the British government ultimately determined that its defeat at Yorktown should prompt peace negotiations leading to American independence and allowing the British to focus more of their resources against competing European powers.

During Jay's time in Spain, a daughter named Susan was born to him and Sarah on July 9, 1780, who lived for only several days, and a second daughter named Maria was born on February 20, 1782, who survived.[38]

In May 1782, Jay learned that he was among five men appointed by Congress to negotiate a peace treaty with Great Britain to be performed by American and British diplomats in Paris. The family left Madrid on May 22, 1782, in further service of the states, arriving in Paris on June 23, 1782. John, Sarah, and Maria Jay moved into an apartment that had been reserved for them at the Hotel de la Chine opposite the Compagnie des Indes (the French East India Company). Personally and professionally, the Jays would enjoy the grandeur and sites of Paris more than the life they had left behind in Madrid.[39]

The five men appointed by Congress to negotiate a peace treaty with Great Britain were Benjamin Franklin, John Adams, Thomas Jefferson, Henry Laurens, and John Jay. Jefferson declined the assignment. Laurens, the former president of the Second Continental Congress, was captured by the British while crossing the Atlantic and imprisoned at the Tower of London until December 31, 1781. Adams was initially delayed in reaching Paris. In the late summer of 1782, Franklin took ill with kidney stones and other maladies, leaving John Jay as the only American in Paris who was at first able, fit, and present to negotiate.[40]

Figure 2.3. Sarah "Sally" Van Burgh Livingston Jay.

An entire book could be written on the challenges, intrigues, machinations, deceptions, complications, frustrations, personality conflicts, and brilliance of the American negotiations with Great Britain, which resulted in a formal end to the war between the two nations. An initial challenge faced by all of the American negotiators was the directive of Congress, which Jay found greatly offensive, that handcuffed the negotiations to the advice and will of the French government. Jay felt so strongly that the interests of the United States not be subordinated to any foreign power that on one occasion, when the subject of French participation arose, he threw his pipe into a fireplace in anger, and it smashed into multiple pieces. Jay was typically mild-mannered, but on rare occasions he allowed fits of anger to flare. He ultimately dealt with the dilemma by demonstrating that the French government did not truly have American interests for independence at heart, which, in Jay's view, forfeited France's role as a benevolent consigliere to the United States, and which allowed the American negotiators to conduct their work with the British without the prior clearance and approval of France.[41]

A second threshold problem for the American negotiators was that the initial commission given by the British government to Richard Oswald, who was to negotiate with the Americans, expressly stated that a grant of independence was to be negotiated in exchange for peace, rather than being freely granted by King George III prior to negotiating peace terms. A separate commission was given by the British government to Thomas Grenville, who was to negotiate matters with the French foreign minister, Charles Garvier Vergennes. Jay insisted that Great Britain first recognize the independence of the states so that a treaty could follow that would be negotiated directly between representatives of Britain and the American states. Jay suggested and achieved a compromise on this issue, resulting in the British Parliament issuing a new commission authorizing Oswald to negotiate with representatives of the United States, with the issue of formally recognizing American independence to be included within any such treaty.[42]

Jay drafted the initial peace proposals that were presented to the British government, as Benjamin Franklin remained ill, and John Adams had not yet arrived in Paris. Jay proposed that a treaty be reached that 1) recognized the states' independence from Great Britain, 2) provided for the withdrawal of British troops from the former colonies, 3) established a northern boundary favorable to the states, 4) established the United States' western boundary at the Mississippi River, 5) guaranteed American navigation rights upon the Mississippi, and 6) recognized American fishing privileges off the northeastern coast of Canadian North America. The British responded to Jay's proposal by seeking 1) reparations to Loyalists in the United States whose property was destroyed or confiscated during the war, 2) payment of legitimate debts owed to British merchants, 3) a different northern border more favorable to British interests, and 4) a postponement of the issues of fisheries to a later treaty.[43]

The details of each sides' demands required further day-to-day negotiations, which was joined during the fall of 1782 by Franklin and Adams. The three American negotiators—Franklin, Adams, and Jay—collectively created an interesting dynamic that proved to be of benefit to the states. Franklin was the consummate diplomat, a fixture

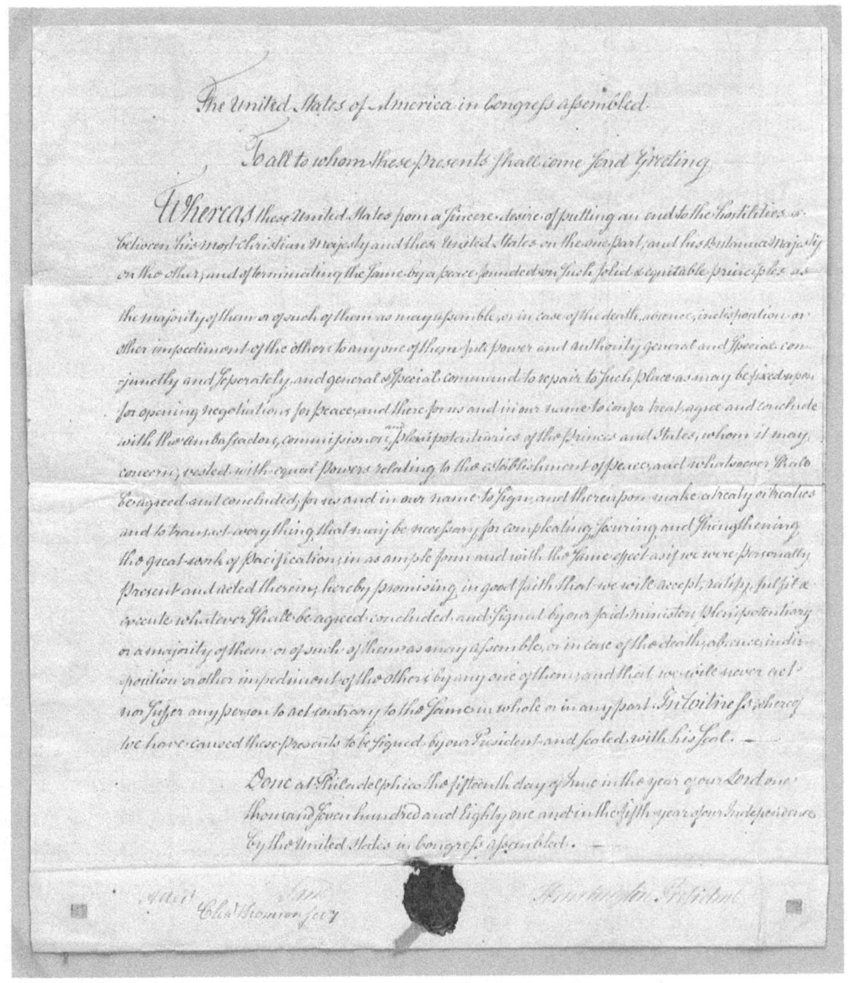

The United States of America in Congress assembled

To all to whom these presents shall come Send Greeting

Whereas these United States from a sincere desire of putting an end to the hostilities between his most Christian Majesty and these United States on the one part, and his Britannic Majesty on the other, and of terminating the same by a peace founded on such solid & equitable principles as

the majority of them or of such of them as may assemble, or in case of the death, absence, indisposition or other impediment of the others to any one of them full power and authority general and special con-junctly and seperately, and general & special command to repair to such place as may be fixed upon for opening negotiations for peace, and there for us and in our name to confer treat, agree and conclude with the Ambassadors, commissioners and plenipotentiaries of the Princes and States, whom it may concern, vested with equal powers relating to the establishment of peace, and whatsoever shall be agreed and concluded, for us and in our name to sign, and thereupon make a treaty or treaties and to transact every thing that may be necessary for compleating, securing and strengthening the great work of pacification, in as ample form and with the same effect as if we were personally present and acted therein; hereby promising in good faith that we will accept, ratify, fulfil & execute whatever shall be agreed, concluded and signed by our said Ministers Plenipotentiary or a majority of them or of such of them as may assemble, or in case of the death, absence, indis-position or other impediment of the others by any one of them; and that we will never act nor suffer any person to act contrary to the same in whole or in any part. In Witness whereof we have caused these presents to be signed by our President and sealed with his seal. —

Done at Philadelphia the fifteenth day of June in the year of our Lord one thousand seven hundred and eighty one and in the fifth year of our Independence By the United States in Congress assembled. —

Attest Chas Thomson Secy   Sam Huntington President

Figure 2.4. Commission to Negotiate a Treaty of Peace.

with French high society, a novel socialite at dinners and parties, and a popular figure with Parisians. John Adams, by contrast, was a brass-tacks personality, sometimes abrasive, seemingly focused at all times on business, and had little patience for diplomatic niceties. Jay was the "balancer" between Franklin and Adams. He appreciated the need for diplomatic decorum, patience, and the development of international relationships, but also remained focused on the important mission at hand. Britain's representatives were Richard Oswald and Henry Strachey throughout the process. When face-to-face negotiations were in progress, Adams would issue demands and threats, Franklin would retreat to jovial expressions and sage anecdotes, and Jay would make the firm, well-reasoned lawyerly arguments addressing the merits of issues that often won over the British representatives. British efforts to obtain meaningful compromises from the American negotiators were generally unsuccessful.

Key terms to what became known as the Treaty of Paris were agreed on by November 30, 1782, but the actual treaty with all of its detail was not signed by the parties at Versailles until September 3, 1783.[44] It was ratified by the Second Continental Congress on January 14, 1784. The treaty gave the Americans most of what they wanted, including independence, a favorable northern boundary through the Great Lakes, a western boundary at the Mississippi, navigation rights, and a British evacuation of military posts. The treaty ceded to the Americans the vast swath of land south of Canada and north of Florida, with significant room for westward expansion to the Mississippi River. Included in the treaty were rights to fish off the northeastern coast, but without the right to dry or cure the catches, and a provision that each country would honor the legitimate debts owed to the citizens of the other. Regarding reparations to Loyalists, the Articles of Confederation did not confer upon the federal government the authority to require the states to provide a mechanism for reparations, but the treaty included a provision that Congress would recommend that the states enact such legislation for the benefit of Loyalists who suffered economic harm because of the war and their loyalty to the Crown. The treaty did not specifically address or foresee issues involving the high seas, such as privateering and the impressment of commercial sailors. As will be seen, treaty provisions regarding the payment of merchant debts and the return of Loyalist properties would become relevant to cases that would later be heard by John Jay and other jurists in the American courts, and the absence of any agreement with the British about privateering and the impressment of sailors would sow the seeds of future conflict between the two nations on the oceans and in the courts.[45]

Henry Laurens, who had been freed by the British from his imprisonment at the Tower of London during the negotiations, spent some time recuperating in southern France and then joined the other negotiators one day before the major final treaty terms were reached. A respected American artist, Benjamin West, was commissioned to paint a portrait of the American and British negotiators of the treaty. West had spent the prior twenty years as a portrait artist of the British king. The British negotiators,

Richard Oswald and Henry Strachey, failed or refused to show up for the portrait, with the most likely explanation being that they did not wish to be memorialized for posterity as the "losers" of America's successful war for independence. The portrait therefore features a table with Jay, John Adams, Benjamin Franklin and his grandson and secretary, William Temple Franklin, and Henry Laurens, with a blank and unfinished section to the table's right where the British negotiators would have appeared.[46]

The American negotiators had the unenviable task of advising their French hosts that a treaty had been reached, despite the earlier understanding that France would play a major role in crafting its terms, and of advising the Congress that France had been cut out of the negotiations despite Congress's directive that France be intimately involved. Had the Americans relied on the French government to negotiate a peace treaty for them it would have taken longer and probably would have been on terms less favorable than what Jay, Franklin, and Adams managed to negotiate on their own. Franklin, who had long cultivated his relationship with the French government and had earned much goodwill from it, smoothed over any ruffled feathers with French Foreign Minister Charles Gravier Vergennes and King Louis XVI and even managed to wrangle an additional loan of money from France to the new American nation.

Franklin admitted to Vergennes that the American negotiators were guilty of neglecting a point of mere *bienseance* and that the British were already flattering themselves for having divided the French from the Americans. Franklin cleverly convinced Vergennes that only a solid French-American friendship could prove the British wrong.[47]

Several members of Congress were angry to learn that France had been marginalized during the peace negotiations, and there were initial calls to reprimand Franklin, Adams, and Jay for their conduct, or alternatively, to recall them from their assignments in Europe altogether. However, when word reached Philadelphia that a peace treaty had been signed on terms that were favorable to the American states, the transgressions of the American negotiators were readily forgotten by the delegates of Congress.[48]

The Treaty of Paris proved to be very popular with the general citizenry of the United States. It has been independently described as "the greatest triumph in the annals of American diplomacy.'[49]

John and Sarah Jay left Europe on June 1, 1784, aboard the *Edward* and arrived back home, at New York harbor, on July 24 of that year. By that time, the Jay family had expanded to include another daughter, Ann, who had been born in Paris on August 13, 1783.

Figure 2.5. Unfinished portrait of the American negotiators of the Treaty of Paris. Pictured from left to right are John Jay, John Adams, Benjamin Franklin, Henry Laurens, and William Temple Franklin.

Jay's intention was to retire from public service. He also intended to devote some time to settling the estate of his father, who had died while Jay was abroad. However, upon his arrival home, Jay learned that the Congress had appointed him as the new American secretary for foreign affairs, a job that he did not refuse. He commenced his activities in that post on December 21, 1784. His salary was initially $4,000, but that was reduced to $3,500 the following year because of general belt-tightening affecting federal employees across the board. The national capital was relocated from Philadelphia to New York in 1785, which was fortuitous for New Yorkers such as Jay. The circumstances allowed Jay to live with his family and work at a fixed location and provided him with an opportunity to reconnect with New York friends, family, attorneys, and political leaders. Jay's New York office was located briefly within New York's City Hall but was then moved to space at the corner of Broad and Pearl Streets in the same building occupied by the infamous Fraunces' Tavern. Jay worked at that location for three and a half years.[50]

At approximately that time, in February 1785, Jay helped found the New York Society for Promoting the Manumission of Slaves. Jay served as its first president. The manumission society initiated lawsuits on behalf of aggrieved slaves, organized boycotts against merchants involved in the slave trade, urged newspapers to decline advertisements for the sale of slaves, and kept watch on the activities of persons involved in the slave trade. The manumission society also managed New York's African Free School, which had fifty-six students within the first year of its founding and which by 1834 educated and equipped more than 1,000 students to take their place in society. In 1788, the state banned slave trading, but the law was riddled with loopholes. Jay remained president of the society until his appointment as US chief justice, leaving the role to avoid any conflict of interest if a case were to arise in court involving any issue of slavery.[51]

Jay was secretary for foreign affairs from late 1784 to March 4, 1789. He defined his role as not merely implementing the will expressed by Congress on matters of international affairs, but also assisting the Congress in formulating its policies. Congress was fortunate to have Jay's guidance, as the members of Congress lacked Jay's experience and knowledge of European diplomacy.[52]

During the latter half of the 1780s, the American states and Great Britain each failed to fulfill certain terms of the Treaty of Paris. The states did not for the most part honor the treaty's commitment to restore property taken from Loyalists, and American debtors felt no obligation to satisfy their financial obligations to British creditors. For its part, Great Britain refused to evacuate its military posts near the new northern and western American borders and significantly restricted American exports into Britain. Nothing could be done to cure these problems, as the Congress had no true authority over the conduct of the independent states.

Relations with Spain grew difficult as well, particularly over the issue of free navigation on the portion of the southern Mississippi River under Spain's control and the establishment of fixed borders between American and Spanish territory. Jay suggested that the United States "forebear" its use of the southern Mississippi River for twenty-five years, without surrendering the "right" to the river, in exchange for a commercial treaty providing for American trade with Spanish colonies and markets. Southern states strongly opposed the idea, deeply distrusted Jay as a result, and called for his dismissal as secretary for foreign affairs.

The issue of navigation rights on the southern Mississippi festered with Spain for several years.

As for France, the relationship between the two countries was overshadowed by the Americans' inability to repay the wartime loans that Congress had received, defaulting on even the interest payments that became due in 1785.[53]

Another vexing international issue during the period was the harassment of American traders by pirates along the Barbary coast of North Africa. American traders had previously enjoyed the protection of the British navy from the Barbary pirates. But with independence from Britain, and there being no American navy of its own, Americans were robbed, killed, and enslaved, and Congress was helpless to do much about it. Without an American navy, Jay suggested that the states consider paying ransoms for the release of their citizens, which was not a popular or adopted proposal. The issue of security on the high seas would reemerge for John Jay a few years later on the docket of the US Supreme Court during his tenure as chief justice.[54]

Jay's time as secretary for foreign affairs demonstrated that the American states were unable to deal effectively with many of the world's major powers and problems. The states had no meaningful army and no navy. Domestically, Congress was dependent on the states for revenue, which was always insufficient. States were embroiled with one another over trade and border disputes, and the separate currencies and legal tender laws of the various states sowed economic confusion and chaos. The great experiment of associating states under the loose Articles of Confederation was failing, and a new continental government needed to be established with greater national, unifying powers. This need was met by the drafting of the proposed United States constitution that "federalized" the states, while at the same time guaranteeing the states' autonomy in most administrative matters and guaranteeing a panoply of rights and freedoms to individual citizens.

The particulars of the new constitution pitted Federalists against Anti-Federalists. The Anti-Federalists were on the side of the debate that sought to assure the greatest amount of authority and autonomy to the states, including the continuance of state currencies, a weak federal executive, and limited federal power overall. Jay was a Federalist, and he supported efforts that were undertaken by the Second Continental Congress to draft a new constitution that would replace the Articles of Confederation to change the dynamic between the federal government and the states in a way that rendered the federal government supreme in certain endeavors. Jay was decisively a continentalist, saying, "It is my first wish to see the United States assume and merit that character of one great nation, whose territory is divided into different States for more convenient government and the more easy and prompt administration of justice, just as our several States are divided into counties and townships for like purposes." The new proposed constitution emerged from the Congress on September 17, 1787.[55]

Jay found a kindred spirit in a fellow New Yorker Alexander Hamilton. Jay and Hamilton decided in the early fall of 1787 to help "sell" the proposed federal constitution to the populace by publishing a series of anonymous articles in newspapers under a single pseudonym. James Madison was invited to join the group. Jay was forty-one years old, Madison thirty-six, and Hamilton in his early thirties when the writing project began. Collectively, the essays became known as the *Federalist Papers*. They were written under a pseudonym, "Publius," consisting of eighty-five essays published between October 1787 and August 1788. The first of the essays ran in New York's semiweekly *Independent Journal* on October 27, 1787. The identity of the authors would not become known for at least several months. Although the *Federalist Papers* were originally intended for a New York audience, they circulated in many other states. The essays became, for supporters, a Federalist bible. The writings made Hamilton, Madison, and Jay the rock-and-roll stars of American Federalist thought.[56]

Jay wrote the essays numbered 2, 3, 4, 5, and 64. No. 2 speaks to the value of unity among the colonies under a single federal government, guided by wise representatives in Congress whose views are recommended, but not imposed, on the people. Nos. 3, 4, and 5 urged the creation of a federalized government for the primary reason of providing the colonies with collective security against foreign powers and threats. No. 64 defined the purpose and procedures for the Senate in a federalized Congress regarding the provision of advice and consent on international treaties, which upon ratification would become the supreme law of the land, and which reflected Jay's personal interest in matters of foreign relations and diplomacy. The reason that Jay did not contribute any essays between No. 5 and No. 64 was that he fell ill during the winter of 1787, before the existence of modern medical technology, immunizations, or prescription medications. When George Washington was presented by Hamilton with a bound copy of the collection of essays, Washington predicted that they "will merit the notice of posterity." Washington's prediction proved to be true. Perhaps no other single document best speaks in detail to the intentions of the framers behind many of the concepts underlying the federal constitution.[57]

The proposed constitution needed to be ratified by at least nine states to become effective for those states. Each state debated its pros and cons. Jay was a leader in the New York debate in favor of ratification. Among other activities, Jay turned to his quill pen to anonymously write an *Address to the People of New York*, which first appeared in April 1788 and set forth reasons why it was in New York's best interests to join the federalized union. The address exhorted all New Yorkers to support the federal constitution that was proposed to the states by the Second Continental Congress.[58]

In mid-April 1788, Jay was seriously injured when he was hit in the head by a rock thrown by a member of an unruly crowd during a riot in Manhattan. The riot was at a jail where a mob was threatening doctors and medical students for having allegedly robbed graves to learn human anatomy. A magistrate had placed the doctors in the jail on a temporary basis for their protection. Jay went to the disturbance with a sword to help defend the jail and its occupants, along with New York Governor George Clinton, General Frederick Von Steuben, General Matthew Clarkson, and others who were bombarded with objects at the scene. Von Steuben was struck by a brick, then Jay by a rock. After Jay was injured, the assembled militia opened fire on the crowd and killed at least three people, which had the effect of dispersing the mob. Jay needed a few weeks to fully recuperate from the injury. The first publication of *An Address to the People of New York* was published during Jay's weeks of convalescence.[59]

The state of New York held a convention at the original courthouse in Poughkeepsie beginning on June 17, 1788. While the convention was in session, New Hampshire and Virginia ratified the federal constitution, making them the ninth and tenth states to do so. Jay, Hamilton, and others undertook a leading role lobbying New York delegates in favor of ratification. On July 26, 1788, New York ratified the proposed constitution by a convention vote of thirty to twenty-seven. It was to become effective on March 4, 1789, the first Wednesday of that month. North Carolina and Rhode Island withheld their ratifications until November 21, 1789, and May 29, 1790, respectively.[60]

This chapter reveals a pattern of John Jay's life in public service. He was needed to undertake intelligence operations in furtherance of revolutionary activities in New York, and did so. He was needed to write New York's constitution, and did so. He was needed to act as the state's first chief judge, and did so. He was needed by Governor Clinton to attend the Second Continental Congress, and did so. After several months as president of the Congress, he was needed to represent the American states to Spain, a potentially key ally, and did so. After the British defeat at Yorktown, Jay was needed to help negotiate a formal peace treaty in Paris, and did so. Jay did not seek, but accepted, his designation by Congress as the American secretary for foreign affairs. When the nation needed to be rallied in favor of a new federal constitution, Jay contributed essays to what became known as the *Federalist Papers*. He likewise stepped forward in the successful effort to obtain New York State's ratification of the US Constitution. Jay had established himself as a "key man" whenever, and wherever, his state or nation required his legal, political, or diplomatic competence, and in each instance, Jay rose to the occasion. The pattern would continue in later years as well.

JAY'S DAYS

The first seventy-seven essays of the Federalist Papers were published in newspapers on an individual, rolling basis. The newspapers included the Independent Journal, *the* New York Packet, *and the* Daily Advertiser, *between October 1787 and August 1788. Later in 1788, the full collection of eighty-five essays was published for the first time as a two-volume bound set. The publisher was J. and A. McLean of New York, New York. The first volume contained the first thirty-six essays. The second volume contained the remaining forty-nine. The first printing was of 500 copies. McLean's edition renumbered some of the essays in an order approved by Hamilton, and later editions followed the numbering used by McLean. An original two-volume set was sold at a Christie's auction on December 16, 2016, for $247,500. Shortly before his deadly duel with Aaron Burr in 1804, Alexander Hamilton made a list of the Federalist essays that he claimed he had authored. In 1818, James Gideon published a new edition of the works with a list of essays prepared by James Madison. The Hamilton and Madison lists overlapped as to fifteen essays, rendering their true authorship uncertain. Some historians have suggested that the disputed essays were products of collaborative efforts between Hamilton* *and Madison, by which both authors could legitimately claim credit for the writings. Other historians have suggested that Hamilton's list, made in haste, might have contained errors, as Hamilton had indisputably misidentified the number of John Jay's essay No. 64. Regardless, there is no dispute today that John Jay was the author of essays 2, 3, 4, 5, and 64.*[61]

Chapter 3

Appointment as the Nation's First Chief Justice

> "I have full confidence that the love which you bear our Country, and a desire to promote general happiness, will not suffer you to hesitate a moment to bring into action the talents, knowledge and integrity which are so necessary to be exercised at the head of that department which must be considered as the Key-stone of our political fabric."
>
> —President George Washington to John Jay
> October 5, 1789

Presidential appointments to the federal judiciary during early American history were not quite as prestigious as they are considered today. In the early 1790s, there were six Supreme Court justices in a nation of approximately four million people. Today, there are nine Supreme Court justices in a nation of approximately 330 million people. For several decades, high judicial positions in the states were considered to be more prestigious than parallel positions in the federal judiciary. One reason was that during the early half of American history, state governments had more power relative to the federal government, in part because of the Tenth Amendment that directed that any powers not expressly delegated to the United States were reserved to the states and the people. Over time, and particularly during the twentieth century, the federal government of the United States assumed more and more responsibilities relative to the states, and the balance in the division of power shifted in favor of the federal government notwithstanding the language of the Tenth Amendment. Loosely, the same can be said of the federal and state judiciaries.[1]

A second reason that federal judgeships were less prestigious than many of their state counterparts was that the federal appellate jurists were required to "ride" multi-state circuits, which was neither desired by many qualified attorneys nor desirable in fact. By contrast, state judges traveled, if at all, within the confines of their own state or county.

Congress established the structure of the federal courts within the broader framework of Article III of the Constitution. The Judiciary Act of 1789 created a federal District Court in each state to hear matters involving minor federal crimes and admiralty and maritime cases. The Circuit Courts, unlike today, were courts of "original jurisdiction," meaning that they had the authority to hear trial-level cases of major federal crimes, civil disputes between parties of different states with a monetary value exceeding $500, as well as appeals from the District Courts. The Circuit Court was required to convene in each state twice per year, but the states were grouped into broader Eastern, Middle, and Southern Circuits. Circuit Courts were composed of three-judge panels consisting of two Supreme Court justices plus the judge of the District Court in the state where the circuit case was heard.[2]

The concept of "circuit riding" had been borrowed from Great Britain, as were many concepts in early American jurisprudence. The Southern Circuit included South Carolina, Georgia, and eventually North Carolina. The Middle Circuit consisted of all states between and including New Jersey and Virginia. The Eastern Circuit included New York State and all of New England. The geographic mass of all of England could fit within New York State, meaning that the Eastern Circuit, not to mention the other circuits, was far larger in size than what was considered the norm in Great Britain. The sheer size of the United States rendered circuit riding more time-consuming, challenging, and physically punishing than it was in the country from which the concept was adopted.[3]

Aggrieved parties at the Circuit Court could appeal unfavorable decisions to the US Supreme Court. Chief Justice Jay, on behalf of himself and his colleagues, complained to President Washington in a letter dated November 13, 1790, that it appeared inappropriate for them to hear the same cases as justices at both the Circuit Courts and then on appeal at the Supreme Court. With that problem unsolved two years later, the justices voiced their complaints directly to Congress by letter dated August 9, 1792, arguing that their dual responsibilities impaired their impartiality and the public's confidence in the courts.[4]

By congressional fiat, the Supreme Court justices were required to travel to the circuits once in the spring and again in the fall and to be at the Supreme Court at the beginning of each February and August for hearing the appeals brought there. Early in the Supreme Court's history, justices would ride the regional circuit that included only their respective home state. That practice changed as of the fall of 1792, after Congress passed legislation requiring the justices to rotate their circuit assignments. Most of the justices were opposed to a rotation of circuit riding. It was least desirable to ride the Southern Circuit because of its geographic size and the cost of its travel, which the non-Southern justices wished to avoid. John Jay was of the opinion, either born of sincerity or convenience, that circuit rotation could only be accomplished through an act of Congress. The Judiciary Act of 1789 required that judges of the District Courts reside in their districts, but there was no similar direction that Supreme Court Justices ride only the circuit that included their home states.[5]

The new legislation that required the Supreme Court justices to rotate their circuit court assignments was a product of intrigue. Justice James Iredell of North Carolina repeatedly and unsuccessfully asked his judicial colleagues during the earliest years of the court's existence to rotate coverage of the circuits as a particular accommodation to him. When that failed, Iredell and his allies in Congress, including Iredell's brother-in-law, Senator Samuel Johnston of North Carolina, prevailed in addressing the issue through legislation that was introduced on March 20, 1792. Indeed, Iredell personally drafted the legislation that Johnston then navigated through Congress on his behalf. The circuit rotations required by the Judiciary Act of 1792 meant that most of the justices would spend even more time traveling than they had earlier, as the travel often was to points more distant from the justices' own home circuits. The primary beneficiary of the new law was Iredell.[6]

This narrative sometimes describes judicial positions with the term "judge," and on other occasions, "justice." There is no practical difference between the two terms, as both pertain equally to judicial officers in the courts. However, in federal and state constitutions, certain judicial offices are identified as "justices," while other judicial offices are identified as "judges." This text endeavors to adhere to the proper constitutional nomenclature wherever and whenever applicable. The chief judicial officer of the US Supreme Court, and the associate officers of that court, are "justices," while the chief judicial officer in New York State is a "judge." Federal district and circuit courts are composed of "judges," whereas New York State Supreme Court jurists at the trial and appellate level are "justices." The term "jurist" is an umbrella term from the dictionary that includes both judges and justices.

The US Constitution is ambiguous as to whether the Supreme Court should have a chief justice at all. Article III, section 1, generically says that "[t]he judicial Power of the United States shall be vested in one supreme [sic] Court, and in such inferior Courts as the Congress may from time to time ordain and establish," and that language says nothing about the Supreme Court being headed by a chief justice. But Article 1, section 3, clause 6, which regards the authority of Congress, mentions that when a president is the subject of an impeachment trial in the Senate, "the Chief Justice shall preside." This singular and cryptic reference to a chief justice, within the legislative branch Article of all places, suggests that the framers of the Constitution had such an office in mind. The first Congress resolved the ambiguity without much debate when it included in the Judiciary Act of 1789 a provision for a "Chief Justice and five associate justices," and with corresponding differences in salary.[7]

George Washington was chosen as the nation's first president with sixty-nine electoral votes. John Adams received thirty-four electoral votes, and John Jay, nine. One of Washington's first responsibilities was to form a Cabinet, and he needed to arrange the political chess pieces so that Alexander Hamilton, Thomas Jefferson, and John Jay would each fill the most prominent of positions. Jay's career had ripened for a high-level appointment within the new administration. He was highly educated for the times. He was intelligent and well-liked by those who knew him. He had maintained a successful law practice until it was interrupted by the movement for independence from Great Britain. He had become a friend and colleague of the most influential men throughout the United States at the First and Second Continental Congresses, and proved his abilities there as an author, negotiator, and tactician. He had successfully negotiated the Treaty of Paris that marked the end of the Revolutionary War and officially recognized the independence of the United States. He had burnished diplomatic skills while representing the states as their minister to Spain and as secretary for foreign affairs. And he had the friendship and respect of a singularly important man—George Washington.[8]

The selection of a chief justice was one of many prominent positions that Washington needed to fill. Jay was strongly considered for appointment to head either the Treasury Department or the State Department. He was not an obvious choice for the Supreme Court, as he had not actually practiced law for at least a decade. But Jay sought the judiciary over other options in the expectation that the Supreme Court would receive a good number of cases involving foreign parties and international law, subjects in which he had a keen interest. Indeed, of the five *Federalist Papers* authored by Jay, four regarded foreign policy and national defense, and the fifth, while ostensibly addressing the role of a federal Senate, focused specifically on the Senate's responsibility of reviewing and ratifying treaties. Alexander Hamilton was thought to be a perfect fit for secretary of the treasury. Jefferson's presence in the Cabinet may have been viewed as a unifying gesture for the new country. Washington ultimately arranged for Hamilton to be secretary of the treasury, Jefferson to be secretary of state, and Jay to be chief justice. For Jay, his nomination as chief justice represented a welcome change of pace. He had spent an entire decade as the US minister to Spain, a negotiator of the Treaty of Paris, and the United States' secretary for foreign affairs. Pivoting his career back to the law, where he also had meaningful prior experience, was a timely career change. Heading the judicial branch of government, which needed to be built from the ground up, would prove challenging but very important to the country.[9]

Jay accepted his nomination for chief justice. The position paid $4,000 a year at the time, while associate justices of the court were each paid $3,500. He was unanimously confirmed by the US Senate without there even being any legislative debate, a concept that is unfathomable for a Supreme Court seat in today's partisan political climate. With that, he ascended to that first and historic judicial position. Jay was not only the first chief justice but also, at age forty-three, the youngest person to ever be appointed to that position in our nation's long history.[10]

President Washington had a number of qualified persons from whom to choose for appointment not only to the Supreme Court, but also for the position of chief justice. Washington's criteria were not focused much on scholarship, but on character, reputation, health, experience, ability, loyalty to the federal concept of government, service in the Revolutionary War and the constitutional ratification process, and geographic diversity. Some factors weighed in favor of potential appointees more than others. John Jay had distinguished himself as a private attorney, but he had a relatively brief tenure as chief judge of the New York State Supreme Court in 1777–78, which was unremarkable. Nevertheless, Jay had considerable other nonlegal and nonjudicial experiences that Washington deemed valuable to a chief justice—coauthorship of the *Federalist Papers*, president of the Continental Congress from 1778 to 1779, minister to Spain from 1779 to 1783, a negotiator of the Treaty of Paris, and secretary for foreign affairs under the Articles of Confederation from 1784 to 1789.

John Rutledge was seemingly disappointed that he was offered a position as an associate justice rather than as chief justice, lamenting that his own "Pretensions to the Office of Chief Justice were at least, equal to Mr. Jay's, in point of Law-Knowledge, with the Additional Weight, of much longer Experience, & much greater Practice." Many persons had speculated that James Wilson would be selected as chief justice. Wilson was one of only six persons who had signed both the Declaration of Independence and the US Constitution, had been an outspoken leader for constitutional ratification in his home state of Pennsylvania, and was an attorney of stellar reputation, intellect, and capability.

While figures such as Rutledge, Wilson, and others might have been entirely acceptable selections for the chief justiceship in 1789, no one had quite the national stature as John Jay, as a result of Jay's success in helping negotiate the Treaty of Paris that ended the Revolutionary War, by which Great Britain formally recognized the independence of the United States. That signal accomplishment alone was difficult for any other contender to match.

John Jay's appointment to the Supreme Court reflects the confidence that President Washington must have had in him and respect for Jay's significant public service during the previous decade. Washington wrote to Jay at the time of the Supreme Court nomination, on October 5, 1789:

> "I have full confidence that the love which you bear our Country, and a desire to promote general happiness, will not suffer you to hesitate a moment to bring into action the talents, knowledge and integrity which are so necessary to be exercised at the head of that department which must be considered as the Key-stone of our political fabric."[11]

At the time of the appointment, Jay was still acting as secretary for foreign affairs, a role he had been performing since 1784 under the Articles of Confederation. Washington asked Jay to serve simultaneously as both secretary of state and chief justice in the newly formed federal government until such time that someone else could be appointed and confirmed as secretary of state. Thus, Jay has the distinction of having performed two high-level federal posts at the same time until Thomas Jefferson became secretary of state on March 22, 1790.[12]

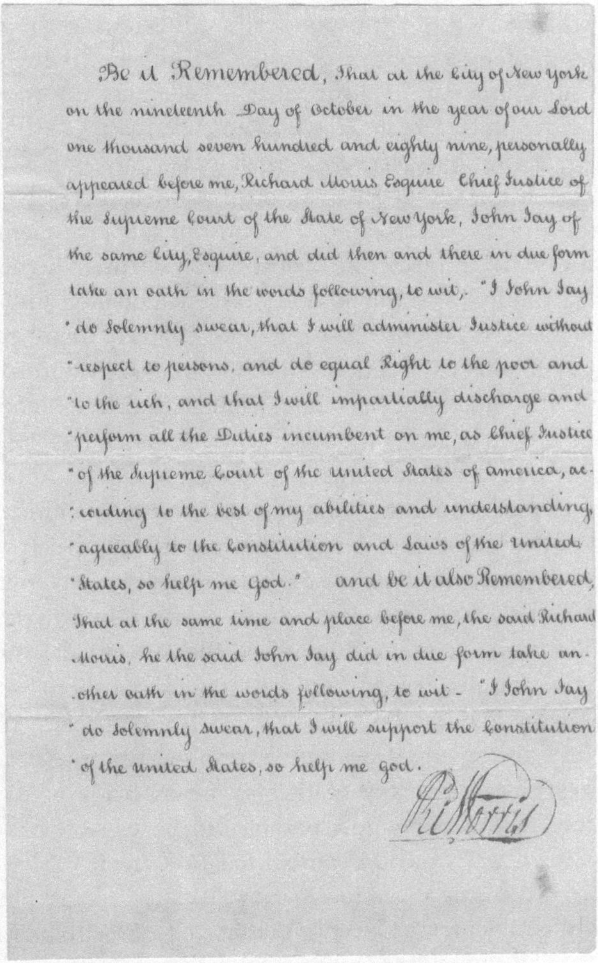

Be it Remembered, That at the City of New York on the nineteenth Day of October in the year of our Lord one thousand seven hundred and eighty nine, personally appeared before me, Richard Morris Esquire Chief Justice of the Supreme Court of the State of New York, John Jay of the same City, Esquire, and did then and there in due form take an oath in the words following, to wit, "I John Jay do Solemnly swear, that I will administer Justice without respect to persons, and do equal Right to the poor and to the rich, and that I will impartially discharge and perform all the Duties incumbent on me, as Chief Justice of the Supreme Court of the United States of America, according to the best of my abilities and understanding, agreeably to the Constitution and Laws of the United States, so help me God." and be it also Remembered, That at the same time and place before me, the said Richard Morris, he the said John Jay did in due form take another oath in the words following, to wit - "I John Jay do Solemnly swear, that I will support the Constitution of the United States, so help me God.

Ri Morris

Figure 3.1. John Jay's oath of office as US chief justice.

Washington also appointed to the Supreme Court the original five associate justices. They were John Blair of Virginia, William Cushing of Massachusetts, Robert H. Harrison of Maryland, John Rutledge of South Carolina, and James Wilson of Pennsylvania. The appointments reflect the bench's geographic diversity representing, as it did, the south, mid-Atlantic, northeast, and New England states. Justice Harrison never actually sat with the court, having declined the appointment after his confirmation by the US Senate due to an illness. Harrison's seat on the court was filled by the replacement appointment of James Iredell of North Carolina. Certainly, the selection of a geographically diverse court was wise for Washington politically. But viewing the court from the standpoint of rank politics does not do justice to the selections. All of the appointees were distinguished Federalist attorneys of high caliber. Washington selected men who had contributed to the American Revolution and who had otherwise participated meaningfully in public life. All of the associate justices had distinguished themselves either as representatives of their states at the constitutional convention or in helping assure ratification of the Constitution in their home states, or both. Four of the initial six appointees (seven including Justice Iredell) already had judicial experience on the highest courts of their home states.[13]

The lack of judicial experience did not necessarily disqualify anyone from receiving a Supreme Court appointment from President Washington. The judicial experience that John Jay had gained as chief judge of New York certainly enhanced his qualifications but did not amount to particularly deep or significant bona fides as a courtroom jurist. The same can be said of the judicial experience of James Iredell, which was limited to six months. James Wilson had no formal judicial experience before his appointment to the US Supreme Court but was known as a brilliant thinker and attorney. To some extent, Washington's mix of justices for the Supreme Court foreshadowed future patterns. Throughout later history, presidential appointees to the federal courts have represented a healthy mix of individuals drawn from lower courts, the bar, and academia.

The geographic diversity of the Jay Court made logistical sense, as the justices of the Supreme Court would be expected to "ride the circuits" by hearing cases in the various federal Circuit Courts while the Supreme Court was not in session in New York and, later, Philadelphia.

Initially, two Supreme Court justices were to sit with a district judge in every circuit of the country, twice a year, to form a three-judge panel hearing cases in those states. The justices riding the circuits, periodically fanning out throughout the states, helped "sell" the new constitutional structure to the populace. The justices were all men of stature, known in their home states and regions, and during their business travels explained the workings of the new federal structure to the lawyers, litigants, jurors, grand jurors, and local folk. It was good advertisement for cementing the legitimacy of the new federal government. Senator William Paterson of New Jersey, who helped author the Judiciary Act of 1789 and who would later become a Supreme Court justice himself, described the justices' circuit riding in effusive terms:

"[Y]ou carry Law to their Homes, Courts to their Doors [and] meet every Citizen in his own state." For this reason, President Washington might have been wise to have selected for the Supreme Court jurists who understood the Revolution and also helped shape the federal Constitution that arose from it. Filling the court with high-profiled men of stature may have been as important, if not more so, than selecting jurists on the sole basis of academic reputation or extensive prior experience in courtrooms.[14]

Figure 3.2. John Jay's Supreme Court portrait by Gilbert Stuart. Jay wore regalia he had received when awarded an honorary degree from Harvard College on July 21, 1790.

Figures 3.3–3.6. Portraits of US Supreme Court Justices John Rutledge, William Cushing, James Wilson, and John Blair Jr.

Washington was acutely aware that the Supreme Court justices, riding the circuits, would also make significant and ongoing contact with the national citizenry. He specifically invited the justices to report to him information they derived from the people and their impressions of the national mood.[15]

Circuit riding had the additional benefit of saving the cash-strapped federal government the cost of paying salaries to an additional layer of jurists occupying the circuit courts. The various benefits the federal government received from circuit riding caused the practice to remain part of the Supreme Court job description for many decades to come.[16]

The Supreme Court was assisted by a clerk. The first clerk of the court was John Tucker, who was appointed in New York on February 3, 1790, and served until sometime after the February 1991 Term in Philadelphia. He was succeeded by Samuel Bayard, who was sworn in on the first day of the August 1791 Term. The clerk's role was to receive documents, maintain the court's official correspondence, accept filing fees, maintain the court's ledgers and calendars, issue the official decisions of the justices, and otherwise be the office administrator of the court.[17]

The government's reliance on the circuit riding of jurists, to proselytize the virtues of the new federal Constitution, had its desired effect during the earliest years of the new republic. The convening of a federal court was a big event in cities where it occurred. Public show was made of local attorneys being sworn in as members of the federal bar. The John Jay Papers maintained at Columbia University include handwritten copies of the charges he gave to grand juries in the Eastern and Middle Circuits, where he lauded the benefits of the federal Constitution. The various justices' charges to grand juries, which extolled the virtues of the federalized court system, were open to the public. The proceedings legitimized the federal courts in the eyes of the public, as they were draped with judicial rituals, pomp and circumstance, and a reverence for due process and fairness. The local newspaper coverage was typically favorable.[18]

The justices of the Supreme Court, including John Jay, came to loathe the burdens associated with riding the circuits. Jay's distaste for circuit riding was a product of a number of factors. The food in country inns was not particularly good and was inferior to the dining he could afford and enjoy at home. Lodging was also inferior to the comforts of home at a day and age when it was not unusual for travelers to share beds and rooms with total strangers. Some of the circuit travel occurred at difficult times of the year during, for instance, months of cold and snow and or times of rain and oppressive heat. The travel was in addition to the trips that Jay and his colleagues were required to make to Philadelphia for the February and August Terms of the Supreme Court each year. Today, airlines have direct flights between major cities on the Eastern seaboard, where flight time in the air is only one or two hours. In the 1790s, travel was in an era of slow, horse-drawn transportation on poor roads, no matter the weather and without the aid of Google Maps or MapQuest. The travel associated with riding the circuits throughout the year took its physical toll on everyone involved. And, perhaps most significantly, the travel took Jay away from his wife, Sarah, his children, and friends in New York for much of each year.[19]

An additional minor point about circuit riding is that it required Jay and his colleagues to travel with their personal law libraries. Today, all courts are equipped with their own library of book and computer resources that judges and clerks rely on for legal authority. Entire law libraries are available to everyone, anywhere in the world, through legal research programs now accessible on computers, cell phones and tablets. During Jay's time, however, courthouses were not well equipped with resource materials, so judicial travel included the burden of transporting a bulky and burdensome collection of one's own law books. The need explains the design of the "Barrister's Bookcase," which are individual shelf compartments stackable one on top of the other to form a full furniture piece. If properly made, each separated compartment could be turned onto its back with its glass swing door facing up, carried by side handles without removing any books from the inside, and then reassembled right-side-up at the destination. Barrister bookcases are commonplace at some courthouses and law firm offices today, though without the side handles for purposes of transport.[20]

The expenses of travel were an issue too. Travel expenses incurred by riding the circuits were paid for by each justice out of his own pocket, with no reimbursement from the federal government. Members of Congress, by contrast, were allotted travel compensation consisting of $6.00 for each day they attended session and an additional $6.00 for every twenty miles they were required to travel to attend. The justices' salaries, while comfortable for the time, were not as impressive as their face amounts suggested because a portion of the incomes was diminished by significant travel expenses throughout much of the year. Indeed, during the spring of 1792, the justices exchanged correspondences among themselves about a proposal to accept a $500 reduction to their individual salaries in exchange for Congress relieving them of their circuit riding duties.[21]

Circuit travel required the justices of the Supreme Court to communicate with family, friends, fellow jurists, and other governmental colleagues by mail. There was, of course, no television or radio news then, nor any modern methods of electronic communication. A colonial mail service originated during the 1770s used by persons and organizations resisting the British and to bypass the Royal Post. The mail system operated throughout most of the eastern colonies, where mail was posted and collected at designated mail offices, taverns, or post riders' homes. During the Revolutionary War, a portion of the continental mail was nevertheless intercepted by the British, rendering its use for resistance activities risky. Letters were often privately entrusted to friends traveling to or near the recipients. By 1789, there were seventy-five official post offices serving a population of three million people. The cost of postage

Figure 3.7. John Jay's barrister bookshelves.

was based on the number of slices of paper being sent and the distance to the recipient. Envelopes were not used, as any envelope counted as a slice of paper. Letter paper was therefore folded and sealed at the crease with paste or hot wax. Stamps were not yet used, as the cost of postage was computed and paid for at the point of mailing. Letter writers tended to fill pages to the four edges, avoiding white spaces and large margins, to make the most use of the available surface area. Handwriting mattered, as did the quality of the quill pens which had to be periodically sharpened, like pencils today. For historians, the "record" of the time consists of official government documents, personal diaries and journals, and letters exchanged between people memorializing the events of the day.[22]

Jay's dislike for riding the circuits was shared by his fellow justices on the Supreme Court. Justice Iredell remarked in a lengthy letter to John Jay and associate justices Cushing and Wilson, dated February 11, 1791, that "no judge can conscientiously undertake to ride the Southern Circuit constantly, and perform the other parts of his duty." Iredell calculated in a letter to his colleague, Thomas Johnson, dated March 15, 1792, that he had traveled 1,800 miles riding the Southern Circuit on three occasions, which does not necessarily include his travel to and from Philadelphia. Several months later, on August 9, 1792, all of the justices of the Supreme Court sent a joint letter to Congress requesting that they be relieved from "the toilsome Journies [sic] through different climates and seasons, which [they] are called upon to undertake." The justices complained that the task of holding twenty-seven circuit courts a year, in different states from New Hampshire to Georgia, plus two sessions of the Supreme Court in Philadelphia during "severe" times of the year, was too burdensome given the size of the United States and the number of judges. The justices complained, "[W]e cannot reconcile ourselves to the idea of existing in exile from our families and of being subjected to a kind of life, on which we cannot reflect, without experiencing sensations and emotions, more easy to conceive than proper for us to express." Congress was not unsympathetic to the complaint, but its sympathies were tempered by the belief that keeping judges on the road put them in touch with the "great mass of the community" and prevented the Supreme Court from becoming a centralized, metropolitan institution. Congress decided to split the issue in 1793 by reducing the number of Supreme Court justices sitting on Circuit Court panels from two to one. The practical effect of the change was that six Supreme Court justices were required to ride the three circuits once a year instead of twice a year. The reduction was not enough to alleviate the complaints about circuit riding, as a further letter was sent by the justices to Congress on February 18, 1894, about the continuing burden.[23]

Circuit riding was related to another peculiarity that was set forth in the original Judiciary Act of 1789. By requiring Supreme Court justices to sit on Circuit Court panels, some of the cases they would help decide in the circuits would inevitably be appealed to the Supreme Court. The same justices, in the Supreme Court, would then be called upon to help review their own lower court decisions. This oddity, which was apparent on its face, was not fixed by Congress for more than an entire century, when it was abolished in the Judiciary Act of 1891. In their letter to Congress dated August 9, 1792, the Supreme Court justices argued this additional reason for eliminating circuit riding from their duties. The members of the Jay Court wrote that "appointing the same men finally to correct in one capacity, the errors which they themselves may have committed in another, is a distinction unfriendly to impartial justice, and that confidence in the Supreme Court, which it is so essential to the public Interest should be reposed in it." The plea fell, at that time, on deaf ears.[24]

In any event, the US Supreme Court convened for the first time on the second floor of the Royal Exchange Building, at the end of Broad Street in Manhattan, on February 1, 1790. It was a convenient location, as Jay and his family resided nearby at lower Broadway, across the street from the New York residence of George Washington. Lacking a quorum, the first session of the court was adjourned to the next day. During the first official session of court, the justices broke British tradition by not wearing white wigs. The February 1790 Term lasted for ten days, during which the jurists admitted attorneys to the court, determined the form of the seals for the various federal courts, appointed a clerk, and formulated procedural rules. Jay proposed that court procedures follow those of the English Courts of King's Bench and Chancery.[25] Attorneys seeking admission to the US Supreme Court needed to demonstrate at least three years of practice before the highest court of a state, good moral character, and legal ability. The earliest attorneys sworn in as members of the Supreme Court bar were Fisher Ames, Egbert Benson, Elias Boudinot, Edward Livingston, and Robert Morris. There were not yet any cases on the Supreme Court's docket during that session or at the next, conducted in August of 1790.[26]

Figure 3.8. The Royal Exchange Building in lower Manhattan.

The Supreme Court's very first case was *VanStophorst v Maryland*, which was filed a year later, for the February Term of 1791. The court sat for that Term at City Hall in Philadelphia. The filing was likely accompanied by some fanfare. Arguably, and ironically, it became one of the least significant cases of the Jay Court. The *VanStophorst* suit was commenced by Dutch creditors who sought to recover the principal and interest on overdue Revolutionary War loans made by them to the state of Maryland. The original loan was for 300,000 Dutch florins, extendable to 600,000 florins, plus 5 percent interest per year and certain service fees, payable at the end of ten years. Interest on the loan could be paid by Maryland by making annual deliveries of tobacco. The state of Maryland had approved the loan but not the agreement on the payment of its interest. A settlement of the parties' dispute over repayment had been reached between the Dutch creditors and representatives of the state, but the Maryland legislature refused to approve the terms of the deal. The parties had agreed to submit their dispute to a panel of four arbitrators that included then-Secretary for Foreign Affairs John Jay, New York Chancellor Robert R. Livingston Jr., New York City Mayor James

Duane, and constitutional convention delegate Rufus King. Before the arbitrators did any actual work, the parties decided to instead negotiate a direct settlement with each other. But thereafter, no settlement agreement was reached.[27]

With the settlement off, the Dutch creditors sought to take depositions of certain witnesses in Holland, which procedurally required the appointment of foreign commissioners to represent the parties at the depositions. Maryland did not object to the taking of depositions in Holland. The state's decision to even appear in the case was controversial, as it represented a potential waiver of "sovereign immunity" that states otherwise enjoy that would, when recognized, make the states off-limits to liability in the federal courts.

The Supreme Court therefore appointed Dutch attorneys to act as commissioners who would certify the anticipated deposition transcripts, and noted in its order that the depositions "shall be read and received as evidence at trial." That order caused Anti-Federalists in Maryland, who opposed centralized federal power, to fear that the case was establishing undesirable precedent that the individual states were subject to lawsuits in the federal courts and did not enjoy sovereign immunity from them. That fear, in turn, caused the Maryland legislature to reverse its earlier opposition to the proposed settlement of the dispute. Once the case was settled and Maryland paid the agreed-upon money to its creditors, the *VanStophorst* case at the Supreme Court was dismissed, as its issues had been rendered academic.[28]

The *VanStophorst* matter was dismissed before any oral argument could be held on it. The Supreme Court's first filed case went nowhere in the end. *VanStophorst* is not treated in this narrative among the cases "decided" by the Jay Court, because the matter was settled by the parties without being resolved by the court on the merits.

Another early Supreme Court case, *Collet v Collet*, was also a misfire. John and James Collet jointly owned the vessel *Swift*, which had made at least three trade voyages to Jamaica. The owners were unable to resolve the financial accounts among themselves, causing John Collet to commence a lawsuit in the state court of Pennsylvania, which was litigated there from December 1786 to November 29, 1790. Ultimately, James Collet was awarded 384.8.5 British pounds, and the amount was affirmed by the Pennsylvania Court of Common Pleas.[29]

John Collet sought to avoid the Pennsylvania judgment by commencing a suit in the federal Circuit Court. Nowadays, such a case would be dismissed under a doctrine called *res judicata*, which prohibits the relitigation of a matter that has already been decided for the same parties on its merits by another court. That aside, and absent any question of federal constitutional law, the federal court could only hear the case if John and James Collet were citizens of different states. John Collet's complaint claimed that James was a citizen of New York and John a citizen of Pennsylvania. James established that he was actually a citizen of Pennsylvania rather than New York, which would have divested the Circuit Court of jurisdiction to hear the case between two fellow Pennsylvanians. John, however, was allowed to then amend his complaint to claim that he was actually a citizen of Great Britain, as he had been born there and never changed his allegiance to Pennsylvania. Unfortunately for John Collet, James's attorney, Moses Levy, produced a certificate that John had taken an oath of allegiance to Pennsylvania on April 30, 1790. Levy also produced a second certificate identifying John Collet as commander of the vessel *Pigou*, which was registered as an American vessel upon an oath that its commander was an American citizen. John Collet's attorneys, Attorney General Edmund Randolph, acting in a private capacity, and Jonathan Dickinson Sergeant, argued that the Pennsylvania oath was null and void, as only the federal government could naturalize citizens under the new 1789 Constitution. Thus, the case presented a novel question of whether state governments, the federal government, or both were authorized to naturalize citizens under the Naturalization Act of 1790.[30]

The Circuit Court panel hearing the case consisted of Justices James Wilson and John Blair, who were riding the circuit, and Judge Richard Peters of the District Court for the District of Pennsylvania. They unanimously found that the federal government's authority to perform the naturalization of citizens was concurrent with that of the states, rendering John Collet's oath of allegiance to Pennsylvania a valid exercise. Therefore, as John and James were both citizens of Pennsylvania, the federal courts had no authority to hear the case and dismissed it. John Collet appealed to the US Supreme Court and obtained a writ directing that the record of the case be transferred to it. The matter was to be heard by the Supreme Court during its August 1792 Term. On June 30, 1792, the certified record of the case was delivered to the clerk of the Supreme Court, but on the same day, John Collet's attorneys discontinued the appeal, and it was withdrawn from the court's calendar without any argument or decision.[31]

Cases that would be of more importance to the new nation were on the event horizon.

JAY'S DAYS

Circuit riding of the Supreme Court was almost permanently eliminated in the waning days of President John Adams's administration, six years after John Jay's tenure ended as chief justice. The Midnight Judges Act of 1801 was an attempt by the outgoing president and the Federalist Congress to expand the number of judgeships in the circuit courts and other courts and eliminate the need for Supreme Court justices to ride the circuits. The new judicial offices would, of course, be filled by Federalists ahead of the Democratic-Republican administration of incoming President Thomas Jefferson. The Midnight Judges Act received its name because some of the newly appointed jurists were reportedly signing their commissions as late as midnight of President Adams's last day in office. The Act was repealed during the early days of the Jefferson administration before the Supreme Court justices could derive any long-term benefit from it. Another ninety years would pass before the circuit riding of Supreme Court justices would be fully eliminated.[32]

Chapter 4

The Supreme Court's First Argued Case

West v Barnes (1791)

"1 Aug. opened Court. decided in the case of West v Barnes that Writs of error to remove causes from Ct. Courts can regularly issue only from this Court. Qu. is not 10 Days too Short a time."

—John Jay Diary Entry
August 1, 1791

William West was the first person in the nation's history who would take a case for argument at the United States Supreme Court. He was a well-known and likeable figure in Rhode Island during the time leading up to his case. West was a farmer, a brigadier general during the Revolutionary War, an outspoken Anti-Federalist, and had served as a non-lawyer state judge in Scituate, Rhode Island. He was a solid citizen. The background of his Supreme Court case, *West v Barnes*, fuses together unique elements of Rhode Island's economics, law, and politics during the period.[1]

Each state under the Articles of Confederation had its own separate currency. The Revolutionary War era had been good for Rhode Island merchants but not good for its farmers. Many farmers were either financially ruined or struggled mightily. The paper money issued by the state of Rhode Island had depreciated to such a degree that by 1781, the state refused to take its own currency for the payment of taxes and debts owed to it. Conditions only worsened during the next five years when, in May 1786, the state's farmer-friendly General Assembly appropriated

100,000 British pounds worth of state paper currency to finance loans to qualified farmers, secured by the farmers' real estate. It passed legislation declaring its paper currency to be equal to its face value in gold and silver and declared that the paper currency be lawful tender for the payment of debts. The same legislation also provided that if any private creditor refused to accept the paper currency as payment toward debts, the debtor could apply to post the payment in paper form with the state's Superior Court in exchange for a judicial certificate satisfying the debt. If, after three months, the creditor refused to collect the money posted at the court, the unclaimed money was to be transferred by the court to the state's General Treasury.[2]

Free markets typically work better than governmental interventionism. Rhode Island's efforts to artificially prop up the value of its currency were doomed to fail and, ultimately, did fail to stabilize the state's crumbling monetary system. The exchange rate for the paper currency, which was at a ratio of six coin shillings for nine paper bills when the initial law was enacted in July 1786, crashed to a ratio of six to ninety by July 1789. Creditors refused to accept the almost worthless paper as payment, demanding instead payment in precious metal coins. Shops closed. Provisions could not be obtained. There were land foreclosures. Citizens of Rhode Island left for better lives in other states.[3]

As Rhode Island's paper currency steadily and painfully devalued, the General Assembly sought to put teeth into its laws by criminalizing persons unwilling to accept the paper currency and imposing penalties. Penalties included fines, the loss of the right to vote, the loss of the right to seek public office, and, ultimately, the prosecution of creditors without any right to a trial by jury.[4]

Before too long, a criminal case appeared on a Rhode Island court docket involving a creditor's alleged violation of the state's currency laws. The case was *Trevett v Weeden*, where it was alleged that defendant John Weeden had refused to accept paper currency as payment from the customers of his butcher shop. It received considerable public attention. The trial of Weeden was held before state Superior Court Judges David Howell, Joseph Hazard, and Thomas Tillinghast on September 25, 1786. Henry Goodwin prosecuted the matter. Attorneys James Mitchell Varnum and Henry Marchant defended Weeden, arguing that the currency law was invalid because it forced creditors to accept worthless paper as payment and because it denied creditors the fundamental right to a jury. Varnum and Marchant provided their trial services to Weeden free of charge on the ground that the issue of the case was of great importance to the residents of their state. No doubt, the publicity derived from a high-profile case is good for any private attorney's law practice, which might have been payment enough to them.[5]

At the end of the trial's evidence and argument, Judge David Howell announced that the court's decision was to dismiss the case. Howell did so without any meaningful explanation of the decision other than to say that the currency-related penal law was "repugnant and unconstitutional." The judges must have known at the time that their decision would be controversial. The concept that a court could declare a law unconstitutional was not universally accepted at the time and was not yet an agreed-upon check and balance between the branches of governments in colonial America. Judge Howell was a man of stature in Rhode Island—he was a graduate of Princeton University, a well-known and accomplished attorney, and a delegate to the Continental Congress from 1782 to 1785 before assuming the bench. While Rhode Island's merchant class was very pleased with the court's decision, the farmers, who were already suffering financially, voiced their complaints to their elected legislators.[6]

The Rhode Island General Assembly, which was controlled by the farmers rather than by the merchants, was angered by the decision as well. The following month, the General Assembly summoned the judges of the Superior Court to the state capital to account for themselves in daring to declare that one of its enactments was unconstitutional.[7] Their mere act of summoning the judges to the capital was a deliberate effort to humiliate the state's judiciary. A reasoned defense of the decision was given by the judges, including a spirited discourse by Judge Howell on the floor of the General Assembly that lasted for almost six hours.[8] The General Assembly then considered whether the judges had given a satisfactory explanation of their judgment in Weeden's case. The General Assembly voted that the judges' explanations were *not* satisfactory to them, which prompted a follow-up motion that each of the judges be fired from his office.[9] On November 4, 1786, before a vote on the latest motion was taken, the judges fought back by demanding that they be afforded a hearing on "certain and specific charges" at a "proper and legal tribunal."[10] With further negotiations, which included many discussions behind closed doors as typical of political bodies, the General Assembly passed a Resolution stating that the judgment in *Trevett v Weeden* was supported by no satisfactory reasons. But because the judges were not charged with any criminality themselves, they were "discharged from any further attendance upon this Assembly on that account," which fell short of dismissing them from their jobs.[11]

As for the state's controversial and failing currency laws, the state government simply ignored the Superior Court's ruling about their unconstitutionality and continued to make policy as if the statutes remained valid and enforceable. Under the circumstances, the citizens of Rhode Island, whether merchants or farmers, could choose for themselves whether to abide by the laws and use paper currency in commercial transactions or ignore the laws with the expectation that its punitive aspects might not be enforced by the state courts.

The judges who presided over *Trevett v Weeden* would be subject to further retribution. Their ruling convinced the state's General Assembly that it should undertake measures to gain greater control over the judiciary rather than passively accept any authority of the judiciary to declare its enactments unconstitutional. The General Assembly quickly

Figure 4.1. Hon. David Howell.

changed the laws to vest in itself the sole authority to appoint the state's judges to only one-year terms, subject to reappointment each year. On May 2, 1787, all five judges of the state's Superior Court applied for their first reappointment to the court under the new law. While Chief Judge Paul Mumford managed to muster enough support in the state's legislature for reappointment, the other four judges, including Howell, Hazard, and Tillinghast, were ousted from the judiciary. The legislature's action proved the maxim that sometimes revenge is best served cold.[12]

The currency crisis continued to worsen to the point that other states passed measures to retaliate against Rhode Island for its worthless paper-money legislation, and Connecticut excluded Rhode Island citizens from its courts. Those events awakened the Rhode Island legislature to considering a repeal of its onerous currency laws. Two repeal proposals in previous years had failed, but that was before Rhode Island began receiving retaliatory pressure to repeal from other states. On September 19, 1789, the General Assembly "suspended" its interventionist currency laws until the following month and then repealed them altogether on October 12, 1789.[13]

The economic divide between merchants and farmers in Rhode Island during the 1880s forged a divide between the two groups that was political as well. The merchants, who lived closer to the Atlantic coast, were Federalists who favored the ratification of the constitution that had emerged from the Constitutional Convention in Philadelphia on September 17, 1787. The Federalists sought to enact a national constitution that conferred federal authority over the states in certain areas of public affairs, such as in the conduct of foreign policy and providing a national defense, the declaration of wars, the regulation of interstate commerce, the establishment of a post office, the existence of a federal court system, the collection of national taxes, and the coining of a national form of money. By contrast, the farmers of Rhode Island were Anti-Federalists occupying much of the state's inland, and they were concerned about tax policy and the payment of state debts. Anti-Federalists wanted a weak form of centralized government, weak executive authority, and the circulation of paper money that would help them pay their debts. Politically, Anti-Federalists had the upper hand in Rhode Island in the late 1880s, as the farmers handily outnumbered the merchants. They not only controlled the state's General Assembly, but also assured that Rhode Island would not even send any delegates to the Constitutional Convention in 1787 because of their opposition to the concept of concentrated federal power. Indeed, Rhode Island refused to ratify the new federal constitution from 1787 through 1789 as the other original states were doing so because the clause in the proposed constitution prohibiting the states from impairing contracts could potentially interfere with Rhode Island's then-existing farmer-friendly currency laws.[14]

Which brings the narrative back to William West and his forthcoming litigation in the federal courts. William West had entered into a molasses business that lost him a significant amount of money and threw him into debt. He had financed his molasses business with a twenty-year mortgage on his extensive Rhode Island farm in favor of Joseph Jenckes, a Providence merchant, and other members of Jenckes's family. West sold the molasses at a loss. The promissory note on the mortgage was for an original sum of 2,174 pounds, and it had been paid down over time to where the debt had been reduced to 1,593 pounds. With further time, West fell behind on his remaining mortgage payments and, being a responsible person, considered ways to raise money that would enable him to pay his creditors and keep his farm.[15]

West, given his exemplary war service, was granted special permission by the Rhode Island state legislature in 1785 to conduct a lottery of 1,950 acres of his real estate, along with some of his cows, horses, oxen, and sheep. While gambling and land lotteries might seem out of place in colonies that were founded on strong and sometimes strict religious principles, and would be unusual for raising private money by today's standards, they were not unheard-of at that time of American colonial history. West planned to use the profits from the lottery toward the satisfaction of his mortgaged debt.[16]

The lottery was successfully held, and West did, in fact, try to apply the proceeds toward the retirement of his debt. On September 12, 1789, West offered to pay the Jenckes family the full balance due on the loan using Rhode Island's paper currency. The Jenckes family refused to accept the paper currency as payment, as the paper money had considerably devalued from the time of the original loan, and they were unwilling to absorb a steep loss of its value. The Jenckes family insisted that they instead be paid for the full amount of the debt in gold or silver coins.[17]

With the parties at an impasse, West, following the provisions of the currency law enacted in August 1786, paid the disputed money to the state's Superior Court on September 16, 1789. The court directed the Jenckeses to appear on the issue ten days later. No one attended the court appearance on behalf of the Jenckes family on the scheduled date,

Figure 4.2. William West's farmhouse in Scituate, Rhode Island.

and as a result, the court, following the statute that had been enacted, issued a certificate that officially discharged West of the debt. At this point in the story, one might expect that there is no further story to tell. However, the validity of Rhode Island's currency statutes had been called into question by the earlier ruling in *Trevett v Weeden*, and the Jenckes family refused to concede that the debt to them had been satisfied.[18]

A member of the Jenckes family was David Leonard Barnes, who was a co-party to the debt, a husband of one of the Jenckes's sisters, and a graduate of Harvard College. Barnes was a smart young attorney who agreed to represent the family in connection with the payment controversy. At that time, and until 1801, cases were eligible to be heard in the federal circuit courts if the controversy exceeded $500 in value and if the parties were citizens of different states.[19] Here, the value of the dispute met the monetary threshold. Additionally, because West lived in Rhode Island and Barnes lived in Massachusetts, the circuit court was authorized to hear Barnes's claim.[20]

Barnes filed a suit in the Circuit Court in Rhode Island at its courthouse in Newport. The relief that was sought from the court was an order ejecting West from the property as a result of West's failure to "pay" the debt on the mortgaged property. In opposition to the ejectment suit, West argued that he had offered to pay the entire debt using the state's currency and, upon its rejection, had paid the full amount into the court as authorized by Rhode Island law. Moreover, at the time West paid the money into the court, Rhode Island's currency law had not yet been actually repealed by the state legislature.[21]

The three-judge panel of the Circuit Court consisted during the summer of 1790 of Chief Justice John Jay and associate Supreme Court Justice William Cushing, who were riding the Eastern Circuit, and Rhode Island District Court Judge Henry Marchant. Marchant had been one of two attorneys who had earlier represented butcher John Weeden, without charging a fee, during Weeden's currency trial in September 1786. The result of that trial had been popular with the Federalist merchants in Rhode Island, so perhaps there is no surprise that Marchant later received an appointment from President George Washington to the federal District Court for the District of Rhode Island after that state's eventual ratification of the national Constitution. Politics aside, Judge Marchant

Figure 4.3. David Leonard Barnes.

had a solid curriculum vitae for appointment to a seat on the federal court on the merits. He was a graduate of the College of Philadelphia, which is now known as the University of Pennsylvania; practiced law in Newport; served as the state's attorney general during the 1770s; attended the Second Continental Congress; and was a member of the Rhode Island General Assembly during the latter part of the 1880s. However, one cannot ignore that in hearing the case between Barnes and West over the relevance and enforceability of Rhode Island's paper currency laws, Marchant would not be expected to be sympathetic to the arguments of farmer William West.[22]

West had spent some time on a Rhode Island state court, but it is doubtful that he had any meaningful legal training or was learned in the law, as was somewhat common for provincial judges in the late 1700s. His primary occupation was that of a farmer. Perhaps owing to this, West made what might be viewed in hindsight as a cardinal error—he decided to represent himself at the Circuit Court *pro se*, which, in this case, placed him at a disadvantage against attorney Barnes and the legally trained judges.[23]

The three-judge Circuit Court consisting of Jay, Cushing, and Marchant was persuaded by Barnes's legal argument that West's debt had *not* been paid and that Barnes could proceed with an ejectment of West from the property. Whatever arguments West made in opposition were unavailing. The Circuit Court failed to specify any written ground for its decision.[24]

According to the *Providence Gazette* regarding subsequent related proceedings, the Circuit Court rendered its decision against William West based on a developed set of facts and a reasoned application of law. West had posted his mortgage payoff with the state's Superior Court on September 16, 1789. The state's currency laws had been suspended by the General Assembly three days later, on September 19, 1789, before being fully repealed the following month. Therefore, when the Superior Court originally directed that the Jenckes appear before it on the issue ten days after West's posting of the money, on September 26, 1789, the scheduled court appearance was on a date when the currency law was already suspended and no longer operational. As a result, as explained by the *Providence Gazette*, the certificate issued by the Superior Court to William West on September 26, 1789, discharging his debt to the Jenckes, was itself null and void and provided West with no viable defense to Barnes's claim for ejectment from the premises. There was a logic to that legal reasoning by the Circuit Court.[25] Perhaps, when West was issued his court certificate that purportedly satisfied his debt, the slow means of communication at the time prevented the state court from being aware that Rhode Island's currency laws had already been suspended.

The paper money paid by William West to the state Superior Court had reverted to the state. One might wonder why, upon the Circuit Court's determination that William West's payment to the court was null and void, the state of Rhode Island did not simply refund the money to West. While there appears to be nothing specific on this question in the historical record, the answer may lie in the fact that the individual states, as sovereigns, were immune to lawsuits by their own citizens. The proceeds paid by West into the court had reverted into the Rhode Island treasury, and the cash-strapped state might have been unable or unwilling to pay it back, knowing that as a sovereign it was immune to any claim by West that the money was rightfully his. If so, West was placed into the unenviable position of having paid the face value of the debt to the state court using paper money while being expected to pay the same debt a second time to the Jenckes family in gold or silver coin. The prospect placed William West on the verge of financial ruination.

His back against a wall, West decided to appeal the Circuit Court's decision to the US Supreme Court. The decision to appeal was, in and of itself, suspect, as two of the justices at the Supreme Court who would hear the case in Philadelphia—Jay and Cushing—had already ruled against him. Such was the Catch-22 of a judicial system that, at the time, allowed appellate judges to hear appeals of the same cases they had already decided in courts below. In the interim, legal historians may only speculate about how many appeals to the US Supreme Court had never been undertaken by aggrieved parties, because one-third of the Supreme Court justices had already ruled against the would-be appellant. William West might have calculated that he had no choice but to undertake an appeal to the Supreme Court, as he was financially ruined by the Circuit Court's determination, and a successful appeal to the Supreme Court provided his only hope.[26]

Congress had enacted the Judiciary Act of 1789, which contained the original procedural rules governing the conduct and practices of the federal courts. One of its procedural rules required that the appealing party secure a "writ of error" whenever an appeal was contemplated to an appellate court. The writ of error was a document loosely akin to what is today known as a "notice of appeal." The writ of error served an important legal purpose of documenting that a party intended to pursue an appeal of an unsatisfactory court determination. An additional purpose served by the writ was to order the transfer of the court file from the lower court to the higher court for purposes of the appeal. Congress, in the Judiciary Act of 1789, did not clearly specify whether the writ should be issued by the court being appealed *to* or the court being appealed *from*. The Judiciary Act merely said, in section 14, that federal courts issue writs "necessary for the exercise of their respective jurisdictions, and agreeable to the principles and usages of law." The "principles and usages of law" appear to be a reference to past practices, and the past practice was for writs of error to issue from the higher court to the lower one. Adding to the confusion, another provision of the Judiciary Act, section 23, stated that a writ of error had the effect of staying the enforcement of the judgment if filed with the lower court within ten days of the judgment. Arguably, Congress would not have intended for that provision to have no practical effect for parties from states far from Philadelphia, who would be geographically unable to secure a writ from the Supreme Court and file it with a lower court in the home state within the span of a mere ten days. Nevertheless, because only higher courts can issue commands to lower courts, the prevailing opinion was that West, as the appealing party, was required to have a writ of error certified within ten days of the Circuit Court's ruling by the clerk of the court to which the appeal would be taken—in his case, by the US Supreme Court. The certification of an appropriate writ of error, within the specified time frame, at the correct court, was a statutory condition to West's right to later have his appeal heard by the Supreme Court on its merits.[27]

The filing rule was onerous and impractical for many appeals that potentially might be heard at the Supreme Court for reasons that are already obvious. It required parties or their attorneys to travel from far-off states to Philadelphia, where the Supreme Court sat at the time, to secure their writs of error. This, during an era of horseback transportation on poor roads, required a commitment of time and expense that was difficult or impossible for many persons to afford or accomplish within only ten days of an adverse ruling. The filing rule was especially unfair to litigants whose cases were heard in lower courts farthest from Philadelphia, such as in the states of New Hampshire and Georgia.

West, given his limited legal background, either did not fully appreciate the need to obtain his writ from the clerk of the Supreme Court in Philadelphia, perhaps deeming the trip impossible, or he simply did not understand the writ requirements. For whatever reason, West secured a writ of error from the clerk of the Circuit Court at the courthouse in Newport, Rhode Island, along with an authenticated transcript of the proceedings there. West posted an appeal bond, and the clerk in Newport issued a citation ordering Barnes to appear on the case at the US Supreme Court in Philadelphia. On July 23, 1791, West sent the writ of error and the Circuit Court's file to the clerk of the US Supreme Court with a request that the matter be added to the court's docket. No writ was ever secured by West from the clerk of the Supreme Court in Philadelphia before the mandatory ten-day deadline, or after.[28]

West then hired William Bradford Jr., the attorney general of the Commonwealth of Pennsylvania, to represent him in the forthcoming proceedings at the Supreme Court. Bradford was known to all or most of the justices of the Supreme Court. He was a graduate of Princeton University and had served as a lieutenant colonel in General Washington's army during the Revolutionary War, including an assignment at Valley Forge. He was a prominent attorney and an appointee to his position as Pennsylvania's attorney general. In those days, there was no prohibition against a state's attorney general simultaneously representing clients in private litigations.[29]

The case of *West v Barnes* was docketed for the August 1791 Term of the Supreme Court. Oral argument was entertained on August 2, 1791. A court reporter, Alexander Dallas, was hired to make a record of the argument, as it was the first time that a record of contested proceedings would need to be prepared at the Supreme Court. Dallas had been a struggling attorney who was born in Jamaica, educated in England, migrated to America in 1783, and was admitted to the practice of law in Pennsylvania two years later. Dallas was a logical choice for the position, as he had already transcribed and published many accounts of cases decided in the Pennsylvania and Delaware state courts.[30]

At oral argument, William Bradford made a motion to the Supreme Court that it accept the writ of error that his client had secured from the clerk of the Circuit Court in Newport. West was not present for the argument, as he had remained in Rhode Island. Bradford's request that the Supreme Court "rejoin to the errors assigned to this cause" was, in effect, a request that the Supreme Court overlook the problem with the writ as minor, insignificant, correctable, and nonprejudicial to any party.[31]

Figure 4.4. Pennsylvania Attorney General William Bradford.

David Leonard Barnes, who had made the 300-mile trip to Philadelphia from his Massachusetts home, was admitted to the bar of the Supreme Court the same morning that the case was heard in order for him to be permitted to make arguments to the justices. Barnes objected to Bradford's motion and to the validity of any writ issued, as it had been issued by the clerk of an incorrect court. Barnes strenuously argued that under the rules governing appeals to the Supreme Court, West was under an unyielding obligation to secure a writ of error from the clerk of the Supreme Court in Philadelphia, a task that West admittedly did not perform. In response, Bradford maintained that the issuance of a writ of error was a mere ministerial task, so it did not matter whether the writ originated from one court or the other. Bradford also argued the inequity of effectively denying any American citizen the right to appeal any case to the Supreme Court if residing more than ten days of travel from Philadelphia.[32]

The *West* case had two broad tiers of analysis to it, one involving the procedural requirements of the ten-day rule for writs of error, which was the subject of Bradford's motion, and the second being the substantive merits of the appeal itself. In such circumstances, courts will typically address procedural issues first, and if the proponent of a claim or an appeal can successfully surmount procedural obstacles, courts will then consider the merits. If procedural obstacles cannot be overcome, there is no need for courts to reach the merits of an argument. Because there were not yet any other active cases on the court's docket, there was no reason to delay the issuance of a written decision on Bradford's motion. The first-ever decision of the US Supreme Court was released the day following the oral argument, which represents a dispositional speed that is almost unprecedented by today's standards.

All of the members of the Supreme Court were sympathetic to West's procedural difficulty and Bradford's motion to cure it. But in a certain percentage of cases, including this one, appellate justices' hands are tied by the language of statutes that govern aspects of a case in controversy. A ruling in favor of West would have required that the Supreme Court ignore, or rewrite, the controlling federal statute defining the ten-day rule for the filing of writs of error and the identity of the court from which the writs must issue. The justices would not undertake the activist role of deciding the issue contrary to the "principles and usages of law" that were requirements of the statute.[33]

In the 1790s, the practice at the Supreme Court was for each justice to render a separate opinion, *seriatim*. The winner or loser in any appeal would be determined by examining each justice's opinion to mathematically calculate which party received a majority in its favor and which did not. The practice followed that which had long existed in the English courts. The Supreme Court did not, as it does today, render a single majority opinion from one justice, accompanied by any separate concurrences or dissents by other justices. The modern practice of issuing consolidated majority and dissenting opinions was not commenced until 1796, during the tenure of Chief Justice Oliver Ellsworth.[34]

All of the justices wrote separate analytical opinions in *West v Barnes* quoting, in the fashion and flourish typical of the time, English law, Sir Edward Coke, William Blackstone, and others. The end result, however, was a unanimous opinion that Congress had intended in the Judiciary Act for the writs of error to be issued in the manner consistent with past procedures and practices. The past practices required that there be a timely writ of error secured from the clerk of the *higher* court—in this case, the Supreme Court—and absent that, the Supreme Court

Figure 4.5. Courtroom at Old City Hall, Philadelphia.

was without jurisdiction to hear the appeal at all. In other words, the procedural obstacle faced by West prevented the court from reaching the merits of his case, and West's appeal was dismissed by application of a procedural technicality. Only Congress could alter the language and meaning of its statute and rectify whatever injustices the rule visited upon litigants of far-off states. The full court did not pass judgment on whether the decision of the Circuit Court, which had included Chief Justice Jay and Justice Cushing, was or was not correct on its merits. But for West's procedural obstacle, *West v Barnes* might have provided the US Supreme Court with its first occasion to consider whether it had to authority to pass judgment on the constitutionality of a state statute.[35]

The justices delivered their opinions on the case in reverse seniority order. Justice Iredell found the language of the Judiciary Law to be unclear. He concluded that the writ of error needed to be issued by only the Circuit Court or the Supreme Court, but not by either, because the existence of overlapping responsibilities would sow confusion. As between the two courts, Iredell believed that it would be "absurd" to expect the Circuit Court to issue a writ to itself and that it was "natural and obvious" that the writ be issued by the Supreme Court because that was the forum being asked to render a legal remedy. While Iredell recognized the unfairness of that result to geographically distant appellants such as William West, only the Congress could correct that defect in the law. Justice Blair reasoned that writs of error were by definition "returnable" only in the court hearing the matter, which in this instance was the

Supreme Court, and that any impracticality contained in the Judiciary Law could only be corrected by the Congress. Justice Wilson agreed with Justice Iredell that the Circuit Courts cannot issue writs to themselves to transfer a file to the Supreme Court, as writs are mandatory directives, and agreed with Justice Blair that any inconveniences caused by the law could only be corrected by the Congress. Justice Cushing's opinion mirrored that of Wilson.[36]

Justice Jay's opinion was the briefest, perhaps aided by the fact that it was announced last. Jay merely stated that as the other justices of the Supreme Court had already set forth their reasonings, "I need only, therefore, suggest my concurrence with my Brethren."[37]

Ironically, Jay's sentiments about the legal issue presented by *West v Barnes* were better expressed by him in his diary. For an entry made at the beginning of the case, Jay wrote, "1 Aug. opened Court. decided in the case of West v Barnes that Writs of error to remove causes from Ct. Courts can regularly issue only from this Court. Qu. is not 10 Days too Short a time." In other words, consistent with his official decision, William West's inability to reach Philadelphia to file the writ of error at the Supreme Court, within ten days of the Rhode Island determination, was irrelevant. All that was relevant, in Jay's view, was whether the writ was issued by the US Supreme Court as required by the controlling provision of the Judiciary Act. The diary entry is a rare glimpse into the private thinking of John Jay in real time, as his other diary entries, and personal letters to family, friends, and colleagues, typically avoided any detailed discussion of cases pending at the court.[38]

Although the Supreme Court justices each issued separate opinions ruling against West, the court reporter, Alexander Dallas, did not publish any of them officially. Instead, Dallas published a single official summary opinion only a few lines long. The summary opinion framed Bradford's motion, noted Barnes's opposition to it, and reflected the unanimous view that "writs of error to remove causes to this court from inferior courts, can regularly issue only from the clerk's office of this court." The summary opinion ends with a flat-sounding, two-word conclusory sentence that reads, "Motion refused." William West lost again.[39]

The Supreme Court's decision to deny Bradford's motion to accept the erroneous writ of error appears to have been correct under the procedural law that existed at the time, as the justices of the Supreme Court had no authority to rule in any manner other than as they did. As Justice Iredell noted in his individual opinion, the role of courts

Figure 4.6. Alexander Dallas.

is to "construe, not amend, acts of Legislation." It was an important distinction for the Supreme Court to draw in its first decided case, as it recognized early in the court's history the separation of powers between the judicial and legislative branches of the federal government. The Supreme Court's decision set a tone. The concept that the role of courts is to interpret and apply laws, but not rewrite them, has carried forward in all the years since. The guiding principle established by *West v Barnes* was more important in the long run than the inequity that resulted to William West individually. Had the Supreme Court decided in favor of William West by contorting the language of the Judiciary Act, the confusion and uncertainties that would have followed in later decades, with courts unpredictably ignoring legislative mandates to reach feel-good results suiting the whims of the moment, would have been significant and damaging. In that sense, William West is a tragic figure, a sacrificial lamb to the broader concept that legislators—not judges—write the laws. That concept has provided the nation's judicial system with a measure of stability and predictability in the many decades that have followed, though at William West's expense.[40]

Indeed, one of the key roles of any judge is to recognize the difference in cases where a decision can be rendered based on what is "fair" or "just," such as where courts may exercise discretion in the length of a jail sentence or the amount of a fine, versus where courts are handcuffed to black letter law that dictates a result, such as the untimeliness of a lawsuit or the absence of a duty between parties. *West v Barnes* is an example of a case where the statutory law dictated what the Supreme Court's decision needed to be, regardless of whether it was fair to William West or, potentially, to any other parties interested in an appeal from states too far from Philadelphia for appellate remedies to have any practical meaning. In a sense, the Jay Court faced, in its first-ever argued case, the basic question of whether the Supreme Court should be used as a "gas pedal" to proactively reach a well-intentioned result regardless of the language of the relevant statutory law, or a "brake" upon the assertion of unfettered judicial authority as to keep the judiciary within the confines of controlling statutory language enacted by Congress. In *West v Barnes*, the Supreme Court applied the brake and transmitted a clarion signal to the federal courts throughout the country that they do the same.

Justice Iredell was so upset by the Supreme Court's ruling, of which he was a part, that he personally lobbied President Washington for an amendment to the Judiciary Act to eliminate the onerous and impractical requirements for writs of error. The harsh procedural result visited upon William West was the catalyst for a change in the rules for certifying writs of error, which were amended in 1792 to allow future such filings to occur at the Circuit Courts that were more local to the litigants. The amendment of the procedure had no effect on the Supreme Court's earlier opinion against William West because the ameliorative effects of the 1792 amendment were prospective only.[41]

The dispute between William West and David Leonard Barnes was not entirely over after the US Supreme Court disposed of the case. After the Supreme Court dismissed West's appeal because of the improper writ of error, Barnes returned to the Circuit Court in Rhode Island in November 1791 for its further assistance in actually ejecting the West family from the property. The further litigation was necessitated by the fact that the marshal in Scituate was willing to eject West, as he had lost the lawsuit, but refused to eject West's family members who were not named in the earlier court papers. The issues of the case were rehashed during that later proceeding, resulting in the article in the *Providence*

Gazette that explained the Circuit Court's legal reasoning in favor of Barnes on the merits of the original case.[42]

Was justice done in the case of William West at the Supreme Court level? The answer to that question depends on an unknowable: if the Supreme Court had reached the merits of the appeal but had then agreed with the Circuit Court that West's payment certificate was null and void, then West would still have lost his appeal. West needed to surmount the procedural flaw of his case *and* convince a majority of Supreme Court justices that the Circuit Court had erred on the merits. Two of those six jurists had already decided the merits of the case against West when the case was first heard at the Circuit Court. An appeal is unsuccessful if it results in a 3–3 tie. The odds of William West prevailing at the Supreme Court on the merits, by obtaining the votes of all four of the remaining four justices, or by changing the minds of Jay or Cushing to help establish a majority vote, were mathematically unlikely.

By today's standards, *West v Barnes* is not recognized as a beacon of earth-shattering legal principles, but it is historically noteworthy in two respects. First, *West v Barnes* was the first case decided by the Jay Court upon oral argument of the parties, and for that reason alone it is deserving of special recognition. Second, the case signaled that the Supreme Court would not render decisions in ways that would rewrite or ignore the language or intent of statutes passed by the US Congress. The Supreme Court's decision helped define the novel concept of a separation of powers between the judicial and other branches of government, with the judiciary deferring to the role of Congress in drafting legislation using words of its choosing. While that concept is well accepted and noncontroversial today, its pronouncement in 1791 was a bigger deal. In the years ahead, the early federal courts would generally read their authority narrowly, reluctant to act unless it was clear that they could do so. *West v Barnes* was the earliest sign that the Jay Court would practice judicial restraint. While unfairness and impoverishment were caused to William West, West was sacrificed to the broader concept that legislators, and not judges, write law, which has provided our national judiciary with stability and predictability in the many decades that followed.[43]

JAY'S DAYS

William West eventually lost his farm as a result of the case and the ejectment proceedings that followed over a period of years. He vowed to never pay the *debt to David Leonard Barnes, claiming it to be unjust. His property devolved to his children and sons-in-law in July 1792. Litigation between West and Barnes continued into mid-1793 over Barnes's separate suit in Rhode Island to recover the $1,500 appeal bond that West had posted when the writ of error was issued, to be paid to whichever party prevailed at the Supreme Court. West lost the lawsuit over the appeal bond on default and, in addition to the value of the bond, was ordered to pay Barnes additional damages of $90 and court costs of $59.90. West spent some time in a debtors' prison and died in poverty in 1816.*

Ironically, Rhode Island's aggressive currency laws, which were specifically designed to help farmers like William West, tragically proved to be West's financial undoing.[44]

A mere three weeks after the Supreme Court's decision was rendered in West v Barnes, *West's attorney, William Bradford, was appointed to a seat on the Pennsylvania Supreme Court. Three years beyond that, Bradford was appointed to the position of US attorney general by President Washington after Edmund Randolph's position in the Cabinet shifted from US attorney general to secretary of state. Bradford died young on August 23, 1795, while still a member of Washington's Cabinet, three weeks before his fortieth birthday.*

David Leonard Barnes, having won at age thirty-one the first-ever case argued at the US Supreme Court, continued to practice law until 1801, when he was appointed by President Thomas Jefferson as a judge of the federal District Court for the District of Rhode Island. Barnes died in Providence on November 3, 1812, while still serving as a federal judge, at the relatively young age of fifty-two.

Superior Court Judge David Howell, who was part of a panel that found Rhode Island's currency law unconstitutional, and who vigorously defended his ruling on the floor of the state's General Assembly, did not suffer as a result of his ouster from the state's judiciary the following year. In 1801, Howell was appointed by President Thomas Jefferson as the United States attorney for Rhode Island. On November 13, 1812, Howell was appointed by President James Madison to the seat on the District Court for the District of Rhode Island, which had become vacant upon the death of Judge David Leonard Barnes. Howell died on July 30, 1824, at the age of seventy-seven, while still holding his federal judicial office.[45]

Chapter 5

Grappling with the Separation of Powers

In Re *Hayburn* (1792), Plus Ex Parte *Chandler* and *United States v Todd* (unreported, 1794)

> ". . . the late decision of the Judges of the United States, in the circuit court of Pennsylvania, declaring an act of the present session of Congress *unconstitutional*, must be a matter of high gratification to every republican and friend of liberty . . . it affords just hope that any existing law of Congress, which may be supposed to trench upon the constitutional rights of individuals, or of states, will, at convenient seasons, undergo a revision . . ."
>
> —*National Gazette*
> April 16, 1792

The early 1790s was the first of many postwar periods in American history. A total of 217,000 men fought for the Continental Army during the war, though there were never more than approximately 48,000 soldiers at any one time, and no more than 13,000 in any one place. The major battles of the war, fought between the first on April 19, 1775, and the last on October 10, 1781, were at Lexington and Concord (MA), Fort Ticonderoga (NY), Bunker Hill (MA), Brooklyn (NY), Trenton (NJ), Princeton (NJ), Brandywine (PA), Germantown (PA), Saratoga (NY), Monmouth (NJ), Savannah (GA), Charleston (SC), Camden (SC), Cowpens (SC), and Yorktown (VA). Statistics from the US Department of

Veteran Affairs for all military conflicts reveal that in the Revolutionary War, there were 4,435 battlefield deaths and 6,188 nonlethal woundings.[1]

The United States has made a point throughout its history of taking care of its veterans, including those who fought the British in the Revolutionary War. After the federal government was formed in 1789, an early priority of the new government was to take care of the war casualties who were not necessarily being treated well by the financially strapped states. There were three categories of persons who were to receive benefits—soldiers who received debilitating injuries during service in the war, war widows, and orphans.

A pension law became necessary because some of the states had fallen into arrears in making their veteran payments, and some people entitled to pensions had not submitted on time the paperwork required of them at the state level. Pension issues and problems were splintered among the various states, and a solution was for the federal government to assume responsibility for many of the pensioners. The secretary of war was to become the chief administrator of a national pension system. By March 1792, there were 1,358 noncommissioned officers and privates on the incumbent pension lists, none of whom received payments exceeding the sum of $5.00 per month. The entire list of all pensioners of all descriptions was 1,472, and with no federal pension law, that number would slowly but steadily decrease as a result of time and attrition. And there was a large number of veterans, widows, and orphans who were not enrolled in any pension system.[2]

Congress stepped forward on March 23, 1792, by enacting An Act to Provide for the Settlement of the Claims of Widows and Orphans Barred by the Limitations Heretofore Established, and to Regulate the Claims to Invalid Pensions. The legislation is otherwise known as the Invalid Pensions Act of 1792. The term "invalid" is not used in the sense of being illegitimate (in-*VAL*-id), but in the sense of physical disability (*IN*-val-id).[3]

Section 1 of the Invalid Pensions Act of 1792 provided a two-year extension to the statute of limitations for any claims by the widows and orphans of army officers, measured from legislation passed by the defunct Continental Congress in 1785 and 1787. Such persons could seek from the government payments equal to seven years of half-pay. The Act provided for eligible pensioners to receive benefits until their disabilities ceased or until death, whichever was to occur first in a given instance.[4]

Commissioned and noncommissioned officers, soldiers, and sailors disabled by wounds incurred during the Revolutionary War, and who did not desert from service, were entitled in section 2 to be placed on a pension list and paid a pension. For a veteran to be placed on the pension list, war service and a war-related injury needed to be documented. The statute required the veteran to present a certificate from his former commanding officer confirming the disability and its relationship to the war, as well as affidavits from two other individuals confirming the same information. The veteran was also required to present three affidavits from reputable freeholders of the county, city, or town where the veteran resided, describing from their knowledge the veteran's mode of life, employment, labor, or means of support during the previous twelve months. The obvious purpose of these requirements was to guard against fraudulent claims and ensure pension payments went only to those persons deserving of them.[5]

In 1792, there was no federal bureaucracy in place to process the paperwork of perhaps several hundreds of veteran applicants. Congress needed to develop a mechanism for administratively reviewing the veterans' applications and their supporting documentation. Congress chose in section 2 of the statute to require that the justices of the federal Circuit Courts act as pension "commissioners." In that role, the justices were to meet each claimant, examine their wounds, make inquiry, review paperwork, form an assessment of each claimant's degree of war-related disability, and calculate what percentage of monthly pay the veteran should receive that would be proportional to the degree of physical disability. The justices were to certify their conclusions and forward them to the secretary of war. To assure that circuit-riding justices would be available to veterans for reviewing their applications, Congress directed in section 3 of the Act that the circuit justices, when holding court, remain at their court locations for at least five days to afford veterans sufficient opportunity to make their claims for relief. Court clerks were directed by the law to advertise in advance the dates that the circuit judges would be available at a particular court location so that veterans would have notice of when and where their applications could be presented.[6]

The circuit justices did not have the final word in approving the veterans' applications. Section 4 of the Act directed the secretary of war to receive and review the proofs of disabilities and place the names of the approved applicants on the United States pension list. Congress reserved to itself the final say in keeping any veteran's name on—or removing it from—the pension list.[7]

The enactment of the Invalid Pensions Act of 1792 raised a host of nightmarish constitutional and administrative issues. One constitutional problem was that the involvement of jurists in nonjudicial, administrative responsibilities was not provided for in Article III of the Constitution, which defined the role of the judicial branch of the federal government. The review of veterans' pension applications was a task that did not involve any litigated case brought to the court between adverse parties. The Circuit Courts were largely composed of Supreme Court justices riding the circuits, and their findings of fact and conclusions were supposed to be the last, not first, resorts.

A second constitutional problem was that the Act called for the justices' pension findings to be reviewed by the secretary of war, who was part of the executive branch, and by Congress, the legislative branch. The 1789 Constitution created three separate branches of government, none of which was designed to be subject to the decision-making oversight of the other.

A further problem with the Act was that it added to the justices' overall workload, which was already exacerbated by the constant demands of travel. The requirement that each justice remain at the Circuit Court for not fewer than five days added to the burden and could only have the effect of rendering travel and schedules less efficient.

In defense of Congress, public officials in Philadelphia, as well as in the states, were still in the process of navigating the separation of powers between the various branches of the federal government, and the division of responsibilities between the federal government on the one hand and the states on the other. The Invalid Pensions Act of 1792 can be viewed with hindsight as one of various growing pains encountered by government officials and the public under the new constitutional framework.

The Invalid Pensions Act of 1792 became law on March 23 of that year, meaning that it was enacted during a time of the year when the Supreme Court justices were scattered about the country riding the circuits. The February 1792 Term of the Supreme Court had already concluded, and the justices would not all be together again in Philadelphia until the commencement of the August Term later in the year. The justices of the Supreme Court were therefore unable to easily confer with each other about how they should respond to the new law or coordinate discussion with the various District Court judges around the country who likewise sat on the Circuit Courts. How the judiciary would respond to the new law was an open question during the spring and early summer of 1792. Many of the justices viewed the law as unconstitutional on its face, and in fact, it certainly was. But how the justices actually responded to the law varied from circuit to circuit.

In the Eastern Circuit, Justices John Jay and William Cushing and Judge James Duane of the District Court of New York agreed to perform the tasks imposed on them by the Invalid Pensions Act of 1792. They did so in an apparent effort to cooperate as much as possible with the mandates of Congress and to further the noble purpose of the legislation of providing benefits to veterans disabled while in the service of the states and country. Privately, they each believed that the pension law was unconstitutional, as they wrote in a letter to President Washington on April 10, 1792. In the letter, Jay, Cushing, and Duane explained to George Washington that the processing of pensions was not consistent with the judicial functions of the courts as defined by Article III of the Constitution, because the Act permitted other branches of government to review their determinations. But the letter stopped short of actually using the word "unconstitutional" and did not represent any official or binding opinion on the issue.[8]

Figure 5.1. Hon. James Duane.

Although Jay, Cushing, and Duane *privately* believed the pension law suffered from significant constitutional infirmities, their *public* handling of the issue was quite different. Publicly, Jay and his colleagues drew a fictional distinction between their role as jurists on the one hand and their role as pension "commissioners" on the other. Jay was of the opinion, while sitting in the Circuit Court with Cushing and Duane, that the Invalid Pensions Act could be sustained and enforced if it were construed as requiring jurists to act on pension applications solely in the role of "commissioners." To underscore the distinction between jurists and commissioners, Jay instituted a procedure at the Eastern Circuit by which pension applications would not be considered until after court had closed for the day. For Jay in particular, who had served as both chief justice and secretary of state at the same time until the appointment of Thomas Jefferson to the Cabinet, the wearing of "two hats" in the furtherance of public service was not a disqualifier of one because of the other.[9]

Jay's reasoning for implementing the law was, nevertheless, quite a stretch. In separating the role of a circuit court justice from that of a pension commissioner, Jay necessarily chose to turn a blind eye to the constitutional defects of the law that he and his New York colleagues had noted to Washington, such as placement of nonjudicial administrative duties upon judicial officers, and the executive and congressional review of the justices' pension recommendations. This suggests that there was a compelling desire on Jay's part to avoid a circumstance, in the new life of the American Republic, where one branch of government would openly defy the directives of a law passed by Congress and thereby trigger unwanted constitutional uncertainty. Jay's professional background was steeped in the art of diplomacy. While the role and legitimacy of the federal government is concretized today, its existence in the 1790s was experimental, untested, and fragile. The concept of judicial review, where the judiciary may declare legislation unconstitutional, was still not settled law, and there was not yet any case pending before Jay and his New York colleagues where the concept of judicial review could be considered. The approach to the pension law by Jay, Cushing, and Duane was therefore one of domestic diplomacy and accommodation, perhaps with a view toward lobbying for a change of the law to correct its infirmities later. Viewed in that light, any difference between Jay's public and private views of the law was not a product of dishonesty, but rather was a well-intentioned effort by Jay to bend over backward to creatively sustain the 1792 law and avoid publicly describing it unconstitutional.

The justices in the Circuit Court in New York summarized their *official* position on the Act as follows:

> "That as the objects of this act are exceedingly benevolent, and do real Honor to the humanity and justice of Congress, and as the Judges desire to manifest on all proper occasions, and in every proper manner their high respect for the national legislature, they will execute this act in the capacity of Commissioners."[10]

The Invalid Pensions Act of 1792 received a different reception at the Southern Circuit. On June 8, 1792, Supreme Court Justice James Iredell in North Carolina, and that state's District Judge, John Sitgraeves, wrote to President Washington to inform him of their belief that the law was unconstitutional. A review of the letter reveals that the justices in North Carolina had already been informed of what Jay, Cushing, and Duane had decided to do in New York and in the rest of the Eastern Circuit. The Southern Circuit justices stopped short of rendering a definitive opinion on whether there was a viable distinction between jurists and commissioners, recognizing, as they did, that no actual application or case was pending before them raising that issue. However, even assuming that jurists could independently act as pension commissioners, Iredell and Sitgraeves informally advised the president that the law was unconstitutional on its face because the judges' pension determinations were reviewable by the executive branch. The letter from the jurists of the Southern Circuit was less accommodative than the one Washington had received from Jay, Cushing, and Duane.[11]

The Southern Circuit's letter to President Washington was signed by only two justices—Iredell and Sitgraeves—rather than three. The reason is that Justice John Rutledge of South Carolina had recently resigned from the Supreme Court to become chief justice of his state's Court of Common Pleas and Sessions. Rutledge's vacancy would be filled by Justice Thomas Johnson of Maryland, but Johnson did not begin his Supreme Court duties until August 6, 1792.

The harshest treatment of the Invalid Pensions Act of 1792 was seen in the Middle Circuit. The Circuit Court for the Middle Circuit, while sitting in Pennsylvania, consisted of Supreme Court Justices James Wilson and John Blair and District Court Judge Richard Peters of the District of Pennsylvania. A Pennsylvania veteran, William Hayburn, presented a pension application and supporting materials to the Circuit Court there. The three jurists outright refused to entertain the application. In open court, oral opinions were announced that the pension law was constitutionally defective for two reasons—that it imposed nonjuridical duties upon the court and that any decision from the court was subject to executive and legislative review not authorized by the Constitution. An original handwritten version of the Middle Circuit's decision in *Hayburn* is held by the National Archives and Records Administration. The reasoning of the Circuit Court justices in Pennsylvania was repeated by them in a letter to President Washington and to their Supreme Court colleagues dated April 18, 1792. The Pennsylvania justices reminded President Washington in their letter that the Constitution was the supreme law of the land, and that he [Washington] was responsible for assuring the faithful execution of that law. The Middle Circuit justices took no pleasure in their actions, describing their approach as necessary but "far from being pleasant," and explained that the Act "excited feelings in us, which we hope never to experience again."[12]

The result of the Middle Circuit's approach was, in effect, a declaration that the Invalid Pensions Act of 1792 was unconstitutional, if not in law, in fact. At least, that is how events were perceived. A letter from Attorney General Edmund Randolph to President Washington, dated April 5, 1792, described a chance encounter between Randolph and Justice Wilson on Sixth Street in Philadelphia. In their street conversation, Wilson informed Randolph that he and Justice John Blair strongly doubted the constitutionality of the law. Congress debated on April 13, 1792, how it should respond to the Middle Circuit's declaration that the pension law was not enforceable. Congress referred the issue to a committee that was appointed to determine the facts, but ultimately it did nothing. Separately, on April 15, 1792, James Madison wrote to Henry Lee of Virginia that the Pennsylvania justices in the Middle Circuit had declared the law "unconstitutional and void."[13]

That the Circuit Court for the Middle Circuit found the Invalid Pensions Act unconstitutional was also the interpretation given by some in the popular press. An Anti-Federalist newspaper in Philadelphia, the *National Gazette*, urged the US Congress on April 16, 1792, to correct its unconstitutional error. It wrote,

> "A correspondent remarks that the late decision of the Judges of the United States, in the circuit court of Pennsylvania, declaring an act of the present session of Congress *unconstitutional*, must be a matter of high gratification to every republican and friend of liberty since it assures the people of ample protection to their constitutional rights and privileges, against any attempt of legislative or executive oppression. And whilst we view the exercise of this noble prerogative of the judges in the hands of such able, wise, and independent men, as composed the present judiciary of the United States; it affords just hope that any existing law of Congress, which may be supposed to trench upon the constitutional rights of individuals, or of states, will, at convenient seasons, undergo a revision . . ."[14]

Federalists in and out of Congress did not take kindly to the Middle Circuit's uppity decision, and serious calls were made for the impeachment of the justices. By contrast, Anti-Federalists defended the determination of the Middle Circuit justices. Benjamin Franklin Bache, the editor of another Philadelphia newspaper, the *General Advertiser*, belittled any talk of impeachment for the court's refusal to implement an unconstitutional law. Bache editorialized that members of "Congress were wrapped up in the cloak of infallibility which has been torn from the shoulders of the Pope; and that it was damnable heresy and sacrilege to doubt the constitutional orthodoxy of any decision of theirs, once written on calf skin."[15] The Anti-Federalists began to see the courts as a guarantor of states' and individuals' rights against congressional overreach. And, in the apparent view of Benjamin Franklin Bache, the judiciary was better positioned to determine matters of constitutional law, as the Pope on matters of Catholic religious doctrine.

As a matter of legal analysis, the public or private positions taken by various justices at the Circuit Courts, that the Invalid Pensions Act of 1792 was constitutionally flawed, was correct. Not enforcing the Act, however, steered the government into uncharted waters on how the three branches of government might respond to the stalemate. Also, the Middle Circuit's refusal to follow the directives of the pension law was not accommodating to William Hayburn or other veterans seeking federal government benefits in that region of the country, and there was a humane desire to give war veterans whatever they were legally and administratively due.

The executive and legislative branches had institutional interests in seeing the pension law enforced. US Attorney General Edmund Randolph filed a writ of *mandamus* at the Supreme Court in Philadelphia for consideration during the August 1792 Term of the court. *Mandamus* is a legal term for when a court is requested to issue an order compelling a governmental actor to perform a duty that it is obligated to perform. Randolph's application was filed by him in his capacity as attorney general of the United States, and not on behalf of William Hayburn or any other client. The *mandamus* that was sought in this instance was an order that the Circuit Court justices in the Middle Circuit perform the administrative functions that Congress imposed upon them under the Invalid Pensions Act of 1792. Thus was born the case of In Re *Hayburn*.[16]

Oral argument was conducted on the writ of *mandamus* at the Supreme Court beginning on August 8, 1792. Attorney General Randolph argued in favor of the writ of *mandamus* on behalf of the United States. While there were many points that could be argued about the law, Chief Justice Jay interrupted Randolph soon after the argument began and inquired of Randolph whether he was "officially authorized to move for a *mandamus*." Jay and some of the associate justices were not convinced that the attorney general of the United States could argue in favor of a writ of *mandamus* without receiving prior authorization to do so by the president. President Washington did not apparently direct Randolph to seek the writ. Today, there is no question that attorneys general may commence actions and proceedings in courts of law without specific direction or approval from the president of the United States. In 1792, the answer to Jay's concern was less certain. An additional concern was whether Randolph, as the attorney general within the executive branch, had any right to involve himself in matters pertaining to the workings of the circuit courts. As reported by Philadelphia's *Federal Gazette* on August 18, 1792, there was a question of "whether it was part of the duty of the attorney general of the United States, to superintend the decisions of the inferior courts, and if to him they appeared improper, to move the supreme court for a revision."[17]

Questioning Randolph's authority to argue the writ was another instance where the Jay Court focused first on threshold procedural issues before reaching the core merits of the matters before it. The Supreme Court had done so in *West v Barnes* the year before, and the pattern continued here.

Randolph responded to Jay's inquiry with a lengthy and erudite argument about the role and responsibilities of the attorney general, referring to well-developed legal precedents from England and from some from the American states. Indeed, Randolph's argument about his authority lasted for several days, touching only tangentially upon the merits of the writ and the pension law. The length of Randolph's argument suggests that he was not winning over a majority of the Jay Court and was unwilling to risk a denial of the writ on mere procedural grounds. Today, attorneys are typically subject to predetermined time limits for their oral arguments to appellate judges. Reasonable time limits are a product of the size of appellate caseloads and practical necessity. In August 1792, there was an acknowledgment that Randolph's writ of *mandamus* presented the Jay Court with a matter of great historic significance, forcing the Supreme Court to consider whether it had the authority to declare a federal statute unconstitutional, and if so, whether to actually make such a declaration. The justices of the Supreme Court took the issues seriously and had the time to ensure that they would get their decision "right."

Specifically, Randolph made three arguments as to why his writ of *mandamus* should be entertained by the Supreme Court on the merits. The first was that his responsibilities as attorney general were essentially the same as those of his counterpart in the British government, where the *mandamus* application, or something similar, would be entertained. Second, Randolph argued that a specific provision of the Judiciary Act of 1789 authorized him to prosecute and conduct suits in the Supreme Court on any matters in which the United States shall be "concerned," which was wide-sweeping language. And third, Randolph argued that because the president in the executive branch of government had the responsibility of faithfully executing the nation's laws, he implicitly possessed the authority to pursue applications in the courts designed to aid in the enforcement of those laws. It was this final argument that raised the related issue, of greatest concern to some of the justices, of whether the writ of *mandamus* needed to be filed by Randolph at President Washington's specific request and direction.[18]

On the question of Attorney General Randolph's authority to proceed, the justices split by a vote of 3 to 3. The official record of the Supreme Court does not reveal which justices voted which way, but Philadelphia's *Federal Gazette* reported that Justices Jay, Wilson, and Cushing were opposed to permitting Randolph to proceed, and Justices

Figure 5.2. US Attorney General Edmund Randolph.

Blair, Iredell, and Johnson were willing to let Randolph do so. By not having a majority of the court in his favor, Randolph and his application for a writ of *mandamus* failed and could not proceed on the merits.[19]

The broader implications of *Hayburn* and the Invalid Pensions Act of 1792 were too important to leave to the unsatisfying result that the attorney general had no authority to seek relief from the Supreme Court on the issue. The obvious fix would have been for Randolph to obtain authorization from George Washington to pursue the writ and return to the Supreme Court. However, Washington might have wanted to keep himself one step removed from the controversy, particularly as he had already received communications from some of the justices about the constitutional problems raised by the pension law. Randolph had one other option available to him for circumventing the belief of three justices that he had no authority to seek the writ on behalf of the United States. He returned to the Supreme Court anew, this time as a private attorney for William Hayburn himself. No law, rule, or regulation existed at the time preventing the attorney general of the United States from representing private clients in courts of law, and in fact he had already done so on behalf of the plaintiffs in the earlier short-lived Supreme Court case of *VanStophorst v Maryland*.

The merits of *Hayburn* were now placed back on the table. In hearing the merits, the Jay Court demonstrated a willingness to entertain applications involving only one party. Unlike typical cases and controversies where there are at least two parties involved in a dispute, there was no "respondent" at the Supreme Court arguing against Randolph's application.

Oral argument of the writ of *mandamus* resumed, this time squarely on the merits of the issues raised by the writ. Randolph did not argue that there were no circumstances where the circuit courts could not refuse to perform nonjudicial duties. Rather, he argued that the Middle Circuit's refusal in this particular instance was inappropriate.[20]

The *Hayburn* case once again reflected the problem of requiring Supreme Court justices to ride the circuits and decide cases pending in those courts. Here, with respect to the 1792 pension law, Justices John Jay and William Cushing had already made known their public view that the law could be enforced by drawing a distinction between jurists and pension commissioners. Supreme Court Justice James Iredell had already documented his belief from North Carolina that the pension law was unconstitutional, though he reserved his consideration of whether the circuit court justices could properly and separately act as commissioners. Justices James Wilson and John Blair were also on record, from their prior ruling in Pennsylvania, that the pension law was unconstitutional and therefore unenforceable. By today's standards, each of these jurists would have a conflict of interest hearing Attorney General Randolph's *mandamus* application at the Supreme Court, as they had already expressed their opinions on the legality of the very issue they were now being asked to review on appeal. But such conflicts were not of particular concern to the bench and bar of the 1790s.

One Supreme Court justice who represented a "clean slate" on the constitutionality of the pension law was the court's newest appointee, Thomas Johnson of Maryland. Johnson, despite being the least senior justice at the Supreme Court, might have held the greatest clout within the court in the *Hayburn* case. The reason involves the mathematical dynamics of the Jay Court. Two justices—Wilson and Blair—had already held that the law was both unconstitutional and unenforceable. Two justices—Jay and Cushing—had already officially determined that the law could be enforced by members of the judiciary acting not as jurists, but separately as commissioners. One justice—Iredell—was on record that the law was unconstitutional, while perhaps leaving open the possibility of enforcing the law along the lines suggested by Jay and Cushing. Subject to hearing argument in Hayburn's case, and subject to any jurist changing his mind, the Jay Court appeared to be divided on the issue 2–2, with Iredell's position uncertain as to the writ's ultimate result. If those votes all remained the same, and with a minimum of four justices needed to sustain Randolph's writ, Justice Johnson was likely the most important vote among equals. If he viewed the pension law to be unconstitutional, there would be at least three, and perhaps four votes with Iredell, for striking the Act down, and the writ would not prevail. If Johnson voted that the law was enforceable through the actions of separate "commissioners," his vote, and perhaps that of Iredell, would provide three or four votes the other way. Johnson's vote should be seen as more of a swing vote than Iredell's, as Iredell had already made known his belief that the pension law was unconstitutional to the extent judge-commissioner pension determinations were subject to review by the secretary of war. Procedurally, if the court were to split 3–3 on the question, the writ of *mandamus*, without a majority vote, would not be issued, and the Circuit Court's ruling in Pennsylvania against William Hayburn would stand.[21]

The distinction that John Jay and William Cushing had made in New York, that the pension law could be enforced by the justices acting in separate personal capacities as commissioners, was threadbare and unconvincing. The statute passed by Congress designated the justices of the Circuit Courts as the governmental agents responsible for processing the pension applications. No distinction was made in the language of the statute between their judicial duties and their personal duties as pension commissioners. Indeed, given the language of the statute, one had to first be a justice of a Circuit Court to qualify as a pension commissioner, further erasing any line between the juridical and administrative responsibilities of the officeholder.

The Jay Court was faced with two obvious outcomes depending on the votes. The first was to follow the earlier reasoning of Justices John Jay and William Cushing by directing the justices at the various circuits to process pension applications as intended by the 1792 statute.

The second potential outcome was to invoke the authority of judicial review and find that the statute was unconstitutional. The latter outcome would have been of great legal significance, and no one could reliably predict the consequences that such a Supreme Court ruling would have on the relationship between the branches of federal

Figure 5.3. US Supreme Court Justice Thomas Johnson.

government and upon the stability of the new US Constitution. As to these two potential outcomes, the members of the Jay Court must have engaged in serious and deliberative discussions and, very possibly, heated arguments. Appellate courts generally try to resolve cases with as much consensus among the judges as possible. To reach consensus, appellate justices will debate and reason with one another in an effort for some to persuade others toward a particular point of view. Personal collegiality among appellate justices helps foster professional consensus, but building consensus at the early Supreme Court may have been more challenging because of the justices' frequent circuit-riding that kept them apart most of the year. Where a uniform consensus is not possible, justices divide into a majority outcome and a dissent outcome, whereupon jurists rush to their quill pens (or, today, their laptops) and expound upon their viewpoints in written opinions.

Clearly, there was sentiment within the Jay Court, particularly from John Jay himself and William Cushing, to find some way to avoid any ruling that the pension law was unconstitutional, even if it meant bending over backwards to do so. Indeed, today, legislation is presumed to be constitutional, and the burden is on the party challenging a law to demonstrate its unconstitutional infirmities. But the problem for the Jay Court in *Hayburn* appears to be that if a majority of its justices truly believed that the Invalid Pensions Act of 1792 was unconstitutional—as all or most did on one level or another—the logical outcome would need to be a striking down of the law in its entirety. If there was sentiment to avoid doing so at almost any cost, then a *third* potential outcome needed to be found for resolving Hayburn's writ application.

The members of the Jay Court found that third alternative, between the extremes of issuing the writ of *mandamus* and refusing to do so at all. The third alternative appears to have been a political compromise, to adjourn *Hayburn* without a decision from the August 1792 Term of the court to the February 1793 Term. The official opinion of the court prepared by Alexander Dallas simply and flatly said, "THE COURT observed, that they would hold the motion under advisement, until the next term."[22]

In a letter to James Madison, Edmund Randolph was dismissive of John Jay, criticizing Jay's legal reasonings and forms of expression. Randolph may have been bitter, as he failed to prevail on his initial arguments as attorney general that he could pursue the writ of *mandamus* on behalf of the United States, and then failed to obtain the *mandamus* relief on the merits when he returned to the court in a private capacity on behalf of Hayburn himself. Indeed, by adjourning the matter to the following February, the Jay Court left in place the ruling of the Middle Circuit that the pension law was unconstitutional, at least during the interim.[23]

History suggests that in adjourning *Hayburn*, John Jay and the court might have acted quite shrewdly, though politically. The adjournment afforded the US Congress, which was acutely aware of the judiciary's concerns, the time that was needed for it to correct the defective law. Were the law amended to correct its constitutional infirmities, the Congress would likely avoid a majority opinion in *Hayburn* that would not only strike down the specific pension law, but pronounce the broader doctrine of judicial review on a national level that would potentially affect future legislative enactments as well. Jay personally knew many of the members of Congress and might have had confidence that, if given time, the legislature would do the "right thing" by addressing the constitutional defects of the pension law.

The Congress did, in fact, correct the pension statute by replacing it with the Invalid Pensions Act of 1793. Efforts to amend the law began on November 7, 1792, when President Washington shared with Congress the letter he had previously received from the Southern Circuit justices, Iredell and Sitgraeves, explaining the exiting law's unconstitutionality. On December 1, 1792, a committee of the House of Representatives proposed some repeal-and-replace language to the pension law that addressed the relevant constitutional concerns. Law revisions were debated in the Congress in January and February 1793. The 1793 version of the law was enacted on February 28, 1793, before the Jay Court took up the *Hayburn* case for a second time.[24]

The timing of the 1793 Act is significant. One might expect that for a matter of *Hayburn*'s importance, the Supreme Court would have revisited the case early in its February Term. The fact that the Jay Court delayed further consideration of the matter through the entire month of February 1793 suggests that the court was aware of efforts that were underway in Congress to amend the law, and the justices were willing to wait out the political circumstances and hear other cases in the meantime. Moreover, the Jay Court had a convenient excuse to hold off further consideration of *Hayburn*, as it also had on its February docket another significant hot-button case, *Chisholm v Georgia*, which is the subject of the next chapter.

The 1793 version of the pension law repealed virtually all of the objectionable sections of the 1792 legislation and established alternative application procedures that did not involve the circuit courts. The 1793 version did require judges of the District Courts to take oaths from pension applicants, or refer the task to three persons commissioned by the judge, and to then transmit the applications to the secretary of war for review and processing. The new procedure did not involve judicial evaluations, recommendations, or fact findings, and no portion of the district judges' tasks was subject to review by the executive or legislative branches.[25]

Once the 1793 law replaced the 1792 version, the *Hayburn* case was dismissed for having been rendered academic. William Hayburn and other pension applicants were required to follow the new procedures set forth in the 1793 law. In the end, the Jay Court avoided having to declare congressional legislation unconstitutional, and Congress avoided the embarrassment of having its 1792 law struck down. The Middle Circuit's ruling in *Hayburn* remained on the books and was binding within that circuit, but it did not matter, as no further pension claims would be presented to the justices of the circuit courts under the 1792 version of the law. The bigger question of judicial review would remain unresolved for another decade until the 1803 case of *Marbury v Madison*, when the doctrine was declared and established.[26]

There is good reason to believe that Justice Johnson viewed the Invalid Pensions Act of 1792 to be unconstitutional and unenforceable. The pension law was still viable outside the Middle District during the time between the August 1792 and February 1793 Terms of the Supreme Court. In late October 1792, Justice Johnson refused to process pension applications while sitting at the Circuit Court in South Carolina. No doubt the US Congress took note of Johnson's ruling in South Carolina and likely calculated that if the Jay Court were to render a decision in *Hayburn* on the merits the following February, the minimum number of votes for finding the pension law unconstitutional and unenforceable had likely been reached. This development must only have had the effect of spurring Congress to correct the defects in the pension law, rather than stand idle and watch the Supreme Court strike it down in February 1793.[27]

Clearly the justices of the Jay Court finessed the *Hayburn* case in a way that avoided declaring the congressional pension legislation unconstitutional. They acted politically in doing so. However, many of the same justices, while riding the circuits, were not so deferential to statutes of the individual states that ran afoul of federal constitutional principles. In 1791, Chief Justice Jay and Justice William Cushing, riding the Eastern Circuit with District Judge Richard Law, struck down a Connecticut statute that had permitted juries in two separate cases to deduct wartime interest from prewar British debt awards. The reasoning, which the justices applied in both *Deblois v Hawley* and *Elliot v Sage*, was that the Connecticut statute violated Article 4 of the Treaty of Paris, which provided that British and American creditors meet no lawful impediment to the recovery of the full value of their debts. In 1792, Chief Justice Jay and District Judge Henry Marchant, while hearing the case of *Champion v Casey* in the Eastern Circuit, struck down as unconstitutional a Rhode Island statute that had granted the defendant a three-year extension to repay his private debts on the ground that it violated the freedom-to-contract guarantee of Article I, section 10, of the federal Constitution. The same year, while Justice Oliver Ellsworth was sitting in the Southern Circuit with Judge John Sitgraeves, a North Carolinian war debt confiscation statute was struck down in *Hamilton v Eaton* on the ground that it violated the terms of the Treaty of Paris. In

1794, in *Skinner v May*, Justice William Cushing and District Judge John Lowell, sitting together in the Eastern Circuit, declared unconstitutional a Massachusetts anti-slave trade reward statute on the ground that it violated Congress' sole authority to regulate international commerce under Article 1, section 1, of the federal Constitution. And during that same year, Justice William Paterson, while sitting in the Middle Circuit, heard the case of *Vanhorne's Lessee v Dorrance*, where he declared unconstitutional a Pennsylvania statute that divested title of one person to real estate and vested it in another without just compensation. These cases from the Circuit Courts demonstrate that Jay, Ellsworth, Cushing, and Paterson were not shy about striking down *state* laws that violated federal constitutional principles. Doing so, where and when warranted, enabled the federal judiciary to flex its muscles and establish the continentalism and supremacy of the federal court system. By contrast, the Jay Court's handling of *Hayburn* suggests that the same justices were far more respectful and deferential toward the enactments of the US Congress, which helped avoid any potential constitutional crisis between the branches of the new and untested federal government.[28]

A footnote to In Re *Hayburn* is two related pension cases that were heard by the Jay Court during the February 1794 Term. The first of these cases was *Ex Parte Chandler*. Records of the case are sparse. War veteran John Chandler of Connecticut had earlier been approved for a pension by the Eastern Circuit, but for whatever reason his name was not included on the secretary of war's approved list. Chandler, though counsel William Edmund, filed a writ of *mandamus* to compel the secretary of war to add Chandler's name to the list. After two rounds of oral argument, the writ was denied by oral decision rendered February 14, 1794, but in the absence of an adequate record, legal historians must speculate as to *why*. One possible explanation is that if the justices then believed the 1792 law to be unconstitutional, the processing of Chandler's application by the Eastern Circuit was null and void. Another possible explanation is that if the 1792 law was constitutional, the Supreme Court believed it had no authority to compel the secretary of war to add Chandler's name to the list, as the secretary of war was vested with discretion about whether to do so in such matters. A third, long-shot explanation is that the Supreme Court justices may have merely believed that Chandler's evidence of a war-related disability was lacking. The true reasoning is lost to history.[29]

The second *Hayburn*-related case was *United States v Todd*. Justices John Jay and William Cushing were in New York when they announced their view in April 1792, prior to *Hayburn*, that they could properly hear pension applications in their personal capacities as "commissioners." Their circuit riding then took them to Connecticut in early May of that year. On May 2, 1792, Justices Jay and Cushing, along with District Judge Richard Law of the District of Connecticut, processed and approved a pension application presented to them in New Haven by a war veteran, Yale Todd. Todd's paperwork was in order, and the circuit justices recommended that Todd be placed on the federal government's pension list. They specifically determined that because of his injuries, Todd be paid at a rate of two-thirds of his former monthly wages of $8.33, plus the sum of $150 for arrears. The recommendation was approved by Secretary of War Henry Knox and by Congress. Todd then received both his $150 of arrears and $22.91 representing the period of time to September 2, 1792.[30]

The United States government eventually took the position that pension applications approved by circuit court justices under the original 1792 law were invalid for the very reasons of its unconstitutionality as debated throughout In Re *Hayburn* during the August 1792 Term of the Supreme Court. The United States sought to recoup from pensioners the monies paid to them under the 1792 law, including the $172.91 total that had been paid to Yale Todd. A suit titled *United States v Todd* was filed at the Supreme Court for the stated amount on the assumption that the Supreme Court could act as a court of original jurisdiction. The United States was represented by then–Attorney General William Bradford, while Todd was represented by an attorney named William Hillhouse. The parties to the case agreed on all of the salient facts. They further agreed that if the circuit justices in the Eastern Circuit, sitting in Connecticut, were constitutionally authorized to act as commissioners in Todd's pension approval process, then Todd should keep the $172.91 that had been paid to him by the government. Conversely, the parties also agreed that if the circuit court judges could not properly act as commissioners, then a judgment should be rendered in favor of the United States for the amount paid.[31]

The Supreme Court, including Justices Jay and Cushing, unanimously determined during the February 1794 Term that the pension power imposed on the circuit courts was not judicial power and therefore was unconstitutional and could not be enforced. The Jay Court further reasoned that because Todd's pension was approved under an unconstitutional pretense and paid to him under that same pretense, the US government was entitled to have Todd repay his ill-begotten $172.91. The Supreme Court's opinion was unreported but recounted in detail in a later case. The Supreme Court's only official decision on the case was the innocuous language that "Judgment be entered for the plaintiff."[32]

The result in *United States v Todd* reveals that by 1794, all of the justices of the Jay Court understood that the Invalid Pension Act of 1792 was unconstitutional. It would not be a leap to conclude that the same basis explains the Supreme Court's unreported reasoning for denying the writ of *mandamus* in Ex Parte *Chandler*. The opinions of Justices Wilson and Blair in the *Todd* case were consistent with their views of the law's unconstitutionality as expressed by them in their letter to President Washington on April 18, 1792, and as expressed by Justice Iredell in his letter to President Washington on June 8, 1792. By the February 1794 Term of the court, the infirmities of the 1792 pension law had been corrected, so there was no longer any pressure on Jay and Cushing to maintain their earlier public posture that circuit court justices could separately and properly act on pension applications as commissioners. Further, the Jay Court's determinations in *Chandler* and *Todd* cannot be viewed as an assertion of judicial review, as the 1792 pension law was no longer on the books for any court to actually strike down.

JAY'S DAYS

Edmund Randolph continued to serve in Washington's Cabinet as attorney general until January 26, 1794. On January 2, 1794, he began new duties as secretary of state in place of Thomas Jefferson, who had resigned from the position. Thus, for most of January, Randolph occupied two positions in the Cabinet simultaneously until William Bradford was confirmed as the new attorney general. Randolph would only serve as secretary of state until August 20, 1795. That month, the British government intercepted a communique between the French minister, Jean Antoine Joseph Fauchet, and Randolph, suggesting that Randolph had shared confidential Cabinet information with the French government and also maligned the good faith and character of the Washington administration. The British shared the intercept with President Washington. During a Cabinet meeting, Washington presented the communique to Randolph and demanded an explanation. Confronted, Randolph had no good explanation and resigned from the government. He returned to his native Virginia to practice law. Randolph's most famous case in private practice was representing Aaron Burr in Burr's infamous trial for treason, which resulted in Burr's acquittal in 1807. Randolph died on September 12, 1813, at the age of sixty. Randolph County in present-day West Virginia bears his name.[33]

Chapter 6

Sovereign Immunity and an Impetus for the 11th Amendment

Chisholm v Georgia (1793)

> "An Alien had a Right to Sue any State . . . But as soon as I, an Alien, brought an Action against Massachusetts, The Congress have repealed and Annulled that Article of the Constitution, and thereby have deprived me of the only means for obtaining redress of the Wrongs done me by Massachusetts, And of Receiving Satisfaction for a lawful demand. . . . And that the Old Proverb is True, Might Overcomes Right."
>
> —Letter of William Vassall to James Lloyd
> August 7, 1794

There is a misimpression that the first great case of constitutional significance was *Marbury v Madison*, decided by the US Supreme Court in 1803 when John Marshall was chief justice. The reason for this misimpression may be that in law schools, *Marbury v Madison* is the first case that is typically read by law students in their introductory course on constitutional law. That *Marbury* is emphasized does not necessarily mean there were not other significant constitutional cases before it. In fact, the first case decided by the Supreme Court of far-reaching constitutional dimension was actually *Chisholm v Georgia*. It is not a focus of law schools, not because it was an unimportant decision for its time, but because its result was later negated by the ratification of the 11th

Amendment. *Chisholm* is, in fact, a significant constitutional case because it addressed an unsettled question of law that affected all of the states and a wide universe of creditors and helped prompt the nation's first constitutional amendment beyond the original ten.[1]

May a private citizen in one state file a lawsuit in federal court that names another state as a defendant? In other words, may a private creditor federally sue a state to collect on a debt owed by the state where the creditor does not live? On the one hand, it might be argued that every state in the union is entitled to immunity from lawsuits because a state is a sovereign entity. On the other hand, it might be argued that with the ratification of the 1789 Constitution, the only true sovereign was the federal government and a citizen's own state, clearing the way for individual lawsuits against any of the other individual states. This question might not sound significant today, but it was important and prominent in the early 1790s. The legal issue was a subject of unresolved debate. Much money rode on the outcome of the question. The financially shaky states owed debts to many persons. The question of whether the states were entitled to "sovereign immunity" would need to be addressed early in the nation's legal history on whether individual states could be subject to the authority and liability of the federal courts. The Jay Court addressed the question squarely in the 1793 case of *Chisholm v Georgia*. It might arguably represent the most important case of constitutional dimension during John Jay's tenure at the US Supreme Court.

The issue of state sovereign immunity in the federal courts did not appear suddenly and unexpectedly. It was the subject of significant debate in the 1780s and 1790s. During those times, the states were preeminent political entities. Americans did not define themselves as citizens of the United States, but as "New Yorkers," or "Virginians," or citizens of whatever other state where they lived. Attitudes and loyalties were state-centric. The individual states had provided the militias that comprised the continental army. The states were the only entities that could levy taxes directly on their citizens. The limited forms of transportation made the states seem farther away from each other than they seem today. If laws needed to be passed to govern the public's conduct, the citizenry did not think in terms of national legislation and national debate, but instead looked to their local legislators and their state capitals. The creation of a federal government raised concerns about the extent to which federal authority would impinge upon state sovereignty, including whether state states could be subjected to lawsuits in the federal courts.

State sovereignty, including whether the states would be subject to the coercive jurisdiction of federal courts, was actively but informally discussed and debated by Federalists and Anti-Federalists at the Second Continental Congress while the federal Constitution was being drafted in Philadelphia. The draft of Article III, section 2, of the proposed constitution, later adopted, authorized the federal courts to hear lawsuits "between a State and Citizens of another State." Anti-Federalists were upset with any language that might permit the federal courts to coerce states into complying with federal court judgments. The Articles of Confederation had permitted no such federal intrusion into state sovereignty. Anti-Federalists, who were distrustful of expanded federal power, sought to protect state sovereignty at all levels, including keeping the federal judiciary out of the states' hair.

Prominent Federalists such as Alexander Hamilton, James Madison, and John Marshall tried to appease the Anti-Federalists by arguing that the ability of federal courts to hear cases "between a State and Citizens of another State" referred only to when the states chose to commence suits as *plaintiffs*, but that the states could not be sued as *defendants*. Indeed, Hamilton, in *Federalist Papers* 81, rejected the notion that states could be made defendants in federal court without their consent. Hamilton wrote, "To what purpose would it be to authorize suits against States for the debts they owe? How could recoveries be enforced? It is evident that it could not be done without waging war against the contracting State," a result Hamilton concluded was "unwarrantable." Similar sentiments had been expressed by opinion leaders James Madison and John Marshall. With those arguments, the Anti-Federalists were sufficiently appeased that the judiciary article of the new Constitution was not a device that could be coercively used *against* the sovereign states. Unfortunately for all concerned, there appears to have been no formal debate on this question by the Committee of Detail at the Constitutional Convention, which included as one of its members future Supreme Court Justice James Wilson of Pennsylvania. As a result, the language of Article III, section 2, was never tweaked to ensure that the federal courts could only hear cases involving the states when those states were postured as plaintiffs rather than as defendants. What was left was constitutional language that was subject to two different interpretations in the earliest days of the new union, and the differing interpretations were gaping and significant.[2]

With hindsight, the language of the 1789 Constitution should have been written to clearly resolve the question of whether the states could be sued in federal courts and whether the federal courts could hear foreign debt collection cases brought against the states and enforce those judgments. Instead, Article III was written in a way that was short on detail in certain respects, vague, and ambiguous. The first Congress had an opportunity to resolve some of the ambiguities upon enacting the Judiciary Act of 1789, but focused only on procedure without addressing the potentially explosive issues of jurisdiction upon the states. For clearly and finally addressing whether the states could be sued in the federal courts, the founding fathers had, in effect, kicked the can to Congress. When Congress had an opportunity to address those same issues in the Judiciary Act, it kicked the can further. The can, twice kicked, landed at the Jay Court.

The various states and individuals made many purchases during the Revolutionary War, both war related and not. By the early 1790s, many states were heavily in debt and virtually bankrupt. The thirteen original states had borrowed more than $200 million to fund their efforts during the Revolutionary War. Much of that debt was no longer owned by the original creditors, having been assigned or sold at discounts to others at home and abroad, including speculators. There were many British and American merchants and creditors who wished to collect on these debts owed by the states, but getting the states to actually pay them proved to be a difficult endeavor. Under the Articles of Confederation, each state was sovereign and immune from lawsuits in the courts absent their consent to be sued, and the states were therefore free to pay their debts whenever, and however, they pleased, if at all. What was politically galling for the states was to spend limited financial resources satisfying debts owed by assignment or purchase to British merchants or to American creditors who were loyalists to the British Crown. There was sentiment that limited resources instead be paid, if at all, to creditors who were independent of the taint of British commerce and sympathies.[3]

Yet Article 4 of the 1783 Treaty of Paris, negotiated by John Jay and others, guaranteed that American and British creditors each be entitled to the full value in sterling money of all bona fide previously contracted debts without impediment from the other country's laws. Making matters worse for the states, Article III, section 2, of the Constitution contained the ambiguously phrased language that federal courts could hear lawsuits between a state and citizens of another state. Suits by British creditors against the states and private individuals called American debt preferences into question, and it would not be long before those preferences would come into conflict with US obligations under the Treaty of Paris.

The issue of sovereign immunity in the courts could have come to a head in the previously seen Supreme Court case of *VanStophorst v Maryland*, which involved a claim by Dutch creditors against the state of Maryland. But Maryland did not assert a sovereign immunity defense and, fearing a potentially adverse ruling on that issue, ultimately settled that case with the plaintiffs. The issue had been dodged in *VanStophorst*, as no court was required to consider, much less decide, any questions of sovereign immunity in that case. But the issue would not be subdued in the courts for long.

One merchant who was owed war-related money was Robert Farquhar. The state of Georgia had purchased supplies of cloth from Farquhar for its use by Georgia soldiers during the Revolutionary War. The value of the purchase was 64,000 pounds sterling. Farquhar died after the transaction, but a collection suit was commenced in federal court by the executor of Farquhar's estate, plaintiff Alexander Chisholm. Chisholm was a South Carolinian, and the litigation was brought in federal court because plaintiff Chisholm and defendant Georgia were citizens of different states.[4]

The *Chisholm* case was of particular interest to the many merchants and creditors who were owed money by the states, particularly debts accrued during the war with Britain, as any recognition of a blanket sovereign immunity in favor of states would render future debt collection against them impossible. By contrast, many of the states, near bankruptcy, were not capable of paying their debts and hoped to rely on the doctrine of sovereign immunity to avoid the debts they could not satisfy. Given the number of creditors owed money by states, multiplied by the number of states themselves, the issue of whether states could be sued for payment, or avoid such suits by invoking the protection of sovereign immunity, was a significant one. Justice Iredell stated that as to the issue of state sovereignty, "[a] general question of great importance here occurs," and Justice Wilson likewise described *Chisholm* as "a case of uncommon magnitude." Today's law schools should take greater note.[5]

The *Chisholm* case was initially brought in the Circuit Court for the Southern Circuit, in Georgia, in 1791. A summons was served on

Georgia Governor Edward Telfair and Georgia Attorney General Thomas P. Carnes directing that the state appear in court on April 25, 1791, to answer the claim. Telfair answered the claim by denying that the federal court had any jurisdiction over the matter, as Georgia was an independent and sovereign state. No one appears to have raised the point that the debt in question arose a decade before the federal constitution was adopted and what effect, if any, that fact might have on the dispute. Justice James Iredell, sitting with District Judge Nathaniel Pendleton, decided that neither the US Constitution nor the Judiciary Act of 1789 gave individuals the right to sue any state in the federal courts. Iredell particularly believed that under Article III, section 2, of the Constitution, only the US Supreme Court possessed original jurisdiction to hear cases where a state was one of the parties. As will be seen, Justice Iredell felt strongly about his view that the states could not be sued as defendants in the federal courts, at least not at the district or circuit court levels.[6]

The plaintiff, Alexander Chisholm, appealed to the US Supreme Court. He was represented by an individual already familiar here, Attorney General Edmund Randolph, acting in a private capacity. It was not Randolph's first foray into the Supreme Court, as he had represented the Dutch plaintiffs in the *VanStophorst* matter in 1791 and appeared at the court again in the *Hayburn* pension case in 1792.

Chisholm's matter was originally scheduled at the Supreme Court for the August 1792 Term of the court. No attorney appeared in court on behalf of the state of Georgia as a result of the state's decision to boycott the proceeding on the ground of sovereign immunity. Randolph therefore requested that judgment be rendered against Georgia if the state were to fail to appear in defense of the case at the following Term. The case was re-calendared for the February 1793 Term, and once again, no representative of the state appeared in Georgia's defense. Instead, Georgia sent a written protest to the Supreme Court, through Alexander Dallas and attorney Jared Ingersoll, denying the Supreme Court's jurisdiction to entertain the case. Georgia's absence from the courtroom visually underscored its claim to sovereign immunity but at the same time prevented the state from arguing to the judges the finer legal points in its favor.[7]

The plaintiff's case proceeded and was argued against an "empty chair." A large audience attended to watch the argument. Edmund Randolph's arguments to the Jay Court focused on three separate components. First, he argued that under the Constitution, Article III, section 2, gave the courts jurisdiction over "controversies between a state and citizens of another state, which by its terms is not limited to when the state is only a plaintiff." The language of the Constitution could not be plainer, which was to the benefit of plaintiff Alexander Chisholm. Second, he argued that under the Judiciary Act of 1789, the Supreme Court was given jurisdiction over all cases "where a state shall be a party." The language's reference to "all" cases demonstrated that states may sue and be sued, even in their capacities as defendants. Moreover, the word "party" is an umbrella term that denotes both plaintiffs and defendants. Third, Randolph engaged in a public policy argument, that if states could not be sued in federal courts, they could "enjoy the high privilege of acting thus eminently wrong, without controul [sic]." He concluded the point by arguing that morality and the common good necessitated "that some [judicial] check should be found" to render a state's wrongful conduct punishable.[8]

Even if the Supreme Court were to rule against Georgia, there lingered an open question of whether the state, or any other state similarly situated, would respect and adhere to any judgment of the Supreme Court. Randolph, when confronted with that issue, merely acknowledged the "painful possibilities" of such a development. But he also said, with cautious optimism, "let me hope and pray, that not a single star in the American constellation will ever suffer its lustre [sic] to be diminished by hostility against the sentence of a court, which itself has adopted." Such eloquence was known to many of the attorneys and judges during the period, including Jay, and has been partially lost to the legal profession in the two centuries that followed.[9]

Justice Thomas Johnson, who had earlier replaced Justice John Rutledge, had resigned from the Supreme Court effective January 16, 1793. The court therefore had only five justices during the February 1793 Term instead of six, as there was insufficient time for President Washington to select Johnson's replacement and for the Congress to confirm any such nominee in time for the February cases. Johnson's replacement, Justice William Paterson of New Jersey, was confirmed by the Senate by voice acclamation on March 4, 1793, and officially began his duties at the court seven days later. As quickly as President Washington had nominated Paterson to the Supreme Court and as quickly as Paterson was confirmed by the Senate, Paterson did not commence his judicial duties until after the February 1793 Term had already ended.

The ultimate question of the *Chisholm* case was framed by different justices in different ways. John Jay defined the issue in language that was clear and concise: "Is a State suable by individual citizens of another State?" Associate Justice Wilson used more grandiose language: "The question to be determined is, whether this State [Georgia], so respectable, and whose claim soars so high, is amenable to the jurisdiction of the Supreme Court of the United States? This question, important in itself, will depend on others, more important still; and, may, perhaps, be ultimately resolved into one, no less radical than this—'do the people of the United States form a Nation?' "[10]

The justices focused in varying degrees on the specific language of the Constitution at Article III, section 2, which provides, "[t]he judicial power of the United States shall extend to . . . controversies between a State and citizens of another State." Each justice of the court issued a separate opinion under their own individual names, read orally in a crowded courtroom in the order of least senior, James Iredell, to the most senior, Chief Justice John Jay. The decisions were read by the justices on February 18, 1793.[11]

In a 4–1 disposition, the majority of the Supreme Court, including Chief Justice Jay, held that Article III, section 2, of the federal Constitution and the Judiciary Act of 1789 erased the sovereign immunity of states and conferred on the federal courts jurisdictional authority to hear disputes between a state and a citizen of another state. The 4–1 holding of the court is merely an arithmetic description of five justices' separate opinions. The holding was consistent with Federalist views that favored strong central governance but went well beyond the limitations argued by Alexander Hamilton in *Federalist Paper* 81.[12]

Within the majority of justices, Justice Blair voted in favor of Alexander Chisholm on the ground that the there was no basis in the constitutional language to distinguish between states as plaintiffs or defendants—"[b]oth cases, I have no doubt, were intended." Justice Wilson, who had a unique view of the Constitution's drafting as a member of the convention's Committee of Detail, relied on the plain language of Article III, section 2, that states could be sued in federal courts. He also agreed with Edmund Randolph's argument that if states could enter into contracts with no intention of honoring their terms, other provisions of the Constitution that protected the inviolability of contracts would have no meaning. Justice Cushing's reasoning was similar to that of Justice Blair, reliant on constitutional language "that is expressly extended to 'controversies between a State and citizens of another State.' "[13]

Jay's view on the question was that the individual states had no immunity in matters involving state affairs. His analysis was more complex than that of all of his colleagues, with the possible exception of Wilson. In Jay's view, the British Crown was the sovereign power during the colonial period, and its sovereignty transferred to the federal government upon the ratification of the US Constitution in 1789. Jay reasoned that because the states were mere subsets of sovereign people in a federalized union, they were not entitled to the immunity that was conferred exclusively on the federal government. He drew a distinction between the United States and European nations; that in Europe, the people were subjects of the sovereign, whereas in the United States the sovereigns were without subjects, and sovereign officials acted merely as agents of the people. Jay specifically noted that "the people are the sovereigns of this country and consequently[,] fellow citizens and joint sovereigns cannot be degraded by appearing with each other in their own [state] courts to have their controversies determined." But citizens of one state, suing another state in a federal court, were a different matter. Jay also observed in his *Chisholm* opinion that denying individuals the right to sue a state, while permitting them to sue lesser municipalities, does "not correspond with the equal rights we claim; with the equality we profess to admire and maintain, and with that popular sovereignty in which every citizen partakes." In the end, Jay was persuaded by the plain words found in the Constitution at Article III, section 2, that the federal courts had jurisdiction over cases "between a State and Citizens of another State" could not be reasonably construed to apply only when the state is a plaintiff, but must equally apply to when the state is a defendant sued by a foreign state citizen.[14]

The majority of the justices of the Supreme Court, therefore, voted in favor of an expansive view of federal judicial authority to resolve disputes between individuals and other states over debt collection. In *Chisholm*, the majority of justices on the Supreme Court willingly hit the gas pedal in liberally invoking wide federal court authority, unlike in *West v Barnes*, where the Supreme Court applied a brake against expanding the court's authority.

The decision in *Chisholm v Georgia* was not unanimous. The sole dissenter, not surprisingly, was Justice James Iredell, who had heard the same case when it was first litigated at the Southern Circuit in Georgia. Iredell reasoned in his dissenting opinion that under common law, the states were immune from suits just as the British Crown had been when the American colonies were first settled, and that suits could only be maintained if the state waived its immunity, which Georgia had clearly not done here. Iredell was of the further opinion that there was no intention for the federal courts to have greater jurisdiction over the states than the state courts had before the federal Constitution existed, and it had previously been understood that the individual states could not be sued without their consent. Iredell's views in favor of state sovereignty went a step further than the position he had taken on the same case at the Southern Circuit, because he was no longer willing to concede by the time the matter was at the Supreme Court that states could be sued in the first instance at the Supreme Court itself, under Article III, section 2, of the Constitution.[15]

The Supreme Court, perhaps uncertain whether Georgia would defy its 4–1 ruling, gave Georgia a further opportunity to appear in court to be heard as to why a judgment should not be rendered against it on default, and to be heard on the amount of the judgment to be entered. The matter that remained, of fixing the amount of the judgment, with or without the input of Georgia, was scheduled for the August 1793 Term. It was rescheduled to the February 1794 Term and then further rescheduled to February 1795. There was a good reason for the delays in determining the amount of money that Georgia would be required to pay: whether the Supreme Court's decision in *Chisholm* would be nullified by the proposal and passage of an 11th Amendment to the Constitution.[16]

Meanwhile, there was money to be made by attorneys in the prosecution and defense of debt claims against states due to the sheer number and size of the unpaid debts. Attorney General Edmund Randolph, acting as private counsel, commenced other similar suits before and after his argument in *Chisholm*. One of his private clients was William Vassall. Vassall was a purported Loyalist to the British Crown with a Harvard education. He had lived in Boston but fled to a London suburb in 1775 because of the Revolutionary War. The Commonwealth of Massachusetts barred him from returning at that time, seized his property, and mortgaged his home. Later, Article 6 of the Treaty of Paris prohibited each party to the treaty from confiscating the property of any person as a result of conduct during the war. Relying on the Treaty of Paris, Vassall sought the return of his property. He maintained that he had never been hostile to the commonwealth of Massachusetts and was non-political, but had moved to England to conduct his business of trading Jamaican sugar without the disruption of the war. Massachusetts, in blatant defiance of the Treaty of Paris, passed a statute that all previously seized property would be mortgaged, and if the mortgage was not redeemed by the original owner, the property would be confiscated by the commonwealth.[17]

Vassall's efforts to obtain the property or compensation for its value were therefore stymied for the first half of the 1780s. It was worth Vassall's effort to fight for the property, as it was a mansion located on a hilltop surrounded by gardens with a magnificent view of Boston Harbor. The mortgage on the property imposed by the commonwealth was purchased by Pascal Nelson Smith in 1780, who later sold it to Mary Hayley. In 1786, Vassall purchased the mortgage from Hayley and regained the title to the home, but Massachusetts law prohibited absentee Loyalists like Vassall from occupying redeemed property absent permission from the governor. Permission was denied in this instance. Unable to live at the Boston property, Vassall sold it back to Mary Hayley and her new husband in 1789, but was still deprived of the original value of the home and all of its contents.[18]

The 1789 Constitution, and section 13 of the Judiciary Act of 1789, both contained language that federal courts had authority to hear suits between aliens and a state. Vassall, at age seventy-seven, decided to sue Massachusetts in a federal court, hired Edmund Randolph, filed papers at the Supreme Court, and was authorized to serve the papers upon the Commonwealth of Massachusetts one week before *Chisholm* was to be argued in Philadelphia.[19]

The historical significance and controversy of *Chisholm* did not end with the mere publication of its 4–1 decision. The decision prompted an uproar from Anti-Federalists and even from some Federalists. John Jay's son William, writing of *Chisholm* years later, described the case as having "instantly aroused that morbid sensibility on the subject of State rights which had opposed so many obstacles to the establishment of the federal government." The various states were rocked by *Chisholm*'s holding and pushed for the enactment of an 11th Amendment to circumvent the Supreme Court's ruling. Many Anti-Federalists believed that they had been hoodwinked by Federalists in the drafting of the judiciary article of the Constitution, having relied in good faith on the representations that the states could not be sued as defendants in the federal courts. It did not help matters that all of the justices of the Supreme Court who heard the *Chisholm* case were Federalists. The states were all affected by the outcome of *Chisholm v Georgia*, and many of them refused to take the decision lying down. The greatest outrage did not initially originate from Georgia, as one might imagine, but from Massachusetts.[20]

The states' dislike of the *Chisholm* decision is graphically illustrated by the actions of Massachusetts Governor John Hancock, the first signer of the Declaration of Independence in 1776. After the decision was rendered in *Chisholm*, Hancock and the commonwealth's attorney general, James Sullivan, were served with subpoenas directing them to appear at the Supreme Court in the newly filed case of *Vassall v Massachusetts*. Hancock was angry and responded by calling a special session of the commonwealth's legislature, then known as the General Court. The term "General Court" was holdover nomenclature from the days of the Massachusetts Bay Colony. Hancock was living his last days and was too ill to read to the legislators his own address, much less travel to Philadelphia to comply with the subpoena. The secretary of state read the address to the legislators instead, advising that the commonwealth had three choices in light of *Chisholm v Georgia*. One choice was to make provision for defending cases such as *Vassall* in court. The second was to support a constitutional amendment that would correct the Supreme Court's "misinterpretation" of Article III, section 2, of the federal Constitution. The third, if *Chisholm* was properly decided on the law, was to seek an amendment of the Constitution anyway to "secure [to] the states severally, in the enjoyment of that share of sovereignty, which was intended that they should retain and possess" under a federal system of government. The matter was adjourned for the Massachusetts legislature to examine the issue further by committee, issue a report, and debate then what the commonwealth's policy should be. The General Court reconvened for a special session in late September and debated *Chisholm* and *Vassall* for three days.[21]

On September 27, 1793, the General Court determined that Massachusetts would *not* appear or answer in the *Vassall* case on the ground that compelling a state to defend itself in a federal court was "unnecessary and inexpedient" and was an "exercise dangerous to the peace, safety and independence of the several States." Thus, Massachusetts placed itself in open defiance of the Supreme Court. The Massachusetts legislature also instructed the commonwealth's representatives in the US Senate and House of Representatives to seek an amendment to the US Constitution that recognized state sovereign immunity from lawsuits initiated by citizens of other states. In fact, Massachusetts' congressional delegation was already a step ahead of the commonwealth's legislature.

Figure 6.1. Massachusetts Governor John Hancock.

Governor Hancock had achieved his goal of obtaining a viable plan to combat *Chisholm*, but he would not appear in public again, as he died eleven days later. Lieutenant Governor Samuel Adams, who assumed gubernatorial responsibilities upon Hancock's death, sent copies of the legislature's resolutions to the other states on October 9, 1793. The announcement that Massachusetts would defy the Supreme Court's ruling in *Chisholm*, and refuse to appear at the Supreme Court to defend itself from Vassall's claims, was a clarion call to other states to do likewise.[22]

Events in Massachusetts did not go unnoticed in Virginia. Governor Henry Lee recommended on November 13, 1793, that the Virginia General Assembly call for a constitutional amendment not only prohibiting citizens from suing other states, but also prohibiting the federal government from suing any state as well. The Virginia legislature complied. Similar resolutions were passed by the legislatures in Connecticut, North Carolina, and New Hampshire. In South Carolina, Maryland, and Georgia, one house of their bicameral legislatures passed similar resolutions as well, before later events overtook the matter, and both Pennsylvania and Delaware appointed special committees to examine the issue.[23]

Cooler heads did not prevail in Georgia. The state of Georgia was so distressed by the ruling in *Chisholm* that on November 9, 1793, its House of Representatives passed a Resolution providing that anyone who prosecuted a case against the state, as otherwise allowed by *Chisholm*, would be "declared guilty of a felony, and suffer death, without the benefit of clergy, by being *hanged*." However, developments at the nation's capital in early 1794 rendered further consideration of the unique death penalty proposal unnecessary, and the necks of Georgia's creditors thankfully remained safe from deadly nooses.[24]

Article V of the US Constitution sets forth the mechanism for amending the Constitution. Article V requires that both houses of Congress approve any proposed constitutional amendment by at least a two-thirds majority of each, which must then be approved by three-quarters of the states. There is an alternate method for amending the Constitution that involves the calling of a constitutional convention, a procedure not applicable here. The states, which sought a constitutional amendment to recognize their sovereign immunity that was denied to them by the Supreme Court, decided to accomplish their goal by means of a congressional proposal and state approvals. Their approach made sense, as US senators at the time were appointed by state legislatures, and as the approval by three-quarters of the states of a sovereign immunity amendment would not be particularly difficult to obtain given the states' self-interest in the outcome.

Legislation for amending the Constitution, to recognize the sovereign immunity of the states, was proposed in the US Congress as early as one day after the *Chisholm* decision was rendered. The first sovereignty proposal was introduced on February 19, 1793, by Massachusetts Representative Theodore Sedgwick, who, using far-reaching language, suggested "that no State shall be liable to be made a party defendant in any of the Judicial Courts . . . of the United States, at the suit of any . . . citizen or foreigners." The proposed language would have prohibited lawsuits against the states in the federal courts by any person or business, foreign or domestic.

Sedgwick's language would not be used, as Congress preferred a more narrowly worded amendment. Narrower language was proposed the following day by Senator Caleb Strong of Massachusetts, which was the primary language that Congress eventually considered and voted on. The

Senate debated Strong's language on February 25, 1793, but Congress recessed, and its further consideration of the issue was delayed until it reconvened on December 2, 1793. In the meantime, attention to the issue shifted to the states.[25]

The proposed 11th Amendment was ultimately voted on by Congress less than a year from the issuance of the *Chisholm* decision. Its final language provided that "[t]he Judicial power of the United States shall not be construed to extend to any suit in law or equity, commenced or prosecuted against one of the United States by Citizens of another state, or by Citizens or Subjects of any Foreign State." The narrower language proposed by Senator Strong differed from the broader language of Representative Sedgwick in that under Strong's version, the states were protected only from suits brought by individuals of foreign states, or by suits from foreign states themselves. The language of the 11th Amendment was identical to that proposed by Senator Strong except for substituting the words "be construed to" for "extend to" to render it more explanatory and by changing some stylistic capitalizations. The proposal for recognizing the sovereign immunity of states was passed by the US Senate on January 14, 1794, by a lopsided vote of 23–2. The House of Representatives also approved the proposal by a lopsided vote of 81–9, which occurred there on March 4, 1794.[26]

The proposed constitutional amendment then went to the states for approval. Because there were fifteen states by that time, the 11th Amendment needed to be approved by at least twelve states to become the supreme law of the land. New York and Rhode Island approved of the amendment on March 27 and March 31 of 1794, the same month that the proposal emerged from Congress. Connecticut gave its assent on May 8, 1794. New Hampshire and Massachusetts approved on June 16 and 26, 1794. Three more states—Vermont, Virginia, and Georgia—approved the amendment on November 9, 18, and 29, 1794. Kentucky and Maryland approved it on December 7 and 26, 1794. Delaware agreed on January 23, 1795. The final, twelfth state was North Carolina, which approved the 11th Amendment on February 7, 1795. With that approval, the 11th Amendment was added to the constitutional framework, and its language has never been modified or revoked. The approval process represents lightning speed for a constitutional amendment—less than one year from the *Chisholm* decision for the proposed amendment to clear both houses of Congress, and less than another year for the approval process to run its course in three-quarters of the states.[27]

Ratification of the 11th Amendment by the twelfth state, North Carolina, did not automatically amend the Constitution. Some of the states, while having ratified the proposed amendment, did not officially notify Congress that they had done so. On March 2, 1797, Congress passed a Resolution urging President John Adams to undertake the mundane task of inquiring of the states whether they had ratified the proposed 11th Amendment, even though everyone knew that a sufficient number of states had already done so. On January 8, 1798, President Adams stated in a Message to Congress that the 11th Amendment had been approved by the requisite number of states and was part of the Constitution, and for that reason, historical literature often references the amendment as a product of 1798 rather than 1795.[28]

By the 11th Amendment, the Supreme Court's holding in *Chisholm* was circumvented and nullified, and Justice Iredell's dissent prevailed as a matter of new constitutional policy. It was the first time that the federal constitution was amended beyond the original ten amendments contained in the Bill of Rights. The *Chisholm* decision had been poorly received by both Federalists and Anti-Federalists, and the reactions to it at the state legislative level, and in Congress, allowed for some rare and constructive bipartisanship between the political competitors. That

Figure 6.2. US Supreme Court Justice James Iredell.

said, the majority's holding in *Chisholm* likely would have resulted in the ratification of the 11th Amendment regardless of the precise language or reasoning used by any particular justice to justify his decision in the case.

Three dangling questions were left unresolved by the ratification of the 11th Amendment. One was whether its effect was retroactive, or prospective only. Perhaps predictably, the issue found its way to the US Supreme Court in the 1798 case of *Hollingsworth v Virginia* under Chief Justice Oliver Ellsworth. There, the court unanimously held that the 11th Amendment retroactively divested the judiciary of jurisdiction to hear any cases by individuals against the states. The holding in *Hollingsworth* makes sense if, as appears to be the case, the 11th Amendment was not written as an *alteration* to the US Constitution, but rather as a mere *explanation* of its original terms. Put another way, the 11th Amendment is not really a constitutional amendment at all, despite its treatment as such. As a result of *Hollingsworth*, all federal suits that were pending against states by citizens of other states were summarily dismissed. To this day, states are immune from foreign citizen suits in the federal courts absent either an expressed voluntary waiver of that immunity or by the exercise of certain remedial powers permitted under the 14th Amendment.[29]

The second dangling question left in the wake of the 11th Amendment was whether citizens of a state could sue their *own* state. The language of the 11th Amendment did not address that immunity question directly. Unlike the issue of retroactivity, which was resolved by the courts promptly, the issue of citizens suing their own states was not definitively resolved until almost 100 years later, in the 1890 case of *Hans v Louisiana*. The US Supreme Court held in *Hans* that courts could not hear suits by citizens against their own states, even when the suit raised questions of federal law, because of the states' entitlement to sovereign immunity. *Hans* included an interesting discussion of *Chisholm v Georgia*, particularly of the dissent in *Chisholm* by Justice Iredell. With the Supreme Court's ruling in *Hans*, state sovereignty circled back to the form initially proposed to the US Congress by Massachusetts Representative Theodore Sedgwick, which Congress at the time had viewed as too broad.[30]

The ratification of the 11th Amendment raised a third set of questions that are purely academic. Did the Jay Court interpret the US Constitution on the issue of state sovereignty in a way that was actually "wrong," and the 11th Amendment was ratified to restore its true meaning? Or, alternatively, was the Jay Court's interpretation of the Constitution "right," and the 11th Amendment was ratified at the urging of the states to *change* the Constitution's original meaning and intent? Reasonable minds can differ in answering those questions. A concurring opinion in *Hans* by Justice John Marshall Harlan defended the majority of the judges who heard *Chisholm*, stating that "the decision in that case was based upon a sound interpretation of the constitution as that instrument then was." While the ratification of the 11th Amendment ultimately renders the questions academic, the stronger argument appears to be that of John Jay and most of his colleagues, that the plain language of the Constitution permitted lawsuits by individual citizens of a state against other states. The problem was caused not by the Jay Court's misreading of the constitutional terms, but by the Constitutional Convention's wording of Article III, section 2, in a manner that was contrary to the informal understandings that had been reached between Federalists and Anti-Federalists about the limits of federal authority over the states. A constitutional policy contrary to that reached in *Chisholm v Georgia* required an amendment to the federal Constitution to *clarify* the intent of the Constitutional Convention that was not accurately expressed in the Constitution itself. The end result was a nullification of *Chisholm*'s holding. To this day, few US Supreme Court cases have ever been nullified by constitutional amendment.[31]

Despite the *Chisholm* decision, the state of Georgia refused to pay any money to Alexander Chisholm. In so doing, Georgia answered Edmund Randolph's rhetorical eloquence at the Supreme Court by allowing the luster of its star to be diminished in the American constellation. The Supreme Court had the authority at the time to award payment, but it had no enforcement mechanisms for making Georgia comply. As a result, Alexander Chisholm, having won his case at the nation's highest court, never collected any of the money that he was owed. Any hope that he might have had at collecting the award was destroyed with the ratification of the 11th Amendment and the retroactive application that it was given in *Hollingsworth v Virginia*.

John Jay's assignment after the February 1793 Term, when *Chisholm* was decided, was to ride the Southern Circuit with James Iredell, where further debt collection cases were addressed. The difference was that whereas *Chisholm* involved a debt collection claim against a state, the cases Jay and Iredell encountered in the Southern Circuit were between private individuals. The Southern Circuit included the District of Virginia. Almost half of all of the American debt to British creditors was owed by residents of Virginia, and naturally there were several dozens of private debt collection cases pending in the federal courts in Virginia when Jay and Iredell arrived there. They were joined on the circuit by Virginia District Judge Cyrus Griffin.[32]

Virginia had enacted a blatantly anti-British sequestration statute on October 20, 1777, which allowed its state's creditors to pay their British debts to the state using depreciated state currency and for the debts to then be deemed discharged. The 1777 law was a primary defense raised by the Virginia debtors in response to the lawsuits commenced against them by British creditors. Complicating matters was a provision of the 1783 Treaty of Paris, which had been negotiated by John Jay, where each party to the treaty had agreed, in Article 4, that its creditors would not meet "lawful impediments to the recovery of the full value in sterling money of all *bona fide* [pre-war] debts" from the other. Certainly, the 1777 Virginia law, which had never been repealed, was an impediment to effective British debt collection in Virginia. The circumstance troubled John Jay greatly as he arrived in Richmond and began hearing British debt collection cases on the docket, including one case for 3,111 pounds titled *Ware, Administrator of Jones v Hylton.*[33]

Many of the British creditors were represented by Patrick Henry, who was already famous for his oratorical skills, and John Marshall, who would become a famous jurist in his own right before too long. Henry argued his cases from the heart, that given the plunder and destruction caused by the British during the Revolutionary War, Virginia had every right to enact a law that subjected British debts to confiscation by the Virginia commonwealth. Marshall argued his cases from the mind, that because Virginia enacted its statute in 1777 while it was an independent and sovereign nation, the law could not be abrogated by either the later federal constitution or the later Treaty of Paris. Henry and Marshall also argued that the Treaty of Paris was no longer binding as a result of various British violations of the treaty's terms. The latter argument must not have sat well with John Jay because Jay, as a negotiator the treaty, likely felt invested in its continued viability and its stabilizing influence on British-American relations.[34]

Jay and Iredell agreed that federal law, including ratified and binding international treaties, were supreme and enforceable over any contradictory state statute. They also agreed that the Circuit Court should not address the validity or invalidity of the Treaty of Paris, as doing so would wade into political issues that courts typically seek to avoid. However, Iredell and Griffin believed that the Virginia law was not necessarily "contradictory" to the Treaty of Paris, as the treaty did not nullify the private right of Virginia creditors to satisfy their various British debts by making payments to the state, even in devalued currency. Jay, the internationalist and diplomat, believed otherwise, that the Treaty of Paris could permissibly alter the private rights of Virginia citizens where, as here, those rights represented "lawful impediments" to the recovery by British creditors of the full value of bona fide debts owed to them prior to the treaty. Jay saw no good arising from a situation where Americans would expect to recover debts against British subjects in British courts, while British creditors could not effectively do so against American debtors in Virginia courts. He also believed that any British violations of the Treaty of Paris did not excuse Americans from upholding the treaty provisions that bound them. Jay believed, as he did when drafting the language of the Treaty of Paris, that debts fairly contracted should be honestly paid, a concept consistent with his Episcopal religious beliefs and the experiences Jay knew of his merchant father.[35]

The British collection cases involving the 1777 sequestration law such as *Ware, Administrator of Jones v Hylton* were 2–1 decisions, with Jay on the losing end. But the Virginia debtors were only protected to the extent that they had paid money to the state toward satisfaction of the same debts. The debtors lost their arguments on some of their defenses, such as their claim that the Virginia statute was not subject to the general supremacy of the Treaty of Paris and that the treaty was no longer valid or enforceable.

Significantly, *Ware* went to the US Supreme Court fewer than two years later, when John Jay was occupied by other matters and unable to hear the case. John Marshall and Alexander Campbell appeared at the Supreme Court on behalf of the Virginia debtors, Daniel Hylton & Co. and Frances Eppes. The creditors were represented by a battery of attorneys including Edward Tilghman, Alexander Willcocks, and William Lewis, all of Philadelphia. There, John Jay's point of view on the law was vindicated by a unanimous Supreme Court in 1794. The Supreme Court held in *Ware* that the Treaty of Paris was in full force and effect despite any violations that may have been committed by the British since its ratification. Additionally, the Supreme Court held not only that the Treaty of Paris was the supreme law of the land, but that its provisions meant that Virginia debtors were obligated to satisfy their British creditors directly, notwithstanding any payments made to the Commonwealth of Virginia under the state's 1777 sequestration law.[36]

A consequence of the Supreme Court's decision was that all of the money that had been paid by debtors to the Commonwealth of Virginia to discharge their British debts had to be paid again. This was on its face an inequitable and unsatisfactory result for Virginia debtors. The British creditors and the American debtors naturally looked to the Virginia statehouse to disgorge the monies that the commonwealth had received toward payment of the debts. As one might imagine, the money was no longer in the state's coffers, as it had been spent long before on war-related and other public expenses. There was no expectation that the federal government would financially bail out the states on this issue. The Virginia legislature, strapped for cash and near bankruptcy, sought to solve the problem created by *Ware* by issuing interest-bearing certificates payable to the debtors who earlier had made payments to the commonwealth, but that was of only partial consolation to the debtors who remained obligated to satisfy the ongoing debts to their British creditors. The terms of the Treaty of Paris had been upheld, and the American debtors who used Virginia's sequestration law had to pay a significant price—twice.[37]

JAY'S DAYS

True to its word, the Commonwealth of Massachusetts never appeared at the Supreme Court to defend itself in Vassall v Massachusetts. *The Supreme Court maintained several debt collection suits against states on its docket through 1796, which included the Vassall matter. But there was no enthusiasm for creditors to prosecute their cases or for the Supreme Court to adjudicate them, as Congress had passed the language of the 11th Amendment by early 1794 and as twelve states had ratified the 11th Amendment by early 1795. The Vassall case was officially dismissed at the Supreme Court in 1797. The passage of the 11th Amendment by Congress was all that William Vassall needed to hear to know that he would never be compensated by the Commonwealth of Massachusetts for the value of his confiscated bucolic property overlooking Boston Harbor. He wrote in a letter to James Lloyd dated August 7, 1794, after Congress had acted, that "my Action falls of Course." Such were the vagaries of being supportive of the British Crown during a war that Great Britain would lose and that Massachusetts' legislators would keenly and vindictively remember.*

In the same letter to James Lloyd, Vassall wrote that under the federal constitution, "An Alien had a Right to Sue any State for a Legal demand at the Supreme Judicial Court of the United States, But as soon as I, an Alien, brought an Action against Massachusetts, The Congress have repealed and Annulled that Article of the Constitution, and thereby have deprived me of the only means for obtaining redress of the Wrongs done me by Massachusetts, And of Receiving Satisfaction for a lawful demand. I find by sorrowful Experience, that an Individual will strive in vain to Compel a Legislature or an Absolute Power to do him Justice; And that the Old Proverb is True, Might Overcomes Right." Vassall's letter suggests that in his mind, the passage of the 11th Amendment was all about him. In fact, it was about the much broader issue of states' rights that had divided Federalists and Anti-Federalists for years, having nothing to do with William Vassall in particular. Despite Vassall's loss at the Supreme Court, he died in 1800 at the age of eighty-four as a still-wealthy man.[38]

Chapter 7

Resisting Political Pressure from the Executive Branch

Pagan v Hooper (1793)

> "I procured a writ of Error in the case of Hooper v Pagan, and immediately on Mr. Judge Wilson's return to the City waited on him in order to procure a citation; but this he did not think proper to grant; nothing further can therefore be done in that line. . ."
>
> —Benjamin R. Morgan to Thomas P. Anthony
> June 8, 1792

Privateering on the high seas occurred frequently in the latter 1700s against the merchant vessels of nations that were at war with one another. *Pagan v Hooper* was the first case presented to the Supreme Court where privateering was part of the underlying facts, but in this instance, issues of privateering were not central to the outcome. No actual "case" was heard on its merits by John Jay and his colleagues, because the justices determined that the Supreme Court was without the authority to hear the appeal. What sets *Pagan v Hooper* apart, however, is that the Supreme Court refused to hear the case despite political pressure that was brought to bear by the Washington administration for it to do so, to further the diplomatic relationship between Great Britain and the United States. This case therefore merits its own chapter, unlike earlier matters that were not fully argued to conclusion such as *VanStophorst v Maryland* and *Collet v Collet*.

The dispute that would lead to *Pagan v Hooper* had its origins in the now-outmoded practice of privateering against merchant vessels. Privateering was nothing new in the late 1700s. Any nation with a weak navy could supplement its power on the high seas during wartime, by allowing private ships to assist the war effort on behalf of the government. The ships were privately owned, equipped, expensed, staffed with crews, weaponized, and operated—hence the term "privateer." The ship's owner typically obtained authority from a government to conduct activities on its behalf by being issued a formal commission, also sometimes known as a "letter of marque." Armed with that legal authority, the privateer could capture the merchant vessels of an enemy nation, or neutral vessels carrying enemy cargo. Privateers would naturally conduct their operations near ports of trade. Captured merchant vessels, known then as "prizes," were escorted to a mainland port after capture. Perishable cargo would be immediately sold, and the proceeds of the sales would be placed into an escrow account for later disbursement. The fate of the vessel, its non-perishable cargo, and any proceeds in escrow, would then be determined by a "prize court" established by the nation that sponsored the privateer. Prize courts examined whether the captured vessel was a "lawful" prize, meaning that it was owned by, or carried the cargo of, an enemy nation. If so, the privateer could sell the prize and its cargo and keep all of the proceeds. The ultimate effect of privateering was the sponsor nation's disruption of the commerce of another nation with which it was at war.[1]

Prize courts were adjudicative. They were often, but not always, fair. Prize court procedures varied from country to country. Typically, a privateer needed to merely establish that he had a "reasonable suspicion" that the captured vessel was engaged in commerce on behalf of an enemy nation. If established, the burden of proof shifted to the original owner of the seized vessel to establish that the vessel and its cargo was not owned by the enemy nation or its subjects. Official ship documents and manifests, which might normally be considered unimpeachable evidence of the vessel's true pedigree and purpose, were always examined because they addressed the ship's ownership, destination, and cargo "out of its own mouth." However, official documents were not always considered conclusive out of concern that they could be phony versions specifically manufactured for use in prize court proceedings. As a result, the rules governing the burden of proof favored the privateer and disfavored the merchant whose vessel was seized. The ultimate burden of proof was different from that applied in the official courts of the United States, where the burden of proof in civil and criminal matters is upon the proponent of a case.[2]

Privateering was practiced by the American states and by Great Britain during the Revolutionary War. Under the Articles of Confederation, individual states issued letters of marque to privateers, and recognized the legitimacy of prize courts for resolving claims between the privateers and the original owners of the seized vessels and cargo. The Second Continental Congress passed resolutions regulating the imprisonment, treatment, and exchange of merchant sailors captured on prize vessels. For the merchants involved, the loss of occasional ships or cargo was merely an unfortunate cost of doing business. The practice of privateering was not internationally abolished until the Declaration of Paris issued in 1856.[3]

Privateering was different than "piracy." Piracy was without government sanction, was not subject to adjudicative prize courts, and was independent of any war between nations. Piracy was criminal. Privateering, by contrast, accomplished many military and economic governmentally sanctioned purposes. It was potentially profitable for those engaged in the business. It cost the sponsor government virtually nothing. The sponsor government augmented its power on the seas and harassed an enemy nation by interrupting its trade between ports. The "losers" were primarily the merchants whose vessels were commandeered, and secondarily, the home country of the merchants whose commercial trade was disrupted.

When the Revolutionary War came to its conclusion, Preliminary Articles of Peace were agreed upon between the American states and Great Britain, approved by Congress on April 15, 1783. In those days, when communications were slow, privateers at sea continued their incursions against enemy vessels unaware that the war had ceased. The preliminary peace terms dealt with this problem by providing that vessels at sea were given a grace period where their privateering activities would be recognized as valid, even if occurring after the preliminary terms of peace had been exchanged. The farther a ship was from shore, the longer the grace period extended. The grace periods, depending upon location and distance, were twelve days, one month, two months, and five months.[4]

With that all as background, the Pagan brothers were successful loyalist Scottish merchants during the years leading to the Revolutionary War. They operated trading vessels to and from ports along the northeast coast of North America. Their vessels were seized by American privateers during the war, prompting them to obtain letters of marque from Great Britain to lawfully arm their own vessels for privateering. On March 25, 1783, one of their vessels, the sloop *Industry*, captured the American brigantine *Thomas*, which was owned by Stephen Hooper of Newburyport, Massachusetts. The capture occurred 50 days after the cessation of Revolutionary War hostilities outside of the one-month grace period of the Preliminary Articles of Peace, but within the two-month period. According to Hooper, the capture occurred within the waters between the English Channel and the Canary Islands, an area subject to a defined grace period of only one month, rendering the capture unlawful. The Pagans disputed the location of the capture, and claimed that the time and place of the capture fell within a longer grace period, rendering it lawful.[5]

The *Thomas* was brought to present-day Penobscot, Maine, an area controlled at the time by Great Britain. The matter was heard at a prize court at Halifax, Nova Scotia, where a prize judge determined that the capture was not lawful, presumably on the basis of the capture's location and date. The prize court ordered the return of the *Thomas* and its cargo to its original owner, Hooper. Under British law, the losing party at a prize court had a right to appeal an unsatisfying determination to the High Court of Appeals in Prize Causes, in London, and the Pagans exercised that right by filing the necessary paperwork there. During the appeal, the Pagans refused to return the *Thomas* to Hooper. After much haggling, the parties agreed to sell the *Thomas* and its cargo and hold the proceeds for whichever party prevailed at the High Court. The Pagans sold the property but retained all of the proceeds, and then in an apparent act of bad faith, took no further efforts to advance their appeal at the High Court.[6]

Aggrieved, Hooper initiated a law suit in the Massachusetts Court of Common Pleas in Salem, Massachusetts, and obtained from that court the arrest of Thomas Pagan, one of the three Pagan brothers. In June of 1789, a jury at the Court of Common Pleas awarded Hooper, who had won his earlier case at the prize court, 3,374 British pounds, slightly less than the 3,500 pounds that Hooper had sought. Pagan and Hooper each appealed the judgment to the Supreme Judicial Court of the Commonwealth of Massachusetts, Pagan on the ground that the jury verdict was in error, and Hooper on the ground that the jury had not awarded him all the money to which he believed himself entitled. The Supreme Judicial Court presided over a second jury trial, which resulted once again in a jury verdict in favor of Hooper, but only for the amount of 3,009.2.10 British pounds.[7]

The Pagans appealed to the Supreme Judicial Court of the Commonwealth of Massachusetts a second time raising an important question which would not be decided by the US Supreme Court until *Glass v Sloop Betsey* in 1794. The question was whether "common law" courts such as those in Massachusetts had the authority to hear matters involving privateering, or whether prize courts were the sole arbiters of those disputes in "admiralty." The justices of the Supreme Judicial Court in Massachusetts decided the appeal against the Pagans, noting that their earlier trial there did not depend upon whether the *Thomas* had been captured as a lawful prize, but only upon the more narrow issue of whether the Pagans had breached their later separate agreement to proceed with an appeal of the capture dispute at the High Court in London and pay the proceeds of the vessel's and cargo's sale to the party that prevailed there—which was a question of basic common law. By this point in the parties' dispute, Hooper had prevailed in all legal proceedings, though not for quite as much money as he had wished.[8]

Roughly four years later, the Pagans revived their dormant appeal at the High Court of Appeals in Prize Cases, without delivering to Hooper the documents that would have invited him to defend the matter in London. The High Court rendered a decree in the Pagans favor based solely on Hooper's failure to appear in his defense of the High Court appeal. The High Court did not reach any of the merits of the parties' prize dispute. Hooper paid no immediate attention to the High Court's decree. Hooper likely ignored the High Court's decree because it was invalid without his having received notice of the appeal and an opportunity to be heard on it.[9]

Thomas Pagan used the High Court's decree to seek yet another trial at the Supreme Judicial Court of Massachusetts. By doing so while physically within the Commonwealth, Thomas Pagan was arrested on the original unpaid judgment and jailed during the third week of June 1790. The Supreme Judicial Court of Massachusetts denied Pagan's request for yet another new trial. Pagan would remain in custody in Boston for another three and a half years for his failure to pay Hooper's earlier Massachusetts judgment.[10]

The British government initiated diplomatic efforts on behalf of the Pagans, perhaps enhanced by Thomas Pagan's continuing loss of freedom. Overtures were directed by Britain's counsel in Boston, Thomas

MacDonogh, to Massachusetts Governor John Hancock. Hancock referred Britain's request for political assistance to the Commonwealth's legislature, which, after investigation, directed that the Supreme Judicial Court consider whether there should be yet another new trial. The Supreme Judicial Court complied with the legislature's directive and entertained argument by the parties on the issue. In the end, at that court, the Pagans were again denied a new trial, in a decision rendered on June 25, 1791.[11]

British diplomatic efforts on behalf of the Pagans, spearheaded by Lord Grenville and Foreign Minister George Hammond, were initiated again, this time on the federal level with Secretary of State Thomas Jefferson. Jefferson referred the matter to Attorney General Edmund Randolph. Hammond's instructions from his government were to pursue the Pagans' interests "in the strongest manner." The official papers of Thomas Jefferson suggest that for the next two years, the Pagan matter occupied the diplomatic attentions of Hammond and Jefferson "more than any diplomatic issue save of neutral rights and the disputed provisions of the Treaty of Paris." Hammond, though only in his very late twenties, pursued the interests of the Pagans tenaciously. Jefferson also acted as a liaison between Hammond and Randolph, transmitting letters and communications between the two.[12]

Figures 7.1–7.2. British Prime Minister William "Lord" Grenville and British Foreign Minister George Hammond.

For his part, Randolph obtained the court records from Massachusetts to determine whether the Pagans had any legal options. After a review of the relevant documents, Randolph urged the Pagans through diplomatic channels to resolve the matter by an appeal to the U.S. Supreme Court. The Pagans and the British government were not satisfied with that advice, as they wished to avoid further court proceedings and instead sought some form of direct relief from the general US government. Jefferson made clear that given the separation of powers that existed between the various branches of the American government, the Pagans needed to exhaust their judicial remedies before the Washington Administration could consider the matter further.[13]

The reason the Pagans were reluctant to undertake an appeal at the US Supreme Court, despite Attorney General Randolph's advice that they do so, was that the Pagans' own attorneys were of the legal opinion that the Supreme Court was without authority to hear it. There was, at best, an open threshold question about whether the Supreme Court could hear the matter. Section 25 of the Judiciary Act limited the Supreme Court's authority to hear appeals from the highest courts of the states (as distinguished from the lower federal courts) only in certain categories of cases, including matters involving federal law and matters where the alleged error appeared "on the face of the record." Here, the Supreme Judicial Court in Massachusetts clearly explained that its decision did not involve the propriety of the prize court's determination in Halifax nor an interpretation of the Preliminary Articles of Peace, but instead merely involved the alleged common law failure of the Pagans to pay Hooper the proceeds realized from the sale of the *Thomas* and its contents under their escrow agreement. The case presented no issue of federal law, nor was there error on the face of its record.[14]

The Pagans hired attorney Benjamin R. Morgan to initiate their appeal at the US Supreme Court. When Morgan presented a proposed writ of error to the Supreme Court on behalf of the Pagans, which would have directed Stephen Hooper to defend an appeal there, Justice James Wilson refused to sign it. In Justice Wilson's view, the US Supreme Court did not have the authority to hear the case. Morgan wrote to his colleague Thomas P. Anthony on June 8, 1792, that "I procured a writ of Error in the case of *Hooper v Pagan*, and immediately on Mr. Judge Wilson's return to the City waited on him in order to procure a citation; but this he did not think proper to grant; nothing further can therefore be done in that line. . ." The latter statement that "nothing further can therefore be done in that line" proved to be less than prophetic, as Wilson may not have been aware, or underestimated, the political and diplomatic clout that Attorney General Randolph and British Minister Hammond would continue to exert on the subject.[15]

Justice Wilson's decision to not sign the proposed writ of error was made by examining only the original 1789 judgment of the Supreme Judicial Court of Massachusetts that was presented to him by Morgan. Wilson was prevailed upon, as a result of pressure from Attorney General Randolph, to reexamine the proposed writ as then supplemented by the Massachusetts' court's decisions rendered in 1790 and 1791, including reference to the default judgment in the Pagans' favor from the High Court in London. On that basis, Wilson signed the proposed writ of error and directed that the parties be heard at the US Supreme Court. Wilson's decision to do so reflects a spirit of cooperation that existed between the executive and judicial branches of government, which is not permitted under the separation of powers as defined and understood today.[16]

Wilson's writ of error contained an error of its own. It misidentified the Massachusetts court that was ordered to transfer its file to Philadelphia as the "Supreme Court," rather than the "Supreme Judicial Court of the Commonwealth of Massachusetts." Catching the error, Chief Judge Francis Dana of that court refused to honor the writ at all, but advised John Jay in a letter dated December 19, 1792, that he would entertain any new writ issued in a proper form. Jay might have been within his rights to be annoyed at the gamesmanship of the Massachusetts court, but on the other hand, Jay had always been a stickler for legal detail in his own right. Whether to issue a new writ of error was taken up by the full Jay Court at its February 1793 Term.[17]

Attorney Edward Tilghman appeared at the US Supreme Court on behalf of the Pagans. When pressed by Chief Judge Jay to identify a basis under Judiciary Act section 25 that would allow the US Supreme Court to hear the appeal from a state court, Tilghman, in an admirable example of attorney ethics and honesty, admitted that no legal basis existed. Attorney General Randolph was present for the oral argument on the proposed writ even though he did not represent any party to the dispute. Randolph did not like Tilghman's answer to Jay's question. Randolph was permitted to address the jurists and urged that a writ of error be issued given the diplomatic importance of exhausting all possible options in the courts. In essence, Randolph, as the attorney general of the executive branch of government, was seeking the assistance of the judicial branch as a favor, to grease the diplomatic relationship between the United States and Great Britain.[18]

Jay and his fellow justices were unconvinced by Randolph's inter-branch request for assistance. There was no federal question at issue, and no error was apparent on the face of the state court record. On February 16, 1793, the Supreme Court unanimously decided not to execute the new proposed writ of error, and not allow any appeal of the matter to proceed, on the ground that there was no jurisdiction on which they could properly do so. In other words, no jurisdiction meant no jurisdiction.[19]

The importance of this proceeding in the Supreme Court has nothing to do with the merits of the case. By all accounts, the Supreme Judicial Court of the Commonwealth of Massachusetts resolved the issues correctly the first, second, and third times that they were calendared and addressed. Rather, by refusing to sign the writ of error as urged by Attorney General Edmund Randolph, the Supreme Court established that the judicial branch of government was, in this additional way, independent of the executive branch, at least on matters of black letter law. The Supreme Court refused to allow itself to be used as a tool of

Figure 7.3. Chief Justice Francis Dana of the Massachusetts Supreme Judicial Court.

diplomacy between the federal government and the British foreign ministry. The case of *Pagan v Hooper* helped the early US Supreme Court define the separation of powers between the executive and judicial branches of government. The Jay Court's handling of the matter was the correct course for it to have taken under the facts and law of the case and under the Constitution. While diplomatic pressure appears to have motivated the Massachusetts legislature to successfully urge the Supreme Judicial Court of the Commonwealth to hear the Pagan-Hooper matter for its final time there, the US Supreme Court ultimately held itself to a higher standard. Jay sought to see the judiciary cooperate with other branches of government, as in *Hayburn*, where Jay navigated the case in a manner that avoided having the judiciary declare the Invalid Pensions Act unconstitutional; yet, in *Pagan v Hooper*, Jay and his colleagues demonstrated that there is a limit to how far the judiciary's interbranch cooperation could go.

JAY'S DAYS

After the US Supreme Court refused to hear the matter involving Thomas Pagan and Stephen Hooper, diplomatic efforts continued to be pressed by the British government for a resolution favorable to the Pagans. Minister Hammond argued that once all potential remedies had been exhausted at the US Supreme Court, the Washington administration became empowered to provide the Pagans with extra-judicial relief. Jefferson, however, interpreted the Law of Nations to require that the Pagans not only exhaust judicial remedies, but also demonstrate that the judicial proceedings resulted in a "gross & palpable injustice." In a letter dated March 13, 1793, Jefferson asked Randolph for an opinion about the propriety of the Pagan-Hooper proceedings in Massachusetts and at the Supreme Court based on that "gross & palpable injustice" standard. Two days later, Randolph responded by advising that the Pagans had suffered no injustice, and that the Supreme Court's refusal to sign a writ of error would have made no difference to the outcome of the case on the merits. By letter dated April 18, 1793, Jefferson advised Hammond that the Pagans had incurred no injustice as would justify the Washington Administration providing them with any form of extrajudicial relief. Months later, Hammond made further efforts on behalf of the Pagans, arguing that Supreme Court's refusal to entertain the Pagans' writ of error was proof that there was no adequate judicial remedy, and therefore, the Washington administration was duty-bound to provide extrajudicial relief. In letters dated

September 5 and September 13, 1793, Randolph refused to yield the point to Jefferson, and Jefferson refused to yield it to Hammond. Hammond advised Lord Grenville in correspondence dated October 12, 1793, that all efforts on behalf of the Pagans failed, bitterly attributing the result to the Washington Administration's procrastination and reluctance to involve itself in the dispute, to the continuing detriment of Thomas Pagan's fortune and health. Diplomatic efforts by the British government ceased when it became apparent that they would bear no fruit, and Thomas Pagan needed to consider other options in order to be released from debtor's prison. In February 1794, the Pagans and Hooper reached a settlement of the dispute, which resulted, finally, in Thomas Pagan's release from debtor's imprisonment.[20]

Chapter 8

The Supreme Court's Only Reported Jury Trial and the Supremacy of Special Jurors

The Three Appeals of *Georgia v Brailsford* (1792, 1793, and 1794)

> "Go then, Gentlemen, from the bar, without any impressions of favor or prejudice for one party or the other; weigh well the merits of the case, and do on this, as you ought do on every occasion, equal and impartial justice."
>
> —Chief Judge John Jay to the jurors
> February 7, 1794

The only "reported" jury trial conducted in the history of the US Supreme Court was in the case of *Brailsford v Georgia* in 1794. The case is unique and historically significant for that reason alone. But the significance of the case goes a step further. In the early 1790s, American law was not developed on the question of the precise roles to be played by judges and juries in resolving cases at trial. *Brailsford* was a case that sheds light on the roles of trial judges and juries during the earliest days of the nation.[1]

The underlying facts of *Brailsford* were not complicated. It was yet another war debt collection case of many that were pending in the early federal courts, affected by a debt-related state law. On May 4, 1782, the state of Georgia enacted a law affecting war debts owed to British nationals so that they be paid not to the actual British creditors, but to the state. The law "confiscated to and for the uses and benefit of the state" the "debts[,] dues and demands" owed to British citizens, "except debts or demands due or owing to British [m]erchants, or others, residing in Great Britain." As to British merchants, the debts owed to them were "[s]equestered," which meant that they were to be paid into the Georgia state treasury until otherwise appropriated for use by a state legislature. Many other states had similar laws on the books at the time. The Georgia statute clearly treated differently the "sequestered" debts of British merchants from the "confiscated" debts of other British creditors, a distinction that would be noted as the case proceeded through the courts.[2]

But more importantly, as has already been seen, Article 4 of the 1783 Treaty of Paris recognized the validity of the preexisting debts owed by each nation's creditors to the other. The terms of Article 4 were not enforceable as a practical matter between the time of the treaty's execution and the ratification of the US Constitution in 1789 because in the interim, British creditors were at the mercy of state courts, state judges, and state jurors who tended to side with American debtors. The creation of a federal system of governance in 1789 changed the dynamic and prompted a flood of British debt collection cases into the newly minted federal courts. Samuel Brailsford was one such creditor who, in 1791, sought to avail himself of the federal circuit court sitting in Georgia to recover his debt. The conflict between the Treaty of Paris, which honored each signatory's debt collection, and the Georgia Sequestration Act, which did not, would inevitably require resolution in the federal courts.[3]

Samuel Brailsford was an American living in Britain, but was treated in the case as a British subject. He and two other persons, Robert William Powell and John Hopton, claimed that they were owed 7,005 British pounds on a bond issued in 1774 by a Georgia resident named James Spalding. Spalding was the surviving partner of a business, Kelsall and Spalding. The two additional creditors, Powell and Hopton, were Americans who resided in South Carolina. The value of 7,005 British pounds is worth, in consumer goods, an estimated $1.3 million in today's dollars, meaning that much was at stake for the parties to fight over. The complete difference in the citizenships of the plaintiffs on one side of the dispute and the defendant on the other, and the value of the case, allowed for the case to be properly brought in a federal circuit court. The matter was assigned to Justice James Iredell, who was riding the Southern Circuit, and Judge Nathaniel Pendleton of the District Court of Georgia. By that time, circuit courts were comprised of two jurists rather than three, as by then Congress had reduced the circuit riding of Supreme Court justices by half.[4]

After Brailsford sued Spalding to recover the debt, the attorney general of the state of Georgia filed a petition seeking to intervene in the case as an interested party to the dispute. The state claimed that Spalding's debt was owed not to Brailsford and the other plaintiffs but to itself under its earlier-enacted sequestration law. Spalding was a merchant. The state argued that its law sequestering the debts of British creditors and merchants was enacted a year before the 1783 Treaty of Paris and was therefore "grandfathered," enforceable, and unaffected by the treaty.[5]

The Supreme Court had not yet rendered its 4–1 decision in *Chisholm v Georgia* that the states could be parties in federal law suits as either plaintiffs or defendants. *Chisholm* would not be decided until the following year, 1793. However, as revealed by *Chisholm*, Justice Iredell, who became the lone dissenter in that case, believed that federal courts could not hear any case where a state was a litigant. By coincidence, Iredell happened to be the jurist who fielded Georgia's petition to intervene in Brailsford's case against Spalding. Iredell, true to his beliefs on the law, denied Georgia's petition to intervene in the case on the ground that no state could be a party to a suit pending in a federal court. His denial of the petition would be consistent with his dissent in *Chisholm* the following year. The litigation between Samuel Brailsford and James Spaulding could continue, but not with the state of Georgia as a party to it.

Spalding adopted the state of Georgia's argument that any recompense he might owe was due only to the state, and not to Brailsford, by application of the Georgia Sequestration Act. Brailsford, of course, relied on the Treaty of Paris for the authority that the state sequestration law needed to yield to a superior, international treaty.

The Circuit Court rendered a decision in *Brailsford v Spalding* on May 2, 1792, without Georgia as an intervenor party. The circuit judges, Iredell and Pendleton, closely examined the language of the Georgia Sequestration Act. They determined that the state's "sequester" of debts owed to British merchants and its "confiscation" of debts owed to other British creditors had different meanings. Judge Pendleton determined that debts to merchants were merely "sequestered," and not "confiscated," in recognition that "debts contracted on the faith of commercial intercourse ought to be deemed of a sacred and inviolable nature." Iredell agreed, writing that well-established mercantile customs between nations warranted that commercial debts not be confiscated. Thus, if a debt was merely "sequestered," the state of Georgia could hold the money, at most, only in trust for the creditor, to be paid back at a future date. Pendleton took his analysis one step further in concluding that even if the debt had been "confiscated" by Georgia and became property of the state, the Treaty of Paris superseded the state's right to the proceeds and revived the creditor's right to recover the debt.[6]

The ruling of the Circuit Court did not sit well with the state of Georgia. The Georgia Sequestration Act had, in effect, been nullified by the Southern Circuit, at least as to merchant debts, without Georgia even being a party to the case to be heard on the issue. Georgia therefore applied to the US Supreme Court for an injunction to prohibit Samuel Brailsford from enforcing his rights against the state under the Circuit Court's decision, pending further litigation of the state's rights under its sequestration law. The application for an injunction, known then as a Bill of Equity, was heard at the August 1792 Term of the Supreme Court. The state of Georgia was represented by attorneys John Wereat and Alexander Dallas. Samuel Brailsford was represented by the Attorney General Edmund Randolph, acting in a private capacity.[7]

The Supreme Court determined the Bill of Equity on August 11, 1792, by a 5–1 vote of the justices. It would be the first of three Brailsford-related decisions, known here as *Brailsford I*. Justice Iredell, who was the only member of the Supreme Court who had participated in the earlier decision of the Circuit Court, said that his view on the injunction was "detached from every previous consideration of the merits of the cause." Justices Iredell, Blair, and Cushing noted that the state of Georgia was not made a party to the circuit court case that affected its claimed right to the debt and, on that basis, was entitled have the US marshal hold the disputed proceeds until such time that the US Supreme Court could determine the merits of the appeal. Chief Justice Jay and Justice Wilson, with analyses that were uncharacteristically brief for both, agreed than an injunction should issue pending the Supreme Court's further action on the case. Only Justice Johnson, who had come to the Supreme Court upon the resignation of Justice Rutledge, dissented from his colleagues. Johnson concluded in his opinion that if the state of Georgia was entitled to the disputed money under its sequestration law, it could still separately collect the money under common law, and there was no reason to believe that either Samuel Brailsford or James Spalding were insolvent as to render collection efforts illusive.[8]

The Supreme Court's holding in *Brailsford I* reflects some of the considerations that would later be clarified by courts in determining whether to grant or deny injunctions. Today, injunctions may be granted by federal courts when a well-established four-part test is met. First, there must be a likelihood that the party seeking the injunction will succeed on the ultimate merits of the case. Second, the party seeking the injunction must demonstrate, that absent an injunction, an irreparable harm would be suffered. Third, courts must balance the equities and hardships and discern in whose favor the equitable considerations tip. Fourth, federal courts may consider whether the issuance of an injunction is in the public interest. These four tests must all be established by the party seeking injunctive relief. Similar analyses are also applied today by state jurists handling state cases. The seeds of the current federal four-part test can be seen in *Brailsford I*. Justice Johnson's dissent was focused on the second factor of the four, of what he perceived to be a lack of irreparable harm absent the issuance of an injunction. The other justices appear to have focused mainly on the third prong, that the state of Georgia was not afforded an opportunity to be heard in the case decided by the Circuit Court, and therefore, as a matter of equity, any payment from James Spalding to Samuel Brailsford be stayed as a matter of fairness, with the proceeds held by the US marshal in the interim. The stay was not an indefinite one. Rather, it would remain in effect only until the February 1793 Term of the court and dissolved if no lawsuit was commenced by the state to recover the money by that time.[9]

The *Georgia v Brailsford* case was being aggressively litigated by the parties. That aggressiveness appeared during the next phase of the case, which is referred to here as *Brailsford II*. Edmund Randolph, still representing Samuel Brailsford, filed his own Bill in Equity against the state of Georgia and Spalding to *dissolve* the injunction that the Supreme Court had earlier granted in favor of the state. During the latter part of 1792, the state of Georgia had undertaken no legal action to collect on Spaulding's debt or on the bond that secured it. The application was heard by the Supreme Court during its February 1793 Term. The state of Georgia continued to be represented by attorney Alexander Dallas, but his co-counsel, John Wereat, was substituted by attorney Jared Ingersoll. Justice Thomas Johnson had resigned from the Supreme Court the previous month after serving on the court for a mere 163 days. Because his seat was still unfilled, the Supreme Court operated during the February 1793 Term with five justices instead of six.[10]

Randolph argued that there was no remedy at law for the state of Georgia to recover the debt owed by James Spalding and that even if a remedy did exist, the state had no procedural right to obtain an injunction in the Supreme Court. In his arguments, he found a sympathetic ear with Justice Iredell, who voted to dissolve the injunction on the ground that Georgia was without any remedy at "law," and hence there was no point awarding it injunctive relief. He believed that Georgia's only remedy was to commence a suit in "equity" to obtain custody of Spalding's bond, which invokes the fairness of the courts, rather than at law, which can be for sums certain. He also believed that Georgia could commence no suit at law against Brailsford, as Brailsford was not yet in possession of any proceeds on which a suit could be based. Thus Iredell, who had voted in favor of the issuance of an injunction in *Brailsford I*, changed his mind and voted to dissolve the injunction in *Brailsford II*.

Figure 8.1. Jared Ingersoll.

Iredell was the sole dissenter in what was a 4–1 decision. Chief Justice Jay wrote for himself, Wilson, and Cushing in finding that if the state of Georgia had a right to seek recovery of Spalding's debt under common law, that right warranted a continuation of the injunction in its favor for one more Term. Jay maintained a practical approach. Justice Blair agreed, noting, as in *Brailsford I*, that Georgia had been denied an opportunity to be heard in the debt collection case before the Circuit Court. Justice Blair further observed that if Samuel Brailsford were to be paid the money and return to Great Britain, the state's right and ability to recover the money from him, if owed, could be negatively affected, and "there would be a great danger of a failure of justice."[11]

Notably, the February 1793 Term of court, during which *Brailsford II* was decided, was the same Term when the Supreme Court decided *Chisholm v Georgia*. The justices of the Jay Court therefore were aware that, as a result of *Chisholm*, states could sue and be sued in the federal courts by citizens of other states. This might have been an unfortunate turn of events for Brailsford and his attorney, as any "error" committed by the Circuit Court in Georgia in refusing Georgia the opportunity to intervene in the case merely underscored the prejudice of that decision to the state and rendered an injunction in its favor more warranted. However, nothing in the language of *Brailsford II* suggests that the issues addressed by the Supreme Court in *Chisholm* cross-pollinated the determination made in *Brailsford II*.

The problem for the state of Georgia was that to collect money from Spalding directly, or to obtain title to the bond that Spalding had posted, Georgia needed to commence a form of lawsuit that would be new to American jurisprudence. A wheel needed to be invented. Georgia had no direct claim against Samuel Brailsford, as no money had yet been paid to him that Georgia could claim as its own. A suit against Spalding was also problematic, as Spalding had posted a bond to secure his debt. Also, the Circuit Court in Georgia had already decided that the 7,005 British pounds at issue were owed to Brailsford and not to the state. The state had a claim, if at all, at "common law." Meanwhile, Brailsford was not receiving any of the money that he believed was rightfully his. The attorneys involved in the matter needed to call upon their legal talents to find a way to properly steer the controversy into a court authorized to render a decision and break the logjam.

The parties engaged in what might be viewed today as an unconventional legal maneuver, to "create" a procedurally justiciable controversy that could be heard on the merits by the Supreme Court. On June 3, 1793, while the injunction was still pending, the parties made an agreement about certain fictional facts that would be placed before the Supreme Court. In their agreement, the parties stipulated that Brailsford had already received payment of the money due to him, even though he actually had not been paid anything. Georgia claimed that Brailsford had agreed to pay over the money to the state but that Brailsford denied any such promise was ever made. As a result, there was a justiciable controversy based on Brailsford's alleged breach of promise that could be heard at the Supreme Court.[12]

Thus was born *Brailsford III*. The state of Georgia filed a suit in the US Supreme Court. Georgia continued to be represented by attorneys Alexander Dallas and Jared Ingersoll. Samuel Brailsford was represented by the new US attorney general, William Bradford Jr., acting in a private capacity. Brailsford's earlier counsel, Edmund Randolph, left the case after he became President Washington's secretary of state upon the resignation from that office of Thomas Jefferson. Bradford was assisted by two co-counsels, attorneys Edward Tilghman and William Lewis.[13]

The justices of the Supreme Court likely were aware that the facts underlying the case were fictional, particularly as the injunction that they had previously issued was still in place beyond its August 1793 deadline and would have prevented any payment of the debt. The justices apparently turned a blind eye to the fictional aspects of the facts to reach the merits of the controversy. There was no question that Georgia could bring its claim in the Supreme Court as a court of original jurisdiction, as the *Chisholm* decision, underscoring states' rights to litigate in the federal courts, had been rendered the previous February.[14]

The parties in *Brailsford III* had agreed on a jury trial to fully and finally resolve their dispute. It would be the only jury trial conducted at the US Supreme Court officially reported as such, though the early Supreme Court conducted two "unreported" trials later during the 1790s. Philadelphia was abuzz at the prospect of a jury trial at the Supreme Court, and many persons directly or indirectly tied to the commercial class were interested in the outcome of the case. The concept of a jury trial at an appellate court is out of place today. But in the 1790s, during the earliest years of federal governance, there was legal opinion that when the Supreme Court heard a case under its "original jurisdiction" as set forth in Article III, section 2, of the Constitution, the same rights to a jury trial existed as in lower federal courts and was guaranteed by the

6th Amendment of the Constitution for criminal defendants and by the 7th Amendment in civil cases exceeding $20 in value.[15]

The jury was not composed of randomly selected citizens as is the practice today. Rather, and by agreement of the parties and the court, the jury was a "special jury" composed solely of merchants. The trial began on January 13, 1794, at Philadelphia's Independence Hall, where, by then, the Supreme Court typically convened. The jury pool initially consisted of forty-eight persons, which the two sets of attorneys narrowed to twenty-four. A jury of twelve male jurors was ultimately selected to hear the case, and the matter was bound over to the Supreme Court's February 3, 1794, calendar. *Brailsford III* would be the first case heard during the Supreme Court's February 1794 Term. The evidentiary and deliberative portions of the trial were conducted from February 4 to February 7, 1794.[16]

The facts of the case, including the existence of James Spalding's debt to Samuel Brailsford, were undisputed, with the only remaining issue being whether payment was to be made to Brailsford and his co-creditors or, alternatively, to the state of Georgia. John Jay, being the chief justice among the associate justices present, presided over the trial as a first among equals.[17]

The arguments of the parties tracked what has already been described: the state of Georgia argued through its attorneys, Dallas and Ingersoll, that it was a sovereign state that could enforce its sequestration law unencumbered by the Treaty of Paris and that the treaty could only have prospective, rather than retroactive, effect. Georgia's attorneys also argued that the Spalding debt, while originally "sequestered," had been forfeited to the state because the state had the inherent authority to confiscate the debts of an enemy alien such as Samuel Brailsford.[18]

Brailsford's attorneys argued that under the terms of the Georgia law, the debt at issue was merely and expressly "sequestered" and not "confiscated" and was never legally forfeited to the state. Brailsford's counsel argued that the Treaty of Paris was the supreme law of the land, which superseded any contrary state law and had the effect of reviving Brailsford's right to direct payment of the original debt. Brailsford's attorneys also made a salient point, that nothing Georgia proposed to do affected the right of Brailsford's co-creditors, Powell and Hopton, from being paid (or retaining) their collective two-thirds share of the debt, as Powell and Hopton were residents of South Carolina and not subjects of Great Britain. Finally, attorney William Bradford argued matters that were not included in the official record of the proceedings, that payment to Samuel Brailsford was consistent with mercantile law and custom.[19]

When the attorneys completed their presentations, Jay, as chief justice, needed to deliver the court's instructions to the jurors. The instructions that were to be given were complicated by the lack of clear definition in American jurisprudence over the role of judges and jurors. *Brailsford III* presented questions of both fact and law. Who was to decide which?

The justices of the Jay Court had their own ideas regarding how to divide the roles of judges and jurors in deciding cases. Jay believed that jurors were best at deciding issues of fact and that judges were best at deciding issues of law. But Jay also believed that jurors should have the right to disregard the legal instructions of judges and substitute their own judgments on the law if they so chose. In other words, Jay believed, based on his instruction to the jury in *Brailsford III*, that a judges' instructions on the law were advisory only, and jurors could accept or reject them at their will. The rationale for juries to either apply or disregard the law in rendering verdicts was to ensure that the citizenry, rather than the judges or the government, could control the law and be an essential element to the preservation of individual liberty.[20] The desire to rely on the inherent common sense of jurors was a significant factor for the inclusion of the 7th Amendment, which guaranteed the right to a jury in common law controversies exceeding $20 in value, in the Bill of Rights. On this issue, Jay had a firm ally in Justice James Wilson. Wilson, in addition to his Supreme Court duties, was a professor of law at the University of Philadelphia, later known as the University of Pennsylvania, and delivered law lectures between 1790 and 1792. In 1791, Wilson delivered a lecture where he noted that questions of fact and law were often intertwined. He also noted instances when judges and juries might disagree on the law. Wilson believed that in such instances, judges should instruct juries about the law but at the same time defer to the jurors on ultimate decisions on matters of law. John Jay's instructions to the jury in *Brailsford III* were consistent with Wilson's own previously expressed views.[21]

Jay's instruction to the jurors therefore addressed matters of fact, law, and the authority of the jury to ultimately decide both. He began his jury instructions by advising that the case "has been regarded as of great importance; and doubtless it is so." He complimented the attorneys who made their presentations with what Jay described as "great learning, diligence, and ability," and he commended the jurors for their "particular attention" throughout the proceedings. He also made clear that "[t]he facts comprehended in the case, are agreed; the only point that remains, is to settle what is the law of the land arising from those facts."[22]

Jay then proceeded to address matters of legal substance. Preliminarily, he noted that the portion of Spalding's debt to the co-creditors, Powell and Hopton, was not confiscated by the state of Georgia, as any such confiscation or forfeiture could only be accomplished, as to them, under the laws of South Carolina where they resided. As to Spalding's debt to Samuel Brailsford, the Georgia statute applied only to the extent of a "sequestration" and was not a "confiscation." By virtue of there being a mere sequestration, the debt that was owed to Brailsford, a British subject, was revived under both the law of nations and the 1783 Treaty of Paris that formally ended the Revolutionary War between Great Britain and the newly independent United States. Jay did not disclose in his remarks, though the jurors likely knew, that he had been a chief negotiator of the Treaty of Paris that he described.[23]

Having given instructions on the law, Jay then discussed with the jurors what he described as "the good old rule," that juries decide questions of fact and that courts decide questions of law. However, Jay instructed that the jurors "have nevertheless a right to take upon yourselves to judge of both, and to determine the law as well as the fact in controversy." In other words, Jay, speaking on behalf of the entire court, informed the jurors that while they might consider and respect his instructions on the law, they were free to adopt or reject the legal instructions they were being given and decide the case as they saw fit. It was this instruction that would have allowed the jurors to incorporate into their ultimate decision *lex mercatoria*, the mercantile customs and practices of the day. That instruction suggests that John Jay and his colleagues were seeking to have the jury reach a determination that would be consistent with mercantile norms for inclusion in the earliest development of the nation's laws. Jay concluded his remarks to the jury with an eloquent exhortation: "Go then, Gentlemen, from the bar, without any impressions of favor or prejudice for one party or the other; weigh well the merits of the case, and do on this, as you ought do on every occasion, equal and impartial justice."[24]

A fair reading of the initial instruction to the jury is that it took the jury 90 percent of the way toward a verdict in favor of Samuel Brailsford, absent the jury rejecting John Jay's instructions on the law and choosing to decide the case otherwise. Jay's instructions stopped short of specifically answering the penultimate legal questions of the case. The legal instruction apparently did not satisfy the jurors about the applicable law. After deliberations were underway for what Alexander Dallas described as "some time," the jurors returned to the courtroom and posed to the Supreme Court two specific questions. One was whether the Georgia Sequestration Act completely vested Spalding's debt to the state upon its enactment of the law in 1782. The second question was whether the Treaty of Paris revived the debt in favor of Brailsford when the treaty later became effective. In effect, the jurors were asking the justices of the court to give them the answers to the ultimate legal questions that they, the jurors, had been asked to resolve. The "special jury" had been empaneled either expressly or implicitly to consider mercantile customs in the context of American law. The trial was conducted not for the court to tell the jurors what should be done under the law, but for the jurors to tell the court what should be done. By asking for further instructions on the law, the jurors either did not understand John Jay's first round of instructions on the law, or if they did, were balking at readily deciding questions of law.[25]

John Jay addressed the jury a second time in response to the questions. He assured the jurors that it was appropriate for them to make inquiry of the court if the earlier instructions had been unclear to them. Speaking on behalf of the entire Supreme Court, John Jay advised the jurors in response to their first question that the mere passage of the Georgia Sequestration Act did not, in and of itself, vest Spalding's debt in the state. He further instructed that no sequestration divests the original owner of the thing sequestered, so that Brailsford, during times of both war and peace, remained its true owner. In answer to the second question, Jay instructed that while Spalding's debt may have been sequestered so that it could not be paid to Brailsford during wartime, the Treaty of Paris revived Brailsford's right to recover on the debt.[26]

The jury resumed its deliberations. The deliberations appear to have been quick from that point forward, as Alexander Dallas recorded that the jurors returned a verdict "without going again from the bar." The verdict was in favor of Brailsford, Powell, and Hopton. The jurors had elected to adopt John Jay's instructions on the law. Jay, the former diplomat and internationalist, must have been privately pleased with the result, as it upheld the terms and supremacy of the 1783 Treaty of Paris that he had helped negotiate. Additionally, by having the case decided by a jury rather than the written opinions of justices, the Supreme Court was insulated from the kind of criticisms it had received from the states a year earlier in reaction to *Chisholm v Georgia*.[27]

John Jay's instruction to the jury—the only reported jury instructions in the history of the Supreme Court—has been criticized by some segments of legal academia for potentially permitting "jury nullification." Jury nullification exists when a jury refuses to apply the law to reach a verdict in a case that does not comport with the law. It is seen and discussed most often in the context of criminal cases, such as where a jury acquits the defendant of a crime despite their belief in the defendant's guilt. Jury nullification is based on the belief that the law, either generally applied or as applied in a specific case, can be unfair in a given case, so that an alternative result may be reached. The concept has its supporters and detractors today, but the Jay Court was clearly open-minded to it in 1794. While the criticisms of Jay's jury instructions might be sound based on today's standards, it is unfair to apply them against the legal standards of Jay's time.[28]

The dividing line between judges and juries is now clear and well-defined, unlike the understandings of the bench and the bar in the 1790s. Today, if a matter such as *Brailsford III* were pending in a federal court and its parties agreed on the salient facts, and the penultimate question required an application or interpretation of law, the court would determine the matter without a jury, either by way of deciding a conclusive written motion addressing the controlling legal authorities, or perhaps by means of a non-jury trial. When trials are required today, judges spoon-feed to juries the general and specific law that governs the issues of a case and the manner of the jury deliberation itself. Juries today are the sole arbiters of the facts, but they cannot second-guess judges' instructions about the applicable law. Errors in jury instruction can provide a basis for reversing a jury's verdict in criminal or civil cases and warrant the conduct of a new trial. In the 1790s, however, when there was no unanimous opinion about the precise roles to be played by juries, American procedures needed time to develop those roles in the way that currently works best.

Brailsford III lends itself to several observations. The first is that it exposed the absence in early American jurisprudence of a definition of the roles of judges and juries in deciding questions of law. The proper roles of judges and juries would take several decades to refine. More than one hundred years would pass before cases crystallized the role of judges as being the exclusive arbiters and instructors of the law governing cases. The current practice helps ensure that juries, bound to the law, will render consistent verdicts across the board.

A second observation about *Brailsford III* is that when the early Supreme Court was confronted with issues involving the law of nations and mercantile law, it turned to a "special jury" of merchants to decide the case in a manner consistent with custom and practice. No doubt, the jury's verdict in *Brailsford III* was looked upon favorably by the commercial class of the United States.

A third observation about *Brailsford III* is the competence of Chief Justice Jay. Jay was responsible and careful to ensure that his instructions to the jurors were given on behalf of a unanimous court, and expressly said so. His use of a "special jury" reflects the gravity that Jay attributed to the case to ensure that the case's results would be consistent with mercantile customs. Jay's instructions to the special jury, while respectful, appear to have helped nudge the jury toward a result that correctly recognized the supremacy of the 1783 Treaty of Paris while at the same time being deferential to the ultimate authority of the jury to render whatever determination it saw fit. The jury's verdict in the case was "right" on the law.[29]

A fourth observation about *Brailsford III* is that its precedential value—of expressly allowing juries to apply or not apply a judge's instruction on the law—quietly remained on the law books unmolested by any subsequent Supreme Court for a considerable time. In 1807, Justice John Marshall instructed the jury in Aaron Burr's infamous trial for treason that while they had "heard the opinion of the court on the law of the case," the jurors were to ultimately "find a verdict of guilty or not guilty as their own consciences may direct." In 1895, more than one hundred years after the verdict in *Brailsford III*, Justice John Marshall Harlan rendered a lengthy opinion for the majority in *Sparf v United States*, criticizing the notion that jurors be allowed to decide questions of law and instead explaining why judges must solely determine such matters. *Sparf* involved a murder at sea, and the trial judge had given the jury an instruction that the defendant could not be convicted of the lesser offense of manslaughter. To get around the unanimous jury instruction by John Jay 101 years earlier that was to the contrary, Justice Harlan imaginatively assumed that Jay's instructions to the jury had been inaccurately reported by the court reporter, Alexander Dallas. *Sparf* may be the only case where the Supreme Court rejected its existing precedent on the ground that the earlier decision was a product of typographical errors or misunderstandings. As noted by the lengthy dissenting opinion in *Sparf* by Justice Horace Gray, much of John Jay's charge to the *Brailsford III* jury was reported within quotation marks, and the practice at the Supreme Court at the time was for the court's opinions to be examined and approved by the presiding justice, John Jay, before being sent to a press for printing. It therefore is likely that despite Harlan's unsubstantiated suspicions, John Jay's jury instructions in *Brailsford III* were accurately quoted and reported by Alexander Dallas and reflected the justices' understanding of the law as it existed at that time. In any event, the majority opinion in *Sparf* marked a turning point for the law away from law-finding juries, as in *Brailsford III*, toward the current practice that while juries are called upon to decide issues of fact, judges are the exclusive arbiters of the law.[30]

A final observation about *Brailsford III* is that the Supreme Court reporter, Alexander Dallas, was also one of two attorneys formally representing the state of Georgia at the *Brailsford* trial. He simultaneously acted in two capacities at the trial—as court reporter and as Georgia's co-counsel. No such duality would be permitted in courts today. Court reporters today are required to have no interest in the outcome of the proceedings they cover to ensure the written record is accurate and not slanted in any way to aid a party and to avoid even the appearance of a conflict, impropriety, or inaccuracy. In 1794, perceptions were different. Government generally, and the judiciary specifically, were not as scrupulous in avoiding conflicts of interest or appearances of impropriety as compared with current norms.

By the end of the February 1794 Term of the court, five of the seven cases presided over by John Jay during his tenure as chief justice were debt collection cases of one form or another—*West*, *Chisholm*, and *Brailsford I*, *II*, and *III*. John Jay's next Supreme Court case would present issues of international war and peace and dangers on the high seas, which also were topics of interest to him.

JAY'S DAYS

In the early history of the US Supreme Court, the bound volumes of the decisions published by the court's reporter bore the last name of the reporter. The Georgia v Brailsford trial decision, for example, has an official citation of "3 Dall. 1 (1794)," meaning that Alexander Dallas was the court reporter publishing that year's volume of decisions, which was his third volume overall, and the Brailsford case appears in it at page 1. Dallas's successors over the years were William Cranch (1801–1815), Henry Wheaton (1816–1827), Richard Peters (1828–1842), Benjamin C. Howard (1843–1860), J.S. Black (1861–1862), John William Wallace (1863–1874), and William Tod Otto (1875–1883). The collection of volumes begins for each of them at volume 1. Dallas and his successors worked for the Supreme Court as independent contractors. They recorded the official records, published the court's decisions and orders, and earned money from the sale of their publications. The practice ended in 1883 when the U.S. Reports began publishing official Supreme Court opinions, both prospectively and retroactively, and is the reporting system that is in place today. The U.S. Reports are financed by the federal government, so that volumes are prepared not by independent contractors, but by a private publisher, West Publishing. The retroactive volumes of the U.S. Reports were numbered consecutively from the beginning of the Supreme Court's existence so that there are parallel citations of the cases in the U.S. Reports and the individual reporters' publications for all years until 1883. Brailsford III is therefore correctly cited as either "3 Dall. 1 (1794)" or "3 U.S. 1 (1794)."

Chapter 9

Trouble on the High Seas

Glass v Sloop Betsey (1794)

> "I do not know of any other Cases of Capture in which either the Legislature or the Supreme Court of the United States have given or recognized a right in the District courts to award restitution [for a captured prize vessel]."
>
> —Letter of Peter DuPonceau to Martin Jorris
> April 8, 1795

Challenges to the new nation were not limited to domestic issues. The United States also faced serious challenges in the handling of its foreign policy and national security. The chief foreign policy challenges involved the hostilities between European powers and how those hostilities affected the United States.

France was in the throes of revolutionary upheaval, which included the storming of the Bastille on July 14, 1789; the official fall of the monarchy on September 21, 1792; the trial of King Louis XVI in December 1792; and the King's execution by guillotine at the *Place de la Concorde* on January 23, 1793. Governmental decisions were being made for the French Republic by its National Convention. The pace of events in France was dizzying. France formally declared war on Great Britain and the Netherlands on February 1, 1793, and six days later, on Spain. News of the declarations of war did not reach the United States until late March or early April. George Washington arrived at his home in Mount Vernon on April 2, 1793, to spend some much-needed time overseeing the spring plantings at his farm and to otherwise tend to personal business. His respite from the pressures of governance would not last long. Washington was at Mount Vernon on April 5, 1793, when he received an urgent letter from Treasury Secretary Hamilton informing him of France's declaration of war on Britain, the Netherlands, and Spain. The concern that was foremost in the mind of Washington, and in the minds of the American public for that matter, was how the outbreak of war would affect the United States and whether the United States would be drawn into the hostilities.[1]

The developments abroad were of such significance that Washington cut short his time at Mount Vernon, leaving on April 13 and arriving at his office in Philadelphia four days later. In the interim, Washington sent correspondence to Secretary of State Jefferson instructing him that the policy of the United States government would be that of maintaining "strict neutrality" between France and Great Britain and that steps be taken to hold that neutrality in place. What those steps were to be would be developed in the days ahead and discussed at a Cabinet meeting that was hastily arranged for April 19, 1793.

In the interim, while there is no evidence that President Washington sought the direct advice of John Jay about the crisis, documents show that Alexander Hamilton reached out to Jay for advice in two letters that were both dated April 9, 1793. The first of the two letters addressed, among other things, whether the United States was still bound to the treaties it had reached with the now-overthrown government of King Louis XVI. The second letter inquired of the need for a declaration of neutrality, including a prohibition against individual Americans from assisting either side in the European war. Hamilton and Jay agreed on the need for a neutrality proclamation. On April 11, 1793, Jay sent Hamilton a reply letter that included a hastily drawn draft of a proclamation of neutrality. Jay urged Hamilton, "Let us do every thing that may be right to avoid war; and if without our Fault we shd. be involved in it, there will be little Room for apprehensions about the Issue." Hamilton and Jay also traded in their correspondences views about the consequences of receiving the new foreign minister that the revolutionary government in France was sending to the United States.[2]

Similarly, the Cabinet debated whether Washington should issue a formal declaration of neutrality and whether the new minister of France, Edmond-Charles Genet, should be received by the United States as a representative of a legitimate French government, and if so, whether to do so absolutely or with some qualification. Not surprisingly, Hamilton and Jefferson butted heads over both issues. Hamilton, Secretary of War Henry Knox, and Attorney General Edmund Randolph argued in favor of a declaration of neutrality. Thomas Jefferson urged that such a declaration be held back to be used as diplomatic leverage and argued that, in any event, only Congress was authorized to determine matters of war and peace. As to French Minister Genet, Jefferson believed that not recognizing him would be a breach of the neutrality that the United States hoped to maintain. Hamilton, never the Francophile, had a hard-line response—that the American-French treaties only existed between the United States and the French monarchy and not with the newly proclaimed French Republic, and that any recognition of Minister Genet would be an implicit and ill-advised "election to continue the treaties." Hamilton urged that to preserve neutrality, treaties with France be renounced or at least suspended. On the viability of the treaties, Hamilton was aligned with Knox, while Randolph was aligned with Jefferson's view that treaties bind nations rather than governments. Jay, in his communications with Hamilton, was already on record that treaties with France continued under France's revolutionary government, and therefore the United States was obligated to receive and recognize Minister Genet. Jay's opinion about receiving Minister Genet would have ramifications later, as open personal conflicts would develop between the two men in the months that followed.[3]

While various Cabinet members agreed with the general concept of neutrality between the warring countries, there were differences of opinion about how strict that neutrality should be. Washington had already made clear his preference that neutrality be strict. Jefferson wished for a looser neutrality policy that would allow some accommodations to France around its edges. Jefferson was an admirer of the French Revolution before it turned bloody and saw the revolution there as an extension of America's own. He was also mindful of France's assistance to the states during the Revolutionary War. Hamilton likewise spoke the language of neutrality, but he and his political allies, and the merchant class that was a significant constituency within the Federalist Party, had a soft spot for Great Britain and its commercial interests. Indeed, Hamilton believed that trade with Britain was essential to the fiscal and economic well-being of the United States.[4]

A large segment of the population shared with Great Britain common heritage, common language, and familiarity at some level with the ways of British commerce and common law. Nevertheless, the people of the United States, while perhaps understanding the value of Washington's policy of neutrality, sympathized more with the French. Colonial America's war with Great Britain had concluded only a few years earlier, and there was lingering disdain for the British Crown.

The final policy decisions, of course, were to be made by President Washington. Washington directed Attorney General Randolph to draft a proclamation of neutrality, which, as described by historian Douglas Southall Freeman, would contain language moderate enough for Jefferson but forceful enough for Hamilton. Historian Frank Monaghan suggests in his biography of John Jay published in 1935 that Washington privately instructed Randolph what the declaration should say, influenced by the draft that had already been prepared by Jay for Hamilton. Attorney-historian Walter Stahr, in his biography of John Jay published in 2005, seems to disagree, noting that there is no actual evidence that Jay's draft of a similar proclamation had ever been seen by Washington, Randolph, or other members of the Cabinet besides Hamilton, or that Jay's draft in any way influenced the wording of the final product. In either event, Randolph's draft was presented to and approved by the Cabinet on April 22, 1793. The Proclamation acknowledged the state of war between identified nations and declared that ". . . the duty and interest of the United States require, that [the states] should with sincerity and good faith adopt and pursue a conduct friendly and impartial toward the belligerent Powers." The Proclamation warned citizens of the United States that they would be prosecuted for aiding any of the warring nations, and that if punished by a belligerent nation for aiding another, the United States would afford them no protection. Notably, to sidestep the complication of existing treaties between the United States and France, Washington's Proclamation, though a statement of nonalignment, did not use anywhere the actual word "neutrality." The Proclamation also contained no language about how the existence of American-French treaties would affect the ability of the United States to remain truly neutral.[5]

The following month, Chief Justice Jay published a detailed statement on the origin of and need for American neutrality in the war. In it, he described various international treaties where the United States committed its friendship to Great Britain, France, and other European nations and why the United States needed to remain strictly neutral in its dealings with those nations. By what appears to have been deliberate design, Jay's statement on neutrality was published in newspapers, and it was used as an authoritative explanation of American policy that was then shared with European governments. Today, no judge at any level of federal or state judiciary is permitted to wade into political issues, whether domestic or international. Jay's policy statement, which was originally delivered to a public grand jury in Virginia, is an example of how in the 1790s, there was little "wall" separating the judiciary from the body politic.[6]

Minister Genet arrived in the United States on April 8, 1793, disembarking at Charleston, South Carolina. The French were so loved and admired by Americans that his arrival was greeted with great enthusiasm by the people of Charleston. From there he made his way toward Philadelphia. The French minister was greeted by welcoming and adoring crowds at many stops along the way. The question of how he would be received by the American government, if at all, was left unresolved at the Cabinet meetings of April 19 and 22, 1793. Genet reached Philadelphia on May 16, 1793. A public reception was thrown for Genet on May 17 at his lodgings at the City Hotel, attended by what Jefferson estimated to be 1,000 well-wishers and by what Hamilton estimated to be 500 or 600. There, Genet spoke of the United States as France's "first and best ally," whose population was devoted to the cause of liberty. He met President Washington the next day. During the days and weeks that followed, Genet enjoyed a political honeymoon interacting with American organizations, societies, and newspapers at meetings, ceremonies, and dinners.[7]

Edmond-Charles Genet, also known by the nickname "Citizen Genet," is a unique figure in French and American history. He was born on January 8, 1763. His father was a wealthy and politically well-connected Frenchman. He was a child prodigy able to read English, Swedish, German, Italian, Greek, and Latin by the age of twelve and was an impressive player of the piano as well. At thirteen, he published a translation of a book on Swedish history and was honored with a gold medal by the king of Sweden for the accomplishment. At sixteen, Genet joined the French Army as a lieutenant but never saw battle. At eighteen, he became chief of the French Bureau of Interpretation, but when that was eliminated in 1787, he was appointed secretary to the French diplomatic presence in London. He was then assigned to the French embassy in St. Petersburg, where he was soon promoted as its *charge d'affaires*.[8]

Genet returned to Paris in mid-September 1792, during the French Revolution, and aligned himself with the Girondin governing coalition. The Girondin government needed experienced diplomats because many of the outgoing diplomats who had served the king had fled or been jailed or executed. Although originally designated by the Girondins as the French minister to the Hague, Genet was redesignated as minister to the United States before leaving for his Hague assignment. King Louis XVI was executed by guillotine on January 21, 1793, at the *Place de la Concorde*, and the following day, Genet left Paris for the United States. His transport frigate from the port of Rochefort, *L'Embuscade*, was bound for Philadelphia, but the winds blew it off course and it arrived instead in Charleston, South Carolina.[9]

Genet was highly intelligent, but as the American government would soon find, he was also very aggressive in the pursuit of his goals and hotheaded in demeanor. No one could have imagined when Genet disembarked at Charleston that within the year, he would become a legal and political nemesis to both President Washington and Chief Judge John Jay.

Figure 9.1. French Foreign Minister Edmond-Charles Genet.

The instructions that Minister Genet received from his government were highly ambitious, if not fanciful. Genet was to negotiate a new treaty with the United States, arrange for the early repayment of loans previously made by France to the United States, enlist American support in a mercantile war against Great Britain and Spain, initiate a military campaign to seize the Florida and Louisiana territories from Spain, and mount a similar campaign to seize Canada from Great Britain. The repayment of loans was to help finance France's war in Europe. The French motivation for trying to seize Florida, Louisiana, and Canada was to obtain their wealth while simultaneously denying the territories to its enemies. A new US-French treaty was to solidify the relationship between the two countries on the generally-correct assumption that public opinion in the United States was more favorable to France than it was to Great Britain.[10]

Hostilities between the European powers began to manifest themselves on the high seas and in American territorial waters at an increasing rate. The "high seas" refers to the ocean beyond a country's territorial limits. The United States' territorial limit in the 1790s was the point three nautical miles from its shore, which was the distance that canon shot could reach at the time. One form of the hostilities on the water—the impressment of merchant sailors—was instigated by the British. A different form of hostilities—privateering—was undertaken mainly by the French, notwithstanding France's desire for a new treaty with the United States. Both forms of hostilities threatened the neutrality that the Washington administration hoped to maintain between the warring parties.

American merchant sailors were being captured by the British Royal Navy on the high seas and pressed into service. The impressment of American merchant sailors by the British was a thorny and vexing issue in the 1790s and the decade that followed. The British Royal Navy suffered from a perpetual need for sailors. Conditions on British naval vessels were uncomfortable to say the least, which made the recruitment of volunteers all the more difficult. Beyond recruiting, an average of 5,000 British sailors and marines died *each year* between 1793 and 1815 from diseases, accidents, and combat. The British sought to solve their mariner shortage by the practice of impressment, where "press gangs" seized American sailors from merchant ships commandeered on the high seas and forced them to work aboard British vessels against their will. An estimated 3,000 American sailors were taken in the 1790s and another 7,000 between 1803 and 1812. While the owners of mercantile shipping considered impressment to be an unfortunate cost of doing business, the American public and the US Congress deemed the practice to be unacceptable, and its continuance stoked ill-will by the American public toward the British Crown. In 1806, Thomas Jefferson, who had by then become president, rejected the proposed commercial Monroe-Pinckney Treaty with Britain, as the British refused to include in it a provision ending the impressment of American sailors. In 1807 and 1811, impressment sparked two deadly battles at sea, the first between the *HMS Leopard* and the American frigate *Chesapeake*, and the second between the British warship *Little Belt* and the American *President*. Ultimately, impressment became an issue of such importance that it led to the War of 1812. That war's origins were already in place in 1793.[11]

A further issue on the seas that complicated the American relationship with foreign powers was the practice of seizing merchant ships and cargo as "prizes." Whereas the impressment of American sailors was a problem caused by the British, the capture of merchant vessels in American waters as prizes of war was caused mostly by the French. The procedures for outfitting vessels for privateering, seizing prize ships during wartime, adjudicating the legality of captures in prize courts, and selling the seized ships and their cargoes are described in chapter 7 of this narrative.

The practice of privateering in the early 1790s usually involved French privateers taking vessels that were believed to be commercially connected to Britain, including those operating near American territorial waters. Privateers were known in the French language as *corsairs*. The French had an absolute right to seize such vessels under the terms of two treaties that existed between the United States and France, the 1778 Treaty of Amity and Commerce, and the 1788 Commerce and Consular Convention. In fact, the Treaty of Amity and Commerce, while primarily an agreement about mutual American and French trade and trading rights, contained in Article 19 a provision that expressly assured that each country would protect the other's privateers and crews from harm. Article 17 of the treaty guaranteed French privateers access to American ports and contained a further guarantee that once there, prize vessels shall not be "arrested or seized." Article 22 restricted access to American ports by privateers sponsored by enemies of France. The intent of that provision had been to allow privateers to seize British vessels during the time of the Revolutionary War to benefit the Americans fighting the British and to benefit France in its harassment of British mercantile shipping. The Treaty of Amity and Commerce had no expiration date. The existence of these treaties, which contained terms favorable to the French at the expenses of the British, rendered Washington's neutrality policy problematic. It was for that reason that Alexander Hamilton had argued that the execution of King Louis XVI released the United States from its obligations under the treaties and would make America's policy of neutrality easier to maintain.[12]

France had perfected the practice of privateering. Its navy was weak compared with the combined navies of Great Britain, Spain, and the Netherlands. The French government commissioned privateers to operate not just in European waters, but in the Western Hemisphere as well. Privateering in the Western Hemisphere posed some obvious logistical problems. If captured vessels were to be taken across the Atlantic Ocean to prize courts in France, some would be lost en route or recaptured, perishable cargo would expire, the adjudicative process would be too time-consuming, and the practice would be less profitable. The French government therefore established prize courts in the United States and at its colonies in the Caribbean. American waters were a logical place for French privateers to operate, as there were established trading relationships between British and American merchants that could be harassed, and as the 1778 Treaty of Amity and Commerce gave French privateers virtually free reign to operate in and out of US ports.[13] With time, controversies over privateering landed in the lap of American courts, including the US Supreme Court.

The French government took specific and deliberate steps to encourage privateering along the coastline of the United States after its February 1, 1793, declaration of war against Great Britain and the Netherlands. When Minister Genet arrived in Charleston to assume his diplomatic responsibilities, no one in the Washington administration anticipated that he would undertake steps to aggressively promote privateering in American waters. Genet wasted no time in financially subsidizing the purchase and outfitting of ships to be used by French and American citizens for privateering, issuing commissions to the ship owners, and directing that his subordinate consuls establish prize courts at major American ports. There was no American policy prohibiting him from doing so, and Genet even sought and obtained the approval from South Carolina's governor, William Moultrie.[14]

It took little time for Genet's energetic activities to become widely known, and they were controversial in two particular respects. First, there was a limited number of French citizens residing in the United States from which to recruit privateers and ship crews, which necessitated recruitment from American citizens as well. Article 21 of the Treaty of Amity and Commerce prohibited American citizens from accepting "any commission or letters of marque for arming any ship or ships, to act as privateers against France." In a letter from Secretary of State Jefferson to former French Ambassador Jean Baptiste Ternant dated May 15, 1793, Jefferson stated that the recruitment of American privateers was a violation of President Washington's Proclamation of neutrality and urged that the activity cease. At Washington's direction, Secretary of State Jefferson issued on June 5, 1793, a clear and unambiguous ban on the outfitting of privateer vessels and requested that any ships that were previously equipped leave American ports. Privately, Jefferson believed that vessels that were outfitted for privateering before the neutrality policy was announced should be permitted to operate against British interests. Washington's only concession to Jefferson was to allow prize ships that had already been captured prior to the neutrality announcement not be restored to their original owners, contrary to British demands.[15]

France had an entirely different view of the issue. Article 21 of the Treaty of Amity and Commerce, while prohibiting American privateers from acting *against* French vessels, contained no language prohibiting American privateers from acting against British interests *on behalf* of France. In the further view of the French, American treaty commitments legally trumped any mere executive Proclamation. On that issue the French were correct, as President Washington could not constitutionally promulgate criminal laws or impose criminal sentences by executive fiat. Moreover, the plain language of Article 21 of the Treaty of Amity and Commerce was straightforward and favored the French interpretation. Genet's insistence on continuing privateering sorely damaged his relationship with Washington and members of the president's Cabinet. French-American relations suffered a further blow on June 11, 1793, when President Washington informed Minister Genet that the United States would not be paying France its Revolutionary War debts before they became due.[16]

At Charleston, the frigate *L'Embuscade* essentially blockaded the harbor and began capturing ships, including the *Morning Star* of Britain, the *Success* of Bremen, and the *Wilhelm* of Hamburg, and was already in possession of Britain's *Four Brothers* from its voyage with Genet across the Atlantic. The captain of *L'Embuscade*, John-Baptiste Francois Bompard, was careful to only seize vessels outside the three-mile American territorial limit. Genet ordered that the *Success* and the *Wilhelm* each be released, as France was not at war with the German cities of the Hanseatic League, which included Bremen and Hamburg. But the *Morning Star* and the *Four Brothers* were awarded by a French prize court to its French captors, and the ships and their cargo were sold at public auction. Genet also commissioned additional vessels for privateering, including the *Sans Culottes*, the *Republican*, the *Anti-George*, and, throwing away any pretense of humility, the conspicuously renamed *Citizen Genet*. In the weeks and months ahead, more than five dozen British vessels were commandeered by the French, plus a smaller number from Spain and other nations.[17]

The instances of privateering perturbed the British government greatly. In early July, a British vessel named *Little Sarah* was captured by the *L'Embuscade*, brought to Philadelphia, renamed the *Little Democrate*, and outfitted for further French privateering. The arrival of *Little Sarah* at the same time as another captured vessel, the *Grange*, caused a sensation in Philadelphia. A large crowd, which Thomas Jefferson estimated to be in the thousands of persons, rushed to the waterfront to see the ships' arrival. Jefferson recounted that as the ships came closer, "the British colours [on *Little Sarah*] were seen reversed and the French flying above them," which caused the crowd to "burst into peals of exultation." British Minister Hammond complained loudly to the Washington administration about the seizure. While the Cabinet was disinclined to defend the French conduct, President Washington determined that an advisory opinion was needed from the US Supreme Court about the French recruitment of American privateers, the arming of vessels in American ports, and the legality or illegality of French prize courts operating within the United States. All such questions affected the Washington administration's policy of neutrality.[18]

On July 18, 1793, the Cabinet composed a list of twenty-nine specific questions that Secretary of State Jefferson sent to the Supreme Court, noting that the answers would assist the Cabinet in formulating further policy and be of great importance to the peace of the nation. The questions were not merely intended to seek learned advice from the Jay Court that could be used in the Washington administration's internal decision-making, but, if answered, would be made public to bolster whatever policies that President Washington would set. Answers would provide Washington with the additional benefit of helping him resolve issue conflicts between members of his Cabinet, particularly between Hamilton and Jefferson. While the questions were posed in a letter signed by Thomas Jefferson, it was known and understood that the questions were from Washington himself.[19]

John Jay knew in advance that the request for an advisory opinion would be coming to his court, as he and Washington had been informally discussing these issues. It was uncertain at that time whether, under the separation of powers, the Supreme Court could properly render advisory opinions on any issues. Jay had expressed to Washington some doubts about the procedure. Jefferson's letter acknowledged that whether advice could be sought from the Supreme Court was a threshold issue that the justices were invited to address.[20]

The Supreme Court did not respond to the Cabinet's twenty-nine questions until August 8, 1793. The delay in responding was occasioned by the difficulties of communication between the various justices in the midst of the summer, weeks ahead of the court's August Term. In particular, Justices Cushing and Blair were not readily available to consult with their fellow justices not only as to the twenty-nine questions, but also on whether the questions should be answered at all. Jay advised the president by letter on July 20, 1793, that there would be a delay responding to the inquiry, to which Washington responded three days later that a response could await consultations among all of the justices.[21]

The full complement of justices addressed the inquiry in a letter dated August 8, 1793. Collectively, the justices declined to render any advisory opinion responsive to Jefferson's letter. The justices noted the "lines of separation drawn by the Constitution between the three Departments of government" and that the executive's power to solicit opinions was "purposely as well as expressly limited to the executive Departments." The justices classified themselves as "a court [of] last Resort," meaning that it answers questions of law only through actual cases that came before it. In other words, the justices adopted a "we-won't-touch-it-unless-it-comes-to-us-in-the-constitutionally-correct-and-orthodox-manner" policy. Today, it is universally understood that the US Supreme Court will not render legal advice even to the other branches of government and that all courts are without discretion to provide such advice. The reasons courts avoid advisory opinions are not just constitutional. By not rendering advisory opinions, courts may adjudicate the same or related issues in future cases without there being any appearance of predetermined bias or lack of judicial independence.[22]

The Supreme Court's refusal to provide advisory opinions should have surprised no one. Three of the justices, Wilson, Blair, and Paterson, had been delegates at the Constitutional Convention and were familiar with the writing of the Constitution's executive provisions, including Article II, section 2. That provision provides that the president may require written opinions from the principal officers of each of the "executive departments." Such language does not necessarily exclude parallel advisory opinions from the judiciary. However, during the Constitutional Convention, Charles Pinckney had proposed that the president be given the authority to require opinions from the Supreme Court on important questions of law, and Pinckney's suggestion was rejected. Accordingly, even if the language of the Constitution were to be considered ambiguous on the question of advisory opinions, the Supreme Court would have been within its rights to consider the debate at the Constitutional Convention, of which some justices had direct knowledge, and discern that the framers' true intent was to prohibit advisory opinions from the judiciary.[23]

By late July and early August, the Cabinet, without yet receiving from the Supreme Court any response to its request for an advisory opinion, initiated measures designed to prevent Americans from joining French privateers. In doing so, the Washington administration sent an implicit message to France that it would not be bullied on the issue of privateering. Treasury regulations were issued on August 4, 1793, requiring US customs collectors to notify the government of "any citizen of the United States who shall be found in the service of either of the parties at war." The administration even brought criminal charges against US citizens who enlisted with French privateers, notwithstanding the absence of any penal law statute prohibiting citizens from doing so.[24]

Indeed, a grand jury in Philadelphia rendered an indictment against two American citizens, Gideon Henfield of Massachusetts and John Singleterry of a state unknown, for unlawfully engaging in privateering on behalf of France. Henfield was on board the *Citizen Genet* when its crew captured the Maryland-bound British ship *William* near the capes of Delaware on May 3, 1793, and then brought it to Philadelphia as a prize with Henfield at the helm. Singleterry was on board the captor ship. The prosecution was initiated by the US Attorney William Rawle under the ultimate supervision of Cabinet member Edmund Randolph. Minister Genet vocally protested the arrests and prosecutions and sent

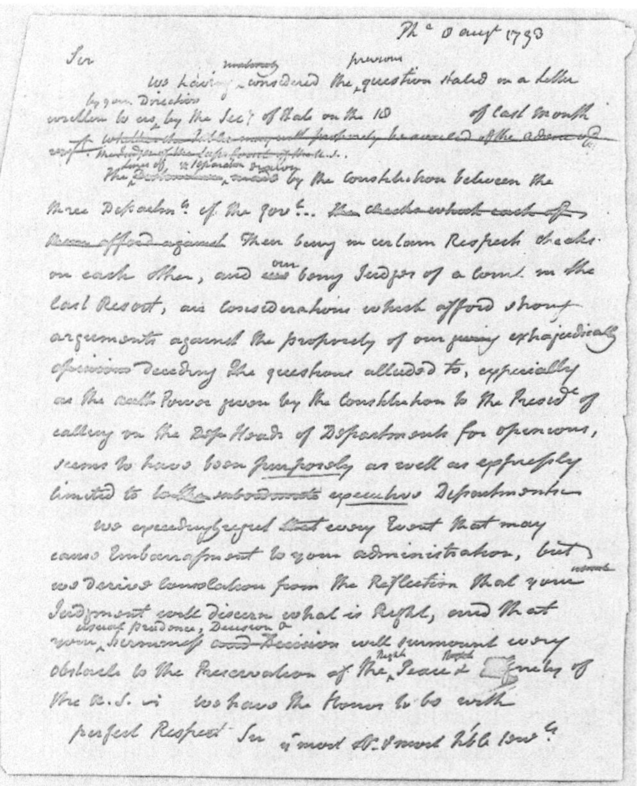

Phª 8 Augt 1793

Sir

We having maturely considered the previous question stated in a letter
written to us by your Direction by the Secy of State on the 18 of last month

The Lines of Separation drawn by the Constitution between the
three Departmts of the Govt... These being in certain Respects checks
on each other, and our being Judges of a Court in the
last Resort, are Considerations which afford strong
arguments against the propriety of our giving extrajudicially
deciding the questions alluded to, especially
as the Power given by the Constitution to the Presidt of
calling on the Heads of Departments for opinions,
seems to have been purposely as well as expressly
limited to executive Departments

We exceedingly regret every Event that may
cause Embarrassment to your administration, but
we derive Consolation from the Reflection that your
Judgment will discern what is Right, and that
your usual prudence, Decision & firmness will surmount every
obstacle to the Preservation of the Rights Peace & Dignity of
the U.S. — We have the Honor to be with
perfect Respect Sir your most obt & most hble Servts

Figure 9.2. Handwritten letter by John Jay to President Washington, dated August 8, 1793.

Secretary of State Jefferson correspondence on May 27, 1793, urging Henfield's and Singleterry's release from custody. Henfield and Singleterry were arraigned on the indictment against them and released on bail pending their trial. Henfield was represented by an accomplished Philadelphia attorney named Peter DuPonceau, whose political sympathies were decidedly with the French, and by Jared Ingersoll and Jonathan Dickinson Sergeant. Henfield's attorneys were paid for by Minister Genet.

Jefferson responded to Genet in a letter of his own, dated June 1, 1793, advising that Henfield's matter was in the American courts and would be "examined by a Jury of his Countrymen, in the presence of Judges of learning and integrity. . ." There was an exchange of additional letters between Jefferson and Genet regarding the prosecution of Gideon

Henfield. On June 5, 1793, Jefferson informed Genet that France's conduct, particularly in using American citizens, was an infringement upon the sovereignty of the United States. Genet responded in correspondence three days later, insisting that letters of marque could be given to any privateer vessel operating in US ports and, using language that might be viewed as intemperate, decrying the Americans' "cowardly abandonment of their true friends in the moment when danger menaces them."[25]

True to Jefferson's initial letter, a trial of Gideon Henfield was conducted before a Philadelphia jury, which commenced on Friday, July 27, 1793. By that time, Singleterry had fled the jurisdiction in violation of the conditions of his bail, and the trial proceeded against Henfield only. Popular opinion seemed to be in favor of Henfield. Henfield's trial defense was twofold—that he was unaware of the American government's policy of neutrality and lacked the intent to violate any law, and that he had become a French citizen and therefore was not in violation of the American government's declaration of neutrality.[26]

At the time of Henfield's trial, there continued to be no penal statute on the books prohibiting any American from helping a foreign country at war against another foreign country. Congress recognized that President Washington's Proclamation was a statement of policy, but it did not have the legal force and effect of legislation passed by Congress. The Henfield prosecution was not wholly without legal authority, as there was already precedent for "common law prosecutions" for violations of the "law of nations." The US Constitution provides in Article I, section 8, that Congress possesses the enumerated power to "define and punish . . . Offenses against the Law of Nations." While there was some academic opinion early in the nation's history that the law of nations mentioned in the Constitution was part of American domestic law and therefore part of the common law jurisdiction of the federal courts to punish, that concept was later rejected in 1812 in the US Supreme Court case of *United States v. Hudson*. In *Hudson*, the Supreme Court held that crimes not recognized by congressional statutes, such as crimes against the law of nations or the laws of war, were *not* punishable. Gideon Henfield's case, however, being several years before 1812, was prosecuted not only for his violation of the law of nations, but also for violating President Washington's executive neutrality proclamation, rendering it even less constitutionally sound.[27]

The *Henfield* trial was conducted in the Circuit Court before Justices James Wilson and James Iredell, who were riding the Middle Circuit, and

Judge Richard Peters of the District Court for the District of Pennsylvania. US Attorney William Rawle acted as the lead prosecutor in the courtroom, assisted by Attorney General Edmund Randolph. Witnesses who testified were Jonas Simmons, John Morgan, Lewis Deblois, and Hilary Baker, whose collective testimonies took an entire day. The evidence included statements uttered by Henfield at the time of his initial arraignment that he was a loyal American who would not knowingly violate President Washington's directives, and evidence that at a later pretrial proceeding, Henfield claimed French citizenship. All pertinent facts of the case, other than the question of Henfield's citizenship, were not disputed. The following day, which was a Saturday, the attorneys gave their closing arguments, and the court gave its instructions to the jury. The jury was given the responsibility of deciding not only matters of fact, but also issues of law. In determining questions of law, Justice Wilson's instructions included an explanation of the relevant law, but his statements to the jurors were purely advisory. On the specific question of expatriation, Justice Wilson told the jurors that an intent to change citizenship needed to be evidenced in some form or fashion, and the mere commission of a crime did not qualify as a surrender of citizenship.[28]

The jury deliberated Gideon Henfield's fate past midnight on Saturday, part of Sunday morning, and all of Monday. On Monday morning, to speed things along, Justice Wilson directed that the jurors receive no food, but water only. Such a lengthy deliberation suggests that there was much to discuss among the jurors and, apparently, divided opinion among them about how to resolve the case. At 7:00 p.m. Monday, after a day that likely was without food, the jury rendered a verdict of "Not Guilty," and Henfield dodged any punishment for his privateering activities. The jurors were not permitted in their verdict to explain the basis for their Not Guilty finding. The crowd of spectators at the courthouse cheered the verdict. Minister Genet was so elated by the verdict that he issued cards to members of the public inviting them to a grand dinner party to meet and honor "Citizen Henfield." Henfield's acquittal gave Genet a green light to continue recruiting Americans in furtherance of French privateering efforts.[29]

The acquittal did not stop Attorney General Randolph from undertaking further efforts to prosecute American citizens for privateering. Although a jury was persuaded by at least one of Henfield's defenses, those defenses, or others, might not necessarily prevail at other trials heard by other juries. Further prosecutions were undertaken in Augusta, Georgia, of Joseph Rivers and three others. The charges were dropped as to one of the defendants there when it was determined that he was a citizen of Great Britain, but the man was tarred and feathered by a mob anyway. The three others, who were held in prison without bail pending trial, were acquitted after their trial in November 1793.[30]

While the verdicts were good news for Gideon Henfield and the Georgia defendants, a message had been sent by the federal government to American citizens that their participation in privateering would not be tolerated without cost.

The *Henfield* and Georgia trials forced Congress to recognize the potential constitutional infirmity of those prosecutions. On June 5, 1794, it enacted legislation imposing criminal penalties on any citizen accepting "a commission to serve a foreign prince or state in war" or to "enter the service of any foreign prince or state . . . as a marine or seaman on board of any vessel of war . . . or privateer." The same legislation regulated the activities of French privateers operating in US ports and authorized the United States to detain any ship, cruiser, or vessel that was outfitted with guns on behalf of a nation at war with another nation at peace with the United States. Such legislation would not have been proposed and approved by Congress without the prior blessing of President Washington. How that legislation was reconcilable with Articles 17, 19, and 22 of the US-French Treaty of Amity and Commerce is an open, and overlooked, question. In fact, the congressional enactments violated the treaty's terms—blatantly.[31]

A second way that Minister Genet's promotion of privateering was controversial involved his establishment of French prize courts within the United States. Secretary of State Jefferson considered the operation of foreign prize courts within the United States to be an unacceptable violation of American sovereignty and neutrality. Jefferson corresponded directly to Genet's consuls, and bypassed Genet in doing so, warning them that they would be subject to prosecution and punishment if they adjudicated prize cases. The fact that Jefferson's letters circumvented Minister Genet demonstrated the extent of Jefferson's pique. Alexander Hamilton realistically summarized Minister Genet's activities as designed "to drag [the United States] into the war, with the humiliation of being plunged into it without even being consulted." It represented an issue where Cabinet Secretaries Jefferson and Hamilton agreed with one another.[32]

The federal government also declared that any judgments rendered by rogue prize courts within the United States were null and void. Notably, however, the federal government took no action to actually stop the sales of prize vessels and cargo at American ports. The government's failure to stop the sales was part of Washington's Solomonic policy of neutrality, publicly prohibiting French prize courts within the United States while simultaneously turning a blind eye to the prize courts' actual activities or to the privateers operating within the prize court system. Privateers holding judgments from prize courts still sold vessels and cargo at full price. More cautious privateers sold vessels and cargo at discounted but still-profitable prices without the imprimatur of any prize court and with the buyer assuming the risk that the original owner might file a legal action to claim title back. The French had no real cause to complain. And as for the British, the Washington administration could explain that it had officially prohibited French prize courts and undertook the prosecution of American citizens who had assisted French privateers.[33]

The upswing in privateering in American waters was a case-by-case problem for the Washington administration and then, ultimately, for the US federal courts. The first specific act of privateering brought to the attention of the Washington administration and the courts was the *L'Embuscade*'s capture of the British vessel, the *Grange*, in April 1793. The capture occurred within a part of the Bay of Delaware that was determined by Attorney General Randolph to be part of American territorial waters. Because the *Grange* was captured in the waters of a neutral country, Randolph determined on May 14, 1793, that restitution was owed by the French to the vessel's British owners. The *Grange* was returned to its original owners out of deference to Randolph's opinion, perhaps influenced by the desire of Minister Genet to make a good early impression on his American hosts. Such amiability would not survive long, as the pace of captures increased.[34]

On June 11, 1793, the British minister to the United States, George Hammond, lodged a protest with Secretary of State Jefferson over the French capture of the British vessel *Catherine*. Hammond demanded an immediate return of the vessel. Washington's Cabinet met the following day to set a policy for handling private and diplomatic requests for the government's assistance in obtaining the return of captured vessels. The policy that was decided on, which furthered the government's desire for neutrality, was to toss the "hot potato" into the hands of the federal courts. Jefferson wrote to Hammond on June 13, 1793, that "the parties interested [be] apprised without delay that they are to take measures as in ordinary civil cases for the support of their rights judicially." The

Cabinet, and Jefferson in his letter, acknowledged an open question of whether the federal courts possessed the jurisdiction to hear cases involving the subject matter of privateering. "Should the decision be in favor of the jurisdiction of the court," Jefferson wrote, "it will follow that all future cases will devolve at once on the individuals interested to be taken care of by themselves, as in other questions of private property provided for by the laws."[35]

Meanwhile, French privateers on the *Citizen Genet,* which was still captained by Pierre Johannene, captured the British vessel, the *William,* two miles from Fort Henry and took it to Philadelphia as a prize. The British owners filed a lawsuit in the federal District Court of Pennsylvania, *Findlay v The William,* seeking return of the vessel and its cargo. The suit was *in rem,* a Latin phrase meaning "against a thing," which is used when a party to a proceeding seeks title and possession of property. The legal parlance at the time described the theory of the case as a "libel" on the property and identified the privateer the "libellant." A deputy marshal of the District Court had been instructed to stop the captor's sale of cargo, which the captors believed to be a violation of the guarantee of Article 17 of the Treaty of Amity and Commerce that captors' vessels not be seized. The cargo was sold at a Philadelphia wharf, but because of the controversy prompted by the involvement of the deputy marshal, it yielded prices below its market value. In court, the privateers' attorney, Peter DuPonceau, sought a dismissal of the case on the ground that under both the law of nations and the terms of the treaty between the United States and France, the United States had no authority to interfere with the disposition of the French prize.[36]

On June 14, 1793, Jefferson received a letter from Minister Genet protesting the US government's "seizure" of the *William,* which he described as a lawful prize. Minister Genet warned that the American action was a violation of treaties between their two countries. He stated in his letter that such disputes are between sovereign states that must be resolved on a diplomatic level and were inappropriate for resolution by the American courts. The pending litigation over the *William* in the District Court neatly fit the policy that Jefferson had earlier explained to Britain's Minister Hammond, that claims regarding captured vessels be treated as private civil matters to be resolved in the courts. Jefferson, being aware of the *Findlay v The William* case, did not immediately respond to Genet's correspondence, perhaps delaying to see what might develop in the District Court.[37]

The administration's policy of referring prize issues to the federal courts suffered a blow within a week, when District Judge Richard Peters held in the *Findlay* case, in a written opinion dated June 21, 1793, that the federal courts lacked jurisdiction to entertain the matter and dismissed the proceeding. Judge Peters framed the legal question as being "[w]hether this court is vested with the power to enquire into the legality of the prize, and to investigate the fact on which all the reasonings are founded?" Judge Peters answered his own question by recognizing the internationally understood practice that "affairs of prizes are only cognizable in the courts of the power making the capture" and "that it never was attempted . . . to erect in a neutral state courts for the trial of prizes." In other words, the fate of captured vessels was the exclusive responsibility of the prize courts. Jefferson was obligated to respond to Minister Genet, which he accomplished by letter dated June 29, 1793. Jefferson explained that because the *William* had been undertaken by an American court, the executive branch of government was without authority to interfere under the constitutional separation of powers, and the federal courts were the exclusive arbiters of whether they possessed jurisdiction to hear the matter. Jefferson's response was of no practical assistance to the French, as it was, in essence, an artful dodge.[38]

In his decision dismissing the *Findlay* case, Judge Peters included an unusual suggestion that the vessel's original owner undertake an appeal to the US Supreme Court, noting that while he [Judge Peters] was bound by legal precedent, perhaps the Supreme Court would not feel so constrained. The owners did not pursue an appeal, instead seeking further redress through political channels. Another case before Judge Peters followed soon thereafter. In *Moxon v. The Fanny*, the British owners of the *Fanny* sought return of their vessel that had been seized as a prize by the French schooner *Sans Culottes* commanded by J. B. P. A. Ferey. Judge Peters dismissed the proceeding for lack of jurisdiction, notwithstanding that the *Fanny* was apparently seized in American territorial waters and brought to an American port. Yet another, consistent, opinion against the federal courts having jurisdiction over prize matters was rendered by Judge Thomas Bee in the District of South Carolina. Similarly, in *Meade v The Brigantine Catherine*, where the vessel at issue was also seized in American waters, Judge James Duane of the District Court in New York held that complaints of this kind involved state sovereigns and that the executive branch of the US government must resolve them rather than the federal courts. The only privateer ruling that was an outlier, where subject matter jurisdiction was found to exist in the courts, was an opinion of Judge John Lowell in the District of Massachusetts. None of the foregoing cases was appealed to the US Supreme Court.[39]

With time, more and more privateer cases reached the federal courts. From 1794 to 1797, there were twenty-four such cases, including fourteen published decisions and ten unpublished decisions, accounting for roughly one-half of the Supreme Court's caseload during the period. No privateer case would impact questions of federal jurisdiction and American government policy more than *Glass v Sloop Betsey*, as it was the first case reviewed by the US Supreme Court regarding French privateering at sea.[40]

The *Betsey* was a sloop that was captured in June 1793 by Captain Pierre Johannene of the *Citizen Genet*. The *Citizen Genet* was the same vessel that had seized the British ship *William* and led to the prosecution and acquittal of Gideon Henfield. The *Betsey* and its cargo were seized in the belief that it was British, but the sloop apparently was owned by a Swedish consortium, and its cargo was both Swedish and American. The capture occurred within two miles of the American coastline near Charleston, and the *Citizen Genet* brought the *Betsey* to the Port of Baltimore for mooring. What particularly distinguished the *Betsey* from other captured vessels was that the *Betsey* was not British, and Sweden was not a belligerent in the European wars. The ship's seizure appears to be an example of aggressive French privateering without restraint.[41]

A sloop, incidentally, is typically a one-mast vessel with a jib and a mainsail. It differs from a cutter, which is a sloop with two foresails and a mainsail. It differs from a ketch, which has two masts and a mizzen mast attached to the rudder head. It also differs from a schooner, which has at least two masts, with one taller than the other. Sloops tend to be smaller than the other described vessels.[42] Though smaller, the *Betsey* and its cargo were valuable enough to warrant litigating in the federal courts.

The *Betsey* was a Swedish merchant ship owned by Swedish subjects on the island of St. Bartholomew carrying a cargo belonging in part to them, in part to Lucas Gibbes and other Swedish subjects, and in part to Alexander S. Glass of New York. In June 1793, it still was not widely known or understood whether acts of privateering committed on American waters would be handled on a diplomatic level or, alternatively, through prize courts or federal courts. Alexander Glass initially approached President Washington for political assistance for the return of his captured sloop. A political resolution to the dispute certainly would have been preferable to Glass than resort to a prize court. The Washington administration was caught in such instances between a rock and a hard place. On the one hand, it felt bound to adhere to the terms of the Treaty of Amity and Commerce between the United States and France, which had guaranteed since 1788 French privateering in American waters and protections at American ports. On the other hand, any sheltering of French privateers was seen by Great Britain as a violation of the Washington administration's stated policy of neutrality between Britain and France. The British government, and the owners of British vessels that had been captured, were angered and frustrated with the American government over these issues. President Washington referred to matter to Secretary of State Jefferson, who passed the issue off to Secretary of War Henry Knox. Ultimately, the Washington administration dealt with the dilemma by informing owners of captured ships, such as the *Betsey*, that such matters could not be resolved by the executive branch and instead had to be addressed by the federal courts. Glass and his co-owners were therefore unceremoniously referred by Secretary of State Jefferson to the courts.[43]

Having been denied political assistance from the Washington administration, Glass had little choice but to commence a proceeding in federal court claiming that he was among the true owners of the *Betsey* and its cargo and to seek custody of the ship, its contents, and an award of money damages. The suit was heard by Judge William Paca at the United States District Court for the District of Maryland. Paca had been a delegate to both continental congresses, was one of Maryland's signers of the Declaration of Independence in 1776, and was a former governor of the state.[44]

Sloop Betsey raised yet again a threshold issue of subject matter jurisdiction—whether France, as the captor nation, possessed sole authority to determine the fate of the *Betsey* and its cargo, or whether the US District Court possessed jurisdiction by virtue of the sloop's capture in American waters and its location at the Port of Baltimore. The case would be difficult for Glass to win, given the cascading opinions from various federal district courts that there was no subject matter jurisdiction for entertaining his form of *in rem* claim in the courts. The French captors were represented in court by attorney James Winchester. In court, Captain Johannene and other witnesses testified to the existence of war between France and Britain, Johannene's commission from the French government, and the capture of the *Betsey* on the sea. Judge Paca did not require evidence of whether the *Betsey* was British or Swedish, believing that if he were to find that the dispute belonged in a prize court, the prize court would determine any question of ownership regarding the vessel or its contents.[45]

Perhaps predictably, in a decision rendered on August 15, 1793, Judge Paca resolved the question in favor of the French-sponsored captor and dismissed Glass's case for lack of subject matter jurisdiction. To do so, Paca was necessarily persuaded that the capture occurred on the high seas rather than within American territorial waters. He determined that while the true identity of the vessel's or cargo's ownership was relevant to any determination by a prize court, it was not relevant in deciding that the District Court lacked jurisdiction to hear the matter in the first place. Paca also determined that the court did not obtain jurisdiction to hear the case merely because the *Betsey* had been brought into an American port after its capture. The United States had not yet developed any body of indigenous law with regard to privateering on the seas. The absence

Figure 9.3. Hon. William Paca.

of indigenous law made it easy for federal district judges such as Judge Paca to default to international law and custom, the law of nations, and the provisions of treaties in determining that the American courts were without authority to hear the claims of vessel owners whose properties had been seized by privateers.[46]

Glass's options narrowed upon losing his case at the District Court. He could appeal the District Court's decision to the federal Circuit Court or, alternatively, contest his claim at a prize court. He and his attorneys chose to appeal within the federal court system, but an appeal would be of no value if, while the case was pending, the *Betsey* was sold. Fortunately for Glass, he obtained an "inhibition" prohibiting a sale, first from Judge Paca until the Circuit Court could decide whether to continue it, and then from Justice William Paterson acting on behalf of the Circuit Court. Today, an inhibition is called an "injunction," which maintains the status quo pending the litigation of a matter. Glass was required to post a $3,000 surety bond to secure damages or expenses incurred by Johannene "to abide the Event of the appeal." As a result, pending appeal, the *Betsey* was held by the US marshal.[47]

Glass followed through with his appeal to the federal Circuit Court sitting in Maryland. Further efforts by Glass to obtain the assistance of members of the Washington administration, such as Secretary of State Jefferson and Secretary of War Knox, were unsuccessful, as the matter was in the hands of the courts and the *Betsey* was held by the marshal. Glass's appeal was filed with the Circuit Court on November 7, 1793, and it was answered by Johannene through his attorney. Each party recounted in their filings the same facts and arguments as had been previously presented to Judge Paca. Oral argument was presented at the Circuit Court on November 8 and 9, 1793. According to the *Maryland Journal*, Glass was represented on the appeal by attorneys Luther Martin, Gustavus Scott, and Robert Smith; and Johannene by James Winchester, all of whom argued "ably and elaborately" to the court. William Paterson of the US Supreme Court, who had been riding the Middle Circuit, heard the case alone, as the Circuit Courts had by then been reduced from three jurists to two and as Judge Paca was unavailable to hear the case. Paterson orally delivered the opinion of the court during the late afternoon on November 9, 1793. He affirmed Judge Paca's determination. Once again, Glass had lost in court, and his options continued to narrow.[48]

To his credit, Paterson recognized the importance and potential novelty of the case. In his opinion affirming Judge Paca's dismissal of the case for lack of jurisdiction, Paterson directed that the dismissal be delayed ten days to give President Washington an opportunity to act, and if no executive action was forthcoming, directed that the dismissal be delayed an additional ten days to allow for an appeal to the US Supreme Court. All parties consented to Paterson's arrangement. A further round of lobbying of Jefferson and Knox was initiated by Glass and his supporters, but once again, actors within the Washington administration refused to get involved. They had no reason to, as any involvement would have necessarily antagonized either the British or the French, and potentially even the Swedes. Moreover, Glass and the Swedes had not exhausted their potential remedies in the courts.[49]

Undaunted, Glass chose to undertake a final appeal to the US Supreme Court, but once again needed an "inhibition" to prevent the sale of the *Betsey* while the further appeal would be pending. Glass's application for an inhibition was initially reviewed by Chief Justice Jay and then granted on November 19, 1793, by Associate Justice James Iredell who, by happenstance, was passing through Baltimore at the time. The $3,000 surety bond was continued. The final paperwork for the appeal was filed on November 27, 1793. The fate of the *Betsey* would need to await resolution of the case by the Jay Court during its upcoming February 1794 Term.[50]

Glass's new attorneys, Edward Tilghman and William Lewis, might have approached the Supreme Court with some degree of trepidation. The case had been decided at both the District Court and Circuit Court with deference to well-worn international law and custom that the captor nation had the exclusive authority to determine the fate of prizes. John Jay had significant background as a diplomat and internationalist. He had spent three years as minister to Spain while the United States was governed by the Articles of Confederation, and he had helped negotiate the Treaty of Paris in which Great Britain formally recognized the independence of the United States. Jay's interest in becoming chief justice was not inspired by any compelling desire to adjudicate only mundane domestic legal issues, and certainly not to ride the circuits, but by the desire to preside over anticipated and important issues of international law. As a result, Jay's diplomatic and internationalist background did not make him appear to be a jurist who would be particularly sympathetic to an *in rem* claim that required a departure from international law and custom. Indeed, Jay's respect for the norms of international law was probably as strong as his respect for the Ten Commandments. Even more problematic for Glass was the presence on the Supreme Court of Justice William Paterson. Paterson, as a justice of the Middle Circuit, had already voted to affirm the determination of the District Court in the same case, which suggested that Paterson had already made up his mind that claims against privateers for seized vessels were not within the scope of federal jurisdiction. Jay and Paterson comprised two of the six justices of the Supreme Court, and if their votes were lost, little more would be required for Glass to lose the appeal altogether. Mathematically, Glass needed to change Justice Paterson's mind, convince Chief Judge Jay of federal court jurisdiction, or obtain favorable votes from all four of the remaining four justices of the Supreme Court to win the appeal. Still, Glass's prospects were potentially better with the Jay Court than with a French prize court, and the Supreme Court's willingness to grant an inhibition while the appeal was pending was a hopeful sign.

Conversely, the captor's attorneys at the Supreme Court, Peter DuPonceau and James Winchester, had every reason to be confident that their client's right to the sloop would be affirmed on appeal. The capture had been upheld at both the District Court and Circuit Court in Maryland. Additionally, legal precedent and the law of nations appeared to be solidly on DuPonceau's side. DuPonceau had aptly noted in a letter to Martin Jorris on April 8, 1795, that "I do not know of any other Cases of Capture in which either the Legislature or the Supreme Court of the United States have given or recognized a right in the District courts to award restitution [for a captured prize vessel]."[51]

Professionally, John Jay must have been excited by *Glass v The Sloop Betsey*. The issues of the case were within his wheelhouse. For the most part, the cases that had already come to the Jay Court had focused on American law, the relationship between the federal government and the states, the relationship between individual citizens and the states, and the relationship between branches of the federal government. Cases of direct international consequence had been, until then, elusive.

Jay and his Supreme Court colleagues entertained argument from the parties over the course of four days, beginning on February 8, 1794. By today's standards, such lengthy oral argument by an appellate court on a single case would be unheard-of. The length of the argument suggests the seriousness of purpose on the part of the parties, attorneys, and jurists. It also suggests that the persons involved recognized that the Jay Court's determination in *Sloop Betsey*, whatever that determination

Figure 9.4. Peter DuPonceau.

might be, would be of great significance to nations, and to many private parties, in the years ahead.

Glass's attorneys argued that regardless of the circumstances of the *Betsey*'s capture, the federal courts had the authority to hear the controversy under its admiralty and maritime jurisdiction because the *Betsey* had been brought to the Port of Baltimore. They argued that Article 17 of the Treaty of Amity and Commerce was not an impediment to their claim to the *Betsey*, as the treaty only protected French privateers who seized ships of France's enemies, which did not include the Americans or the Swedes. They also argued that provisions of the Judiciary Act that limited the court's authority in admiralty matters to "civil" complaints did not distinguish civil matters from activities in furtherance of *war*, but merely highlighted the difference between civil and *criminal*.[52]

DuPonceau made four arguments to the Supreme Court as to why the federal courts were without jurisdiction to hear the dispute. One argument was that the mere presence of the *Betsey* at Baltimore did not, in and of itself, confer jurisdiction upon the court, as there was no underlying federal jurisdiction to hear and determine issues of prizes in the first instance. A second argument was that because prizes are by definition only recognized during times of war under international norms, the controversy was necessarily outside the federal court's civil admiralty and maritime jurisdiction and instead was referable only to a prize court. A third argument was that under international law, custom, and practice, the controversy regarding the *Betsey* was solely between nations—France and Sweden as to the vessel, and France, Sweden, and the United States as to its cargo. Finally, DuPonceau argued that any exercise of jurisdiction over the matter would constitute a violation of Article 17 of the US-French Treaty of Amity and Commerce. DuPonceau only had to prevail on at least one of his four arguments to defeat Glass's appeal. Glass, by contrast, had to persuasively defeat all four of the principal arguments in the minds of at least four of the six justices on the Supreme Court. A 3–3 tie by the Court would leave the Circuit Court's earlier affirmance intact.[53]

At the conclusion of the parties' arguments, the Jay Court reserved its decision. Doing so was not unusual, as it provided the Supreme Court justices an opportunity to consult with each other about the issues of the case and compose written decisions. During that time, the justices, debating the matter among themselves, must have determined that they needed further oral argument by the parties on one additional point of law. The attorneys were invited back to the Supreme Court to argue one discrete issue: whether a foreign country such as France could lawfully operate prize courts within the United States. Clearly, for the justices to ask the attorneys to return to the Supreme Court for additional argument, the subject of that argument must have been important to the determination of the case.[54]

During the supplemental round of oral argument, attorney DuPonceau responded to the issue "that the parties to the appeal did not conceive themselves interested in the point; and that the French minister had given no instructions for arguing it." To appellate advocates and appellate justices, DuPonceau's answer was, on its face, unsatisfying to say the least. Questions from appellate jurists during argument often reflect the very issues that the jurists believe are of importance in rendering a forthcoming decision. The question telegraphed that one or more of the justices of the Supreme Court were concerned about the legality of the French prize courts operating within the territory of the United States. It was among the twenty-nine questions that the Washington administration had earlier posed for an advisory opinion. If the French prize courts were not legal, the natural question that would flow from that would be whether American federal courts would jurisdictionally fill the void by providing an alternate forum for resolving prize disputes. With hindsight, which is always twenty-twenty, DuPonceau should have fielded the question posed to him by arguing in favor of the legitimacy of the French prize courts operating on American soil.[55]

Six days passed between the conclusion of the final oral arguments and the rendering of the court's decision, during which time the justices were discussing, debating, analyzing, deliberating, and writing about the case. The court's decision in *Glass v The Sloop Betsey* was rendered that same February, one year to the month after the French had declared war on Great Britain, the Netherlands, and Spain.[56]

The Jay Court unanimously and surprisingly reversed the decision of the Circuit Court. The court primarily held that no foreign power could maintain "any court of judicature of any kind within the jurisdiction of the United States," absent being authorized to do so by treaty. No such treaty provision existed between the United States and France. Therefore, the Supreme Court reasoned that no prize court could resolve the *Betsey* dispute in the United States, and as a result, the federal court possessed admiralty jurisdiction over the matter instead. The court's ruling was primarily based on the very question that attorney Peter DuPonceau failed to answer during his supplemental oral argument of the case. Implicitly, federal admiralty jurisdiction was found to exist in place of any prize court by virtue of the sloop's presence at the Port of Baltimore. The District Court of Maryland was directed to decide whether Glass and his colleagues were entitled to restitution and "whether such restitution can be made consistently with the laws of nations and the treaties and laws of the United States." The Supreme Court's opinion in *Sloop Betsey* must have been a shock to many persons, as it represented a departure from long-established legal and international norms.[57]

Perhaps more tellingly, the opinion in *Sloop Betsey* was a unanimous one, with the justices of the Supreme Court speaking as a single voice. Its first sentence characterized the justices as "being decidedly of opinion," language evoking strength and certitude. Even Justice Paterson, who had earlier affirmed the District Court's conclusion that federal court jurisdiction was lacking over the *Betsey* controversy, reversed his own thinking in voting with his colleagues. He might have done so because of a sincere change of heart, or, alternatively, he might have believed at the time of his Circuit Court opinion that he should not, as a single judge of a circuit, reach such a sweeping and new determination without the full voice of his Supreme Court brethren. The language used might also have been a signal that while the Supreme Court had earlier declined to provide the Washington administration with an advisory opinion, many of the answers that the administration had sought were being decidedly addressed in the court's opinion.[58]

The substantive portion of the court's opinion in *Sloop Betsey* was surprisingly brief, consisting of only three short paragraphs. It did not reflect the heavy, long-winded, and erudite legalese that was typical of judicial writings from those days. The bulk of the Supreme Court's work product was the summary of the arguments of the parties. It was a shorter opinion than those generally produced by the Jay Court in its earlier cases. The opinion was more conclusory than analytical. No legal authority was cited by the Supreme Court in support of its determination. The brevity of the opinion appears to be out of place given the four days that earlier had been invested in exhaustive and high-minded oral argument on the various technical issues of the case.

Although the Supreme Court's written opinion in *Glass v Sloop Betsey* was uncharacteristically brief, its impact on the law was great. The Jay Court breathed life into the authority of the federal courts to hear and resolve disputes involving captured prizes and, by extension, the meaning of the admiralty and maritime clauses of Article III, section 2, of the US Constitution. The Jay Court not only applied the gas pedal to those clauses, but also "floored it" with a determination that boldly overthrew long-standing international practices under the law of nations.

Glass's victory at the Supreme Court was not comprehensive. The Supreme Court sidestepped two of DuPonceau's four arguments against jurisdiction—that under international law and custom, the dispute was between nations rather than individuals, and that the involvement of federal courts would violate Article 17 of the Treaty of Amity and Commerce. The Supreme Court used language that very carefully and clearly ping-ponged those questions back to the District Court in directing that the District Court decide whether restitution could be awarded consistent with "the law of nations and the treaties and laws of the United

States." It is entirely plausible, with hindsight, that the six justices on the Supreme Court found a way to render a single unanimous opinion only by referring questions about the law of nations and treaties to the District Court. Had those issues instead been addressed head-on by the justices on their merits, the Supreme Court's unanimity might not have been maintained. As chief justice, John Jay might have concluded that in a case of such importance, a unanimous decision of the court would be more forceful and helpful to the other branches of government, even with the remittal of certain discrete issues to the District Court, rather than issuing a fractured opinion from a divided court that potentially would have sustained the legal controversies years into the future. This theory is supported by the brevity of the *Sloop Betsey* opinion, as the less that is written by an appellate court on a matter, the less there is for jurists to disagree about.

The Washington administration must have been very pleased with the Supreme Court's unanimous opinion. It meant that going forward, the headaches associated with French captures of British or other vessels would remain with the judicial branch of government. This, in turn, made it easier for the administration to maintain neutrality between the belligerent nations.

Despite the brevity of the *Sloop Betsey* opinion, and besides representing an early assertion of American admiralty jurisdiction in matters involving foreign interests, the case had other political and military ramifications that were not lost on the governments of Europe. The French government had been willing to allow privateers acting on its behalf to harass and seize British ships in or near American waters in furtherance of the ongoing hostilities between Great Britain and France. The seizure of the *Betsey* appears to be one such example. If the Supreme Court had held that the captor nation (France) was solely possessed of jurisdiction to determine claims involving the ship, consistent with the legal practice in Europe at the time, further commercial ships would predictably be commandeered by the proxies of one country or another, using American territorial waters and ports as a battleground for hostilities between those other nations.

Moreover, the Supreme Court's decision was consistent with the delicate neutrality that the Washington administration was attempting to maintain between France and Great Britain. All of the justices on the Supreme Court had a Federalist view of government, as did President Washington. The Jay Court's opinion supported the Washington administration's carefully crafted policy of neutrality. The opinion gave President Washington and Secretary of State Jefferson the political "cover" to respond to future French or British complaints about nasty privateering issues as belonging solely in the federal courts. The Supreme Court's decision in *Sloop Betsey* also may have had the effect of promoting greater safety, certainty, and reliability to the trade and commercial shipping of the United States. However, there is no hard-and-fast evidence that the Supreme Court's decision was based on any considerations other than the narrow jurisdictional issues apparent on its face.[59]

In *Sloop Betsey*, the Supreme Court made no definitive statement refuting the validity of prize courts under the law of nations. The Supreme Court also made no definitive statement about whether the adjudication of prize issues in the federal courts violated the Treaty of Amity and Commerce. However, in the years that followed, district courts viewed *Sloop Betsey* as an invitation to exercise jurisdiction over the controversies. Those cases included, for example, *Martins v Ballard* in the District Court for the District of South Carolina (Bee, J.) in 1794. *Sloop Betsey* enabled American merchants victimized by privateering to seek redress in the federal courts and forced the privateers to defend their property claims in those same courts. As a result, a monkey wrench was thrown into French plans to damage British commerce through privateering, causing battles that were supposed to be waged on the seas to also be waged in federal courtrooms. The Supreme Court would not refine the rules for prize restitution or address various factual permutations until it heard later cases, particularly in late 1795 and in 1796. The *Sloop Betsey* decision and later cases did not end the practice of French privateering, but merely increased the percentage of captured ship sales that were accomplished without the involvement of prize courts.[60]

And finally, the determination of *Sloop Betsey* confirmed the wisdom of the Supreme Court's earlier refusal to provide Washington's Cabinet with an advisory opinion. Had the Court complied at that time, it might have felt bound to resolve the *Sloop Betsey* case in a way that would be consistent with the earlier advisory opinion. A decision by the Supreme Court at odds with its own earlier advisory opinion would have diminished the court's credibility. By rendering no advisory opinion, the Supreme Court had a free hand to resolve *Sloop Betsey* in whatever manner it deemed necessary and appropriate by the time of its decision. To this day, the US Supreme Court does not issue advisory opinions.[61]

JAY'S DAYS

After Gideon Henfield's trial acquittal and fifteen minutes of fame, he went on a further excursion on the high seas, where he was captured by the British and not heard from again.

One of Minister Genet's attorneys retained to defend the taking of the Sloop Betsey, Peter DuPonceau, was not only an attorney, but also a philosopher, artist, and linguist. He joined the American Philosophical Society in 1791 and served as its president between 1827 and 1844. He was elected as a fellow to the American Academy of Arts and Sciences in 1820. He developed texts that described the languages of native Americans and created a "lexigraphic" approach for understanding the Chinese and Vietnamese languages. He died in Philadelphia on April 1, 1844, at the age of eighty-three.

On June 26, 1812, the US Congress enacted legislation specifically vesting prize jurisdiction in the federal district courts. The legislation also regulated the issuance of letters of marque to armed American vessels for privateering as a naval tactic against Great Britain during the War of 1812.[62]

Chapter 10

Efforts To Criminally Prosecute Chief Justice Jay

The Citizen Genet Affair

> ". . . Mr. Dallas mentioned some things which he had not [previously] said to me, and particularly his [Edmond Charles Genet's] declaration that he would appeal from the President to the people. He did in some part of his declamation to me drop the idea of publishing a narrative or statement of transactions. . ."
>
> —The Papers of Thomas Jefferson
> July 10, 1793

As incomprehensible as it might sound today, there was an effort in 1793 to criminally prosecute John Jay at, of all places, the US Supreme Court, while he was serving there as chief justice. It is an unusual tale in early American history and another example of how, under the young federal constitution, principal actors in the US government were feeling their way through uncharted issues of domestic law, international law, and individual rights. Its primary protagonist was the energetic and irascible minister from France, Edmond-Charles Genet, a principal actor seen in the previous chapter.

July was a celebratory time for American Francophiles, as July 14 was the anniversary of the storming of the Bastille. The festivities of the month in 1793 masked the true tensions that were building between the Washington administration and the French government over difficult issues such as privateering, and beyond the separate issue of the British impressment of sailors. Democracy in both the United States and France was a unifying bond, additionally solidified by France's earlier assistance to the American colonies during the Revolutionary War. Events naturally catapulted debate over American neutrality into the nation's political consciousness. There was some sentiment that the United States should side with France in its war with Great Britain given the ties that had been forged between the two countries during the previous decade. The Washington administration was naturally wary of any efforts that might be undertaken by persons or groups seeking to maneuver the United States into an active wartime alliance with France against Britain.

In July 1793, French privateers had captured the British vessel *Little Sarah* and brought the prize to the Port of Philadelphia. With time, it would prove to be a singularly significant event for Minister Genet, John Jay, and New York Senator Rufus King. The capture of *Little Sarah* resulted in strenuous complaints and demands from the British minister, George Hammond. It was at about that time that Minister Genet changed the name of the captured *Little Sarah* to *La Petite Democrate* and began outfitting the vessel with guns and armaments so that it could be used for further privateering along the American coast. President Washington was not in Philadelphia at the time, as he was on a trip to Mount Vernon. On July 5, a Cabinet meeting was held in the absence of President Washington to discuss, among other things, a week-old report from Pennsylvania Governor Thomas Mifflin that *Little Sarah* was being outfitted for privateering. The Cabinet asked Governor Mifflin to conduct further investigation of the matter.[1]

On July 7, 1793, when Mifflin confirmed that *Little Sarah* had been enhanced with armaments including multiple iron canons and swivels, he informed Secretary of State Thomas Jefferson that the vessel might sail at any time and called out the Pennsylvania militia. Mifflin sent Pennsylvania Secretary of State Alexander Dallas to Genet to ask that the vessel be detained. While Dallas is known by his role as the original court reporter during the US Supreme Court's earliest years, he simultaneously served as Pennsylvania's secretary of state from 1791 to 1801. At midnight, Minister Genet expressed to Alexander Dallas his anger at the Washington administration for committing what Genet believed to be treaty violations with regard to *Little Sarah* and indicated that he would not order the vessel to stay. Dallas was sympathetic to the French. During the conversation between Genet and Dallas, Genet allegedly threatened to appeal the administration's policy directly to the American people. Genet's statement, assuming it was made, revealed on his part a considerable amount of hubris in believing that his exhortations about American policy could be more persuasive among Americans than those of George Washington and the Americans' own government.[2]

Dallas informed Jefferson about the level of Genet's anger, which prompted Jefferson to arrange a meeting of his own with Genet. According to Jefferson, Dallas did not at that time reveal to him Genet's "threat" of appealing American policy over President Washington's head to the American people.[3] Perhaps Dallas thought better of doing so.

The blunt conversation between Jefferson and Genet was in stark contrast with the hoopla accompanying the festivities of the American and French independence celebrations of July 4 and July 14 of that year. On July 7, 1793, Jefferson warned Genet to not put *Little Sarah* at sea for any privateering activities at least until President Washington's return to Philadelphia. Jefferson's request was a meaningful one, given that the Pennsylvania militia had already been mustered and the departure of the ship from its port could spark an incident between the two nations. The two men descended into heated discussion about how long it would take to complete the outfitting of *Little Sarah*, exactly when Washington would return to Philadelphia, and what would happen if *Little Sarah* sailed down river without actually heading out to sea. According to Jefferson, Genet did most of the talking, airing what Jefferson described as "an immense field of declamation and complaint" about American treaty violations and disrespect of the French. Genet also advised that the Little Sarah was not yet ready to set sail, which Jefferson interpreted as an agreement that the vessel would not go anywhere until President Washington's anticipated arrival in Philadelphia, based on Genet's "look and gesture."[4]

Later that same day, Jefferson spoke at Governor Mifflin's house with Mifflin and Dallas. According to Jefferson, Dallas revealed for the first time that Genet had earlier threatened that if "old Washington" did not change his policies toward France, Genet would go over the heads of the administration and appeal directly to American people.[5] Jefferson noted in his papers, ". . . Mr. Dallas mentioned some things which he had not [previously] said to me, and particularly his [Genet's] declaration that he would appeal from the President to the people. He [Genet] did in some part of his declamation to me drop the idea of publishing a narrative or statement of transactions, but he did not on that, nor ever did on any other occasion in my presence, use disrespectful expressions toward the President." In other words, Genet's threat of appealing governmental policy to the American people, such as by publishing a narrative or statement, was cross-corroborated by Dallas and Jefferson, though in Jefferson's case, it was not accompanied by any reference to the president as "old Washington" or other derogatory language.[6]

In the view of members of the Cabinet, and ultimately of George Washington himself, Genet's threat was darker and more worrisome than appeared on its face. Genet had already proven himself an effective agitator in furtherance of French interests, including, in particular, an American alignment with France against Britain. His robust efforts at organizing an extensive fleet of privateers were enough to prove the point. He was not without his supporters among the American populace. Jefferson, Washington, and indeed the entire Cabinet were concerned that Genet's actual threat was to organize Americans in sympathy with France to undertake violence against the American government. None of the participants in the original conversations between Jefferson, Dallas, and Genet over *Little Sarah* could have imagined that they precipitated an unfortunate and embarrassing controversy that ultimately would lead directly to John Jay. The controversy would become popularly known as the "Citizen Genet Affair."[7]

Jefferson negotiated further with Genet and successfully defused the crisis, but only to an extent. Genet advised that *Little Sarah* aka *La Petite Democrate* was not yet ready to set sail, either because the statement was true or perhaps to save face. Jefferson convinced Governor Mifflin to withdraw the state militia from the Philadelphia waterfront. At a rump Cabinet meeting the following day, again without Washington, both Hamilton and Knox were prepared to order the mounting of canons along the Delaware River at Mud Island to prevent *Little Sarah* from sailing. Jefferson was apoplectic at the suggestion, that the move could prove deadly and have costly consequences on French-American relations. Hamilton and Knox ultimately dropped the idea upon Jefferson's assurance that Genet had agreed not to let *Little Sarah* set sail before Washington's return to Philadelphia. The Cabinet bet on Jefferson's ability to trust Genet despite the unresolved dispute about whether Genet had made threats to make French appeals directly to the people of the United States.[8]

Washington was understandably angry about Genet's bellicosity upon his return to Philadelphia on July 8, 1793. Upon Washington's instruction, Jefferson issued a letter to French Minister Genet and British

Minister Hammond advising them that questions were posed to the US Supreme Court about privateering and related subjects and that President Washington "will expect" *Little Sarah* to remain at Philadelphia until such time that an ultimate determination of its fate is made. While Genet may have tacitly promised Jefferson that *Little Sarah* would not sail *before* Washington's return to Philadelphia, Washington had by then returned to Philadelphia, and the extent of Genet's promise was fulfilled. *Little Sarah*, under the name *La Petite Democrate*, then set sail from Philadelphia under the French flag in furtherance of privateering against British vessels and in defiance of President Washington's stated "expectations." Apparently Minister Genet had no interest in hearing whatever the Jay Court might have to say on the subject in an advisory opinion.[9]

Hamilton and Knox argued during a Cabinet meeting that President Washington request the French government to recall Genet as its minister to the United States. While a foreign diplomat is duty bound to comply with the laws of the host nation and immune from punishment for violating those laws, conduct that is contrary to the host country's laws is a ground for requesting a diplomat's recall. Jefferson, perturbed but still a soft touch on matters involving France, urged that Washington not act precipitously and further urged patience to afford the Supreme Court an adequate opportunity to consider the twenty-nine questions that had been posed to it. But Washington decided during the first week of August 1793 to seek Genet's recall. It was a somewhat unusual, though not unprecedented, request. There was a secondary debate within the Cabinet about whether Washington's recall request should be made public, as Hamilton urged, or be kept private, as Jefferson wished. Washington sided with Jefferson on that issue. A letter to the French government underwent various drafts until all writings were finalized on August 23, 1793, and signed by Jefferson as secretary of state. Trans-Atlantic communications were understandably slow, and it would take many weeks for the French government to receive and consider the request, grant or deny it, and then communicate its decision back to the United States. In the interim, Genet continued in his role as France's minister to the United States and continued to foment activities designed to push the American government toward a war against Great Britain.[10]

Washington and his Cabinet could not know that the Girondin coalition government of France would be overthrown within the month by the Jacobin government of Maximilen de Robespierre. The Jacobin government undertook its infamous Reign of Terror between September 5,

1793, and July 27, 1794, resulting in the execution of an estimated 1,400 French citizens. The position of Edmond-Charles Genet, an appointee of the soon-to-be overthrown Girondin government, would become more precarious for reasons independently occurring from the political chaos within his own home country.

John Jay continued to be a trusted and informal confidante of the president and members of the Cabinet. He was consulted about Genet. Jay shared the concerns of his friend, Alexander Hamilton, that the French minister might feel emboldened to organize a portion of the populace against the American government. The new federal republic was still potentially fragile, and revolutionary fervor had been sweeping France for some time. As for what to do about Genet and his threat to appeal policy matters to the American people, Hamilton suggested that Jay, as chief justice, make some form of public statement that would expose Genet's possible machinations and thereby defuse them. Jay agreed. His decision to do so is yet another example of how Supreme Court justices in those days involved themselves in political matters outside the walls of any courthouse.[11]

Jay and New York Senator Rufus King, a fellow Federalist, jointly signed a letter that was published in a New York newspaper, *The Diary*, on August 12, 1793. The letter confirmed rumors that Minister Genet would appeal unfavorable presidential decisions to the American people. Because Jay and King were both New Yorkers, their published letter suggested the subtle but hidden hand of yet another New Yorker, Alexander Hamilton. It is inconceivable that such a letter would have been jointly published by two prominent New York Federalists—one a leading jurist and the other a prominent member of Congress—without prior sanction from the highest levels of the Washington administration. The implication to the American people was to consider their allegiance to Minister Genet or to President Washington, and, likely, allegiances would flow to the latter. The persons involved in the effort must have intended, and believed, that the publication would "expose" Genet and deflate his influence within the United States.[12]

Jay, King, Hamilton, and maybe others might have brought the issue to the public's attention in an effort to not only damage the country's perception of Minister Genet, but perhaps also damage Franco-American relations more broadly and thereby strengthen Anglo-American relations. Such are the intrigues of palace politics. If so, it did not shake the sympathies of many newspapers toward France. Newspapers sympathetic to the Democratic-Republicans maintained that the Jay-King letter proved nothing, and they defended Minister Genet on the ground that George Washington was not such a "consecrated character" that his decisions could not be popularly appealed to the people without criminality.[13]

Genet took Jay's and King's published letter as an affront to his honor. The dispute with Genet had shifted from Jefferson and Dallas, where it originated in private, to Jay and King, where it became public. On August 13, 1793, Genet sent a letter to President Washington that he also sent to newspapers for publication. In it, he lamented that persons who he did not identify by name had subjected him to "personal abuse" in a public attack designed to damage the "esteem" that he held as a representative of the French Republic. Genet wrote "an explicit declaration that I have never intimated to you an intention of appealing to the people." While Genet denied making any threat attributed "to the President," his denial was not considered to be persuasive because he was never accused of uttering his statement directly *to* President Washington. Ironically, the publication of Genet's letter to Washington was an appeal to the American public, of sorts, similar to that which Jay and King had accused the minister of threatening in their own earlier publication.[14]

Diplomatic protocol at the time did not provide for foreign ministers to correspond directly with the president, and for that stated reason, Jefferson publicly announced three days later that there would be no official response to Genet's letter. To Genet, Jefferson's reply was evasive.[15]

Matters festered for the next several weeks, though perhaps by early November it looked as if the issue had finally gone away. It did not. Genet remained angry about his public smackdown by Jay, King, and, by extension, the Washington administration. His potential recall by the French government was a further humiliation that he likely had heard about, which must have stoked his anger at the American officials who were trying to engineer it, on top of all else. Genet decided to up the ante. Although Genet was a brash, impolitic, and sometimes hotheaded person, he also was a quick study about the workings of American courts. Drawing on the US government's common law prosecution of Gideon Henfield earlier in the year for privateering in violation of the federal policy of neutrality, Genet decided that he had legal grounds for a common law prosecution of John Jay and Rufus King, albeit on a different ground—libel.

On November 14, 1793, Genet wrote a letter to Attorney General Edmund Randolph formally asking the US government to criminally prosecute Jay and King for libel. He elegantly wrote "of the scandalous falsity of the charge against me" and asked Randolph "to take such steps, at the ensuing federal court, as the honor of your own country, as well as mine, exact upon such an occasion." That the letter originated from a foreign minister, particularly from a country as pivotal as France, required that it be taken seriously.[16]

If Edmund Randolph had ever discussed the Genet controversy with Washington, Jefferson, Hamilton, or other members of Cabinet, or with Jay or King, he would be required by today's standards to recuse himself from the matter altogether. In modern times, investigative recusals by attorneys general and the appointment of special counsels have been somewhat common, occasioned during the presidential administrations of Richard Nixon, Jimmy Carter, Ronald Reagan, George H. W. Bush, William Clinton, George W. Bush, and Donald Trump. Matters in the 1790s were not as formal, complicated, or legalistic. Randolph was advised that President Washington wished to remain neutral in matters involving Edmond-Charles Genet, as he had been since the time that *Little Sarah* was first captured and outfitted by Genet for privateering activities. Through Jefferson, Washington instructed Randolph "to proceed in this case according to the duties of your office, the laws of the land, and the privileges of the parties concerned." Thomas Jefferson may have been torn by the turn of events, writing to Randolph that, on the one hand, Genet, in his role as a foreign minister, was "peculiarly entitled to the protection of the laws," while, on the other hand, Jay and King were entitled "not to be vexed with groundless prosecutions."[17]

One might wonder how and why Attorney General Randolph needed to take seriously a request that the nation's chief justice and a United States senator be criminally prosecuted for what might be characterized, at worst, as a civil defamation. The answer lies in the fact that in the 1790s, free speech was not known and understood in the same manner as it has been for much of the nation's later history. The First Amendment contains what appears to be an ironclad guarantee that Congress make no law "prohibiting the exercise of free speech; or abridging the freedom of speech." That language, however clear, did not prevent the Federalist-controlled Congress from enacting the Sedition Act, which President John Adams signed into law in 1798. The Sedition Act criminalized the making of false statements against the federal government. Although the Sedition Act was not yet on the books in

1793, it reflects how in the 1790s, the United States citizenry and their representatives in government had a different understanding about the meaning of free speech from what was developed by the courts during later generations. Many other constitutional guarantees set forth in the founding documents, including the provisions of the First, Second, Fourth, Fifth, Sixth, and Eighth Amendments, required many decades, and in many instances more than a century and a half, to develop the meanings broadly attributed to them today.[18]

Moreover, the legal community in the 1790s and many high elected federal officials recognized the concept of "common law prosecutions," without need for the defendant to have violated any particular criminal statute passed by Congress. An individual engaging in conduct violative of a US treaty, for example, could be subjected to criminal prosecution. The concept extended to violations of the internationally recognized law of nations. And in the case of Gideon Henfield, it was extended further to his alleged violation of President Washington's neutrality proclamation. What is puzzling about the recognition of common law prosecutions in those days is that they were seemingly inconsistent with the concept of limited government; that under the Tenth Amendment, the federal government possessed no authority other than that expressly given to it under the Constitution. The Constitution did not expressly provide for common law prosecutions, not in its Judiciary Article (Article III) or otherwise.

Thus, when Edmond-Charles Genet complained to Attorney General Edmund Randolph that he had been libeled by John Jay and Rufus King, in connection with the performance of his diplomatic duties no less, the request for a common law prosecution of Jay and King was not far-fetched at all, and in fact was within the mainstream of legal thought in existence at the time. Because the federal government and its court system were new, there was no decisive legal precedent for anyone to rely on in deciding the issue.

Jay and King must have become concerned that they were in some legal, if not political, peril. To make matters more embarrassing, the US Constitution provided in Article III, section 2, that federal jurisdictional power extended "to all Cases affecting Ambassadors, other public Ministers and Consuls," and that in such cases, "*the Supreme Court shall have original Jurisdiction.*"[19] In other words, if a common law prosecution involving Minister Genet were to be commenced against

Jay and King, the case would not be filed in a lower federal court and work its way up an appellate ladder, but instead would be filed directly and originally with the Supreme Court, where Jay happened to be chief justice.

The language of the Constitution distinguished between "ambassadors" and "ministers." Whereas ministers were diplomats, ambassadors were more respected, as they had a direct relationship with their national leader or king.[20] The Constitution, which gives the Supreme Court original jurisdiction to hear cases involving "Ambassadors, or other public Ministers or Consuls," suggests that the founding fathers intended for the Supreme Court's authority to apply to a broad array of diplomats, regardless of their specific titles. Minister Genet, being the primary representative of France to the United States, certainly met that qualification.

John Jay and Rufus King might have been better advised to keep a low profile in the controversy for the time being, but they did not. Perhaps at the urging of others, they were persuaded to issue a response that President Washington could not, or would not. Jay and King decided that the best defense was a good offense. They jointly drafted another statement intended for publication in New York noting, as though they were lawyers having completed a cross-examination of Genet, that Genet had failed to ever deny making his threatening statement *to Alexander Dallas or Thomas Jefferson*. As if to underscore their new statement's credibility, they asked Treasury Secretary Hamilton and Secretary of War Knox to "certificate" the statement. Hamilton and Knox did so in very late November, and the Jay-King statement was then published in newspapers bearing the two Cabinet members' certifications. Hamilton and Knox were the two Cabinet secretaries who had taken the hardest line against France in earlier meetings, including their belief that the US-French Treaty of Amity and Commerce was abrogated by the overthrow of the French monarchy. Jay's and King's latest letter might have been meant as much for Attorney General Randolph's consumption as for the American public. The "certificate" represented an assurance by Hamilton and Knox that they each heard information about Minister Genet's threat from Governor Mifflin and Secretary of State Jefferson. Hamilton's and Knox's certification was little more than political window dressing, as it reported mere secondhand information, but it added the two men's credibility to whatever credibility Jay and King already had with the public on the subject.[21]

Notably, Jefferson, the cabinet secretary always more partial toward France, was not a signatory to the newly published Jay-King statement, and he did not affix his name to his Cabinet colleagues' "certification" of the document. Jefferson made himself scarce, even though he was the only high-ranking federal official who could speak to the issue from direct conversations with Dallas and Genet.

For his part, Alexander Dallas, who was the immediate recipient of Genet's controversial statement the previous July, also remained silent, perhaps because he had been a vocal supporter of French causes. But after publication of the Jay-Knox letter certificated by Hamilton and Knox, Dallas issued a statement to the public dated December 17, 1793, denying that Minister Genet ever threatened in conversations with him that he [Genet] would appeal issues over Washington's head to the American people. Dallas explained that any "appeal" by Genet was more likely intended to be directed to the US Congress. The explanation was an awkward one, offered several weeks after the controversy had been swirling, and was unsupported by any public statement of Thomas Jefferson. Dallas was irked that the issue was brought to the attention of the public by Jay and King without the courtesy or common sense of consulting with him in the first instance. Significantly, Dallas's public statement, in which he denied any threat by Genet, was contradicted by Jefferson's private notes of his conversation with Dallas and Governor Mifflin on July 7, 1793, where Dallas had described the threat in detail. But those all-important notes were kept hidden from public disclosure by Jefferson himself.[22]

Jefferson's silence on the issue bothered John Jay. He lamented in a letter to Rufus King that Jefferson "remain[ed] as if it were in a background" and that public letters calling on Thomas Jefferson "to admit or deny the facts in question, would have been, and may yet be useful." For Jefferson's part, he might have believed that getting involved in the controversy would unnecessarily complicate the relationship that he needed to have with Genet in handling foreign affairs in his role as US secretary of state. There also might have been a darker explanation for Jefferson's silence in the Citizen Genet Affair. Jefferson was not necessarily aligned with Federalist thinkers in Washington's Cabinet, and he might have had political motivations for distancing himself from others on the subject. He might have been perfectly content to keep silent and let Jay and King twist in the wind of the controversy without coming to their political rescue.[23]

Figure 10.1. Senator Rufus King.

If Attorney General Randolph entertained any thoughts of declining a prosecution of Jay and King on the ground that common law prosecutions were not valid, he could not actually do so. As attorney general, he had authorized and supported the common law prosecution of Gideon Henfield and others. Randolph was boxed in procedurally, perhaps as Genet had calculated, and needed to decide the matter strictly on the basis of whether the case warranted the government's attention. He likely agreed with Jefferson that many rights needed to be taken into account—Genet's as well Jay's and King's.

In the end, Attorney General Randolph chose to punt the Genet football. He wrote to Genet on December 18, 1793, that the federal government would undertake no criminal prosecution of John Jay or Rufus King. On the one hand, Randolph's decision not to prosecute might appear like favoritism toward his governmental colleagues and be supportive of the broader goals of the Washington administration. But such a reading of Randolph's decision would be misplaced. Randolph noted in the same letter that if Genet were inclined, nothing prevented the minister from commencing a private common law prosecution of Jay and King. As noted, any such private litigation would need to be filed directly with the US Supreme Court.[24]

Jay and King were perturbed that Randolph virtually *invited* Genet to commence a private common law prosecution against them. They drafted what would be their third joint letter, this time addressed privately to President Washington, critical of Randolph for his legal advice to Genet and critical of Jefferson for his silence about Genet's threat. Jay and King specifically requested that Jefferson be compelled to make public his notes of his now-infamous meeting with Genet about *Little Sarah* in the belief that those notes would bolster their claims about what Genet had said. Now it was Washington's turn to be perturbed, as he interpreted Jay's and King's complaints as being directed against *him* for having referred the Genet matter to Randolph. One senses that behind closed doors, many persons in the Washington administration involved in the controversy were angry and lashing out. A meeting was called between Washington and Jay for the ostensible purpose of Washington giving Jay a dressing-down and for the two men to iron out their differences. They discussed the matter openly but bluntly. Washington objected to the tenor of the Jay-King letter to him and gave a full-throated defense of his conduct and the conduct of his Cabinet members. In the end, it was agreed that King would deliver to Washington the initial draft of the same letter, which, upon its later delivery, Washington burned by fire, ending the disagreeable subject matter between the men involved. But it did not end the ongoing desire of Genet to initiate a criminal prosecution against Jay and King.[25]

Meanwhile, Genet consulted with two Philadelphia attorneys, Peter DuPonceau, who had successfully defended Gideon Henfield and participated in the *Glass v Sloop Betsey* case, and Joseph Thomas. DuPonceau was excited at the prospect of commencing a suit against Jay and King. He wrote that he was "decidedly of opinion that [they] have committed an offense not only against the local law of this Country, but against the Law of Nations, for which they may be indicted and punished." DuPonceau may have been concerned that commencing the prosecution in the US Supreme Court, where John Jay was chief justice, presented some unique pitfalls, but in the end, he concluded that the Supreme

Court was the proper forum in which to present the case. Genet even arranged for witnesses to be brought to Philadelphia to assist with his case. Genet enlisted the support of Brockholst Livingston, an attorney in New York, to make arrangements for the witnesses. What makes Brockholst Livingston's involvement noteworthy is that he was a younger brother of Sarah Livingston Jay, and he appears to have placed his loyalty to politics ahead of his loyalty to family-in-law.[26]

It is not actually known whether Genet and his attorneys ever filed, or attempted to file, a common law complaint against John Jay and Rufus King at the US Supreme Court. Fortunately for Jay and King, other events rendered the controversy moot before any Supreme Court case could proceed.[27]

President Washington's request to the French government that it withdraw Minister Genet from the United States had been routed in the normal diplomatic course from Secretary of State Jefferson to the American minister to France, Gouverneur Morris. Morris presented the request to the French foreign minister, Francois Louis Michel Chemin des Forgues, on October 8, 1793, in Paris. Des Forgues assured Morris at that time that Genet would be recalled. Two days later, after des Forgues had read the materials provided by Jefferson describing how Genet's conduct was jeopardizing French-American relations, des Forgues informed Morris that not only would Genet be recalled, but he also would be arrested and punished. On October 11, 1793, the Jacobin Committee of Public Safety formally recalled Genet from his position as minister to the United States, and a month later declared that Genet had been part of a Girondin plot to alienate the United States from France. During the same tumultuous time that Genet's fate was being determined by the Committee of Public Safety, the deposed French Queen, Marie Antoinette, was beheaded by guillotine at *Place de la Concorde*, on October 16, 1793.[28]

Meanwhile, to whatever extent Minister Genet did not care for George Washington, the feeling was mutual. The Citizen Genet Affair was a headache Washington did not want or need. By December, Washington still had not heard back from the French government about the American request for Genet's recall from his diplomatic post, and he grew impatient. On December 5, 1793, Washington sent a message to Congress formally advising its members of his request that Minister Genet be recalled, supported by correspondences between Jefferson and Genet, affidavits regarding the seizure of ships, and French government documents regarding the United States. By then, the issue of having Minister Genet recalled to France was public. In January 1794, Washington directed Secretary of State Edmund Randolph, who had succeeded Thomas Jefferson in the job, to draft a message to Congress that he would unilaterally revoke Genet's diplomatic authority within the United States unless Congress objected. The draft was rendered moot when the Washington administration was finally notified that the French government had granted the request that Genet be withdrawn as the country's minister to the United States. The French government's doing so should not have been a great surprise at that time, as the new Jacobin government of France might have been expected to seize upon any excuse to rid itself of the appointees of the prior Girondin government, which the Jacobins had overthrown the previous August.[29]

The new French minister, Jean Antoine Joseph Fauchet, debarked from a ship in Philadelphia on February 20, 1794, to formally replace Genet as the French minister to the United States. Fauchet brought with him additional news. A warrant had been issued by Maximilen de Robespierre's Jacobin government for Genet's arrest. Genet was no longer one of his country's zealous patriots, but had become branded as a counterrevolutionary traitor. Material was published in France claiming that Genet had deliberately sought to provoke a crisis with the United States to alienate the two countries from each other and thereby drive the Americans into the arms of Great Britain. He was also accused of profiting off purchases made from France. The allegations against Genet were fanciful and untrue, but they were taken at face value given the heady and bloody politics that gripped France at the time. France was fully in the midst of its Reign of Terror, and it was understood that if Genet returned to France, he would be guillotined as an enemy of the state.[30]

Genet requested asylum in the United States. The decision about whether to grant asylum belonged to President Washington. Washington was initially disinclined toward the request, as there was no love lost between the two men. Alexander Hamilton, who may have been Genet's fiercest opponent in the Cabinet, urged Washington to grant asylum, particularly if Genet were to agree to forego any common law prosecution of John Jay and Rufus King at the Supreme Court.

There was a law on the books in France that rendered the families of foreign envoys responsible for their acts abroad. Genet had been replaced by a four-man commission led by Jean Antoine Joseph Fauchet. A primary task of the French commissioners was to restore good relations with the United States. Minister Fauchet, perhaps understanding that his new American hosts wanted no prosecution of Jay or King, advised Genet that if he embarrassed their home country by proceeding with the prosecution, Genet's mother and sisters in France could, under French law, be executed. With that, a deal was made, and the Citizen Genet Affair reached its conclusion. Genet received the political asylum he requested, but would pursue no common law prosecution of John Jay or Rufus King for libel.[31]

Genet's life in politics and public service ended at the tender age of thirty-one. In the end, it can be said that Genet overplayed his hand during his tenure as French minister to the United States, but his diplomatic assignment to the United States appears to be what ultimately saved his life from the terror of politics in his homeland at the time.[32]

The controversy between John Jay and Edmond-Charles Genet did not represent John Jay's finest moments in public life. Jay had been drawn into the controversy at the invitation of Alexander Hamilton and engaged the subject in the likely sincere belief that Genet represented a threat to the United States at a particularly perilous time for American international relations. As noted by attorney-historian Walter Stahr, Jay's Federalist colleague, John Adams, claimed years later that he had never been much concerned that Genet would excite violence against the institutions or officers of the United States government. For Jay, the Citizen Genet Affair went from bad to worse at each of its stages and only resolved by the fortuity that other circumstances, well beyond Jay's control, conspired to make the private common law prosecution of him fall by the wayside. Had the case been actually prosecuted, Jay might well have prevailed because the truth of the Jay-King allegations would have provided a legal defense to the alleged defamation, and there may have been enough credible evidence for Jay and King to establish that defense. Alexander Dallas would have been a key witness at any such trial, and apparently his testimony could have been harmful to Jay's and King's defense. Had the case been actually prosecuted, regardless of its outcome, it would not have helped Jay's political reputation or career.[33] Nor would it have enhanced the legitimacy of the US Supreme Court.

JAY'S DAYS

Secretary of War Henry Knox left the Washington administration on December 31, 1794. He tended to various business interests for the next twelve years. On

October 22, 1806, a chicken bone lodged in his throat and became infected. Knox died three days later at the age of fifty-six.[34]

Senator Rufus King went on to further distinction, being the last Federalist to run for the presidency of the United States, which occurred in 1816. He lost the election to Democratic-Republican James Monroe. King continued as New York's US senator until 1825, making him the last Federalist from New York to serve in the Senate. In late 1825 and the first half of 1826, King served as the US minister to Great Britain on behalf of the administration of President John Quincy Adams. He died on April 29, 1827, at the age of seventy-two. He left behind a personal library of 2,200 titles in 3,500 volumes, which is currently maintained by the New York Historical Society.[35]

Alexander Dallas, to whom Minister Genet allegedly made his controversial statement about appealing over President Washington's head to the American people, and who had also worked as the official court reporter at the US Supreme Court, enjoyed a distinguished career as an attorney and public servant. His work editing and publishing court decisions in legal journals in the nation's capital city gave him invaluable visibility and contacts in Philadelphia's elite political and legal circles that enhanced his career. The capstone of his career was his appointment as secretary of the treasury by President Madison in 1814.[36]

Edmond-Charles Genet lived out a comfortable life in the United States. He moved to New York and married Cornelia Clinton, the daughter of New York State Governor George Clinton, on November 6, 1794. The happy couple purchased a 325-acre farm in Jamaica, New York, which they acquired from DeWitt Clinton using Cornelia's dowery and Genet's personal savings. The property was named "Cornelia's Farm." Eight years later, they moved to an even larger estate in East Greenbush overlooking the scenic Hudson River, three miles south of Albany, which they named "Prospect Hill." In 1804, Genet became an American citizen. Ironically, Genet died on France's Independence Day, July 14, 1834, at the age of seventy-one.[37]

Chapter 11

Jay Court Decisions of Lesser Note

Kingsley v Jenkins (1793), Ex Parte *Martin* (1793), and *U.S. v Hopkins* (1794)

> "During the late Vacation Mr. Martin presented me a writ of Error to be allowed. I refused to allow it . . . and for Reasons too obvious to you, to require being mentioned."
>
> —Letter of John Jay to William Cushing
> August 6, 1793

So far this narrative has highlighted the cases decided by the Jay Court that were of significance to major issues and challenges facing the United States in its earliest years as a new nation. There were, however, three other cases where Chief Judge Jay played a role in 1793 and 1794, where the facts and legal principles at issue, while interesting, are not of as much historical consequence. None of these cases was reported in Alexander Dallas's volumes. This chapter provides a brief chronological summary of those cases to complete the narrative of Jay's tenure as chief justice of the Supreme Court.

Kingsley v Jenkins (February 1793)

Ebenezer Kingsley was a wealthy merchant who lived in Hudson, in Columbia County, New York. In 1788 he loaned securities with a face value of $12,432.67 to two merchants and a tavern keeper in Berkshire County, Massachusetts, named Thomas Jenkins, Silas Pepoon, and Anna Bingham. At the time of the loan, the securities were only worth $2,535.81, as their value had decreased from their face value. The securities were to be returned to Kingsley after one year, but the parties agreed on a forbearance for an additional year. The loan recipients likely intended to sell the securities, reinvest the proceeds in better securities, and then return the principal while retaining whatever profits they derived. Unfortunately for Jenkins, Pepoon, and Bingham, their speculation was not successful, and they defaulted in their repayment obligation to Kingsley. During the second year of the extended loan, Kingsley obtained an agreement from Massachusetts Congressman Theodore Sedgwick to guarantee repayment of the loan. When the loan defaulted, Kingsley sought to enforce the guarantee against Sedgwick, but Sedgwick refused to pay what he allegedly owed.[1]

Kingsley therefore commenced two lawsuits. The first was in the Circuit Court in Massachusetts against Theodore Sedgwick to enforce the agreed-on guarantee. In October 1792, a jury rendered a verdict in favor of Sedgwick, and although Kingsley filed a writ of error to appeal to the US Supreme Court, he never followed through with an actual appeal.[2]

The second suit in the Circuit Court was against Jenkins, Pepoon, and Bingham for their alleged breach of the contract. Pepoon and Bingham were arrested and required to post bail, and Jenkins, though never arrested, posted some security as well. A non-jury trial was conducted upon stipulated facts on May 12, 1792, before Chief Judge Jay and Justice William Cushing, who were riding the Eastern Circuit, and Judge John Lowell of the District of Massachusetts. The plaintiff, Kingsley, sought an award of the amount of the loan minus two $100 payments that had been made and minus the $40 value of a yoke of oxen made in exchange for the one-year loan extension. The defendants raised a legal defense that the terms of the loan violated a 1784 Massachusetts law prohibiting a creditor from charging more than 6 percent interest per year on loans. Under that law, the creditor of any usurious loan forfeited repayment of the entire principal and any expectation of interest. The defendants argued that based on the value of the posted securities in July 1788, the $200 payments of money and the $40 value of the oxen represented 8.5 percent interest, and based on the value of the securities in 1789, the same payments equaled approximately 8 percent. However, in 1790, the value of the securities increased, so that, like a seesaw, the

$240 payments of money and oxen represented only approximately 5 percent of the total. The parties likely argued about whether, under the Massachusetts usury law, the interest percentage should be calculated against the value of the loan at the time of its origination, the value at the time repayment was ultimately due, or, given the one-year extension that was given here, the value at some point of time in between.[3]

On May 19, 1792, the Circuit Court rendered a judgment against Kingsley, presumably on the ground of usury. The court's conclusion was mathematically correct if calculated against either the 1788 or 1789 security values. However, as between the three defendants, the Circuit Court ordered that Pepoon and Bingham pay Jenkins $5,393.66 plus $31.16 for court costs. Kingsley, Pepoon, and Bingham filed an appeal at the Supreme Court arguing two points, one being that the Circuit Court erred as a matter of law, and the second being that even if the Circuit Court decided legal matters correctly, it miscalculated the judgment by awarding $2,500 more than what should have been awarded. Kingsley passed away during the latter part of 1792, but his portion of the appeal was still prosecuted in his name.[4]

The Supreme Court heard argument on the appeal on February 9, 11, 13, 14, and 15, 1793. Five justices were present—Jay, Cushing, Wilson, Blair, and Iredell—meaning that two of the five justices had already ruled against the appealing parties at the original trial. Mathematically, the appealing parties need to convince Wilson, Blair, and Iredell to obtain a majority in their favor or convince Jay and/or Cushing that they had erred at the Circuit Court. Jared Ingersoll and Edmund Randolph represented the appealing parties, and William Lewis and Edward Tilghman represented Jenkins. On February 19, 1793, the justices ruled 5–0 in favor of Jenkins and upheld the Circuit Court's award.[5]

JAY'S DAYS

Further lawsuits were initiated between the parties in connection with Jenkins's efforts to collect on his $5,393.66 judgment and Pepoon's and Bingham's efforts to resist paying it. Jenkins won his suit in the Circuit Court for a "writ of execution" in February 1794, and Pepoon and Bingham lost their suit in equity for a ruling that their obligation to pay the judgment be perpetually postponed. Jenkins also filed a lawsuit against the sureties of Pepoon and Bingham to collect on the bail bond they had earlier filed to avoid incarceration. Jenkins lost his case against the sureties. Pepoon and Bingham appealed the loss of their *equitable case to the US Supreme Court, which decided on August 15, 1798, during its February 1798 Term, to affirm the dismissal of the Circuit Court. The bench at that time consisted of Justices Cushing, Iredell, Paterson, and Chase, as by then, John Jay had left the judiciary. It is not known whether Jenkins ever succeeded in collecting on his judgment.*[6]

Ex Parte *Martin* (August 1793)

James Martin was born in Boston to William and Ann Martin. Ann Martin had inherited a significant amount of land in Massachusetts. During the Revolutionary War, her husband, William, was a Loyalist who served as a colonel on behalf of the British Army. In April 1779, the Commonwealth of Massachusetts enacted a statute authorizing it to confiscate the property of Loyalist "absentees." On October 2, 1781, Massachusetts' Inferior Court of Common Pleas rendered a judgment finding that William and Ann Martin had waged war and conspired to wage war against the Commonwealth and then fled the state. On that basis, the court concluded that William and Ann Martin had renounced their Massachusetts citizenship and become aliens, by which Ann's land was confiscated. The court's judgment did not name or include the Martins' son, James.[7]

James Martin had studied law and in 1773 was admitted to the bar of the Court of Common Pleas in Suffolk County, Massachusetts. He lived and worked in the British West Indies during the Revolutionary War but returned to Massachusetts in 1791. At that time, James Martin sought the return of his mother's property that had been confiscated earlier, claiming that because he was born in Boston, he was a citizen of the Commonwealth entitled to bring a legal case seeking the ownership of the land by natural inheritance. Massachusetts opposed Martin's case on the ground that because both of his parents had been declared non-citizen aliens, James, as their son, was an alien with no right to commence lawsuits or own property notwithstanding the city of his birth. Martin's claims would rise or fall on the question of whether he was a citizen of Massachusetts or an alien with no rights in the controversy.[8]

To prosecute his case, Martin sought to be admitted as an attorney to the bar of the Supreme Judicial Court of Massachusetts, where his lawsuit was brought. At the time, Massachusetts required that its admitted attorneys needed to be citizens of the Commonwealth or of another state. To obtain his attorney admission, Martin argued that he had been born in Boston, was admitted to the bar of the Court of Common Pleas, and had practiced law in the British West Indies for more than the number of years required for eligibility to practice law in the Supreme Judicial Court of Massachusetts. Martin might have been quite clever in seeking admission to the bar, because if his application were to be granted, the Supreme Judicial Court would have necessarily found that he was a "citizen" of Massachusetts, which in turn would enable him to seek the return of his mother's confiscated land.[9]

Unfortunately for Martin, the jurists of the Supreme Judicial Court saw through the tactic, as they decided that Martin could only be admitted to the bar if he became naturalized. Martin refused to be naturalized. Martin likely feared that if he were naturalized, he would be conceding that he was not a citizen of Massachusetts at the time his family's property was seized and therefore would not have an actual claim that naturalization could retroactively validate. Because Martin refused to be naturalized, the Supreme Judicial Court denied his application for admission to the bar. Martin returned to the Supreme Judicial Court of Massachusetts in February 1792 offering to take loyalty oaths to the Commonwealth and federal constitutions, but the court continued to insist that there be a full naturalization, which Martin refused to undertake.[10]

Aggrieved, James Martin appealed the denial of his attorney admission to the US Supreme Court. To prepare his writ of error, he needed a copy of the court's order denying him admission to the Supreme Judicial Court of Massachusetts. Martin claimed that when he tried to obtain a copy of court documents that he needed for the writ, the chief judge of the Supreme Judicial Court, Francis Dana, instructed the clerks to not provide a copy of the court's order and had Martin's written application for admission returned to him with his name erased. Without those documents, Martin's writ of error to appeal the matter to the US Supreme Court could not be properly completed and filed.[11]

Martin responded with another legal chess move. He applied for and was granted admission to the bar of the state of New York. He prepared a deposition, sworn under oath, setting forth the history of his admission procedure in Massachusetts including the alleged misconduct of Chief Judge Dana. The misconduct allegations against Dana were significant, as Dana had been a member of the Continental Congress in 1774, 1775, and 1784, and had represented the Congress as its minister to Russia from 1780 to 1783. Martin appeared at the US Supreme

Court on February 4, 1793, with a proposed writ of error, supported by his deposition. The Supreme Court, noting the scurrilous allegations against Massachusetts' Chief Judge Dana, refused to accept the filing unless those allegations were deleted. No deletions were made. Martin returned to the US Supreme Court five days later with an application seeking admission to the bar of the Supreme Court. The application was supported by evidence of Martin's citizenship of the state of New York, his admission to the practice of law in New York, his years of legal practice in the British West Indies, and various letters attesting to his character and fitness to practice law. The application was yet another effort by Martin to obtain an attorney admission that might implicitly acknowledge his citizenship in a state.[12]

Martin's latest attorney admission application could have been easily and properly denied. The rules of the US Supreme Court contained no citizenship requirement. Its rules instead required that an attorney be admitted to the practice of law in any state for at least three years and that the applicant be of good character. Because Martin had not been admitted to the practice of law in New York for the required three years, or in Massachusetts for that matter, his application for admission to the Supreme Court was defective on its face.[13]

It is not clear whether the Supreme Court missed the "three-year rule" as to Martin. After considering Martin's application for a few days, the court ultimately denied it. The Jay Court explained that if it admitted Martin as an attorney to its court, it would, in effect, be deciding the ultimate dispute between Martin and Massachusetts of whether he was a citizen or an alien and affect Martin's land claims in the Commonwealth. The Court would "not thus incidentally determine so important a question." On this point, the Supreme Court's analysis appears to be incorrect because the absence of a citizenship rule at the Supreme Court meant that Martin's admission, if granted, would have implied nothing about his citizenship status in Massachusetts.[14]

Undeterred, James Martin revived his proposed writ of error so that he could again try to appeal the denial of his admission as an attorney of the Supreme Judicial Court of Massachusetts. He removed the offending passages in his deposition about Chief Judge Dana, and this time his proposed writ of error was accepted by the clerk of the US Supreme Court for filing. Whether the writ would be granted, and whether the matter would be placed on the court's calendar for argument at its August

1793 Term, was referred to the chief justice, John Jay. Jay denied the writ without any recorded explanation, which killed Martin's latest effort to appeal. Jay's denial might be explained if the Supreme Court continued to be concerned that a decision on the Massachusetts appeal would inappropriately short-circuit the merits of Martin's citizenship issue with the Commonwealth. Or it could be explained by Martin's noncompliance with the Supreme Court's three-year practice rule.[15]

When the Supreme Court convened for its August 1793 Term, Martin appeared yet again. He requested, and was granted, the opportunity to address all members of the bench who were present regarding the writ of error that had earlier been denied by John Jay. Justice William Cushing was absent for the argument. Once again, Martin's writ was denied, as was discussed by Jay in a letter to Justice Cushing dated August 6, 1793. Jay wrote: "During the late Vacation Mr. Martin presented me a writ of Error to be allowed—I refused to allow it . . . and for Reasons too obvious to you, to require being mentioned." Jay's conclusion would certainly be true if based on Martin's failure to satisfy the three-year rule, which was never expressly stated by anyone at the Supreme Court.[16]

James Martin's last option was to prosecute a common law criminal complaint in Massachusetts against Chief Judge Dana for tampering with his court file. In correspondence dated February 17, 1794, Dana referred to Martin's complaint as "false & scandalous as well as indecent." Martin's case against Dana went nowhere, as the Grand Jury that reviewed the matter decided that if Dana tampered with any court records, the remedy was not a criminal charge, but impeachment from public office by the legislature. No impeachment proceedings were initiated, though with James Martin's tenacity well evidenced, it may be assumed that he approached Massachusetts legislators about the prospect.[17]

JAY'S DAYS

In 1801, James Martin ultimately prevailed in convincing the Supreme Judicial Court of Massachusetts that the confiscation of his mother's property was wrongful. The Court concluded by a 4–1 vote that because the property at issue was titled to Ann Martin only, and not to her husband, William, William Martin's Loyalist hostilities toward the Commonwealth of Massachusetts could not be applied against her. Married women at the time were not deemed to possess any will of their own but instead were presumed to act under the will of their husbands. Because Ann's property should not have been confiscated by Massachusetts in the first instance, her son, James, became entitled to it by inheritance regardless of his citizenship status in Massachusetts. Thus, James Martin's various applications to be admitted as an attorney in Massachusetts and at the US Supreme Court proved in the end to be irrelevant to the ultimate legal question on which he prevailed. Chief Judge Dana was among the four jurists at the Supreme Judicial Court of Massachusetts who ruled in Martin's favor on the merits of his claim.[18]

United States v Hopkins (February 1794)

There was a reason that President Washington made Alexander Hamilton his secretary of the treasury. Hamilton was an innovative, bold, and activist leader of the Federalist movement. An example of Hamilton's boldness is the Funding Act of 1790.[19]

The concept behind the Funding Act of 1790 was to refinance the national debt by obtaining a new loan that would satisfy all of the old outstanding loans. The refinancing included the assumption of war debts that were still unpaid by the states. Certain tax receipts were specifically earmarked to service the principal and interest of the new omnibus debt. The debt instruments of the federal and state governments, which had depreciated in value over time, were exchanged for new secured instruments. State instruments qualified for the federal government's debt reorganization if they were issued before January 1, 1790, and they needed to be "subscribed" to the national debt either at the Treasury Department or through a federal loan officer assigned to each state. It was unclear whether state debt that had already been satisfied or otherwise retired could be subscribed to the federal loan. Rhode Island, Virginia, North Carolina, South Carolina, and Georgia attempted to do so, but Hamilton did not allow it based on his interpretation of the relevant language in the Funding Act. Hamilton and Attorney General Edmund Randolph both reasoned that once a debt certificate was satisfied, the debt no longer existed and therefore could not be assumed by the federal government.[20]

Virginia sought to get around Hamilton and Randolph's interpretation of the Funding Act by passing legislation in December 1792 that allowed holders of its state debt certificates issued after January 1, 1790, to swap those certificates for satisfied certificates issued in Virginia before January 1, 1790, so that the new debts would look like old debts and become eligible for subscription to the federal government.

The federal loan officer in Virginia was John Hopkins. He sought to review Virginia's records to identify which debt certificates issued before January 1, 1790, actually represented new debt. Virginia refused Hopkins access to its debt records. Hopkins responded by refusing to swap any further Virginia debt certificates for federal certificates. Hamilton and Virginia Governor Henry Lee believed the impasse could be resolved if the dispute could be reviewed by the US Supreme Court. The two sides contrived a case, enlisting a Richmond securities broker named Richard Smyth to offer to subscribe $23,454.76 of qualifying debt securities to the federal government, which Hopkins refused, and the interactions between Smyth and Hopkins were documented to create a record for the court. Procedurally, the case was brought to the Supreme Court as a writ of *mandamus*, where Smyth sought from the court an order that Hopkins be required to accept Smyth's debt certificates as part of his ministerial duties.[21]

The matter was heard at the Supreme Court during the February 1794 Term. Edward Tilghman represented Smyth, and the new attorney general, William Bradford, appeared on behalf of the federal government. Oral argument on the *mandamus* was presented to the justices on February 13, 1794. There does not appear to be any record of the arguments themselves. However, Smyth, as the petitioning party, bore the burden of establishing his entitlement to the relief he requested, and in matters of *mandamus*, that entitlement needed to be clear in order for him to prevail.[22]

The Jay Court rendered its decision on February 14, 1794. It rejected Smyth's arguments. According to the Minutes of the Supreme Court, the justices reasoned that the right Smyth sought to enforce under the Funding Act "does not appear sufficiently clear to authorise the Court to issue the Mandamus moved for." In other words, Smyth failed to meet his burden of proof, as Hopkins's refusal to ministerially accept the Virginia debt certificates was not clearly unauthorized under the circumstances of the case. The justices of the court did not appear from the Minutes to have wholeheartedly endorsed the view earlier expressed by Alexander Hamilton that once Virginia debts are satisfied, they could not be exchanged for newer debt to then be swapped for federal securities.

However, Hamilton's view of the issue was the better argument, and the Supreme Court's denial of *mandamus* appears to have been the correct result under the facts and the controlling federal statute.[23]

JAY'S DAYS

The Funding Act of 1790, as related to the case of United States v Hopkins, *relieved the states of significant debt, which in turn allowed them to lower taxes on their citizens. Yet federal taxes were raised to finance the federal government's wraparound obligations. In the end, the seesaw in state and federal tax receipts balanced out.*

Chapter 12

A Final Mission While Chief Justice

> "Damn John Jay! Damn every one that won't damn John Jay! Damn every one that won't put lights in his windows and sit up all night damning John Jay."
>
> —A critic of the Jay Treaty in Boston
> July 1795

No book on John Jay, even one such as this focused on Jay's tenure at the US Supreme Court, would be complete without some acknowledgment of his role in negotiating the Jay Treaty in 1794–1795. It was his final mission on behalf of the federal government, undertaken while he still held the title of chief justice.

War between the various European powers during the last half of the 1700s was more of a norm, not an exception. No nation was more dominant on the high seas than Great Britain, which used its sea power to its advantage wherever, and however, possible. The British and French each had significant commercial trade relationships at various points on the globe. France formally declared war on both Great Britain and the Netherlands on February 1, 1793, and on Spain six days after that. As already seen, the Washington administration dealt with the European conflict by formulating and implementing a policy of neutrality. The United States claimed that, by virtue of its policy of neutrality, American ships could trade noncontraband goods to and from the ports of any of the belligerents. There was significant mercantile trade between the United States and the British West Indies, which continued unmolested during much of 1793. However, in December 1793, British vessels, without warning, began seizing American ships trading in the West Indies, which put the two countries on a path to war. American ship crews were imprisoned or abandoned, and valuable cargos were confiscated. Making matters worse, word reached Congress in February 1794 that the governor-general of Canada, Lord Dorchester, had exhorted Native American Indian bands in Ohio to engage in hostilities against the Americans in the expectation that, with British help, the Native Americans would be able to set their own boundaries with the United States. And the British continued holding western outposts in violation of the Treaty of Paris, which guaranteed its continued control of the fur trade with the Native Americans.[1]

Anti-British sentiment swept through the various states, which included mobs mistreating British sailors, the tarring and feathering of pro-British Americans, the creation of volunteer defense companies, and calls for war. Trade with Britain was the major source of revenue for the federal government. The commercial class, which had influence with the federal government, sought to avoid war at almost all cost. Cooler heads prevailed on the governmental levels, with the British and the United States agreeing that it would be worthwhile to attempt negotiating peace before either side fired the first shots.[2]

Washington considered the appointment of four possible negotiators—Vice President Adams, Treasury Secretary Hamilton, Secretary of State Jefferson, and Chief Justice Jay. Jay happened to be in Philadelphia the same month hearing circuit court cases in Philadelphia. Adams was not particularly adept at the art of diplomacy, and Jefferson was not entirely trustworthy because of his Francophilia. Opposition arose to Hamilton among some of the US senators involved in the discussions. Hamilton wrote to Washington on April 14, 1794, recommending John Jay as "the only man in whose qualifications for success there would be a thorough confidence, and him whom alone it would be advisable to send."[3]

Persuaded, Washington arranged for a meeting with Jay on April 15, 1794, where the president asked Jay to accept the mission. Jay responded by requesting a little time to consider it. Later that same day, by obvious coordination, Jay was personally lobbied by Hamilton and Senators Rufus King, George Cabot, Caleb Strong, and Oliver Ellsworth to accept the assignment.[4]

Jay was torn between his strong personal preference not to go to Britain and his sense of duty to the country to help prevent a potentially avoidable war. He wrote Sarah on April 15, 1794, that "I find myself in a dilemma between personal considerations and public ones. Nothing can be much more distant from every wish on my own account. I feel the impulse of duty strongly." He added, looking at the bigger picture, that "If it should please God to make me instrumental to the continuance of peace and in preventing the Effusion of Blood and other Evils and Miseries incident to War we shall both have Reason to rejoice." Four days later, Jay again wrote to Sarah that "no appointment ever operated more unpleasantly upon me: but the public considerations which were urged and the manner in which it was pressed, strongly impressed me with a conviction that to refuse it would be to desert my Duty for the Sake of my Ease and domestic concerns & comforts."[5]

Sarah responded on April 22, 1794, "Your superiority in fortitude as well as every other virtue I am aware of, yet I know too well your tenderness for your family to doubt the pangs of separation—Your own conflicts are sufficient: they need not be augmented by the addition of mine." She added in the same letter that the children "were exceedingly affected when they received the tidings—& intreated [sic] me to endeavor to dissuade you from accepting an Appointment that subject us to so painful a separation." But nowhere in the letter did Sarah actually ask her husband not to make the trip.[6]

There were other complications. Any trip abroad to negotiate a treaty would take at least several months. If Jay harbored any ambitions of running for the New York State governorship in the election scheduled for April 1795, which was considered a possibility for him, the trip abroad could interfere with those plans and with serving in the office if elected. The success or failure of the mission could impact Jay as a potential candidate for the presidency in 1796 were George Washington to retire after two terms in office.

There was an additional question of a constitutional nature, of whether a justice of the Supreme Court could permissibly and simultaneously act as the nation's envoy to negotiate a treaty with another nation abroad. The Constitution prohibited members of Congress from accepting dual federal appointments but did not have similar language as to federal judges. This question was resolved by simply ignoring it. For several months in 1789 and 1790, Jay had served simultaneously as both chief justice and secretary of state until the confirmation of Thomas Jefferson on March 22, 1790, and the current circumstances were similar in nature.[7]

The US Senate, which needed to confirm the envoy appointment, broke along partisan lines but confirmed Jay's appointment by a vote of 18 to 8. With that confirmation, Washington had an appointee with significant diplomatic experience, the gravitas unique to that of a chief justice of the United States, and the confidence of the country.[8]

These events led to the hopeful morning at the Manhattan waterfront when Jay, while retaining his title of chief justice, bid farewell to cheering crowds and celebratory cannon fire and set sail on May 12, 1794, aboard the *Ohio* for his twenty-six-day voyage to the British Isles. It must have been a heady day. Jay likely dreaded the seasickness he knew he would experience as a result of his earlier trans-Atlantic voyages to Europe and back. One consolation was that he had the confidence and goodwill of a nation behind him, bolstered by the cheers of the crowd that formed at the waterfront to see him off on his voyage. Indeed, based on what was known then, a successful mission might conceivably springboard Jay from the Supreme Court to the US presidency at the conclusion of George Washington's second term. As written by John Adams, who eyed the presidency for himself, if Jay's peace mission to Britain proved successful, it would "recommend him to the choice of the people for president as soon as a vacancy shall happen."[9]

Jay's instructions bound him to two non-negotiable conditions. The first was that he could agree to nothing that conflicted with American treaty commitments to France. The second was that he could not agree to any commercial treaty with Britain that did not guarantee American shipping free and unfettered access to the British West Indies. Jay also was given suggestions and recommendations on many related issues. John Trumbull, the famous painter, was chosen to be the mission's secretary, and Jay's son, Peter Augustus, was chosen to be Jay's private secretary. The trip to Britain therefore flipped the family members who had accompanied Jay to Spain years before; Sarah, who had accompanied her husband then, remained at home, while Peter Augustus, who did not go to Spain, went to Britain with his father.[10]

One item of leverage that Jay might have wielded over the British was the possibility that absent a peace treaty, the United States could join an armed-neutrality agreement already in existence between Sweden and Denmark, with its possible expansion to include the Baltic powers and Russia. Shortly after Jay's departure for Europe, the Washington administration received a formal invitation from Sweden and Denmark to join their alliance of neutrals. While Secretary of State Edmund Randolph favored acceptance of the invitation in the belief that it would strengthen Jay's hand abroad, Alexander Hamilton opposed doing so for fear that it would antagonize the British and jeopardize Jay's mission. Unfortunately for Jay, Hamilton not only succeeded in persuading President Washington against joining the alliance of neutrals, but also informed the British minister in the United States, George Hammond, of Washington's decision. As a result, whatever leverage Jay thought he might have had in his negotiations with the British, he did not have, and it gave the British foreign minister, Lord Grenville, little incentive to compromise during the negotiations that followed his receipt of that news.[11]

Negotiations ran from June 23 to November 19, 1794. From the American point of view, the final product was very disappointing. The official title of the document was the "Treaty of Amity, Commerce, and Navigation, Between His Britannick Majesty; and the United States of America, by Their President, with the advice and consent of Their Senate." In the United States, it was more simply called the Jay Treaty. Overall, it was much closer to what the British initially envisioned than what the Americans had hoped for. On the surface, Jay managed to largely maintain the two non-negotiable requirements of his mission regarding the sanctity of treaty commitments with France and "access" to West Indian ports. However, the guarantee of American access to West Indian ports was illusory, as the treaty also provided that American merchants were prohibited from carrying molasses, sugar, coffee, cocoa, or cotton in their own vessels from British-controlled islands or from the United States to any other part of the world. There was limited practicality to having "access" to West Indian ports if American merchants were unable to trade their most common staples.[12]

Most broadly, the Jay Treaty established in Article 1 a peace between the United States and Great Britain. In Article 2, Britain agreed to withdraw all troops from its garrisons in the western states by June 1, 1796. In Article 3, both parties acknowledged their reciprocal rights to the free navigation of American waterways including on the Mississippi River and agreed to maintain equal trade tariffs on each other's commerce. In Articles 4 and 5, the parties agreed on further negotiation about disputed boundaries, a tool that Jay had observed earlier in life as clerk to the Boundary Commission that resolved border disputes between New York and New Jersey. In Articles 6 through 8, the United States agreed to guarantee the payment of debts owed to British creditors that could not be collected because of legal impediments imposed by the states, and restitution for captured or condemned British properties to be determined by members of a board of commissioners. Articles 12 through 18 defined much of the parties' free trade agreement including the restrictions on American trading of molasses, sugar, coffee, cocoa, and cotton, and the right of Great Britain to seize enemies' defined property. Article 12 limited the size of cargo on American ships bound for the West Indies to a maximum of seventy tons, though ships of that size or less were too small to safely cross the Atlantic Ocean. Articles 24 and 25 arguably conflicted with the US-French Treaty of Amity and Commerce in that it allowed privateers commissioned by either party to use the other's ports and prohibited belligerent nations from using each other's ports for arming privateer vessels or selling commandeered goods there. On the positive side of the ledger for the Americans, the Jay Treaty did not make the federal government responsible for interest on any debts that it guaranteed, it did not change the nation's northwest boundary, and it did not provide British merchants with a free-trade entrance to the American west through Canada. In letters to Washington, Hamilton, Randolph, Ellsworth, and King, Jay explained that he did not believe further concessions from Britain were possible, and that, overall, the treaty would be beneficial to the United States.[13]

Jay remained in Britain an extra six months to avoid traveling on the Atlantic Ocean during the turbulent winter months, endured further seasickness during the trip home in the spring, and arrived in New York Harbor aboard the *Severn* on May 28, 1795. Jay was greeted by a multitude of people who cheered and escorted him to his house. There was celebratory gunfire at the Battery and on Governors Island, and church bells were rung throughout the city.[14]

A copy of the treaty reached the United States before Jay did. Politically, the Federalists "owned" the treaty. President Washington could not have been very pleased with it. The treaty reached the president in Philadelphia on March 6, 1795, three days after an adjournment of the Senate, and Washington kept the terms of it confidential until the Senate reconvened on June 8 to consider it. Even then, the terms were not made publicly available. The effort to keep the terms of the treaty confidential was a telling indication that the Washington administration and Congress instinctively knew that it would not be well received by the populace.[15]

Senate debate about the treaty was partisan and bitter. On June 24, 1795, the Jay Treaty was ratified by the Senate by a party-line vote of 20 to 10, the minimum number necessary to meet the required two-thirds threshold for treaties. The ratification was a qualified one, as it did not include Article 12, which limited the products that could be traded with the British West Indies and the size of American trading ships. The Senate also required that none of its members disclose the terms of the treaty to the public, which is further proof that the legislators knew that it would not be popular.[16]

The secrecy surrounding the terms of the Jay Treaty did not last long. Excerpts "leaked" to the Philadelphia *Aurora General Advertiser*, an Anti-Federalist newspaper published six days a week by Benjamin Franklin's grandson, Benjamin Franklin Bache. The excerpts were published on June 29, 1795, and three days later, a full version was published by the same newspaper.[17]

The disclosure played into the hands of both the Democratic-Republicans and the French, as the national public's reaction to the US-British treaty was one of incredulity and anger. Details of the Jay Treaty provoked a nearly yearlong public controversy of an intensity rarely matched in American history. Had the terms of the treaty been disclosed to the public before the Senate's debate, its ratification might not have been possible. For many days in July there were heated public meetings, mobs, protests, speeches, condemnations, the burning of effigies of John Jay, the lowering of flags to half-mast, the burning of the British Union Jack, newspaper editorials excoriating Jay and the treaty, and some violence. In Philadelphia, Jay's effigy was pilloried, guillotined, burned, and then blown up. The trading restrictions set forth in Article 12 of the treaty were deemed particularly insulting and galling. The public's wrath was directed at the Federalists generally and at John Jay specifically. A poem circulated that began, "The British brib'd that scoundrel Jay, To pass his country's rights away." A critic in Boston wrote, "Damn John Jay! Damn every one that won't damn John Jay! Damn every one that won't put lights in his windows and sit up all night damning John Jay!" Had there been a modern-day public opinion poll at the time, John Jay's favorability ratings likely would have not fared well.[18]

On July 18, 1795, an angry crowd confronted Alexander Hamilton in lower Manhattan, when he was hit by one of many rocks thrown his way, and the injury drew blood. On another occasion, a mob marched with the American and French flags to Jay's residence in Manhattan, where they then burned a copy of the treaty. Newspapers sympathetic to France and the Democratic-Republicans excoriated Jay and the Federalist Senate. Thomas Jefferson, emerging as the undisputed leader of the Democratic-Republicans, denounced the Jay Treaty in no uncertain terms. He described it as "a monument of folly or venality . . . universally execrated." A society in South Carolina passed a resolution that every constitutional means be used to bring John Jay to trial and justice and that he

> "not escape, if guilty, that punishment which will at once wipe off the temporary stain laid upon us, and be a warning to TRAITORS hereafter how they sport with the interests and feelings of their fellow citizens. He was instructed, or he was not: If he was, we will drop the curtain; if not, and he acted of and from himself, we shall lament the want of a GUILLOTINE."[19]

In Congress, Democratic-Republicans launched a concerted and sustained public attack on the Jay Treaty, even urging that the House of Representatives, which it controlled, not appropriate the funds necessary to implement the treaty's terms. Public opinion swung away from the Federalists for having "sold out" American interests. Public opinion, which favored the French over the British as a result of the Revolutionary War, became even more pro-French and anti-British because of the treaty.[20]

Jay is said to have quipped that because of the unpopularity of the treaty, he could travel at night from Boston to Philadelphia guided solely by the light of his burning effigies.[21]

In the face of broad public opposition, President Washington faced the difficult decision of whether to sign the treaty ratified by the Senate. He expressed his view in a letter to Edmund Randolph on July 22, 1795, that "[m]y opinion respecting the treaty is the same now that it was, namely, not favorable to it, but that it is better to ratifie [sic] it in the manner the Senate have advised (& with the reservation already mentioned) than to suffer matters to remain as they are, unsettled." Washington signed the Jay Treaty on August 14, 1795, subject to the excision of Article 12. Great Britain signed the treaty on October 28, 1795, and its provisions other than those of Article 12 became effective on February 29, 1796.[22]

Figure 12.1. Drawing of John Jay hanged in effigy.

Washington's signature on the treaty had a calming effect on the nation, but not entirely. With time, public opinion toward the treaty moderated. War with Great Britain was averted at a time when the United States had no credible army, no navy, and no defense against British troops stationed at the western forts. In April 1796, the Democratic-Republican controlled House of Representatives approved the funds necessary to implement the terms of the treaty. In more than two centuries that followed, historians have debated whether the Jay Treaty surrendered too much to the British while securing too little for the United States or whether a lopsided deal that averted another war, which the Americans likely would have lost, proved to be a fair bargain for the United States in the years that followed it.[23]

Jay was confident that the treaty would prove wise with time. He wrote in a letter to Henry Lee on July 11, 1795, that "[t]he treaty is as it is; and the time will certainly come when it will very universally receive exactly what degree of commendation or censure, which to candid and enlightened minds, it shall appear to deserve." Weeks later, he expressed a similar fatalistic sentiment to James Duane, that "[a]s to the treaty, it will speak for itself: it has been maliciously slandered, and very ably defended. But no calumny on the one hand, nor eloquence on the other, can make it worse or better than it is. At a future day it will generally be seen in its true colours, and in its proper point of view."[24]

Meanwhile, the Supreme Court heard five cases during its February 1795 Term while John Jay was still abroad negotiating the Jay Treaty. The February 1795 Term was a particularly active one for the court, as cases that had been long percolating became ripe for resolutions. The cases included *Oswald v State of New York*, *Penhallow v Doane's Administrators*, *Bingham v Cabot*, *Ex Parte Corbly, Lockery, Hamilton and Segwick*, and *United States v Laurance*.[25] While Jay was not in Philadelphia to hear those cases, they were decided while he still remained the nation's chief justice.

There is relevance between the Supreme Court cases decided during the February 1795 Term and Jay's absence from the court. Jay, as chief justice, had been a consensus builder among his judicial colleagues. Before he left for Britain, many of the cases decided by the Supreme Court were unanimous, and when they were not, there was never more than one dissenter. Jay's efforts as a consensus builder reflect his prior experiences as a diplomat handling delicate matters of foreign affairs and negotiation, such as those he displayed while negotiating the Treaty of Paris. Jay's talents at forging consensus among his judicial colleagues is particularly evidenced by his adept handling of the invalid pensioners issues of *Hayburn* and the prize court issues of *Sloop Betsey*. But once Jay left for Britain, decision-making at the Supreme Court became openly fractured in certain cases. A most striking example is *Bingham v Cabot*, a maritime prize dispute that presented multiple issues for the Supreme Court, where the judges split their votes 3–1 on the adequacy of an appellate record, 2–1 and "1 not ready to vote" on whether the case was eligible for a common law trial in Massachusetts, 3–"1 abstain" on the propriety of an important evidentiary ruling, and 2–2 on whether the appellant was entitled to a new trial to cure prior judicial errors. The various voting combinations among the justices varied from issue to issue. In other words, the justices, without John Jay's presence, were divided in ways never previously seen at the court.[26]

John Jay's return to the United States upon concluding the Jay Treaty marked the end of his tenure as chief justice of the Supreme Court. Jay resigned from the court effective June 29, 1795, and his juridical skills were lost to the court. Upon Jay's resignation, President Washington immediately named Justice John Rutledge chief justice by means of a Senate recess appointment. Rutledge was one of the Washington's original appointees to the Supreme Court, but had resigned from the court on March 4, 1791, to become chief justice of the South Carolina Court of Common Pleas and Sessions. The recess appointment meant that Rutledge would serve as chief justice subject to confirmation by the Senate when it next convened, which was not until December 1795. Rutledge made a major political mistake on July 16, 1795, by publicly criticizing the Jay Treaty. That criticism earned him Federalist enemies in the Senate, and when his confirmation as chief justice was voted on, he was not approved by a vote of 14 to 10.[27]

JAY'S DAYS

Lord Grenville, who negotiated the Jay Treaty for Great Britain as secretary of foreign affairs, became prime minister on February 11, 1806, but served in that capacity only until March 31, 1807, when he and his coalition of ministers were ousted from power. His most significant accomplishment as prime minister was the abolishment of the British slave trade in 1807.[28]

John Rutledge did not take well the US Senate's rejection of his nomination as chief justice. Distraught, he jumped off a wharf in Charleston in an effort to commit suicide. He was saved by two slaves but resigned from the Supreme Court within two days of the event, and his public career was over. While John Jay's tenure as chief justice spanned almost six years, Rutledge's tenure as chief justice was fewer than six months.[29]

Chapter 13

After the Supreme Court

> "We have both passed the usual Term of human life, or (as the lawyers say) our leases have expired, and we are holding over."
>
> —Letter of John Jay to Lindley Murray
> April 24, 1821

Jay's resignation from the Supreme Court as of June 29, 1795, was prompted by good reason. He had been elected governor of New York State in the election held in April 1795, shortly before his return home from Britain. The votes were still being counted when Jay sailed into New York Harbor. He was ultimately declared to be the winner over New York Chief Judge Robert Yates by 1,589 votes of 25,373 cast, roughly equal to a 53 percent to 47 percent margin. Jay's tally may have benefited from the fact that voters were aware he was overseas on the peoples' business, negotiating with the British to avoid another war. The job of governor paid $4,000 a year, and it had the benefit of eliminating for Jay year-round travels to and from Philadelphia and throughout the circuits. By then, the Jay family, which originally included Peter Augustus, born in New York; Maria, born in Madrid; and Ann, born in Paris, had grown to also include son William, born on June 16, 1789; and daughter Sarah Louisa, born on February 20, 1792. Jay accepted his election as governor out of deference to the interests of his family and out of loyalty to his many political friends who had successfully advanced his candidacy while he had been abroad.[1]

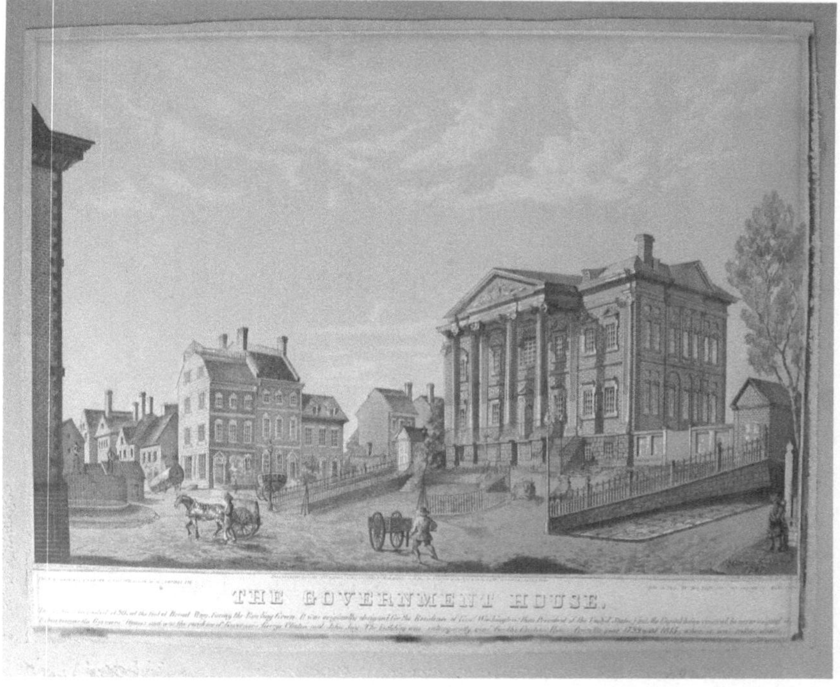

Figure 13.1. Government House.

Jay's election as governor might have also benefited from the voters' recollection that three years earlier, in the gubernatorial election between the Jay and then-incumbent governor George Clinton, Clinton had lost the statewide popular vote but nevertheless was declared the winner through procedural machinations that invalidated the votes of Otsego, Tioga, and Clinton Counties and took away Jay's numerical margin of victory. Jay had not actively campaigned for the governorship in 1792, as he was focused at that time on Supreme Court duties including the *Hayburn* pensioners case.

The 1792 gubernatorial campaign run against Jay was nasty. Clinton supporters and Clinton-friendly newspapers did their best to smear and besmirch Jay's accomplishments and reputation, and misrepresented his abolitionist views on slavery to white propertied voters. Jay never responded to the attacks against him. Clintonians sought to invalidate the votes that had been cast in Otsego, Tioga, and Clinton counties by contesting the hypertechnical manner in which those ballots were physically delivered to the secretary of state for inclusion in the statewide totals. There were many sound arguments as to why the contested ballots should have been counted, but a twelve-member canvas board controlled by Governor Clinton voted 7–4 to exclude them and then, contrary to custom, burned the ballots. With that, the statewide vote total flipped in favor of Clinton by 108 votes, and the theft of the election was completed. True to his character, Jay was equanimous about his electoral defeat and accepted it without apparent complaint, even though his election as governor would have ended his Supreme Court traveling and anchored him to his family in New York. Jay's wife, Sarah, was more disappointed than her husband with the loss of the 1792 election and made no secret of her angry feelings about the ultimate result. The 1792 election controversy caused deep and lasting divisions among New Yorkers, prompting incidents at that time of violence in Kingston, Albany, and New York City, and earned Governor Clinton the uncomplimentary nickname of "the Usurper." The controversy over the 1792 election likely left a bad taste in the mouths of voters sympathetic to John Jay that was still fresh in 1795. Jay's election as governor in 1795 represented vindication for what had been stolen from him in 1792.[2]

Jay acquitted himself well as New York's governor. During his first term in office, Jay dealt with two epidemics of yellow fever, the second of which killed one of every thirty residents of the city of New York. He initiated an official statewide day of Thanksgiving. Governor Jay, instead of purging Clintonians from state offices, removed no officials for political affiliation and filled vacancies on the basis of merit. He raised the deficient salaries of the state's judges; eliminated the death penalty for all offenses other than for treason, murder, and robbery of churches; oversaw the construction of New York's first statewide prison; fortified New York Harbor with an arsenal and weapons; and created the office of comptroller to better manage the state's finances. The capital was moved in 1797 to Albany, which remains its location today. Jay's time in office was successful and resulted in his nomination by the Federalists for reelection in 1798 for another three-year term.[3]

What made the election of 1798 unusual is that the Democratic-Republicans nominated for governor Robert R. Livingston Jr., who, by coincidence, had been John Jay's closest friend while in college and his law partner when the two men began their careers as attorneys. The friendship had already soured over issues of Jay's chief justiceship, Livingston's attacks on Jay during the 1792 campaign for governor, and the controversial terms of the Jay Treaty. Jay won the 1798 election by a wider margin than he had three years earlier, with 2,380 votes to spare, and won many legislative districts where successful candidates for other offices were Democratic-Republicans. The election represented a new high-water mark for the Federalist party in New York State. Livingston's loss to Jay in the election, which ended his longer-term aspirations for elective office, did nothing to repair the damaged relationship between them.[4]

Jay's second term as governor was groundbreaking, as he succeeded in signing into law important antislavery legislation. There were various factors in Jay's life that led him to abolitionism. One was his religiosity steeped, as it was, in the dignity of mankind as part of a divine and inclusive creation. A second was the example of his father, Peter Jay, who had treated his own slaves during John's childhood as part of his own family. In a March 1765 letter, Peter Jay identified his slaves by name and described their medical problems, and explained that because of "this

Figure 13.2. Robert R. Livingston Jr.

distressed condition of my family, I cannot be spared from home to visit my friends in town." As an adult, John Jay treated his own slaves as if they were family as well. A third factor behind Jay's views may have been his observation of the harsh slavery conditions at sugar plantations in Martinique during his voyage with Sarah to Spain. Fourth, Jay regretted that he had not been successful in obtaining an antislavery provision in the New York State Constitution that he drafted in 1777. Fifth, Jay had helped form the New York Manumission Society in 1785 and fulfilled the role of its first president. Sixth, Jay recognized the inconsistency of being opposed to slavery while at the same time being a slaveholder. He wrote of the hypocrisy of men fighting for freedom in the Revolutionary War while keeping others in slavery. Throughout his life, he freed his slaves after "their faithful services shall have afforded a reasonable retribution." Some of the slaves he freed remained with the family as employees for customary wages. And finally, Jay had numerous lifetime writings expressing his profound distaste for the institution of slavery. Jay's belief in the sovereignty of the people extended, in his view, to all people, calling slavery repugnant to the national concept that all men are created equal, endowed by their creator with inalienable rights such as life, liberty, and the pursuit of happiness. By the time Jay was in his second term as New York State's governor, he was finally positioned to make a meaningful and lasting impact on the issue.[5]

In 1799, Governor Jay signed into law groundbreaking legislation called An Act for the Gradual Abolition of Slavery, providing freedom to all children born to New York slaves after July 4, 1799. It was stunning for its time. The legislation did not free existing slaves, but abolished slavery gradually through time and attrition. Jay would have preferred to abolish slavery in New York outright, but he faced the political reality that to accomplish anything, he needed to forge a compromise between those who favored its abolition and those who did not, on disputed terms.[6]

Four attempts had been made with the state legislature to pass an antislavery bill from 1797 to 1799 before a fifth attempt proved successful. Each of the first four attempts was bogged down with differences between New York's Assembly and Senate over a host of collateral issues such as whether freed slaves could own property, vote in elections, hold public office, intermarry, or give testimony against whites in state courts. The bill that eventually passed freed males born after July 4, 1799, upon reaching age twenty-eight, and females at age twenty-five. Slaves born before July 4, 1799, remained so for life but were legally reclassified as indentured servants. The legislation was silent on all questions of legal and civil rights that had blocked the previous proposals, which was an unfortunate but necessary compromise for any bill to pass at all. Historically, the abolitionist legislation may be viewed as Jay's most significant accomplishment during his years as governor. Given how many years the legislation preceded the Civil War, Jay and the legislation receive insufficient historical recognition for the prescient and forward thinking they represented. The law set into motion a gradual ending of slavery within the state over a period of years, well ahead of Civil War and the ratification of the 13th Amendment to the federal constitution in 1865.[7]

Many of Jay's friends urged him to run for a third term as governor in the election that was to be held in 1801. Jay, despite the earlier controversy over the treaty that bore his name, was personally popular and trusted in New York and had proven himself as an effective state executive. But Jay refused to run. He explained to the committee members who solicited his nomination for a third term that "[t]he period has now nearly arrived, at which I have for many years intended to retire from the cares of public life, and for which I have for more than ten years preparing." He had inherited a farm in Bedford and steadfastly intended to retire there with Sarah at the end of his term in office in June 1801. Jay was determined to close the book on his life of public service.[8]

But there was one further last-ditch effort to keep John Jay from a comfortable retirement in Bedford. The effort came not from any New Yorkers, but from outgoing President John Adams.

Chief Justice Oliver Ellsworth announced his resignation from the US Supreme Court effective December 15, 1800, while the votes from the 1800 election were still being tabulated. Each passing day made Adams's defeat in the electoral college increasingly likely. Adams, with very little time left to his only presidential term, nominated John Jay for reappointment to his former position as chief justice, but he did so without consulting Jay in advance. Adams obtained quick confirmation of the nomination by the Senate. Adams wrote to Jay on December 19, 1800, that his appointment marked "to the public the spot where, in my opinion, the greatest mass worth remained collected in one individual," and provided Jay "a great opportunity to render a most signal service to your country."[9]

Jay was not pleased with the prospect of a Jefferson presidency. On some purely intellectual level, Jay might have been tempted to accept his renomination as chief justice. Jay had invested much time and energy in high government service both at home and abroad. A strong Federalist judiciary could act as a potential counterbalance to an incoming Jefferson administration. Jay never previously turned down a strong call for public service. But those who knew Jay, and of his determination to begin retirement, believed that Adams's nomination would be refused.[10]

Jay was in Albany when Adams's letter reached him. The language of the letter was compelling and persuasive, perhaps reflecting Adams's recognition of the need to "reel" Jay into the idea of returning to his former role at the Supreme Court. As predicted by family and friends in New York who had heard rumors of the nomination, Jay declined the offer. His first obligation was to his wife and family. In his responsive letter to President Adams written January 2, 1801, Jay declined on the ground that circuit riding was too burdensome on the justices and that prior efforts to relieve the Supreme Court justices of their onerous travels had proven unsuccessful or inadequate. Jay concluded that "the propriety of expediency of my returning to the bench under the present system [would] give countenance to the neglect and indifference with which the opinions and remonstrances of the judges on this important subject have been treated."[11]

Jay's letter declining the chief justice appointment took approximately a week to reach President Adams. It was handed to Adams by Secretary of State John Marshall on January 30, 1801. After reading the letter, Adams turned to Marshall and asked, "Who shall I nominate now?" According to Marshall's account of the conversation, he responded to the president that he did not know. Adams hesitated for a moment and then said, "I believe I must nominate you." Marshall was formally nominated as chief justice the following day and then promptly confirmed by the US Senate.[12]

Notable historians such as David McCullough suggest that Adams already had Marshall in mind to be the next chief justice. It nevertheless is equally plausible that Adams had been taken off guard by Jay's refusal to return to the high court. Indeed, given the limited number of weeks that Adams had left in office, he might not have wasted valuable time offering the chief justiceship to John Jay if he had truly expected Jay to turn it down. And, had President Adams so desired John Marshall to become chief justice, he could have nominated Marshall for the position in the first instance without involving John Jay at all. Marshall was only forty-five years old at the time, meaning that he could potentially serve as chief justice for many years into the future. In fact, John Marshall remained as the nation's chief justice for thirty-four years, dying in office on July 6, 1835. Marshall survived almost all of the early founders of the Republic as well as the Federalist Party, which disbanded in 1824.[13]

Chief Justice John Marshall made his mark on the US Supreme Court and is widely considered as among the greatest jurists to ever hold the office. The most notable decision rendered during his tenure is that of *Marbury v Madison*, which recognized in 1803 the all-important doctrine of judicial review by which the judicial branch of government determines the constitutionality of enacted legislation. Judicial review is the doctrine the Jay Court narrowly avoided in its handling of the *Hayburn* case in 1792. The doctrine became a crucial mechanism in the checks and balances among the three branches of the federal government. Relatedly, Marshall wrote for the court the landmark ruling in *Fletcher v Peck* in 1810, which was the first time the US Supreme Court held that a state statute was unconstitutional. Another notable opinion of Chief Justice Marshall, rendered near the end of his tenure at the Supreme Court, was the 1824 case of *Gibbons v Ogden*, which established federal supremacy in matters involving interstate commerce.[14]

Would American jurisprudence have developed differently if John Jay had accepted President Adams's reappointment as chief justice? Jay's record at the court reflected a cautious and reserved approach to judicial power, deferential and cooperative with the other branches of government when possible. The same cannot be said of Marshall. While the doctrine of judicial review in *Marbury v Madison* likely would have become the law of the land at some point in the development of American checks and balances, it might not have occurred as early as 1803 had Marshall not become chief justice. US presidents often seek to fill the federal judiciary with relatively young jurists when possible to extend the influence of a presidency well beyond its finite term. Marshall's tenure proves that point. But Marshall, a Federalist, would not have served on the US Supreme Court were it not for the threshold decision by John Jay to decline the reappointment as chief justice.

In any event, retirement awaited Jay after the conclusion of his second gubernatorial term. He could not retire to his family's home in Rye, as his brother Peter was residing there. There was a family-owned bucolic farmland in Bedford, New York, in the northeastern quadrant of Westchester County, which Jay had inherited and had leased to tenants. A 287-acre parcel of the property had originally been purchased by Jay's maternal grandfather, Jacobus Van Cortlandt, which Jay inherited in 1785. Two years later, Jay inherited an adjoining 316 acres from an aunt, rendering the combined total slightly more than 600 acres. Toward the end of Jay's final term as governor, he converted a modest farmhouse on the property into a three-story dwelling by employing contractors from various trades. The farm produced mainly wheat, butter, apples, and pears. Jay moved to the Bedford farm when his gubernatorial term expired in June 1801, and Sarah, who was ill and not able to travel from Albany, did not join him there until the early fall of 1801. Jay, now retired at the age of fifty-five after a distinguished career as a lawyer, judge, and public servant, finally ended his job-related travels to spend quality time as a gentleman farmer with his wife.[15]

It was not to be. Sarah was in poor health at the time of Jay's retirement. Her health declined precipitously during May 1802. She died on May 28, 1802, with her husband and family members at her bedside, after living at the Bedford farmhouse for little more than half of a year. She was only forty-five years old at the time of her death. Immediately

Figure 13.3. The John Jay Homestead in Katonah, New York.

upon Sarah's passing, Jay took the family to an adjoining room and read from chapter 15 of First Corinthians.[16]

John Jay would remain at the house as a widower for twenty-seven years after his wife's death, but was at all times surrounded by family to varying degrees. Jay's daughter, Ann, assumed the role of the female head of the household under the traditions of the time in the absence of her mother. Jay maintained daily routines that included morning prayers before breakfast involving family and the household help, and a Bible reading and evening prayers precisely at 9:00 p.m. He was an avid chess player. Jay and Ann were joined at the Bedford farm in 1812 by Jay's son William and his new wife, Augusta McVickar, who then filled the home with their five children. Jay's other children, Peter Augustus and Maria, visited from time to time from their homes, Peter Augustus from New York City and Maria from Albany. Jay's brother, Peter, died in 1813. Jay's youngest daughter, Sarah Louisa, who split most of her time between New York City and Albany, died after a brief illness in 1818, possibly from a ruptured appendix. William, an attorney, suffered from poor eyesight, which caused him to abandon the active practice of law in favor of managing the family farm in Bedford. William nevertheless served as a judge on New York's Court of Common Pleas from 1818 to 1820 and as a judge of the Westchester County Court from 1820 to 1842 at a time when Westchester maintained county courthouses at both White Plains and at Jay's home town of Bedford. William was a staunch abolitionist. He also authored a biography of his father, which was published in 1833.[17]

When once asked by a friend how Jay occupied his mind in retirement, he responded that "I have a long life to look back upon, and an eternity to look forward to."[18]

After Jay's death, his two surviving daughters, Ann, who never married, and Maria, who had become a widow, lived together in New York City and died within eight days of one another on November 13 and November 21, 1856, respectively. William was the longest-surviving child of John and Sarah Jay, living to the year 1858.[19]

What of Jay as a potential president of the United States? Did "retirement" from the New York governorship in 1801, and the death of Sarah Jay in 1802, provide Jay with the opportunity and incentive to consider the presidency? No justice of the US Supreme Court has ever become president of the United States. The opposite occurred once, when ex-President Howard Taft, who left the White House in 1913, was appointed chief justice of the US Supreme Court in 1921.

There does not appear to be any evidence in Jay's personal record that he ever possessed any desire for the presidency. Jay discouraged the opportunity to run for New York State's first governorship in 1777. When he agreed to seek the governorship in 1792, he felt that the office should seek the man, not the man seek the office, and for that reason, he never campaigned for election. There is no reason to believe that he had any different view of the presidency. Many of the public services Jay performed throughout his career were not actively sought by him but were instead endeavors that other persons had asked him to undertake. Jay's experience as an attorney, judge, diplomat, and governor of what soon became the nation's largest state might have made him an ideal candidate for the Federalists to run in a national election. Yet when his best opportunity to run for president arose upon President Washington's retirement in 1796, Governor Jay did not actively seek the office and received only five votes in the electoral college, all from the state of Connecticut. Jay significantly trailed Adams, Jefferson, Pinckney, Burr, and a small handful of other candidates in popular and electoral college support that year. The reason might be a confluence of factors—that other candidates actively sought support for the office, that Jay's role in negotiating the Jay Treaty still rendered him too radioactive to be a top-tier candidate for the presidency at that time, and that Jay simply did not aspire to the job. Moreover, Jay was distrusted by southern states from his days as secretary for foreign affairs under the Articles of Confederation, when he had unpopularly suggested that the states suspend navigation rights upon the Mississippi River to secure a treaty with Spain.[20]

By 1800, there was no point to Jay making a challenge for the presidency against fellow Federalist John Adams, whom Jay liked and respected over the years from their work together in both Philadelphia and Paris. In that election cycle, Jay received only one unsolicited vote in the electoral college, which was from Rhode Island. Four years later, in 1804, Jay was fully and happily retired, approaching sixty years of age, and the Federalist Party was in a rapid state of decline. Politics sometimes requires a merger of the man and the moment. Jay had the experience and talent to be a capable president, but the moment seems to have eluded both him and history.[21]

A defining event in John Jay's professional trajectory might have been his loss in the race for the New York State governorship in 1792. Had the Clintonians not stolen that election, Jay may not have been asked by President Washington to negotiate the Jay Treaty with Great Britain in 1794–95. Had Jay not negotiated the treaty with Great Britain, he, as a governor of New York, would have enjoyed a greater degree of national popularity by 1796 when the timing of a presidential draft would have been more in his favor.

John Jay's retirement was a true retirement. It is in stark contrast with that of Thomas Jefferson, who, post-presidency, founded the University of Virginia, advised successors, received a steady stream of visitors, and maintained ongoing correspondences. Jay made a minor exception for the American Bible Society that was formed in 1816, for which he served as vice president and then as president for seven years. He wrote to his son, Peter Augustus, "The Bible is the best of all Books, for it is the word of God, and teaches us the way to be happy in this world and in the next. Continue, therefore to read it, and regulate your life by its precepts." He and Peter Augustus joined the American Antiquarian Society on June 1, 1814. Jay joined a Sunday school society and a group called Educating Pious Youth for the Ministry.[22]

Jay's activities with the American Bible Society and the Sunday school society fit neatly into his inner religiosity. He made references to God, Divine Providence, and religion in many of his most important writings, including his Address to the People of Great Britain, jury charges as chief judge of New York and chief justice of the United States, Federalist Papers Nos. 2 and 5, his draft of the original New York State Constitution, his draft of a neutrality declaration for President Washington, his opinion in *Chisholm v Georgia*, his countless correspondences with friends and colleagues, and his creation of the first recognized day of Thanksgiving in the state of New York. The confidence and comfort that Jay took from his religious faith centered his public and private life before and during his retirement.

In retirement, Jay was distraught by the War of 1812 between the United States and Britain, as it effectively scuttled the Jay Treaty that he had so assiduously negotiated almost two decades earlier. The Jay Treaty forestalled a war between the United States and Great Britain, but did not ultimately succeed in preventing it altogether. The United States was in a better position to fight a war with Great Britain in 1812 than it would have been in the mid-1790s, and to that extent, the Jay Treaty served an important and useful national purpose. The Jay Treaty did not address the problem of British impressment of American marine merchants and sailors, which festered with time and greatly contributed to the war. Jay deliberately avoided any public comment about the War of 1812. Privately, in a letter dated July 28, 1812, he was of the view that the war was "neither necessary, nor expedient, nor seasonable," but because it had "been constitutionally declared," the citizenry was obligated to support it.[23]

Jay publicly broke his political silence during retirement on only one occasion, in the autumn of 1819. He wrote a letter that was widely published in newspapers regarding the possible admission of Missouri as a state of the union. In the letter, Jay wrote that slavery "not be introduced nor permitted in any of the new states [and that it be] abolished in all of them." The issue of Missouri's admission to the union was resolved by the infamous Missouri Compromise of 1820, which admitted Missouri as a slave state and Maine as a free state and divided the remaining territory of the Louisiana Purchase along the 36°30' latitude line.[24]

During retirement, Jay's decisions from the Supreme Court remained on the books as "good law" but for the *Chisholm* case from its nullification by the ratification of the 11th Amendment. Also during Jay's retirement, slavery in New York State was incrementally abolished under the legislation that he had signed into law in 1799.

Health was an issue for Jay during his retirement years. He was always lean of build and, in his later years, somewhat frail. At various times in his retirement, Jay suffered from piles, fever, influenza, inflammation of the eyes, acute rheumatism, bilious attacks, and an obstruction of the liver. He complained in a letter to John Adams in 1821 that he had not enjoyed a single day of good health for any of the previous nine years. All or most of Jay's various physical ailments likely could be cured or controlled by modern-day medical science. In 1825, he suffered a slight stroke. Family members managed his financial affairs later in life. In 1827, he received a severe hand injury while taking a piece of firewood off a stack for his fire. Jay was philosophical about his age and health, commiserating in an April 24, 1821, letter to Lindley Murray, his fellow clerk when they worked together for Benjamin Kissam, that "[w]e have both passed the usual Term of human life, or (as the lawyers say) our leases have expired, and we are holding over. To be thus circumstanced, is not very important to those who expect to remove from their present abodes to better habitations, and to enjoy them in Perpetuity."[25]

On the evening of May 14, 1829, Jay suffered what appears to have been a stroke, which prevented him from speaking but did not affect his mind. Jay died at his farmhouse at approximately noon on May 17, 1829, at the age of eighty-three. Perhaps fittingly, Jay passed away in the library located on the first floor of his home, surrounded by the

Figure 13.4. John Jay's desk at the Jay Homestead.

law books that had for so long served him well. Upon hearing word of John Jay's death, the New York State Supreme Court closed throughout the state as a sign of mourning, and by an order of Congress a bust of John Jay was placed where the US Supreme Court heard its cases. Jay's funeral in Bedford was not ostentatious, in accordance with his wishes. Indeed, he had directed that when the time came for his funeral, there be "No scarfs—no rings. Instead thereof, I give two hundred dollars to any one poor deserving widow or orphan of this town, whom my children shall select."[26]

Jay's remains are interred at the Jay Family cemetery in Rye, New York.[27]

Chapter 14

History's Verdict

> "I have long been convinced that human fame was a bubble which, whether swelled by the breath of the wise, the good, the ignorant, or malicious, must burst with the globe we inhabit. I am not among the number of those who give it a place among the motives of their actions."
>
> —John Jay

John Jay was never elected president or vice president of the United States. His face does not appear on the cliffs of Mt. Rushmore. His image is not on any denomination of US coin or paper money. Because of schedule commitments, he was not a signer of the Declaration of Independence. While his namesake is found at the John Jay College of Criminal Justice in Manhattan and at certain high schools in the Hudson Valley region of New York, Jay's name does not identify any bridges, tunnels, airports, municipalities, or landmarks of great significance. Jay was not a character included in the musical and movie *1776* and has not been the subject of a Broadway musical like *Hamilton*. Yet John Jay left behind a lasting legacy in his roles as an author of the *Federalist Papers*, intelligence officer, secretary for foreign affairs, negotiator of two significant international treaties, governor of New York State, and, most relevant here, as the nation's first chief justice of the Supreme Court.

Jay has not been placed by historians into the exclusive first tier of the nation's founding fathers. That tier is occupied by Washington, Adams, Jefferson, Franklin, Hamilton, and Madison. He is, however, perceived as at the top of the second tier. Placement in the second tier may underestimate the impact of his overall accomplishments. His absence from the top tier of American founders is a product, in part, of his never having been elected to a national public office. It might also be explained from history's mixed reviews of the Jay Treaty that he negotiated with Great Britain.

The primary focus of this book, of course, is John Jay's cases and role at the US Supreme Court and the manner in which Jay's personal and professional background influenced how those cases were decided.

The cases heard by the Supreme Court during John Jay's tenure as chief justice were nothing short of compelling, and each was significant in its unique individual ways. Each case provides insight into the broader issues and challenges facing the United States during the earliest years of the nation's existence, particularly in matters of constitutional and statutory interpretation, debt collection, and privateering. The earliest days of the United States, under its new federal Constitution, were tumultuous and new, and the nature of those times was reflected by the uncharted issues addressed by the Jay Court. The justices who held seats on the Jay Court bore heavy responsibilities to the government of which they were a part, the litigants who appeared before them, and the history they were making. No one was the face of those responsibilities more than the chief justice himself, John Jay.

Parallels between Jay's life experiences and his view of cases at the Supreme Court can be drawn. Jay was a stickler for detail, including his knowledge of the rules at his boarding school and his refusal to provide transcripts of the New York–New Jersey Border Commission. That same attention to detail is seen in Jay's adherence to the plain language of the controlling statutes, such as the writ of error requirements at issue in *West v Barnes*, and of the US Constitution itself, such as the right of citizens to sue states other than their own, as was at issue in *Chisholm v Georgia*. As a founding father, Jay was invested in the success and stability of the new federal government and therefore bent over backward in his handling of In Re *Hayburn* to avoid declaring the Invalid Pensions Act of 1792 unconstitutional. Jay's sensitivity to creditor rights, from the debt collection efforts of his father, his debt collection clients as an attorney, and the debt collection provisions he helped negotiate in the Treaty of Paris, influenced his charge to the special jury in *Brailsford III*. Jay's background as an international diplomat also influenced his view of *Brailsford III* in recognizing the supremacy of international treaty provisions over inconsistent state laws. And while the Supreme Court's decision in *Glass v Sloop Betsey* surprisingly broke with the international law recognized by European nations at the time, it fit Jay's background of advocating for the independence, security, and continentalism of the United States. As a contributing author of the *Federalist Papers*, Jay understood the need for a separation of powers between the branches of government. The separateness of the judicial branch was recognized by the Jay Court's refusal to be influenced by the Washington administration in *Pagan v Hooper* and its refusal to provide Washington's Cabinet with an Advisory Opinion about issues of French privateering. An understanding of Jay's Supreme Court decisions therefore should include an understanding not only of the issues addressed by the court, but of the man as well.

Jay performed his public duties without regard to his popularity with the public. Indeed, there were times when he was unpopular. He was seriously injured when struck by a rock thrown by a member of a mob in mid-April 1788. The Jay Court's majority decision in *Chisholm v Georgia* was so unpopular with the states that it prompted the enactment of an 11th Amendment to the Constitution. Later, the terms of the Jay Treaty were also unpopular that they resulted in threats against Jay's life and hanging of his effigies. Jay's opposition to slavery was opposed by those in New York invested in the old order, but it did not deter Jay from the state legislation that phased out slavery over time. Jay performed his duties based on what he believed to be right, without regard to popularity or approval.

Being "first" in an important job is not always easy. The broader and longer-term significance of the Jay Court's cases included the precedent that the court set as to how disputes were to be decided. The judges adhered closely to the plain language of the Constitution and laws. They left to the Congress the responsibility of curing problems with statutory language, as in *West v Barnes* and In Re *Hayburn*. They left to the Congress and states the responsibility of clarifying whether sovereign states could be sued through the addition of the 11th Amendment. They avoided taking the steps, which did not occur until a decade later, of declaring any law passed by Congress as unconstitutional. They declined to render advisory opinions, which adhered closely to the separation of powers. Interbranch constitutional crises were assiduously avoided. From 1789 to 1795, the Jay Court was not at all "activist," but played a cooperative judicial role that was generally supportive of the overall goals of the legislative and executive branches of government. Such an approach may be understood given the need of national leaders at that time to promote the stability of the newly formed federal system of governance. The judiciary has grown into a more fiercely independent branches of government today, as it should and must be in a system based on checks and balances.

The *Chisholm v Georgia* case is worthy of an additional, final observation. The nation needed to sift through many early issues of constitutional interpretation, including the meaning and extent of state sovereign immunity. *Chisholm* was a catalyst for the resolution of that issue. Whether the Jay Court decided *Chisholm* correctly or incorrectly on the law is beside the point. There has been a running debate in this country about whether our federal Constitution should be interpreted as originally intended by the founding fathers as reflected by its plain language or whether the Constitution is a living, breathing document that is subject to changing interpretations over time. In John Jay's days, there was no such debate. The Constitution was new, and jurists in the federal judiciary interpreted and applied its language as plainly written by its authors and ratified by the states. The intentions of the Framers are best discerned by an application of the language expressed by the Constitution itself, and as such, language would have been interpreted by those who ratified it. There was not during Jay's days any effort, and almost certainly not even any thought of trying, to interpret constitutional language in any manner other than from what was plainly written. Even in *Glass v Sloop Betsey*, where federal admiralty and maritime authority was interpreted broadly, Jay and his colleagues arguably relied on plain constitutional language to reach their conclusion.

Well more than a century would pass before lawyers, judges, and academics developed the concept of more loosely interpreting constitutional language to suit the purposes of changing times. To an even greater extreme, there have been some constitutional critics in recent years who unfortunately describe the constitution as outdated and no longer relevant and a product of a bygone age. As between the two general schools of thought—originalism versus flexibility for changing times—John Jay and his judicial colleagues might have counseled future generations to adhere to the former and reject the latter. Originalists today fall into two competing camps. The first is that the Constitution be interpreted in accordance with the intentions of its drafters. The second is that the Constitution be interpreted based on its plain language. Any daylight between those two originalist schools appears only rarely. John Jay and almost all of his Supreme Court colleagues were in the second of those two competing schools. Perhaps no case illustrates that point more than *Chisholm*, where the Supreme Court gave effect to the actual language of the Constitution even though the intentions of the Founders differed on whether the states could be sued in federal courts.

In any event, the plain language of the Constitution is a beacon that provides attorneys, jurists, and the public with enduring legal certainty and stability. It is the one document that maximizes and preserves individual rights and liberties against the tyranny and intrusion of government so long as it is consistently and properly interpreted and applied by the courts over time without prevarications. Concerns about tyranny and intrusion are as valid and prevalent today as they were in the 1790s, perhaps even more so given the extent of modern technologies and the rise of the regulatory state. If modifications are needed to the Constitution to adjust for changing attitudes, a built-in mechanism exists for formally amending it—as begun with the ratification of 11th Amendment in the wake of *Chisholm* and as repeated on sixteen additional occasions thereafter.[1]

And how does John Jay's tenure as chief justice, and the various governmental services he undertook during his professional lifetime in the broader sense, reflect on *him*?

John Jay appears to have been a humble public servant not driven by an obsession for personal political advancement or fame. Evidence that he was not obsessed with political self-promotion can be seen in multiple ways: he spent several years performing the peoples' business in Spain, France, and England. He never actively sought election to the governorship of the state of New York in 1792, when the election was stolen from him, or in 1795, when he won the office outright. He never actively sought the presidency, not in 1796, when he received five electoral college votes, or after John Adams's defeat in 1800, which cleared the way for a new national leader of the Federalist Party. In 1800, he declined the opportunity to return to his former position as chief justice of the Supreme Court, favoring instead a settled life in Bedford as a gentleman farmer. Even in retirement, he avoided interjecting himself into national and New York State politics, making only one limited exception regarding the controversial admission of Missouri as a new state of the union. These aspects of Jay's life should be interpreted as meaning that he was not a man driven by boundless self-ambition or self-promotion, but was instead engaged in a selfless form of public service to the extent that he believed he could be of contributory value to the nation.

Jay's own words support the conclusion that he did not pursue a public career for himself, but did so to be of service to others. He once wrote, "I have long been convinced that human fame was a bubble which, whether swelled by the breath of the wise, the good, the ignorant, or malicious, must burst with the globe we inhabit. I am not among the number of those who give it a place among the motives of their actions." What motivated John Jay's public career, rather than fame or self-promotion, was a sense of responsibility to be of service to his state and nation. He wrote, "I joined myself to the first assertors [sic] of the American cause, because I thought it my duty; and because I considered caution and neutrality, however secure, as being no less wrong than dishonourable." Being of service was consistent with his deeply rooted Christian religious beliefs.[2]

Jay's life was not without risk. There were, of course, natural risks of disease and death, such as from the smallpox that afflicted certain members of his family and the yellow fever that killed a significant number of persons in New York City during different years. Those aside, he risked his life as a spymaster in Fishkill during the Revolutionary War in 1776–77, fortuitously missed being captured by the British in Martinique during his voyage to Spain in late 1779, was seriously injured when struck by a rock defending physicians from a mob in New York in 1788, and was a hated figure threatened and hanged in effigy once the terms of the Jay Treaty became known to the public during the latter half of 1795. Any one of those events could have led to something worse for him. Symbolically, even his tombstone today bears damage caused by what appears to be a bullet, fired at an unknown time by an unknown person under unknown circumstances.

Jay's value to his state and nation was seen in a variety of professional roles. His value was enhanced in part by his education, intellect, clarity of oral and written expression, personal religiosity, work ethic, levelheadedness, professional restraint, seriousness of purpose, political talents, and ability to reach political compromise when needed. That he was highly regarded, even by his political adversaries, speaks volumes. Jay's unanimous confirmation as the nation's first chief justice without the need for debate in the US Senate also evidences the confidence in which Jay was held by his political peers. No nominee to the US Supreme Court today can expect confirmation to the office without an in-depth investigation and vetting, controversial debate in the Congress, and an animated level of partisan voting and gamesmanship. The esteem in which Jay was held by the members of rival political parties does not match today's highly charged partisan political climate and speaks to a time when public servants in the highest of national offices were committed to a unified common good.

JAY'S DAYS

Three public high schools are named after John Jay in the general region where he lived and practiced law—John Jay High School in Cross River, Westchester County, which opened in 1956; John Jay Senior High School in East Fishkill, Dutchess County, which opened in 1969; and the John Jay High School in the Park Slope section of Brooklyn, New York (until its closure in 2004).

Jay is also the namesake of the John Jay College of Criminal Justice, which is part of the university system of the city of New York. The college is located on West 59th Street in Manhattan and offers degrees in criminal justice, forensic science, forensic psychology, and public affairs.

John Jay Park is located between East 76th Street and East 78th Street near the FDR Drive in Manhattan.

Also named after the first chief justice are two Jay Streets in New York City. One is in the west Tribeca section of Manhattan. The second is across the East River at the MetroTech Center in Brooklyn Heights.[3]

The John Jay Institute headquartered in Langhorne, Pennsylvania, is a philanthropic organization founded in 2005 that funds and promotes post-collegiate faith-based academic fellowships to prepare leaders for careers in public service.

In 1997, the US Central Intelligence Agency opened a Liaison Conference Center at its headquarters in Langley, Virginia, with three rooms named after three founding fathers—George Washington, for his acquisition of foreign intelligence during the Revolutionary War; Benjamin Franklin, for his covert activities against the British during the same war; and John Jay, for the counterintelligence operations he conducted in New York's Hudson Valley during the revolutionary period.[4]

Jay's boyhood homesite in Rye, New York, is today managed by the not-for-profit Jay Heritage Center and is available for public tours and other activities.

The John Jay Homestead in Bedford, New York, where Jay lived as an adult, was handed down over the years to various Jay descendants, and its dwelling and property were offered in 1946 as a possible headquarters of the newly formed United Nations, though the offer was declined. After the death of Eleanor Jay Iselin in 1953, Iselin's heirs arranged in 1959 for the property to be purchased by the state of New York, which performed renovations and opened the site to the public in 1965. The John Jay Homestead State Historical Site in Bedford, New York, now reduced to fifty-nine acres, is open for tours most days of the week, which vary depending on the time of the year.[5]

Acknowledgments

A book project of this type, involving research into persons and events from more than two centuries ago, is not accomplished by a single author. Instead, the work product reflects the time, effort, and expertise of other persons consulted by the author who are dedicated to history and accuracy and who expect no recognition for their contributions in exchange for their insights. Recognition of their expertise and assistance is nevertheless richly deserved. I therefore thank the following persons who helped make the research and writing of this book more complete, well-rounded, accurate, and interesting, and which has resulted in what I believe to be a better end product than I would have been able to produce strictly on my own:

Thanks to New York Chief Judge Janet DiFiore, whom I have known, as of this writing, for thirty-seven years. Judge DiFiore, who is John Jay's linear successor at New York State's highest court, was enthusiastic about this book from its inception. Coincidentally, we first spoke of this book project mere days after the New York Court of Appeals completed a calendar conducted in historic Ulster County, where John Jay had sat during his early tenure as chief judge in 1777.

Thanks to Dr. Robb K. Haberman of the Butler Rare Book & Manuscript Library of Columbia University. Dr. Haberman helped me navigate the John Jay Papers at Columbia, including in particular Jay's diary and other writings. Meredith Self and Tara Craig of the Columbia University library system were also particularly helpful providing and granting permissions for the use of digital images.

Thanks to attorney-historian Walter Stahr, author of the leading biography of John Jay's life, whom I fortuitously met one day at the rare book archives of Columbia University, and for the helpful conversations that followed. Walter Stahr's biography of John Jay will be the leading authority on Jay's overall life for decades to come.

Thanks to attorney-historian Paul Rheingold for his information and exchange of ideas about the practice of law in New York in the 1770s and the specifics of Jay's law practice before taking the bench as New York's Chief Judge.

Thanks to the staff of the John Jay Homestead State Historical Site in Bedford, New York, specifically Director Heather Iannucci, Collections Manager Arthur Benware, and Interpretive Programs Assistant Bethany White, for their information, archival acquisitions, and to the general staff at the site for their informative tours. Relatedly, thanks to Jim Stickel of the New York State Office of Parks, Recreation, and Historic Preservation for digital images and permissions for their use.

Similarly, thanks to the staff at the Jay Heritage Center in Rye, New York, including Alan Drewry, for his knowledge of the Jay family and the Jay house.

I thank Michael Rinella, Senior Acquisitions Editor of SUNY Press, for recognizing the value of this transcript as part of SUNY's constitutional series and in bringing this book to publication within the state of New York, where it belongs. Thanks also to SUNY Press's Senior Production Editor Ryan Morris for overseeing the manuscripts production, copy editor Laura Tendler for her many helpful edits, and Kate Seburyamo for the efforts that she is undertaking marketing the book.

In the same vein, I appreciate the work and guidance of my book agent, Tim Hays of Hays Media, LLC.

Thanks to those who proofread the raw manuscript, including Chief Judge DiFiore, Tony Galvao, Tim Hays, and Michele Dillon.

Thanks to Andrea Adovasio for her assistance with manuscripts.

And thanks to my countless friends in the New York State court system, in academia, in politics from various political parties over the years, and in my personal and family life, for affording me this opportunity to memorialize the judicial achievements of John Jay in the hope that this enriches our common legal posterity.

Notes

Chapter 1

1. *New York Daily Gazette*, May 12, 1794; Monaghan, *John Jay*, 370.

2. Jay, *Life of John Jay*, 1, 10. Different texts about Jay's life identify different dates of birth in December 1745. John Jay's son, William, who published a biography of his father, identified his father's date of birth as December 12, which is the date used here. The Jay Heritage Center in Rye, New York, displays a family tree drawn on the wall of a rear room of the mansion, which is consistent with a timeline of births reconstructed at the Jay Homestead in Katonah, New York. New York City, as we know it today, consists of the boroughs of Manhattan, Brooklyn, Bronx, Queens, and Staten Island, which were consolidated into a single city in 1898. During John Jay's lifetime, New York City referred only to the island of Manhattan and a strip of southwestern Bronx, as the surrounding areas were separate municipalities. Reference in this narrative to New York City, or to the City of New York, refers to the municipal borders that existed during Jay's lifetime.

3. Family Tree, Jay Homestead Historic Site; Stahr, *John Jay*, 3–4; Webster, *Can a Chief Justice Love God?*, 3.

4. Monaghan, *John Jay*, 22; Stahr, *John Jay*, 3–4; Webster, *Can a Chief Justice Love God?*, 3.

5. Johnson, *John Jay*, 1. The Episcopal Church was the American version of the Church of England. This narrative refers to the Anglican Church prior to American independence from England, and the Episcopal Church after that.

6. Johnson, *John Jay*, 2; Stahr, *John Jay*, 4; Webster, *Can a Chief Justice Love God?*, 3.

7. Stahr, *John Jay*, 5; Historicalstatistics.org, "Currency Converter." Other methods for comparing the worth of old currencies involve wage rates and the value of gold or silver.

8. Webster, *Can a Chief Justice Love God?*, 4.

9. Johnson, *John Jay*, 2; Stahr, *John Jay*, 8–11; Van Santvoord, George, *Sketches*, 5; Webster, *Can a Chief Justice Love God?*, 3–4.

10. Jay, *Life of John Jay*, 15; Morris, *John Jay: Making of a Revolutionary*, 55; Monaghan, *John Jay*, 30; Pellew, *John Jay: American Statesman*, 12; Stahr, *John Jay*, 14.

11. Jay to Livingston April 2, 1765, Nuxoll, ed., 1 *Selected Papers of John Jay*, 35; Johnson, *John Jay*, 2; Stahr, *John Jay*, 13. Gouverneur Morris's first name has nothing to do with a public title, but was a family name.

12. Den Hartog, *Patriotism & Piety*, 22; Johnson, *John Jay*, 2–3; Morris, *John Jay: Nation and the Court*, 4; Stahr, *John Jay*, 12.

13. Chroust, "Legal Profession in Colonial America," 356–57.

14. Johnson, "Lawyer in a Time of Transition," 1260; Johnson, *John Jay: Colonial Lawyer*, 7.

15. Arthur J. Morris Law Library, "Papers of Benjamin Kissam, 1755–1776"; Johnson, "Lawyer in a Time of Transition," 1261; Peter Jay to John Jay Aug. 23, 1763, Nuxoll, ed., 1 *Selected Papers of John Jay*, 26; Morris, 1 *Correspondence and Public Papers of John Jay*, 48–49; Peter Jay to John Jay January 16, 1764, 1 *Correspondence and Public Papers of John Jay*, 51–52.

16. Van Santvoord, *Sketches*, 6; Johnson, "Lawyer in a Time of Transition," 1263; Jay to Peloquin October 9, 1764, Johnston, 4 *Correspondence and Public Papers of John Jay*, 178–79.

17. Johnson, *John Jay*, 3; Van Santvoord, *Sketches*, 6.

18. Johnson, "Lawyer in a Time of Transition," 1268–69; Stahr, *John Jay*, 20–21.

19. Blum et al., eds., *National Experience*, 85.

20. Blum et al., eds., *National Experience*, 85–87; Johnson, *John Jay*, 4; Stahr, *John Jay*, 22, 25; Engelman, "Cadwallader Colden and the New York Stamp Act Riots," 572; Johnson, "Lawyer in a Time of Transition," 1267. The courts managed to stay open for the trials of criminal matters.

21. Jay to Livingston May 1, 1765, Nuxoll, ed., 1 *The Selected Papers of John Jay*, 44; Johnson, *John Jay*, 4.

22. Blum et al., eds., *National Experience*, 87; Historical Society of the New York Courts, "Crown v William Prendergast."

23. Kissam to Jay August 25, 1766, Nuxoll, ed., 1 *Selected Papers of John Jay*, 48; Johnson, "Lawyer in a Time of Transition," 1270; Mark and Handlin, "Land Cases in Colonial New York," 169.

24. Johnson, *John Jay*, 4–5; Historical Society of the New York Courts, "Crown v William Prendergast"; Mark and Handlin, "Land Cases in Colonial New York," 194; Morris, *John Jay: Nation and the Court*, 4–5. Prendergast's name is sometimes misspelled as Pendergast.

25. Johnson, "Lawyer in a Time of Transition," 1268–69; Morris, *John Jay: Making of a Revolutionary*, 84; Webster, *Can a Chief Justice Love God?*, 5.

26. Johnson, "Lawyer in a Time of Transition," 1272; Stahr, *John Jay*, 19.

27. Johnson, *John Jay: Colonial Lawyer*, 58–59; Johnson, "Lawyer in a Time of Transition," 1273; Stahr, *John Jay*, 19–20.

28. Johnson, *John Jay: Colonial Lawyer*, 92 n. 3; White, *John Jay: Diplomat of the American Experiment*, 38; Johnson, "Lawyer in a Time of Transition," 1274.

29. University of Groningen, "Biographies—Jared Ingersoll"; Stahr, *John Jay*, 26.

30. Johnson, *John Jay: Colonial Lawyer*, 72; Monaghan, *John Jay*, 41–42; Stahr, *John Jay*, 26; Johnson, *John Jay*, 5.

31. Johnson, *John Jay: Colonial Lawyer*, 72–74; Johnson, *John Jay*, 5–6; Stahr, *John Jay*, 26–27.

32. Columbia University Digital Library Collection, *Papers of John Jay*, doc. 03610; Rheingold, "Practicing Trial Lawyer," 34; Johnson, *John Jay: Colonial Lawyer*, 98–101; Stahr, *John Jay*, 29. A concise summary of John Jay's various cases and trials has been published by Paul D. Rheingold in "John Jay: Practicing Trial Lawyer for Seven Years," 15 *Judicial Notice* 31 (2020).

33. Johnson, "Lawyer in a Time of Transition," 1278–79.

34. *Papers of John Jay Rare Book and Manuscript Collection*, Box 62; Columbia University Digital Library Collection, *Papers of John Jay*, doc. 03607; Johnson, "Lawyer in a Time of Transition," 1278.

35. Johnson, *John Jay: Colonial Lawyer*, 85.

36. Columbia University Digital Library Collection, *Papers of John Jay*, docs. 03609, 03610, 03611, 03620, 08188.

37. Johnson, *John Jay: Colonial Lawyer*, 84.

38. Kissam to Jay November 6, 1769, *Papers of John Jay*, Columbia Digital Library, apt://columbia.edu/columbia.jay/data/jjbw/06726/06726001.TIF; Johnson, "Lawyer in a Time of Transition," 127576; Morris, *Making of a Revolutionary*, 71; Johnson, *John Jay*, 6; Johnson, *John Jay: Colonial Lawyer*, 76, 92; Jay, *Life of John Jay*, 22.

39. Jay, *Life of John Jay*, 23; Johnson, *John Jay*, 6; Stahr, *John Jay*, 28; Johnson, *Colonial Lawyer*, 92. Troup would become a lieutenant colonel in the Continental Army during the Revolutionary War and later serve as a judge of the United States District Court for the District of New York.

40. Historicalstatistics.org, "Currency Converter"; Johnson, *John Jay*, 6; Stahr, *John Jay*, 30; Johnson, "Lawyer in a Time of Transition," 1277, 1282.

41. Johnson, "Lawyer in a Time of Transition," 1277.

42. Johnson, "Lawyer in a Time of Transition," 1267–68.

43. Johnson, "Lawyer in a Time of Transition," 1269; Monaghan, *John Jay*, 39, 42–43; Stahr, *John Jay*, 19, 27–28, 30; Morris, *Nation and the Court*, 5; Pellew, *American Statesman*, 17–18.

44. Stahr, *John Jay*, 30–32; Webster, *Can a Chief Justice Love God?*, 5.

45. Columbia.edu, "History."

46. University of Virginia Arthur J. Morris Law Library, "Benjamin Kissam."
47. Garner, "Remembering Lindley Murray."

Chapter 2

1. Blum et al., eds., *National Experience*, 93–94.

2. Jay, *Life of John Jay*, 28–29; Monaghan, *John Jay*, 53; Stahr, *John Jay*, 34.

3. Monaghan, *John Jay*, 57; Stahr, *John Jay*, 35. Georgia did not attend the congress, as it needed British help dealing with attacks from the Creek Indians.

4. "Address to the People of Great Britain," Ford, ed., 1 *Journals of the Continental Congress, 1774–1789*, 84–85; Morris, *Nation and the Court*, 6; Webster, *Can a Chief Justice Love God?*, 8; Jay, *Life of John Jay*, 30; Monaghan, *John Jay*, 60–61; Stahr, *John Jay*, 41–42.

5. "Notes of John Adams" dated September 26–27, 1774," Smith, ed., 1 *Letters of Delegates to Congress, 1774–1789*, 105; Stahr, *John Jay*, 39.

6. Jay to Livingston January 1, 1775, *Papers of John Jay*, Columbia Digital Library, apt://columbia.edu/columbia.jay/data/jjbw/01104/01104001.TIF; Morris, *John Jay: Making of a Revolutionary*, 139; Monaghan, *John Jay*, 65–67; Stahr, *John Jay*, 44–45; Force, 2 *American Archives*, 4th series, 427–28, 471; Jay, *Life of John Jay*, 32; Monaghan, *John Jay*, 67; Stahr, *John Jay*, 45.

7. Ford, ed., 2 *Journals of the Continental Congress, 1774–1789*, 49–52, 68–74, 80; Smith, ed., "Notes of John Dickinson May 23–25, 1775" and "Olive Branch Petition," 1 *Letters of Delegates to Congress, 1774–1789*, 371–76, 440–42; Stahr, *John Jay*, 47–48.

8. Ford, ed., 2 *Journals of the Continental Congress, 1774–1789*, 97–99, 105–23; Blum et al., eds., *National Experience*, 98.

9. Blum et al., eds., *National Experience*, 98.

10. Smith, ed., "Notes of Lord Drummond of January 1776," 3 *Letters of Delegates to Congress, 1774–1789*, 23–24, 32–40; Monaghan, *John Jay*, 77.

11. Troup to Jay October 30, 1775, and John Jay to Sarah Jay December 23, 1775, *Papers of John Jay*, Columbia Digital Library, apt://columbia.edu/columbia.jay/data/jjbw/07170/07170001.TIF (Troup), and apt://columbia.edu/columbia.jay/data/jjbw/05305/05305001.TIF (rate of compensation); Morris, *John Jay: Making of a Revolutionary*, 177, 212.

12. Family Tree, Jay Homestead Historic Site; Monaghan, *John Jay*, 79.

13. Blum et al., eds., *National Experience*, 98; US Department of Veteran's Affairs, "America's Wars."

14. "Resolutions of the New York Convention Approving the Declaration of Independence," Johnston, 1 *Correspondence and Public Papers of John Jay*, 72–73; Resolutions Dated July 9, 1776, 1 *Journals of the Provincial Congress*, 518; Jay, *Life of John Jay*, 44; Morris, *John Jay: Nation and the Court*, 8; Webster, *Can a Chief Justice Love God?*, 8; White, *John Jay: Diplomat of the American Experiment*, 57–58.

15. Force, 6 *American Archives*, 4th series, 1154–66, 1364–70, 1410; Meltzer and Mensch, *The First Conspiracy*, 201–2, 238–80, 308–9; Morris, *Making of a Revolutionary*, 278; Freeman, *Washington*, 275–76; Monaghan, *John Jay*, 82; Stahr, *John Jay*, 59–60.

16. Jay, *Life of John Jay*, 49–50; Johnson, *John Jay*, 13; Meltzer and Mensch, *The First Conspiracy*, 353; Monaghan, *John Jay*, 90–91; Morris, *Making of a Revolutionary*, 331; Pellew, *John Jay, American Statesman*, 60 (identifying the date of the first meeting as September 26); Stahr, *John Jay*, 67; Webster, *Can a Chief Justice Love God?*, 7. Charlotte County ran at that time from Saratoga northward to the Canadian border and included land that is now part of western Vermont. In 1784, the county's name was changed to Washington County in honor of General Washington.

17. Peter Jay to John Jay September 22, 1776, John Jay to Sarah Livingston September 29, 1776, Frederick Jay to John Jay October 19, 1776, and John Jay to Sarah Jay October 19, 1776, *Papers of John Jay*, Columbia Digital Library, apt://columbia.edu/columbia.jay/data/jjbw/07870/07870001.TIF, apt://columbia.edu/columbia.jay/data/jjbw/08013/08013001.TIF, apt://columbia.edu/columbia.jay/data/jjbw/06313/06313001.TIF, apt://columbia.edu/columbia.jay/data/jjbw/08024/08024001.TIF; Morris, *Making of a Revolutionary*, 318–21; *Life of John Jay*, 58; MacDonald, "Fishkill and Its Role in the Revolution," 19.

18. Monaghan, *John Jay*, 91; Morris, *Making of a Revolutionary*, 333–36, 338–40; Stahr, *John Jay*, 68–70; Webster, *Can a Chief Justice Love God?*, 9; Cooper, *The Spy*.

19. "Minutes of the Committee for Detecting Conspiracies," Morris, *Making of a Revolutionary*, 348, and 346 (as to Robinson's later-revealed British loyalties). Robinson, despite the sound of his first name, "Beverly," was a man.

20. Morris, *Making of a Revolutionary*, 389, 391; Jay, *Life of John Jay*, 68; Monaghan, *John Jay*, 93–94; Pellew, *John Jay: American Statesman*, 58; Stahr, *John Jay*, 74–75, 77–78; Webster, *Can a Chief Justice Love God?*, 9; Morris, *Nation and the Court*, 10–11.

21. 1 *Journals of the Provincial Congress*, 844–46, 866–69; Den Hartog, *Patriotism & Piety*, 24; Morris, *Making of a Revolutionary*, 391–93; Stahr, *John Jay*, 77–78; Morris, *Nation and the Court*, 12–15; Pellew, *American Statesman*, 76; Monaghan, *John Jay*, 94–95; N.Y. Const., Art. XXXV (1777).

22. Jay to Livingston and G. Morris April 29, 1777, *Papers of John Jay*, Columbia Digital Library, apt://columbia.edu/columbia.jay/data/jjbw/02819/02819001.TIF; Johnston, 1 *Corrrespondences and Public Papers of John Jay*, 397–402; Jay, *Life of John Jay*, 69–70; Morris, *Making of a Revolutionary*, 393; Morris, *Nation and the Court*, 16; Buckley, "The Governor—From Figurehead to Prime Minister," 869; Stahr, *John Jay*, 75, 79; Monaghan, *John Jay*, 95–96; Pellew, *American Statesman*, 78.

23. Jay to Yates May 15, 1777, *Papers of John Jay*, Columbia Digital Library, apt://columbia.edu/columbia.jay/data/jjbw/08580/08580001.TIF; Johnston,

1 *Correspondence and Public Papers of John Jay*, 137; Monaghan, *John Jay*, 98–99; Stahr, *John Jay*, 80.

24. 1 *Journals of the Provincial Congress*, 916–18; Jay, *Life of John Jay*, 70; The Historical Society of the Courts of the State of New York, "Duely & Constantly Kept," 12; Monaghan, *John Jay*, 99; Stahr, *John Jay*, 80.

25. Minutes of the Supreme Court of Judicature, September 1777, Box 12; Morris, *Making of a Revolutionary*, 478; Jay, *Life of John Jay*, 79, 81, 83; Monaghan, *John Jay*, 101; Pellew, *American Statesman*, 89.

26. Minutes of the Supreme Court of Judicature, September 1777, Box 12.

27. Stahr, "John Jay as New York's First Chief Justice," 7.

28. Morris, *Nation and the Court*, 16, 17; Stahr, "John Jay as New York's First Chief Justice," 7;

29. Morris, *Making of a Revolutionary*, 478–79; Pellew, *American Statesman*, 87 (as to robberies); Stahr, "John Jay as New York's First Chief Justice," 7; Clinton to Morris May 14, 1778, Hastings, ed., 3 *Public Papers of George Clinton*, 309.

30. Hastings, ed., 3 *Clinton Papers*, 144–46, 533–35; Duane to Jay August 22, 1778, Morris, 1 *Making of a Revolutionary*, 493; Jay, *Life of John Jay*, 86; Pellew, *John Jay: American Statesman*, 94; Monaghan, *John Jay*, 105–6; Stahr, *John Jay*, 89.

31. Smith, ed., 11 *Letters of Delegates of Congress*, 1774–1789, 312–17, 324; Ford, ed., 12 *Journals of the Continental Congress*, 1202; Morris, *Making of a Revolutionary*, 507; Jay, *Life of John Jay*, 86–87; Monaghan, *John Jay*, 112, 119–21; Pellew, *American Statesman*, 99; Stahr, *John Jay*, 91–92, 95–96.

32. Livingston to Jay February 20, 1779, Jay to Livingston February 27–28, 1779, Sarah Jay to John Jay, March 5, 1779, and John Jay to Sarah Jay March 21, 1779, Morris, 1 *Making of a Revolutionary*, 563–64, 567–69, 572–73, 578; Morris, *Peacemakers*, 11; Monaghan, *John Jay*, 116, 123; Pellew, *John Jay, American Statesman*, 103; Stahr, *John Jay*, 116.

33. Jay, *Life of John Jay*, 87; Stahr, *John Jay*, 104–5.

34. Monaghan, *John Jay*, 123–25; Pellew, *American Statesman*, 103.

35. William Livingston to Sarah Jay October 7, 1779, and Susannah Jay to Sarah Jay October 9, 1779, *Papers of John Jay*, Columbia Digital Library, apt://columbia.edu/columbia.jay/data/jjbw/06878/06878001.TIF, apt://columbia.edu/columbia.jay/data/jjbw/07352/07352006.TIF; Morris, *Winning of the Peace*, 199–200, 676; Marine Committee to Seth Harding September 17, 1779, and October 17, 1779, Smith, ed., 13 *Letters of Delegates to Congress, 1774–1789*, 510–11 and 14, *Letters of Delegates to Congress, 1774–1789*, 88–89; Monaghan, *John Jay*, 123–25; Stahr, *John Jay*, 117, 123.

36. Johnson, *John Jay*, 19; Webster, *Can a Chief Justice Love God?*, 11, 13; Jay, *Life of John Jay*, 102–4; Monaghan, *John Jay*, 127, 130; Stahr, *John Jay*, 126; Sarah Jay to Susan Livingston August 28, 1780, Morris, *Making of a Revolutionary*, 705.

37. Morris, *Winning of the Peace*, 26–27; Morris, *Peacemakers*, 44–45.

38. Freeman, *Washington*, 490; Johnson, *John Jay*, 21; Stahr, *John Jay*, 134, 144.

39. Jay, *Life of John Jay*, 136; Johnson, *John Jay*, 22, 24; Morris, *Winning of the Peace*, 240; Monaghan, *John Jay*, 183; Stahr, *John Jay*, 145.

40. Johnson, *John Jay*, 24–25; Morris, *Winning of the Peace*, 239; Stahr, *John Jay*, 147; Clark, *Benjamin Franklin*, 381; Monaghan, *John Jay*, 205.

41. Jay, *Life of John Jay*, 128–29; Monaghan, *John Jay*, 173 (quoting from the instructions of Congress), 197, 212; Morris, *Nation and the Court*, 18; Webster, *Can a Chief Justice Love God?*, 15; Pellew, *American Statesman*, 187–88.

42. Johnson, *John Jay*, 24–25; Monaghan, *John Jay*, 191, 203; Stahr, *John Jay*, 156, 158.

43. Monaghan, *John Jay*, 190: Stahr, *John Jay*, 160, 164–65.

44. Clark, *Benjamin Franklin*, 382; Monaghan, *John Jay*, 223.

45. The Definitive Treaty of Peace, Signed at Paris, 1783.

46. Ellis, *The Quartet*, 67; Stahr, *John Jay*, 189. Another excuse for the absence of the British representatives was that Oswald considered himself too homely for his likeness to be painted.

47. Monaghan, *John Jay*, 211–12; Clark, *Benjamin Franklin*, 383.

48. Monaghan, *John Jay*, 213.

49. Ellis, *The Quartet*, 67.

50. Monaghan, *John Jay*, 229, 244; Family Tree, Jay Homestead Historic Site; North, "The 'Amiable' Children of John and Sarah Livingston Jay" (Ann was also called within the family Nancy); Johnson, *John Jay*, 29; Jay, *Life of John Jay*, 189 (identifying the date of commencement as December 23, 1784); Stahr, *John Jay*, 199.

51. Jay, *Life of John Jay*, 234–35; Monaghan, *John Jay*, 234, 318, Stahr, *John Jay*, 237; Kaye, "New York's First Chief the Family Man," 8–9; Slavery in the North, "Emancipation in New York."

52. Monaghan, *John Jay*, 246; Pellew, *John Jay, American Statesman*, 207.

53. Johnson, *John Jay*, 30–31; Stahr, *John Jay*, 200–1, 212–13, 215; Jay, *Life of John Jay*, 236–39; Monaghan, *John Jay*, 259, 264; Pellew, *American Statesman*, 209.

54. Johnson, *John Jay*, 32; Morris, *Nation and the Court*, 23–24; Jay to the American Commissioners March 11, 1785, Guinta, ed., 2 *The Emerging Nation: A Documentary History of the Foreign Relations of the United States*,574–76; Stahr, *John Jay*, 218; Pellew, *John Jay, American Statesman*, 214–15.

55. Jay to Washington June 27, 1786, 4 *Selected Papers of John Jay*, Nuxoll, ed., 354–56; Jay, *Life of John Jay*, 190; Morris, *Nation and the Court*, 36.

56. Monaghan, *John Jay*, 289; Ellis, *American Creation*, 116; Gienapp, *Second Creation*, 154; Stahr, *John Jay*, 248. The *Independent Journal* was also known as the *General Advertiser*.

57. Hamilton, Madison, and Jay, *The Federalist Papers*, passim; Washington to Hamilton August 25, 1788, *Papers of George Washington Digital Edition*;

Johnson, *John Jay*, 33; Monaghan, *John Jay*, 290; Stahr, *John Jay*, 248–49. Ellis, *American Creation*, 117.

58. Library of Congress, "An Address to the People of the State of New York"; Den Hartog, *Patriotism & Piety*, 31; Monaghan, *John Jay*, 292; Morris, *Nation and the Court*, 33.

59. Jay, *Life of John Jay*, 261–62; Monaghan, *John Jay*, 291–92; Morris, *Nation and the Court*, 29; Stahr, *John Jay*, 253; Webster, *Can a Chief Justice Love God?*, 16.

60. Morris, *Nation and the Court*, 36–37; Monaghan, *John Jay*, 296–97; Stahr, *John Jay*, 257, 259, 265; Blum et al., eds., *National Experience*, 128.

61. PBAGalleries, "1st Complete Edition of the *Federalist Papers* in Book Form on May 31st"; Christie's, *The Federalist Papers*.

Chapter 3

1. US Census Bureau, "History: 1790"; US Census Bureau, "Census Bureau Predicts U.S. and World Population"; US Const., 10th Amend. (1789).

2. The Judiciary Act of 1789, ch. 20, secs. 2, 3, 4, 9, 11, 1 Stat. 73–79 (1789).

3. The Judiciary Act of 1789, 1 Stat. 73(4) (1789), as amended and updated 1 Stat. 128 (1790) and 1 Stat. 197 (1791).

4. Jay to Washington November 13, 1790, Mastromarino, ed., 6 *Papers of George Washington*, 649–52; Marcus, 2 *DHSC*, 2–4, 107–8.

5. Pfander, "Judicial Compensation and the Definition of Judicial Power in the Early Republic," 30; Stahr, *John Jay*, 293.

6. Glick, "On the Road: The Supreme Court and the History of Circuit Riding," 1771; Marcus, 2 *DHSC*, 248 n. 6.

7. Wexler, "The First Three Chief Justices," 1375; The Judiciary Act of 1789, sec. 1.

8. Webster, *Can a Chief Justice Love God?*, 16.

9. Freeman, *Washington*, 576; Stahr, *John Jay: Founding Father*, at 271–72.

10. The Compensation Act, ch. 18, 1 Stat. 72 (1789); Glick, "On the Road: The Supreme Court and the History of Circuit Riding," 1769–70; Pfander, "Judicial Compensation and the Definition of Judicial Power in the Early Republic," 20.

11. Casto, *The Supreme Court in the Early Republic*, 56; Marcus, "The Effect (or Non-Effect) of Founders," 1795; Wexler, "The First Three Chief Justices," 1380, 1381; Rodell, *Nine Men*, 60; Washington to Jay October 5, 1789, 4 *Papers of George Washington Digital Edition*, Presidential Series," 137; Marcus, 1 *DHSC*, 11; Morris, *Nation and the Court*, 42.

12. Jay, *Life of John Jay*, 274–75; Johnson, *John Jay*, 35; Marcus, "The Effect (or Non-Effect) of Founders, 1796"; Pellew, *John Jay, American Statesman*, 235. Secretary of State John Marshall performed the same dual roles for approximately two months when he was appointed chief justice in 1801. Marcus, 1 *DHSC*, 154, 155 and n. 1.

13. Casto, *The Supreme Court in the Early Republic*, 54, 65–66; Marcus, 1 *DHSC*, 33; Marcus, "The Effect (or Non-Effect) of Founders," 1797 and 1797 n. 18; Nuxoll, ed., 5 *Selected Papers of John Jay*, xxiv.

14. Marcus, "Is the Supreme Court a Political Institution?," 96–97; Mazzone and Woock, "Federalism as Docket Control," 20; *Papers of John Jay Rare Book and Manuscript Collection*, Box 57; The Judiciary Act of 1789, 1 Stat. 74(4) (1789); Marcus, "The Effect (or Non-Effect) of Founders," 1809.

15. Washington to Jay and the Supreme Court April 3, 1790, Marcus, 2 *DHSC*, 21; Glick, "On the Road: The Supreme Court and the History of Circuit Riding," 1766.

16. Glick, "On the Road: The Supreme Court and the History of Circuit Riding," 1757.

17. Pellew, *John Jay, American Statesman*, 237; Marcus, 1 *DHSC*, 158–60, 166 n 175; 6 *DHSC*, 13.

18. *Papers of John Jay Rare Book and Manuscript Collection*, Box 57.

19. Johnson, *John Jay*, 36.

20. Dillon, "New York State of Mind," 35.

21. Marcus, 2 *DHSC*, 3, 246–51; Pfander, "Judicial Compensation and the Definition of Judicial Power in the Early Republic," 20–21; Act of September 22, 1789, ch. 17, 1 Stat. 70 (1789); Glick, "On the Road: The Supreme Court and the History of Circuit Riding," 1770; Stahr, *John Jay*, 289. The $500 reduction would have needed to be voluntary, as Article III, section 1, of the US Constitution prohibits Congress from reducing judicial compensation during jurists' terms in office to protect the independence of the judicial branch from potential retributive intrusions by the other branches of government.

22. Freeman, North, and Wedge, *Selected Letters of John Jay*, 14–16.

23. Iredell to Jay, Cushing, and Wilson February 11, 1791, *Papers of John Jay*, Columbia Digital Library, apt://columbia.edu/columbia.jay/data/jjbw/03977/03977004.TIF; Marcus, 2 *DHSC*, 130–31, 246, 289–90, 443–44; Nuxoll, ed., 5 *Selected Papers*, 445; Mazzone and Woock, "Federalism as Docket Control," 22; Judiciary Act of 1793, ch. 22, sec. 1, 1 Stat. 333. 333–34; Pfander, "Judicial Compensation and the Definition of Judicial Power in the Early Republic," 33.

24. Judiciary Act of 1891, ch. 22, sec. 1, 1 Stat. 333, 333–34; Marcus, 2 *DHSC*, 290; Mazzone and Woock, "Federalism as Docket Control," 22.

25. Johnson, *John Jay*, 36.

26. Dillon, "New York State of Mind," 31; Monaghan, *John Jay*, 305; Pellew, *American Statesman*, 237; Stahr, *John Jay*, 273. When the federal capital

moved to Philadelphia, the Supreme Court initially met at Independence Hall and then until 1800 at Old City Hall. Supreme Court Historical Society, "Homes of the Court." The Supreme Court began hearing cases at various locations within the US Capitol Building in Washington, DC, between 1800 and 1935. In 1935, the Supreme Court occupied the majestic columned location where it remains today, at 1 First Street. Mazzone and Woock, "Federalism as Docket Control," 19, 21–22.

27. *VanStophorst v Maryland*, 2 US 401 (1791); Monaghan, *John Jay*, 307; Marcus, 5 *DHSC*, 8, 13–15; Smith, "Credible Commitments and the Early American Supreme Court," 92.

28. Marcus, 1 *DHSC*, 201; 5 *DHSC*, 18, 20; Smith, "Credible Commitments and the Early American Supreme Court," 92. A brief account of the case was discussed by the US Supreme Court in *Alden v Maine*, 527 U.S. 706, 726.

29. Marcus, 6 *DHSC*, 27.

30. Marcus, 6 *DHSC*, 27–29; 1 Stat. 103 (1790).

31. Marcus, 1 *DHSC*, 486; 6 *DHSC*, 29.

32. An Act to provide for the More Convenient Organization of the Courts of the United States, ch. 4, sec. 1, 2 Stat. 89 [1801]; The Judiciary Act of 1802, ch. 8, sec. 1, 2 Stat. 132.

Chapter 4

1. American Naval Records Society, *Naval Documents*, 1082–83; Cohen, "Rhode Island Federal Courts: A History," 58; Marcus, 6 *DHSC*, 3–27.

2. American Numismatic Society, "A History of American Currency"; Warren, "Earliest Cases of Judicial Review of State Legislation," 16. "General Assembly" is an umbrella term for Rhode Island's bicameral legislature, which consisted of a lower House of Representatives and an upper Senate.

3. Warren, "Earliest Cases of Judicial Review of State Legislation," 18, 22.

4. Warren, "Earliest Cases of Judicial Review of State Legislation," 17–18.

5. Warren, "Earliest Cases of Judicial Review of State Legislation," 18–20.

6. Warren, "Earliest Cases of Judicial Review of State Legislation," 19.

7. Warren, "Earliest Cases of Judicial Review of State Legislation," 20.

8. Warren, "Earliest Cases of Judicial Review of State Legislation," 20.

9. Warren, "Earliest Cases of Judicial Review of State Legislation," 20.

10. Warren, "Earliest Cases of Judicial Review of State Legislation," 20.

11. *Providence Gazette*, November 11, 1786; Warren, "Earliest Cases of Judicial Review of State Legislation," 20, and 21 (citing a report on *Trevett v Weeden* by David Howell at the Library of Congress).

12. Warren, "Earliest Cases of Judicial Review of State Legislation," 22.

13. *Providence Gazette*, February 28, 1789; Warren, "Earliest Cases of Judicial Review of State Legislation," 22–23.

14. Main, *The Anti-federalists*, 7, 13, 52–53, 116, 212; Warren, "Earliest Cases of Judicial Review of State Legislation," 22. Of the original states, Rhode Island would be the last to ratify the new federal constitution, which did not occur until May 29, 1790. The Washington administration had already been in power for more than a year.

15. Larsen, "West v Barnes," 13, citing *United States Chronicle (Providence)*, December 3, 1789; Cohen, "Rhode Island Federal Courts: A History," 58; Marcus, 6 *DHSC*, 7; Warren, "Earliest Cases of Judicial Review of State Legislation," 23.

16. West, *William West of Scituate, R.I.*, 21.

17. Cohen, "Rhode Island Federal Courts: A History," 57–58; Larsen, "West v Barnes," 13 citing *United States Chronicle (Providence)*, December 3, 1791; Marcus, 6 *DHSC*, 7; Warren, "Earliest Cases of Judicial Review of State Legislation," 23.

18. Marcus, 6 *DHSC*, 8; Warren, "Earliest Cases of Judicial Review of State Legislation," 23–24.

19. The Judiciary Act of 1789, 1 Stat. Ch. 20, sec. 11, 78–79.

20. Cohen, "Rhode Island Federal Courts: A History," 57–58; Larsen, "West v Barnes," 13; Marcus, 6 *DHSC*, 8; The Judiciary Act of 1789, 1 Stat. Ch. 20, sec. 11, 78–79.

21. Warren, "Earliest Cases of Judicial Review of State Legislation," 23–24.

22. Marcus, 6 *DHSC*, 9; United States District Court, District of Rhode Island, "Henry Marchant."

23. Larsen, "West v Barnes," 13.

24. Warren, "Earliest Cases of Judicial Review of State Legislation," 24.

25. *Providence Gazette*, June 16, 1792; Marcus, 6 *DHSC*, 11. September 26 was a Saturday in 1789. It is unclear whether the Jenckeses were to actually appear at the Superior Court that day or whether, consistent with today's practice, appearances scheduled for weekends automatically rolled over to the following Monday.

26. The Judiciary Act of 1891, ch. 517, secs. 2 and 3, 26 Stat. 826, 926–27.

27. The Judiciary Act of 1789, ch. 20, 1 Stat. 73, 81–82, 85; Marcus, "Is the Supreme Court a Political Institution?," 100.

28. Marcus, 6 *DHSC*, 9–10; Cohen, "Rhode Island Federal Courts: A History." 58.

29. Cohen, "Rhode Island Federal Courts: A History," 58; Marcus, 6 *DHSC*, 9; United States Department of Justice, "Attorney General: William Bradford."

30. Cohen, "Rhode Island Federal Courts: A History," 58; Marcus, 6 *DHSC*, 9; Joyce, "The Rise of the Supreme Court Reporter," 1295.

31. West v Barnes, 2 U.S. 401.

32. Larsen, "West v Barnes," 11–13, citing Federal Gazette (Philadelphia), August 2–3; Marcus, 6 *DHSC*, 9–10; Marcus, "Is the Supreme Court a Political Institution?," 100; Warren, "Earliest Cases of Judicial Review of State Legislation," 25.

33. Cohen, "Rhode Island Federal Courts: A History," 58; Marcus, 6 *DHSC*, 10.

34. Casto, The Supreme Court in the Early Republic, 111.

35. *West v Barnes*, 2 U.S. at 401; Cohen, "Rhode Island Federal Courts: A History," 58; Larsen, "West v Barnes," 14; Marcus, "Is the Supreme Court a Political Institution?," 101.

36. Marcus, 6 *DHSC*, 18–26.

37. Marcus, 6 *DHSC*, 26.

38. Diary, Papers of John Jay, Columbia Digital Library, https://dlc.library.columbia.edu/jay/ldpd:47754; Marcus, 6 *DHSC*, 13. (Jay's abbreviations and lack of capitalizations are reproduced in the text here as in the original.)

39. *West v Barnes*, 2 U.S. at 401.

40. Marcus, 6 *DHSC*, 10 (italics in original version).

41. Cohen, "Rhode Island Federal Courts: A History," 58–59; Larsen, "West v Barnes," 14; The Process and Compensation Act of 1792, ch. 11, sec. 3, 1 Stat. 243.

42. Marcus, 6 *DHSC*, 11.

43. Henderson, *Courts for a New Nation*, 61.

44. West, *William West of Scituate, R.I.*, 22–23.

45. Cohen, "Rhode Island Federal Courts: A History," 57–59; Marcus, 6 *DHSC*, 11–12; Larsen, "West v. Barnes," 14; United States Department of Justice, "Attorney General: William Bradford."

Chapter 5

1. Civil War Trust, "Revolutionary War—FAQs"; US Dept. of Veteran's Affairs, "America's Wars."

2. Glasson, "History of Military Pension Legislation," 24–25.

3. Invalid Pensions Act of 1792, ch. 11, 1 Stat. 243.

4. Invalid Pensions Act of 1792, ch. 11, sec. 2, 1 Stat. 243.

5. Invalid Pensions Act of 1792, ch. 11, sec. 2, 1 Stat. 243.

6. Invalid Pensions Act of 1792, ch. 11, sec. 2 and 3, 1 Stat. 243; Casto, *The Supreme Court in the Early Republic*, 175.

7. Invalid Pensions Act of 1792, ch. 11, sec. 4, 1 Stat. 243.

8. The letter is contained in an unnumbered footnote in In Re *Hayburn*, 2 U.S. 410.

9. Marcus, "Is the Supreme Court a Political Institution?" 102–3; Marcus, 6 *DHSC*, 34; Casto, *The Supreme Court in the Early Republic*, 176; Gerber, ed., *Seriatim*, 29; Monaghan, *John Jay*, 317; Morris, *Nation and the Court*, 44–45.

10. Minutes of the US Circuit Court for the Circuit of New York, 6 *DHSC*, 370–71.

11. Iredell and Sitgraeves to Washington, June 8, 1792, Haggard and Mastromarino, eds., *Papers of George Washington*, 440–44; Marcus, 6 *DHSC*, 34, 49.

12. Circuit Court Judges in Pennsylvania to Washington April 18, 1792, Haggard and Mastromarino, eds., *Papers of George Washington*, 287–89; Bates, *The Story of the Supreme Court*, 51; Marcus, 6 *DHSC*, 46, 53–55; Monaghan, *John Jay*, 317. In Re *Hayburn*, 2 U.S. at 411–12 including unnumbered footnote; Casto, *The Supreme Court in the Early Republic*, 177.

13. Randolph to Washington April 5, 1792, Haggard and Mastromarino, eds., 10 *Papers of George Washington*, 221–22; Marcus, 6 *DHSC*, 36; Marcus and Teir, "Hayburn's Case: A Misinterpretation of Precedent," 531 n 25, citing ANNALS OF CONG. 556–57 (April 15, 1792).

14. Marcus, 6 *DHSC*, 51–52 (italics in original text).

15. Monaghan, *John Jay*, 317.

16. In Re *Hayburn* 2 U.S. at 409.

17. Marcus, 6 *DHSC*, 37, 38 n. 27; *General Advertiser*, Aug. 16, 1792; Stahr, *John Jay*, 292; Marcus and Teir, "Hayburn's Case: A Misinterpretation of Precedent," 535, citing the *Federal Gazette*, August 18, 1792.

18. Marcus and Teir, "Hayburn's Case: A Misinterpretation of Precedent," 535–36, referring to the Judiciary Act of 1789, ch. 20, sec. 35, 1 Stat. 73, 93 (1789); Stahr, *John Jay*, 292.

19. In Re *Hayburn*, 2 U.S. at 409; Marcus and Teir, "Hayburn's Case: A Misinterpretation of Precedent," 538.

20. Marcus, *DHSC*, 67–68; Stahr, *John Jay*, 292.

21. Marcus, "Is the Supreme Court a Political Institution?," 104.

22. In Re *Hayburn*, 2 U.S. at 409 (italicization as in the original).

23. Randolph to Madison August 12, 1792, Rutland and Mason, eds., *Papers of James Madison*, 348–50; Marcus, 6 *DHSC*, 67–68.

24. Invalid Pensions Act of February 28, 1793, ch. 17, sec. 1, 1 Stat. 324; Marcus, 6 *DHSC*, 39–40.

25. Invalid Pensions Act of February 28, 1793, ch. 17, secs. 1–4, 1 Stat 324.

26. *Marbury v Madison*, 5 U.S. 137 (1803).

27. Minutes of the US Circuit Court for the District of South Carolina for October 26, 1792, 6 *DHSC*, 70.

28. Holt, "To Establish Justice," 1989 *Duke Law Journal* 1421, 1450 n. 94; Hulsebosch, "Being Seen Like a State," 59 *William & Mary Law Review*, 1239, 1296; Marcus, 2 *DHSC*, 123. Treanor, "Judicial Review Before *Marbury*," 519–22; *Hamilton v Eaton*, 11 F.Cas. 336, 340; *Vanhorne's Lessee v Dorrance*, 28 F.Cas. 1012. The citation for the state statute that was declared unconstitutional is Sess. of May 1784, 1784 Conn. *Laws* 283–84.

29. Marcus, 6 *DHSC*, 41–42.

30. *United States v Ferreira*, 54 U.S. 40, 53 (*United States v Todd*, being an unreported opinion, has no citation of its own, but was discussed at length in *Ferreira*); Marcus, 6 *DHSC*, 373.

31. *United States v Ferreira*, 54 U.S. at 53.

32. *United States v Ferreira*, 54 U.S. at 53 (discussion of *U.S. v Todd*); Marcus, "Is the Supreme Court a Political Institution?," 105.

33. Elkins and McKitrick, *The Age of Federalism*, 435–26; Randolph County Commission, "History of Randolph County, WV."

Chapter 6

1. Barnett, "The People or the State?," 1729–30.

2. Clark, "The Eleventh Amendment and the Nature of the Union," 1862, 1877; Hamilton, *Federalist Paper* 81; Bates, *Story of the Supreme Court*, 57.

3. Clark, "Eleventh Amendment," 1863.

4. Casto, *The Supreme Court in the Early Republic*, 188.

5. *Chisholm v Georgia*, 2 U.S. at 432 (1793).

6. *Chisholm v Georgia*, 2 U.S. at 419; Morris, *Nation and the Court*, 49–50; Ragsdale, "Debates on the Federal Judiciary." Governor Telfair's surname is misspelled in the Supreme Court's *Chisholm* opinion with an "s" instead of an "f."

7. Morris, *Nation and the Court*, 50.

8. Morris, *Nation and the Court*, 50; *Chisholm v Georgia*, 2 U.S. at 420–27; Stahr, *John Jay*, 294.

9. *Chisholm v Georgia*, 2 U.S. at 427.

10. *Chisholm v Georgia*, 2 U.S. at 453, 469; O'Connor, *William Paterson: Lawyer and Statesman*, 267; Gerber, ed., *Seriatim*, 138.

11. Morris, *Nation and the Court*, 52.

12. *Chisholm v Georgia*, 2 U.S. at 479.

13. *Chisholm v Georgia*, 2 U.S. at 450, 465–67. The contract provision Justice Wilson referenced is Article I, section 10. Legal historian William R. Casto suggests that by today's standards, Justice Wilson would be required to recuse himself from *Chisholm*, as he was a shareholder of a company in a case called *Hollingsworth v Virginia*, where the litigation would be directly affected by the Supreme Court's decision in *Chisholm*. Casto, *The Supreme Court in the Early Republic*, 195; Gerber, ed., *Seriatim*, 177–78.

14. *Chisholm v Georgia*, 2 U.S. at 471–79.

15. *Chisholm v Georgia*, 2 U.S. at 434–36, 445–46.

16. *Chisholm v Georgia*, 2 U.S. at 478 (as to the August 1793 Term); Morris, *John Jay: Nation and the Court*, 53.

17. Marcus, 5 *DHSC*, 352–53; Clark, "Eleventh Amendment," 1877; Treaty of Paris, Art. 6, 8 Stat. 81.

18. Marcus, 5 *DHSC*, 354, 356–57.

19. Marcus, 5 *DHSC*, 362.

20. Jay, *Life of John Jay*, 297.

21. Marcus, 5 *DHSC*, 364–65; Marcus, "John Hancock's Address to the Massachusetts General Court," 5 *DHSC*, 416–19; Clark, "Eleventh Amendment," 1888.

22. Marcus, "Resolution of the Massachusetts General Court dated Sept. 27, 1793," 5 *DHSC*, 440; Marcus, "Letter from Samuel Adams to Governors of the States, Oct. 8, 1793," 5 *DHSC*, 442–43; Clark, "Eleventh Amendment," 1889–90; Morris, *Nation and the Court*, 64–65. Ragsdale, "Debates on the Federal Judiciary"; Lash, "Leaving the Chisholm Trail," 1581.

23. Ragsdale, "Debates on the Federal Judiciary"; Marcus, "Proceedings of the Virginia House of Delegates, Nov. 28, 1793," 5 *DHSC*, 338–39; Marcus, "Resolution of the Connecticut General Assembly, dated Oct. 29, 1793," 5 *DHSC*, 609–10"; Resolution of the North Carolina General Assembly, dated Jan. 11, 1794," 5 *DHSC*, 615–16; "Proceedings of a Joint Session of the New Hampshire General Court, dated Jan. 23, 1794," 5 *DHSC*, 618; Marcus, "Proceedings of the South Carolina Senate, dated Dec. 17, 1793," 5 *DHSC*, 610–11; "Proceedings of the Maryland House of Delegates, dated Dec. 27. 1793," 5 *DHSC*, 611–12; "Proceedings of the Georgia House of Representatives, Nov. 9, 1793," 5 *DHSC*, 236–37; "Proceedings of the Dec. 30, 1793," 5 *DHSC*, 612–13; "Proceedings of the Delaware Senate, Jan. 10, 1794," 5 *DHSC*, 614–15.

24. Marcus, "Proceedings of the Georgia House of Representatives" as reported in the *Augusta Chronicle*, Nov. 19, 1793, 5 *DHSC*, 236 (emphasis added); Bates, *Story of the Supreme Court*, 56; Ragsdale, "Debates on the Federal Judiciary"; Laws.com, "Understanding the 11th Amendment"; Monaghan, *John Jay*, 309; Morris, John Jay: *Nation and the Court*, 64.

25. Marcus, "Proceedings of the United States House of Representatives, Feb. 19, 1793," 5 *DHSC*, 605–6; Marcus, "Resolution in the United States Senate, Feb. 20, 1793" 5 *DHSC*, 607–8; Casto, *The Supreme Court in the Early Republic*, 197; Welch, "Mr. Sullivan's Trunk," 281–82; Stahr, *John Jay*, 296; Clark, "Eleventh Amendment," 1887 and n. 416.

26. US Const. 11th Amend.; Morris, *John Jay: Nation and the Court*, 65; Clark, "Eleventh Amendment," 1892 and n. 447; Marcus, "Proceedings of the United States House of Representatives, Mar. 4, 1794," 5 *DHSC*, 620–23; Marcus, "Proceedings of the United States Senate, Jan. 14, 1794," 5 *DHSC*, 617.

27. South Carolina approved of the 11th Amendment on December 4, 1797. New Jersey, Pennsylvania, and Tennessee, which became a state on June 17, 1796, never took action on the Amendment.

28. Marcus, "Resolution of the United States Congress, Mar. 2, 1797," 5 *DHSC*, 628; National Archives, "Message of John Adams to Congress"; Marcus, "Message of President John Adams to the United States Congress, Jan. 8, 1798," 5 *DHSC*, 637–38; Clark, "The Eleventh Amendment and the Nature of the Union," 1893. A Message to Congress was what is today known as the annual State of the Union address. In the 1790s, the Message to Congress was in writing. The first State of the Union address delivered to the Congress in person was that of President Woodrow Wilson in 1913.

29. *Hollingsworth v Virginia*, 3 U.S. 378, 382 (1798); *Fitzpatrick v Bitzer*, 427 U.S. 445 (1976).

30. *Hans v Louisiana* 134 U.S. 1 (1890); Welch, "Mr. Sullivan's Trunk," 282.

31. Randy E. Barnett, "The People or the State?," 1737; *Hans v Louisiana*, 134 U.S. 21 (Harlan dissent).

32. Johnson, *John Jay 1745–1829*, 37.

33. *Ware, Administrator of Jones v Hylton*, 3 U.S. 199 (1796), citing Act Va. Oct. 20, 1777; Treaty of Paris, 8 Stat. 81, Art. 4; Casto, *The Supreme Court in the Early Republic*, 99; Johnson, *John Jay*, 37.

34. Marcus, "*Ware v Hylton*," 6 *DHSC*, 211–13; Stahr, *John Jay*, 297.

35. Marcus, "*Ware v Hylton*," 6 *DHSC*, 211; Stahr, *John Jay*, 299; Morris, *Nation and the Courts*, 85–86.

36. *Ware, Administrator of Jones v Hylton*, 3 U.S. at 199, 285 (1796); Marcus, "*Ware v Hylton*," 6 *DHSC*, 214–16; Morris, *Nation and the Courts*, 90.

37. Morris, *John Jay: Nation and the Courts*, 91.

38. Vassall to Lloyd August 7, 1794, Marcus, 5 *DHSC*, 449; Marcus, 5 *DHSC*, 369; Clark, "Eleventh Amendment," 1894.

Chapter 7

1. Sloss, "Judicial Foreign Policy," 151–52; Sweeney, "A Tort Only in Violation of the Law of Nations," 455–56; Casto, *The Supreme Court in the Early Republic*, 77.

2. Colombos, "A Treatise on the Law of Prize," 361–62; Deak and Philip, "Early Prize Court Procedure," 692–93.

3. Wuerth, "The Captures Clause," 1722; Yale Law School Lilian Goldman Library's Avalon Project, Declaration of Paris of April 16, 1856; Marcus, 6 *DHSC*, 296 n. 3.

4. Marcus, 6 *DHSC*, 216; Declaring the Cessation of Arms, as well by Sea as by Land, agreed upon between the United States of America and His Britannic Majesty, para. 2.

5. Marcus, 6 *DHSC*, 215–17.

6. Marcus, 6 *DHSC*, 217.

7. Marcus, 6 *DHSC*, 218 and 218 n. 16 and n. 17.

8. Marcus, 6 *DHSC*, 218.

9. Marcus, 6 *DHSC*, 218–19.

10. Marcus, 6 *DHSC*, 219, 224.

11. Marcus, 6 *DHSC*, 219–20.

12. Marcus, 6 *DHSC*, 220 and 220 n. 35, citing Catanzariti, ed., 22 *Papers of Thomas Jefferson*, 340–41 note.

13. Marcus, 6 *DHSC*, 220–21.

14. Marcus, 6 *DHSC*, 221; Judiciary Act of 1789, sec. 25, 1 Stat. 85–87 (1789).

15. Morgan to Anthony June 8, 1792, Marcus, 6 *DHSC*, 221.

16. Marcus, 6 *DHSC*, 221–22.

17. Dana to Jay December 19, 1792, *Papers of John Jay*, Columbia Digital Library, apt://columbia.edu/columbia.jay/data/jjbw/13127/13127001.TIF; Marcus, 6 *DHSC*, 222 and 220 n. 50, 262.

18. Marcus, 6 *DHSC*, 222.

19. Marcus, 6 *DHSC*, 222–23.

20. Jefferson to Randolph March 13, 1793, Catanzariti, ed., 25 *Papers of Thomas Jefferson*, 379; Randolph to Jefferson March 15, 1793, Catanzariti, ed., 25 *Papers of Thomas Jefferson*, 389; Jefferson to Randolph April 18, 1793, Catanzariti, ed., 25 *Papers of Thomas Jefferson*, 563; Hammond to Jefferson August 19, 1793, Catanzariti, ed., 26 *Papers of Thomas Jefferson*, 724; Randolph to Jefferson September 5, 1793 and Jefferson to Hammond, Catanzariti, ed., 27 *Papers of Thomas Jefferson*, 38, 106; Marcus, 6 *DHSC*, 223–24, 264–68, 273–80.

Chapter 8

1. There apparently were two "unreported" jury trials at the US Supreme Court. Lochlan F. Shelfer, "Special Juries in the Supreme Court," 211. One was *Oswald v State of New York* in 1795, discussion of which may be found at Marcus, 5 *DHSC*, 65–67, but which did not involve John Jay in his capacity as a jurist. Procedural history for *Oswald v State of New York* may also be found at 2 U.S. 401 (1792) and 2 U.S. 415 (1793).

2. Shelfer, "Special Juries," 221, and 223 quoting Georgia Confiscation Act of 1782, secs. 4, 5; *Brailsford I*, 2 U.S. 402.

3. Shelfer, "Special Juries," 221.

4. Marcus, 6 *DHSC*, 73–78; *Brailsford I*, 2 U.S. 402; Stahr, *John Jay*, 308; Historicalstatistics.org, "Historical Currrency Converter."

5. *Brailsford I*, 2 U.S. 402.

6. "Circuit Court Opinion dated May 2, 1792," Marcus, 6 *DHSC*, 96, 98–102 (Pendleton opinion), 106 (Iredell opinion).

7. *Brailsford I*, 2 U.S. 402.

8. *Brailsford I*, 2 U.S. 402.

9. E.g., *Monsanto Co. v Geerston Seed Farms*, 561 U.S. 139, 141 (2010).

10. *Brailsford II*, 2 U.S. 415.

11. *Brailsford II*, 2 U.S. at 418–19.

12. Shelfer, ""Special Juries," 224, and 224 citing Maeva Marcus, "Georgia v Brailsford," 2 *Journal of Supreme Court History* 57, 65 (1996); Marcus, "Agreement of the Parties," 6 *DHSC*, 153.

13. *Brailsford III*, 3 U.S. 1; Marcus, 6 *DHSC*, 85.

14. Shelfer, "Special Juries," 225 and n. 101.

15. Shelfer, "Special Juries," 210.

16. Shelfer, "Special Juries," 225.

17. *Brailsford III*, 3 U.S. 1.

18. *Brailsford III*, 3 U.S. 1.

19. *Brailsford III*, 3 U.S. 1; "William Bradford's, Jr.'s Notes for Argument in the Supreme Court," Marcus, 6 *DHSC*, 163–64.

20. Nelson, "The Province of the Judiciary," 326.

21. Nelson, "The Province of the Judiciary," 326–28; Regnier, "Restoring the Founders' Ideal," 792. Wilson was the first-ever professor of law at the University of Philadelphia and only the second professor of law at any university by that time.

22. *Brailsford III*, 3 U.S. 1.

23. *Brailsford III*, 3 U.S. 1.

24. Shelfer, "Special Juries," 242; *Brailsford III*, 3 U.S. 1.

25. *Brailsford III*, 3 U.S. 1.

26. *Brailsford III*, 3 U.S. 1.

27. *Brailsford III*, 3 U.S. 1.

28. Barone, "Independent Juries," 24; Mulligan, "Jury Nullification," 71.

29. *Brailsford III*, 3 U.S. 1; Blinka, "'This Germ of Rottedness,'" 165.

30. Lahn, "The Demise of the Law-Finding Jury," 561; *Sparf v United States*, 156 U.S. 51, 65, and 156–57 (Gray dissent) (1895); Sunderland, "Verdicts, General and Special," 254; Regnier, "Restoring the Founders' Ideal," 818. The issue in the trial was whether former Vice President Aaron Burr had endeavored to establish an independent nation in what is the present-day southwest United States or whether he merely sought to take possession of 40,000 acres in Texas leased to him by Spain for use as a farm. He was also accused of assembling an armed militia to take control of New Orleans and to separate it and other territory from the United States. Burr was acquitted.

Chapter 9

1. Hamilton to Washington April 5, 1793, Syrett, ed., 14 *Papers of Alexander Hamilton*, 291–92; Doyle, *The Oxford History of the French Revolution*, 194–96; UNC, "Timeline: The Revolutionary and Napoleonic Wars"; Freeman, *Washington*, 620.

2. Washington to Jefferson April 12, 1793, Patrick and Pinheiro, eds., 12 *Papers of George Washington*, 448–49; Hamilton to Jay April 9, 1973 (two letters) and Jay to Hamilton April 11, 1793, Syrett, ed., 14 *Papers of Alexander*

Hamilton, 297–99, 300, 307–10 (abbreviations and capitalizations as in the original); Freeman, *Washington*, 621; Thomas, *American Neutrality in 1793*, 24; Casto, *Supreme Court in the Early Republic*, 74; Ammon, *Genet Mission*, 47; Jay, *Life of John Jay*, 298–99; Monaghan, *John Jay*, 350–51; Casto, *Foreign Affairs and the Constitution in the Age of Fighting Sail*, 28; Pellew, *American Statesman*, 256–57; Reinstein, "Executive Power and the Law of Nations," 426.

3. Ammon, *Genet Mission*, 48–49; Freeman, *Washington*, 621–22; Reinstein, "Executive Power and the Law of Nations," 426; Jay to Hamilton April 11, 1793, Syrett, ed., 14 *Papers of Alexander Hamilton*, 300.

4. Casto, *Foreign Affairs and the Constitution in the Age of Fighting Sail*, 25; Hulsebosch, "The Founders' Foreign Affairs Constitution," 210; Casto, "The Early Supreme Court Justices' Most Significant Opinion," 174–75.

5. "Neutrality Proclamation, 22 April, 1793," *Papers of George Washington*, Patrick and Pinheiro, eds., 474–74; "Proclamation," American State Papers: Foreign Relations; Freeman, *Washington*, 622; Monaghan, *John Jay*, 351; Casto, *Foreign Affairs and the Constitution in the Age of Fighting Sail*, 31.

6. Casto, *Supreme Court in the Early Republic*, 75.

7. Berkin, *A Sovereign People*, 92; Sloss, "Judicial Foreign Policy," 155; Monaghan, *John Jay*, 351; Marcus, 6 *DHSC*, 296 n. 1; Ammon, *Genet Mission*, 55, 59.

8. Ammon, *Genet Mission*, 2, 3–5; Casto, *Foreign Affairs and the Constitution in the Age of Fighting Sail*, 5, 6; Monaghan. *John Jay*, 352.

9. Berkin, *A Sovereign People*, 92; Casto, *Foreign Affairs and the Constitution in the Age of Fighting Sail*, 7–10.

10. Ammon, *Genet Mission*, 26–27; Berkin, *A Sovereign People*, 81; Casto, *Foreign Affairs and the Constitution in the Age of Fighting Sail*, 14.

11. Campbell, *Disasters, Crises, and Accidents in American History*, 53.

12. Williams, *French Assault on American Shipping*, 1; Treaty of Amity and Commerce, 8 Stat. 22, Arts. 17, 19, 22; "Treaty of Amity and Commerce," Yale Law School Lillian Goldman Library's Avalon Project; Blum et al., eds., *National Experience*, 139; Reinstein, "Executive Power and the Law of Nations," 412; Shepherd, *The Adams Chronicles*, 170. The article numbers of the Treaty of Amity and Commerce have two versions, as two articles originally numbered 11 and 12 were "suppressed," resulting in the renumbering of the remaining articles. This book identifies articles based on the original numbering used by the parties.

13. Sloss, "Judicial Foreign Policy," 152.

14. Sloss, "Judicial Foreign Policy," 155; Ammon, *Genet Mission*, 45; Jefferson to G. Morris August 16, 1793, Catanzariti, ed., 26 *Papers of Thomas Jefferson*, 698; Blum et al., eds., *National Experience*, 139; Casto, *Supreme Court in the Early Republic*, 76–77; Flanders, *The Lives and Times of the Chief Justices*, 390; Sloss, "Judicial Foreign Policy," 155.

15. Treaty of Amity and Commerce, 8 Stat. 22, Art. 21; Jefferson to Ternant May 15, 1793, Catanzariti, ed., 26 *Papers of Thomas Jefferson*; Ammon, *Genet Mission*, 67–68.

16. Casto, *Foreign Affairs and the Constitution in the Age of Fighting Sail*, 61; Ammon, *Genet Mission*, 71.

17. Casto, *Foreign Affairs and the Constitution in the Age of Fighting Sail*, 28, 37, 39, 43, 46. The ships and cargo sold for less than they were valued and were purchased by the original owner.

18. Jefferson to Monroe May 5, 1793, Cantanzariti, ed., 26 *Papers of Thomas Jefferson*, 661; Ammon, *Genet Mission*, 51–52, 80; Casto, *Supreme Court in the Early Republic*, 77; Casto, *Foreign Affairs and the Constitution in the Age of Fighting Sail*, 41; Monaghan, *John Jay*, 354–55.

19. Jefferson to the Supreme Court July 18, 1793, Cantanzariti, ed., 26 *Papers of Thomas Jefferson*, 520–21; Marcus, 6 *DHSC*, 747–50; Nuxoll, ed., 5 *Selected Papers of John Jay*, 536–40; Casto, *Supreme Court in the Early Republic*, 78; Casto, "The Early Supreme Court Justices' Most Significant Opinion," 182–83; Casto, *Foreign Affairs and the Constitution in the Age of Fighting Sail*, 111.

20. Jefferson to the Supreme Court July 18, 1793, Cantanzariti, ed., 26 *Papers of Thomas Jefferson*, 520–21; Marcus, 6 *DHSC*, 299, 299 n. 13, 747; Casto, *The Supreme Court in the Early Republic*, 78.

21. Supreme Court to Washington July 20, 1793, and Washington to Supreme Court July 23, 1793, Patrick, ed., 13 *Papers of George Washington*, 256–57, 270; Marcus, 6 *DHSC*, 299–300, 752–53; Nuxoll, ed., 5 *Selected Papers of John Jay*, 541.

22. Supreme Court to Washington August 8, 1793, Patrick, ed., 13 *Papers of George Washington*, 392–93; Marcus, 6 *DHSC*, 755; Morris, *John Jay: Nation and the Court*, 46; Casto, "The Early Supreme Court Justices' Most Significant Opinion," 184–85; Casto, *Foreign Affairs and the Constitution in the Age of Fighting Sail*, 111; Nuxoll, ed., 5 *Selected Papers of John Jay*, 545; Rodell, *Nine Men*, 56.

23. Casto, *The Supreme Court in the Early Republic*, 80.

24. "Institutions to the Collectors of Customs," 1 *American State Papers: Foreign Relations*; Sloss, "Judicial Foreign Policy," 158.

25. *Henfield's Case*, 11 F.Cas. 1099 (Cir. Ct. D. Pa. 1793); Casto, *Supreme Court in the Early Republic*, 82, 135; Casto, *Foreign Affairs and the Constitution in the Age of Fighting Sail*, 48, 86, 91, 94; Berkin, *A Sovereign People*, 109, 126; Genet to Jefferson May 27, 1793, Jefferson to Genet June 1, 1793, Jefferson to Genet June 5, 1793, and Genet to Jefferson June 8, 1793, Catanzariti, ed., 26 *Papers of Thomas Jefferson*, 124 and 159, 160–61, 195–97, 231–34. Singleterry's surname is spelled in some historical literature as "Singletary."

26. Casto, *Foreign Affairs and the Constitution in the Age of Fighting Sail*, 91, 94; Van Santvoord, *Sketches*, 57.

27. U.S. Const. Art. 1, sec. 8, clause 10; *United States v. Hudson*, 11 U.S. 32, 7 Cranch at 34 (1812).

28. Casto, *Foreign Affairs and the Constitution in the Age of Fighting Sail*, 94, 96–97.

29. Casto, *Foreign Affairs and the Constitution in the Age of Fighting Sail*, 97; *Henfield's Case*, 11 F.Cas. 1099, 1122 (Cir. Ct. D. Pa. 1793); Van Santvoord, *Sketches*, 58 and 58 note.

30. Arlyck, "The Courts and Foreign Affairs," 19; Casto, *Foreign Affairs and the Constitution*, 100; Casto, *Foreign Affairs and the Constitution in the Age of Fighting Sail*, 100.

31. Act of June 5, 1794, ch. 50, secs. 1 and 2, 1 Stat. 381, 382–83.

32. Sloss, "Judicial Foreign Policy," 157; Cooke, *Alexander Hamilton*, 131.

33. Jefferson to Hammond May 15, 1793, Catanzariti, ed., 26 *Papers of Thomas Jefferson*, 38; Sloss, "Judicial Foreign Policy," 157.

34. "Opinion of Edmund Randolph May 14, 1793," Catanzariti, ed., 26 *Papers of Thomas Jefferson*, 31–35; Casto, *Foreign Affairs and the Constitution in the Age of Fighting Sail*, 50; Sloss, "Judicial Foreign Policy," 162.

35. Jefferson to Hammond June 13, 1793, Catanzariti, ed., 26 *Papers of Thomas Jefferson*, 270–71.

36. *Findlay v The William*, 9 F.Cas. 57; Genet to Jefferson June 14, 1793, 1 *American State Papers: Foreign Relations*, 152.

37. Genet to Jefferson June 14, 1793, 26 Catanzariti, ed., 26 *Papers of Thomas Jefferson*, 281–83; 1 *American State Papers: Foreign Relations*, 152.

38. *Findlay v The William*, 9 F.Cas. at 59, 61–62; Jefferson to Genet June 29, 1793, Catanzariti, ed., 26 *Papers of Thomas Jefferson*, 400; 1 *American State Papers: Foreign Relations*, 161.

39. Casto, *Foreign Affairs and the Constitution in the Age of Fighting Sail*, 89–90; Casto, *Supreme Court in the Early Republic*, 83–84; *Moxon v The Fanny*, 17 F.Cas. 942, 943 (1793). *Meade v The Brigantine Catherine* is an unreported Opinion described in Sloss, "Judicial Foreign Policy," 165–67, and at 165 n. 98. Judge Duane had been a member of the First and Second Continental Congresses with John Jay. Judge Bee had been a member of South Carolina's delegations to the Second Continental Congress.

40. Sloss, "Judicial Foreign Policy," 147.

41. *Glass v Sloop Betsey*, 3 U.S. 6 (1794).

42. Generally, Vanhorn, "Eighteenth-Century Colonial American Merchant Ship Construction."

43. Lucas Gibbs and Alexander Glass to Jefferson July 8, 1793, and Jefferson to Glass September 10, 1793, National Archives, "Jefferson Papers"; Kevin Alryck, "The Courts and Foreign Affairs at the Founding," 31–32.

44. Casto, *Supreme Court in the Early Republic*, 83.

45. Marcus, 6 *DHSC*, 301–02.

46. *Glass v Sloop Betsey*, 3 U.S. 6 (describing in its first paragraph the procedural history of the case); Marcus, 6 *DHSC*, 302–3; Gerber, ed., *Seriatim*, 28.

47. Goebel Jr., 1 *History of the Supreme Court*, 598; Marcus, 6 *DHSC*, 303–4.

48. Marcus, 6 *DHSC*, 305–6 and 306 n. 48, citing to the *Maryland Journal*, November 12, 1793; *Glass v The Sloop Betsey*, 3 U.S. 6 (describing in its first paragraph the procedural history of the case).

49. Lucas Gibbs to Jefferson November 12, 1793, Marcus, 6 *DHSC*, 306; National Archives, "Jefferson Papers."

50. Goebel Jr., 1 *History of the Supreme Court*, 598–99; Marcus, 6 *DHSC*, 307.

51. DuPonceau to Morris April 8, 1795, Marcus, 6 *DHSC*, 352.

52. *Glass v Sloop Betsey*, 3 U.S. 6.

53. *Glass v Sloop Betsey*, 3 U.S. 6.

54. Marcus, 6 *DHSC*, 309.

55. Casto, *Supreme Court in the Early Republic*, 86; Marcus, 6 *DHSC*, 309.

56. Casto, *Supreme Court in the Early Republic*, 84.

57. *Glass v Sloop Betsey*, 3 U.S. 6. The final paragraph of the opinion ordered that the cause be "remanded" to the District Court of the District of Maryland for a final decision. Today, there is a distinction between a "remand" and a "remittal." Remand is a term that today references the sending of a person into custody, such as by a jail sentence or a criminal defendant's inability to post bail. A "remittal" refers to an appellate court sending a case or an issue to a lower court for further proceedings. Technically, therefore, under today's nomenclature, the final paragraph of the *Sloop Betsey* opinion should have ordered a "remittal" of the cause to the District Court rather than a "remand," but there should be no doubt that all persons involved understood the intent of the Supreme Court.

58. *Glass v Sloop Betsey*, 3 U.S. 6; Marcus, "Is the Supreme Court a Political Institution?," 106.

59. Arlyck, "The Courts and Foreign Affairs," 35. See generally Estes, *The Jay Treaty Debate, Public Opinion, and the Evolution of Early American Culture*.

60. *Martins v Ballard*, 16 F. Cas. 923, 925 (1794); Casto, *Supreme Court in the Early Republic*, 87. Examples of the developing decisional authority included *Talbot v Jansen*, 3 U.S. 133 (1795); *United States v Peters*, 3 U.S. 121 (1795); *The Den Onzekeren*, 3 U.S. 285 (1796), *Hills v Ross*, 3 U.S. 311 (1796), *Moodie v The Ship Phoebe Anne*, 3 U.S. 319 (1796), and *Del Col v Arnold*, 3 U.S. 333 (1796).

61. Dillon, "New York State of Mind," 34.

62. Van Santvoord, *Sketches*, 58, note; Act of June 26, 1812, ch. 107, 2 Stat. 759 (1812).

Chapter 10

1. Notes of Cabinet Meeting July 5, 1793, Cantanzariti, ed., 26 *Papers of Thomas Jefferson*, 437; Casto, "The Early Supreme Court Justices' Most Significant Opinion," 177.

2. Mifflin to Jefferson July 7, 1793, Catanzariti, ed., 26 *Papers of Thomas Jefferson*, 444; Casto, "The Early Supreme Court Justices' Most Significant Opinion," 177; "Memorandum of a Conversation with Edmond Charles Genet,"

Catanzariti, ed., 26 *Papers of Thomas Jefferson*, 464, 466; Ammon, *Genet Mission*, 86; Casto, "The Early Supreme Court Justices' Most Significant Opinion," 177.

3. "Memorandum of a Conversation with Edmond Charles Genet," Catanzariti, ed., 26 *Papers of Thomas Jefferson*, 466.

4. "Memorandum of a Conversation with Edmond Charles Genet," Catanzariti, ed., 26 *Papers of Thomas Jefferson*, 464; Casto, *Foreign Affairs and the Constitution in the Age of Fighting Sail*, 104; "Ammon, *Genet Mission*, 87, 89; Stahr, *John Jay*, 304.

5. "Memorandum of a Conversation with Edmond Charles Genet," Catanzariti, ed., 26 *Papers of Thomas Jefferson*, 466; Casto, *Foreign Affairs and the Constitution in the Age of Fighting Sail*, 105; Casto, "The Early Supreme Court Justices' Most Significant Opinion," 178; Monaghan, *John Jay*, 355.

6. "Memorandum of a Conversation with Edmond Charles Genet," Catanzariti, ed., 26 *Papers of Thomas Jefferson*, 466; Casto, *Foreign Affairs and the Constitution in the Age of Fighting Sail*, 105; Casto, "The Early Supreme Court Justices' Most Significant Opinion," 178; Monaghan, *John Jay*, 355.

7. Stahr, *John Jay*, 304.

8. "Jefferson Memorandum," Catanzariti, ed., 26 *Papers of Thomas Jefferson*, 467; "Dissenting Opinion," Catanzariti, ed., 26 *Papers of Thomas Jefferson*, 449–50; Casto, *Foreign Affairs and the Constitution in the Age of Fighting Sail*, 105–6; Casto, "The Early Supreme Court Justices' Most Significant Opinion," 178; Monaghan, *John Jay*, 355. The area of Mud Island is now known as Fort Mifflin.

9. Jefferson to Genet and Hammond July 12, 1793, Catanzariti, ed., 26 *Jefferson Papers*, 487; Casto, *Foreign Affairs and the Constitution in the Age of Fighting Sail*, 107; Casto, "The Early Supreme Court Justices' Most Significant Opinion," 180; Monaghan, *John Jay*, 355.

10. Jefferson to Genet August 16, 1793, and Cabinet Opinions on Edmond Charles Genet August 1, 1793, August 2, 1793, August 20, 1793, and August 23, 1793, Catanzariti, ed., 26 *Papers of Thomas Jefferson*, 598, 601–3, 685, 730–32, 745–46; Ammon, *Genet Mission*, 92, 107; Reinstein, "Executive Power and the Law of Nations," 427; Stahr, *John Jay*, 305; Berkin, *Sovereign People*, 128–29; Blum et al., eds., *National Experience*, 139; Cooke, *Alexander Hamilton*, 130; Freeman, *Washington*, 633. In 1788, the Second Continental Congress had requested the recall of the French minister to the United States, Count de Moustier, for alienating Congress and for his immoral behaviors, so that the request for the recall of Genet was not unprecedented. Ammon, *Genet Mission*, 23.

11. Ammon, *Genet Mission*, 97; Stahr, *John Jay*, 305.

12. Jay and King to Printers, Nuxoll, ed., 5 *Selected Papers of John Jay*, 562; Berkin, *A Sovereign People*, 133; Casto, *Supreme Court in the Early Republic*, 137; Casto, *Foreign Affairs and the Constitution in the Age of Fighting Sail*, 140; Jay, *Life of John Jay*, 304; Minnigerode, *Jefferson: Friend of France*, 319; Monaghan, *John Jay*, 355–56; Stahr, *John Jay*, 306.

13. Jay, *Life of John Jay*, 305.

14. Genet to Washington August 13, 1793, Patrick, ed., 15 *Papers of George Washington*, 436–38; Berkin, A *Sovereign People*, 133; Minnigerode, *Jefferson: Friend of France*, 323; Casto, *Supreme Court in the Early Republic*, 137; Casto, *Foreign Affairs and the Constitution in the Age of Fighting Sail*, 141.

15. Jefferson to Genet August 16, 1793, Cantanzariti, ed., 26 *Papers of Thomas Jefferson*, 684; Berkin, A *Sovereign People*, 133; Casto, *Foreign Affairs and the Constitution in the Age of Fighting Sail*, 141; Minnigerode, *Jefferson: Friend of France*, 323–24.

16. Genet to Randolph November 14, 1793, Syrett, ed., 15 *Papers of Alexander Hamilton*, 235.

17. Genet to Randolph December 18, 1793, Catanzariti, ed., 27 *Papers of Thomas Jefferson*, 587–88; Casto, *The Supreme Court in the Early Republic*, 137.

18. U.S. Const., 1st Amend.; Act of July 14, 1798, 1 Stat. 596, ch. 73 (1798). The Sedition Act expired in 1800 and was not renewed by Congress.

19. U.S. Const., Art. III, sec. 2 (emphasis added).

20. Casto, *Foreign Affairs and the Constitution in the Age of Fighting Sail*, 3.

21. John Jay and Rufus King Statement, November 26, 1793, Nuxoll, ed., 5 *Selected Papers of John Jay*, 569–74; Casto, *Foreign Affairs and the Constitution in the Age of Fighting Sail*, 147; Stahr, *John Jay*, 306; Minnigerode, *Jefferson: Friend of France*, 320.

22. Casto, "The Early Supreme Court Justices' Most Significant Opinion," 178–79; Minnigerode, *Jefferson: Friend of France*, 330–31; Casto, *Foreign Affairs and the Constitution in the Age of Fighting Sail*, 141.

23. Jay to King December 19, 1793, Nuxoll, ed., 5 *Selected Papers of John Jay*, 579–80; Stahr, *John Jay*, 238; Monaghan, *John Jay*, 358–59.

24. Casto, *Supreme Court in the Early Republic*, 137–38; Casto, *Foreign Affairs and the Constitution in the Age of Fighting Sail*, 147; Stahr, *John Jay*, 307.

25. Monaghan, *John Jay*, 359; Stahr, *John Jay*, 307.

26. DuPonceau and Joseph Thomas to Genet December 23, 1793, cited in Casto, *Supreme Court in the Early Republic*, 139; Casto, *Foreign Affairs and the Constitution in the Age of Fighting Sail*, 150.

27. Casto, *Supreme Court in the Early Republic*, 139; Casto, *Foreign Affairs and the Constitution in the Age of Fighting Sail*, 149.

28. National Archives Founders Online, "The Recall of Edmond Charles Genet."

29. Washington to US Senate and House December 5, 1793, Hoth, ed., 14 *Papers of George Washington*, 474–77; Berkin, *Sovereign People*, 144–45; Reinstein, "Executive Power and the Law of Nations," 428; Blum et al., eds., *National Experience*, 139; Cooke, *Alexander Hamilton*, 130; Catanzariti, ed., 26 *Papers of Thomas Jefferson*, 685.

30. Freeman, *Washington*, 644; Casto, *Supreme Court in the Early Republic*, 139; Ammon, *Genet Mission*, 158; Berkin, *Sovereign People*, 145.

31. Minnigerode, *Jefferson: Friend of France*, 363; Casto, *Supreme Court in the Early Republic*, 139; Ammon, *Genet Mission*, 159; Casto, *Foreign Affairs and the Constitution in the Age of Fighting Sail*, 150.

32. Ammon, *Genet Mission*, 171.

33. Stahr, *John Jay*, 307–8, citing Cappon, ed., 2 *The Adams-Jefferson Letters*, 346–47.

34. Puls, *Henry Knox*, 246–47.

35. Bioguide.congress,gov, "King, Rufus."

36. Joyce, "The Rise of the Supreme Court Reporter," 1295.

37. Ammon, *Genet Mission*, 172, 175, 179; Robinson Library, "Edmond Charles Genet."

Chapter 11

1. Marcus, 6 *DHSC*, 176–78.

2. Marcus, 6 *DHSC*, 178.

3. An Act for the Restraining the Taking of Excessive Usury (March 16, 1784), *The First Laws of the Commonwealth of Massachusetts*, 216–17; Marcus, 6 *DHSC*, 179 and 179 n. 21.

4. Marcus, 6 *DHSC*, 180 and 180 n. 30.

5. Marcus, 1 *DHSC*, 211–12; 6 *DHSC*, 180.

6. Marcus, 1 *DHSC*, 305; 2 *DHSC*, 483; 6 *DHSC*, 181–82.

7. An Act for Confiscating the Estates of Certain Persons Commonly Called Absentees (April 30, 1779), *Acts and Laws*, April 1779 session, 233–36; Marcus, 6 *DHSC*, 199.

8. Marcus, 6 *DHSC*, 200.

9. Marcus, 6 *DHSC*, 200.

10. Marcus, 6 *DHSC*, 201.

11. Marcus, 6 *DHSC*, 202.

12. Marcus, 1 *DHSC*, 207, 210–11; 6 *DHSC*, 200, 202.

13. Marcus, 1 *DHSC*, 177; 6 *DHSC*, 204 n. 26.

14. Marcus, 6 *DHSC*, 203.

15. Marcus, 1 *DHSC*, 212–13; 6 *DHSC*, 203.

16. Jay to Cushing August 6, 1793, Nuxoll, ed., 5 *Selected Papers of John Jay*, 544–45; Marcus, 1 *DHSC*, 218; 6 *DHSC*, 204 and 211 (capitalizations as in the original). Justice Cushing was not present for Martin's application.

17. Dana to Robert Treat Paine February 17, 1794, Marcus, 6 *DHSC*, 204 and 204 n. 33.

18. Marcus, 6 *DHSC*, 205 n. 37.
19. 1 Stat. 138 (1790).
20. 1 Stat. 138 (1790); Marcus, 6 *DHSC*, 356–57.
21. Marcus, 6 *DHSC*, 358–59.
22. Marcus, 6 *DHSC*, 360.
23. Marcus, 1 *DHSC*, 228; 6 *DHSC*, 358, 360.

Chapter 12

1. UNC, "Timeline: The Revolutionary and Napoleonic Wars (1792–1815)"; Blum et al., eds., *National Experience*, 139–40; Monaghan, *John Jay*, 363; Stahr, *John Jay*, 313.

2. Blum et al., eds., *National Experience*, 140. In the late 1700s, the practice of tarring and feathering did not use actual hot tar as we know it today, but pine tar used then in the building of ships. Pine tar does not have to be particularly hot to be sticky, and therefore tarring and feathering typically did not burn the subject or cause serious injury or death.

3. Hamilton to Washington April 14, 1794, Syrett, ed., 16 *Papers of Alexander Hamilton*, 278–79; Monaghan, *John Jay*, 366; Pellew, *John Jay, American Statesman*, 265; Stahr, *John Jay*, 314.

4. Monaghan, *John Jay*, 366; Stahr, *John Jay*, 314–15.

5. John Jay to Sarah Jay April 15, 1794 and April 19, 1794, Nuxoll, ed., 5 *Papers of John Jay*, 606–7, 622–23; Jay, *Life of John Jay*, 311; Monaghan, *John Jay*, 366–67.

6. Sarah Jay to John Jay April 22, 1794, Nuxoll, ed., 5 *Papers of John Jay*, 606–7, 625–26; Freeman, North, and Wedge, *Selected Correspondence of John Jay*, 220–21; Jay, *Life of John Jay*, 310; Monaghan, *John Jay*, 366–67.

7. Stahr, *John Jay*, 315.

8. Jay, *Life of John Jay*, 314; Monaghan, John Jay, 367.

9. John Adams to Abigail Adams April 19, 1794, Hogan et al., eds., 10 *Adams Papers*, 147–49.

10. Monaghan, *John Jay*, 368.

11. Blum et al., eds., *National Experience*, 140.

12. 8 Stat. 116 (1794); Monaghan, *John Jay*, 376, 381 (noting end date as November 13, 1794); Stahr, *John Jay*, 330 (noting end date as November 19, 1794). Stahr, *John Jay*, 328–29.

13. Jay Treaty, 8 Stat. 116 (1794); Johnston, 4 *Correspondence and Public Papers of John Jay*, 137–44; Johnson, *John Jay*, 43.

14. Monaghan, *John Jay*, 387; Stahr, *John Jay*, 333–34; Jay, *Life of John Jay*, 356.

15. Monaghan, *John Jay*, 389; Stahr, *John Jay*, 335.

16. Monaghan, *John Jay*, 390.

17. Freeman, *Washington*, 666; Monaghan, *John Jay*, 390. The Senate "leaker" might have been Virginia Senator Stevens Thomson Mason, as he was the individual who "authorized" Bache to later publish the treaty in full. Gienapp, *Second Creation*, 257.

18. Hulsebosch, "A Civilized Nation," 1039–40; Freeman, *Washington*, 667; Monaghan, *John Jay*, 390–94; Stahr, *John Jay*, 336; Pellew, *American Statesman*, 281; Webster, *Can a Chief Justice Love God?*, 125–26; Johnson, *John Jay*, 44; Gienapp, *Second Creation*, 256 quoting Wimmiam Mumford, *Poems and Compositions in Prose on Several Occasions* (Richmond: Samuel Pleasants, 1798).

19. Freeman, *Washington*, 670; Jay, *Life of John Jay*, 356–57, 360, 362; Jefferson to Thomas Mann Randolph Jr. August 11, 1795, Catanzariti, ed., 28 *Papers of Thomas Jefferson*, 434–35; Brodie, *Thomas Jefferson: An Intimate History*, 370; Monaghan, *John Jay*, 393; Stahr, *John Jay*, 336.

20. Jay, *Life of John Jay*, 368; Hulsebosch, "A Civilized Nation," 1040.

21. Ellis, *American Creation*, 197; Faigman, *Laboratory of Justice*, 34; Stahr, *John Jay*, 337. The specific source of Jay's often-repeated quip is of uncertain origin and is not historically confirmed.

22. Washington to Randolph July 22, 1795, Ebel, ed., 18 *Papers of George Washington*, 403–4; Freeman, Washington, 676; "British-American Diplomacy, The Jay Treaty," Yale Law School Avalon Project.

23. Stahr, *John Jay*, 338.

24. Jay to Henry Lee July 11, 1795, *Papers of John Jay*, Columbia Digital Library, apt://columbia.edu/columbia.jay/data/jjbw/12870/12870001.TIF; Johnson, ed., 4 *Correspondence and Public Papers of John Jay*, 178–79; Jay, *Life of John Jay*, 377.

25. Only *Bingham v Cabot* is officially reported, at 3 U.S. 19 (1795). Information about the other cases may be found at Marcus, 5 *DHSC*, 65–67 (*Oswald*), 6 *DHSC*, 389, 392–96 (Penhallow), 6 *DHSC*, 514–17 (Ex Parte *Corbly*), and 6 *DHSC*, 522–36 (*Laurance*).

26. *Brighan v Cabot*, 3 U.S. 19.

27. Gerber, ed., *Seriatim*, 86; Monaghan. *John Jay*, 406; Wexler, "The First Three Chief Justices," 1385.

28. Spartacus Educational, "Lord Grenville."

29. Marcus, 1 *DHSC*, 780.

Chapter 13

1. Stahr, *John Jay*, 378; Family Tree, Jay Homestead Historic Site; North, "The 'Amiable' Children."

2. Jay, *Life of John Jay*, 285–86, 288; Monaghan, *John Jay*, 326, 336; Pellew, *American Statesman*, 214; Stahr, *John Jay*, 287–88. In a letter to John from Sarah Livingston Jay dated June 10, 1792, the vote of the canvasser board was reported

as 8–3 rather than 7–4. Sarah Jay to John Jay, June 10, 1792, Columbia Digital Library, https://dlc.library.columbia.edu/jay/ldpd:42314.

3. Den Hartog, *Patriotism & Piety*, 38; Jay, *Life of John Jay*, 385, 396; Johnson, *John Jay*, 46; Monaghan, *John Jay*, 410–12; Stahr, *John Jay*, 344–45, 355.

4. Monaghan, *John Jay*, 416; Pellew, *American Statesman*, 292.

5. Buckley, "The Governor—From Figurehead to Prime Minister," 869 note 14; Jay, *Life of John Jay*, 235; Webster, *Can a Chief Justice Love God?*, 111; Kaye, "New York's First Chief the Family Man," 8.

6. An Act for the Gradual Abolition of Slavery, March 29, 1799, 4 Laws of New York State, 22nd Session Ch. 62, 388–89.

7. Kaye, "New York's First Chief the Family Man," 9; An Act for the Gradual Abolition of Slavery, March 29, 1799, 4 Laws of New York State, 22nd Session Ch. 62, 388–89 (1799). The 1799 law was a forerunner to a more expansive abolitionist law passed in 1817. The 1817 law established July 4, 1827 as the date of emancipation for all children born to slaves in New York before July 4, 1799. Nonresidents could still enter New York with their slaves for up to nine months, and part-time state residents were allowed to bring slaves to the state temporarily. See Gradual Emancipation Law, NY. Sess. Laws 1817, p. 137, § 6 (1817). The law was challenged in the New York courts but was found constitutional in *Griffin v Potter*, 14 Wend. 209 (1835). The exceptions for visitors and part-time residents were repealed in 1841. See 1 N.Y. Rev. Stat. c. 20, tit. 7, Part 1, as amended by Act 1841, c. 247 (1841); Slavery in the North, "Emancipation in New York."

8. Van Santvoord, *Sketches*, 83.

9. Adams to Jay December 19, 1800, *Papers of John Jay*, Columbia Digital Library, apt://columbia.edu/columbia.jay/data/jjbw/13333/13333001.tif; Marcus, 1 *DHSC*, 145–46.

10. Johnson, *John Jay 1745–1829*, 47; Stahr, *John Jay*, 363.

11. Jay to Adams January 2, 1801, *Papers of John Jay*, Columbia Digital Library, apt://columbia.edu/columbia.jay/data/jjbw/06430/06430001.tif; Marcus, 4 *DHSC* 146–47; Pellew, *American Statesman*, 301; Stahr, *John Jay*, 363.

12. Stahr, *John Jay*, 364; McCullough, *John Adams*, 560.

13. McCullough, *John Adams*, 560; Supreme Court Historical Society, "Timeline of the Justices—John Marshall"; Blum et al., eds., *National Experience*, 182.

14. *Marbury v Madison*, 5 U.S. 137 (1803); *Fletcher v Peck*, 10 U.S. 87 (1810); *Gibbons v Ogden*, 22 U.S. 1 (1824).

15. John Jay Homestead, "History"; Stahr, *John Jay*, 365–66; Johnson, *John Jay*, 49. Jay's brother Peter was affectionately known within the family as "blind Peter," which distinguished him from other members of the family with the same first name.

16. Jay, *Life of John Jay*, 430; Monaghan, *John Jay*, 428; Stahr, *John Jay*, 367.

17. Jay, *Life of John Jay*, 443, 450; John Jay Homestead, "History"; North, "The 'Amiable' Children"; Monaghan, *John Jay*, 431; New York State Unified Court System, "9th Judicial District, History."

18. Jay, *Life of John Jay*, 444.

19. North, "The 'Amiable' Children."

20. National Archives, "Historical Election Results."

21. National Archives, "Historical Election Results."

22. Morris, *Winning of the Peace*, 709; Webster, *Can a Chief Justice Love God?*, 132; American Antiquarian Society, "Members"; John Jay Homestead, "History"; Jay, *Life of John Jay*, 449–50; Pellew, *American Statesman*, 311; Stahr, *John Jay*, 380.

23. Jay to Van Schaack July 28, 1812, *Papers of John Jay*, Columbia Digital Library, apt://columbia.edu/columbia.jay/data/jjbw/09440/09440001.TIF; Jay, *Life of John Jay*, 445; Stahr, *John Jay*, 372.

24. Jay to Elias Boudinot November 17, 1819, 4 *Correspondence and Public Papers of John Jay*, 430; Stahr, *John Jay*, 372; Blum et al., eds., *National Experience*, 196.

25. Jay to Adams May 7, 1821, Founders Online, National Archives, https://founders.archives.gov/documents/Adams/99-02-02-7487; Jay to Murray April 24, 1821, Papers of John Jay, Columbia Digital Library, apt://columbia.edu/columbia.jay/data/jjbw/09600/09600001.TIF; Monaghan, John Jay, 430–31; Stahr, John Jay, 383.

26. Jay, *Life of John Jay*, 459–60; Monaghan, *John Jay*, 436; Pellew, *American Statesman*, 315.

27. Find a Grave, *John Jay*.

Chapter 14

1. Dillon, "When All Judges Were Originalists," 28; "Baroni, "Celebrating Our Constitution," 14. Woodrow Wilson was among the first persons of national statute to popularize the concept in his book *Constitutional Government in the United States*, originally published in 1908.

2. Jay, *Life of John Jay*, 95.

3. Wordpress.com, "Jay Street"; Moscow, *The Street Book*; BK News, "20 Brooklyn Street Names."

4. CIA, "The Founding Fathers of American Intelligence."

5. John Jay Homestead, "History."

Bibliography

Primary Source Historical Collections

John Adams Collections

American State Papers: Foreign Relations. Vol. 1. "Proclamation" and "Instructions to the Collectors of Customs." Accessed March 15, 2018. http://memory.loc.gov/cgi-bin/ampage?collId=llsp&fileName=001/llsp001.db&Page=140.

Cappon, Lester J., ed. *The Adams-Jefferson Letters: The Complete Correspondence Between Thomas Jefferson and Abigail and John Adams*. Vols. 1, 2. Chapel Hill: University of North Carolina Press, 1959.

Hogan, Margaret A., James Taylor, Sara Martin, Hobson Woodward, Sara B. Sikes, Gregg L. Lint, and Sara Georgini, eds. *The Adams Papers*, "*Adams Family Correspondence*." Vol. 10. Cambridge: Harvard University Press, 2011.

Founders Online, National Archives. "Message of John Adams to Congress Jan. 8, 1798." https://founders.archives.gov/documents/Adams/99-02-02-7487.

Alexander Hamilton Collections

Syrett, Harold C. *The Papers of Alexander Hamilton*. Vols. 14, 15, 16. New York: Columbia University Press, 1969 (Vols. 14–15), 1972 (Vol. 16).

Harold C. Syrett, ed. *The Papers of Alexander Hamilton, Digital Edition*. Charlottesville: University of Virginia Press, Rotunda, 2011. http://rotunda.upress.virginia.edu/founders/default.xqy?keys=ARHN-print-01&mode=TOC.

John Jay Collections

Family Tree provided by the Jay Homestead Historic Site, Katonah, New York. November 12, 2019.

Freeman, Linda M., Louise V. North, and Janet M. Wedge. *Selected Letters of John Jay and Sarah Livingston Jay: Correspondence by or to the First Chief Justice of the United States and His Wife*. Jefferson, NC: McFarland & Company, Inc., Publishers, 2005.

John Jay Papers. New York Historical Society Museum and Library, New York, New York.

Johnston, Henry P., ed. *The Correspondence and Public Papers of John Jay*. Vols. 1–4. New York: G.P. Putnam's Sons, 1890.

Nuxoll, Elizabeth, ed. *The Selected Papers of John Jay*. Vols. 1, 4, 5. Charlottesville: University of Virginia Press, 2010 (Vol. 1), 2015 (Vol. 4), and 2017 (Vol. 5).

The Papers of John Jay. Rare Book and Manuscript Room of Butler Library, Columbia University, New York, New York.

The Papers of John Jay, Digital Edition. Columbia University Digital Library Collection. https://dlc.library.columbia.edu/sites/jay.

Thomas Jefferson Collections

Catanzariti, John, ed. *The Papers of Thomas Jefferson*. Vols. 25, 26, 27, 28. Princeton: Princeton University Press, 1992 (Vol. 25), 1995 (Vol. 26), 1997 (Vol. 27), 2000 (Vol. 28).

George Washington Collections

Ebel, Carol S., ed. *The Papers of George Washington, Presidential Series*. Vol. 18. Charlottesville: University of Virginia Press, 2015.

Haggard, Robert S., and Mark A. Mastromarino, eds. *The Papers of George Washington, Presidential Series*. Vol. 10. Charlottesville: University of Virginia Press, 2002.

Hoth, David R., ed. *The Papers of George Washington, Presidential Series*. Vol. 14. Charlottesville: University of Virginia Press, 2008.

Mastromarino, Mark A., ed. *The Papers of George Washington, Presidential Series*. Vol. 6. Charlottesville: University Press of Virginia, 1996.

The Papers of George Washington, Series 2, Letterbooks 1754 to 1799. Letterbook 30, March 19, 1794–October 11, 1796. Manuscript/Mixed Material. https://www.loc.gov/item/mgw2.030/.

Patrick, Christine Sternberg, ed. *The Papers of George Washington, Presidential Series*. Vol. 13. Charlottesville: University of Virginia Press, 2007.

Patrick, Christine Sternberg, and John C. Pinheiro, eds. *The Papers of George Washington, Presidential Series*. Vol. 12. Charlottesville: University of Virginia Press, 2005.

Miscellaneous Collections

Force, Peter, ed. *American Archives: Consisting of a Collection of Authentic Records, State Papers, Devates, and Letters and Other Notices of Publick Affairs*. Vols. 2, 6. Washington, DC: Government Printing Office, 1837–53.

Ford, Worthington C., Gaillard Hunt, John C. Fitzpatrick, Roscoe R. Hill, Kenneth E. Harris, and Steven D. Tilley, eds. *Journals of the Continental Congress, 1774–1789*. Vols. 1, 2, 12. Washington, DC: Government Printing Office, 1904–76.

Hastings, Hugh, ed. *Public Papers of George Clinton, First Governor of New York, 1777–1795, 1801–1804*. Vol. 3. Albany: State University of New York Press, 1900.

Journals of the Provincial Congress, Provincial Convention, Committee of Safety and Council of Safety of the State of New York. Vols. 1 and 2. Albany: Thurlow Reed, 1842.

Library of Congress, Digital Edition. "An Address to the People of the State of New York." http://https://www.loc.gov/resource/bdsdcc.c0501/?sp=1.

Minute Books of the Supreme Court of Judicature. New York County Clerk's Office, Division of Old Records, Box 12.

The Papers of Benjamin Kissam, 1755–1776. Arthur J. Morris Law Library Special Collections. Charlottesville: University of Virginia. http://archives.law.virginia.edu/records/mss/84-11.

Ragsdale, Bruce A., ed. Federal Judicial History Office. "Debates on the Federal Judiciary: A Documentary History: Vol. 1: 1787–1875" (2013). Accessed July 19, 2019. https://fjc.gov/content/debate-federal-judiciary-documentary-history-volume-I-1787%E2%80%931875.

Smith, Paul H. et al., eds. *Letters to Delegates to Congress, 1774–1789*. Vols. 1–3, 11. Washington, DC: Government Printing Office, 1976–99.

U.S. Government, Naval Documents of the American Revolution. Vol. 3. Washington, DC: United States Government Printing Office, 1968, electronically published by American Naval Records Society. Accessed November 20, 2019. http://ibiblio.org/anrs/docs/E/E3/ndar_v03p06.pdf.

Yale Law School Lillian Goldman Library's Avalon Project. "British-American Diplomacy, The Jay Treaty." Accessed July 3, 2018. http://avalon.law.yale.edu/18th_century/jay.asp.

Yale Law School Lillian Goldman Library's Avalon Project. "Declaration of Paris of April 16, 1856." Accessed September 21, 2018. http://avalon.law.yale.edu/19th_century/decparis.asp.

Yale Law School Lillian Goldman Library's Avalon Project. "Treaty of Amity and Commerce Between the United States and France, February. 6, 1778." Accessed March 11, 2018. http://avalon.law.yale.edu/18th_century/fr1788-1.asp.

Museums and Historic Sites

Bedford Museum at the Bedford Courthouse, Bedford, New York
Fraunces Tavern Museum, New York, New York
Jay Heritage Center, Rye, New York
John Jay Homestead State Historic Site, Bedford, New York
Independence Hall, Philadelphia, Pennsylvania
Old City Hall, Philadelphia, Pennsylvania
Van Wyck Homestead Museum, Fishkill, New York
William Paca House and Garden, Annapolis, Maryland

Photograph Archives

Columbia University, Rare Book and Manuscript Room of the Butler Library
Fenimore Art Museum, Cooperstown, New York
Fraunces Tavern Photo Collection
Jay Heritage Center, Rye, New York
John Jay Homestead State Historic Site, Bedford, New York
Library of Congress, Prints and Photographs Division
Library of Virginia, State Artwork Collection
Massachusetts Historical Society
National Archives and Records Administration
New York Historical Society Museum and Library Digital Collections
US Supreme Court Photograph Archive
Wikimedia Photo Commons
Worcester Art Museum, Worcester, Massachusetts

Book, Articles, and Assorted Internet Sources

Alryck, Kevin. "The Courts and Foreign Affairs at the Founding." 2017 *B.Y.U. L. Rev.* 1 (2017).

American Antiquarian Society. "Members." Accessed June 28, 2018. http://www.americanantiquarian.org/memberlistj.

American Numismatic Society. "A History of American Currency." Accessed March 22, 2018. http://numismatics.org/a-history-of-american-currency/.

Ammon, Harry. *The Genet Mission*. New York: W.W. Norton & Company, Inc., 1973.

Barnett, Randy E. "The People or the State?: Chisholm v. Georgia and Popular Sovereignty." 93 *Virginia Law Review* 1729 (November 2007).

Barone, Patrick T. "Independent Juries: Liberty's Last Defense." 36 *Champion* 24 (December 2012).

Baroni, Michael. "Celebrating Our Constitution." 53 *Orange County Lawyer* 12 (November 2011).

Bates, Earnest Sutherland. *The Story of the Supreme Court*. 1st ed. Indianapolis, IN: Bobbs-Merrill Company Publishers, 1936.

Bioguide.congress.gov. "King, Rufus." Accessed October 1, 2018. http://bioguide.congress.gov/scripts/biodisplay.pl?index=k000212.

BK News. "20 Brooklyn Street Names & the Meaning Behind Them." Accessed September 23, 2018. http://ourbksocial.com/20-brooklyn-street-names-meaning-behind/.

Blinka, Daniel D. "'This Germ of Rottedness': Federal Trials in the New Republic, 1789–1807." 36 *Creighton Law Review* 135 (2003).

Blum, John M., Edmund S. Morgan, Willie Lee Rose, Arthur M. Schlesinger Jr., Kenneth M. Stampp, and C. Vann Woodward. *The National Experience: A History of the United States*. 4th ed. New York: Harcourt Brace Jovanovich, Inc., 1977.

Brodie, Fawn M. *Thomas Jefferson: An Intimate History*. New York: Bantam Books, Inc., 1974.

Campbell, Ballard C. *Disasters, Accidents, and Crises in American History: A Reference Guide to the Nation's Most Catastrophic Events*. New York: Facts on File, 2008.

Casto, William R. *Foreign Affairs and the Constitution in the Age of Fighting Sail*. Columbia: University of South Carolina Press, 2006.

Casto, William. "The Early Supreme Court Justices' Most Significant Opinion." 29 *Ohio Northern University Law Review* 173 (2002).

Casto, William R. *The Supreme Court in the Early Republic: The Chief Justiceships of John Jay and Oliver Ellsworth*. Columbia: University of South Carolina Press, 1995.

Central Intelligence Agency Library, P. K. Rose. "The Founding Fathers of American Intelligence." https://www.cia.gov/library/center-for-the-study-of-intelligence/csi-publications/books-and-monographs/the-founding-fathers-of-american-intelligence/art-1.html.

Christie's Auctions and Private Sales. *The Federalist Papers*. Accessed May 18, 2018. https://www.christies.com/lotfinder/Lot/the-federalist-papers-hamilton-alexander-1739-1802-6052509-details.aspx.

Chroust, Anton-Hermann. "Legal Profession in Colonial America." 33 *Notre Dame Law Review* 350 (1958).

City-Data.com. "Paterson—History." Accessed September 8, 2018. http://www.city-data.com/us-cities/The-Northeast/Paterson-History.html.

Civil War Trust. "Revolutionary War—FAQs." Accessed April 5, 2018. https://www.civilwar.org/learn/articles/american-revolution-faqs.

Clark, Bradford R. "The Eleventh Amendment and the Nature of the Union." 123 *Harvard Law Review* 1817 (June 2010).

Clark, Ronald W. *Benjamin Franklin: A Biography*. New York: Random House, 1983.

Clinton Chamber of Commerce. "A Brief History of Clinton." Accessed September 19, 2018. https://www.clintonnychamber.org/our-history.html.

Cohen, Ira. "Rhode Island Federal Courts: A History." 61 *Fed. Law.* 54 (September 2014).

Colombos, Constantine John. *A Treatise on the Law of Prize*. London: Sweet & Maxwell, Ltd., 1926.

Columbia University in the City of New York. "History." Accessed May 6, 2018. https://www.columbia.edu/content/history.

Cooke, Jacob E. *Alexander Hamilton*. New York: Charles Scribner's Sons, 1982.

Cooper, James Fenimore. *The Spy: A Tale of the Neutral Ground*. New York: Heritage Press, 1963 (reprint).

Deak, Francis, and Philip C. Jessup. "Early Prize Court Procedure: Part One." 82 *Univ. of Pennsylvania Law Review* 677 (May 1934).

Den Hartog. *Patriotism & Piety: Federalist Politics and Religious Struggle in the New American Nation*. Charlottesville: University of Virginia Press, 2015.

Dillon, Mark C. "A New York State of Mind: The Career and Cases of John Jay, the First Chief Justice of the United States." 90 *New York State Bar Journal* 30 (May 2018).

Dillon, Mark C. "U.S. Chief Justice John Jay: When All Judges Were Originalists." 15 *Judicial Notice* 21 (Spring 2020).

Doyle, William. *The Oxford History of the French Revolution*. Oxford: Oxford University Press, 2002.

Elkins, Stanley M., and Eric McKitrick. *The Age of Federalism*. New York: Oxford University Press, 1993.

Ellis, Joseph J. *American Creation*. New York: Vintage Books, 2007.

Ellis, Joseph J. *The Quartet: Orchestrating the Second American Revolution, 1783–1789*. New York: Vintage Books, 2015.

Engelman, F. L. "Cadwallader Colden and the New York Stamp Act Riots." 10 *William & Mary Quarterly* 560 (Spring 1953).

eReferenceDesk. "Clinton County, New York." Accessed September 19, 2018. http://www.ereferencedesk.com/resources/counties/new-york/clinton.html.

Estes, Todd. *The Jay Treaty Debate, Public Opinion, and the Evolution of Early American Culture*. Amherst: University of Massachusetts Press, 2006.

Faigman, David L. *Laboratory of Justice, The Supreme Court's 200 Year Struggle to Integrate Science and the Law*. 1st ed. New York: Henry Holt & Co. 2008.

Find a Grave. "John Jay." Accessed January 15, 2018. https://www.findagrave.com/cemetery/641195/john-jay-cemetery.

Flanders. Henry. *The Lives and Times of the Chief Justices of the Supreme Court of the United States*. Vol. 1. Philadelphia: T. & J.S. Johnson & Co. Law Booksellers and Publishers, 1881.

Freeman, Douglas Southall. *Washington*. New York: Charles Scribner's Sons, 1968.

Garner, Bryan. "Remembering Lindley Murray, an Inspirational Lawyer-Grammarian." *ABA Journal*. Accessed July 8, 2018. http://www.abajournal.com/magazine/article/remembering_lindley_murray_an_inspirational_lawyer-grammarian/news/article/judges_and_the_administrative_state/?icn=sidebar&ici=bottom.

Gerber, Scott Douglas, ed. *Seriatim: The Supreme Court Before John Marshall*. New York: New York University Press, 1998.

Gienapp, Jonathan. *The Second Creation: Fixing the American Constitution in the Founding Era*. Cambridge: Belknap Press of Harvard University Press, 2018.

Goebel, Julius D., Jr. *History of the Supreme Court of the United States, Antecedents and Beginnings to 1801*. Vol. 1. New York: Macmillan Publishing Co., Inc., 1974.

Glick, Joshua. "On the Road: The Supreme Court and the History of Circuit Riding." 24 *Cardozo Law Review* 1753 (April 2003).

Giunta, Mary A., J. Dane Hartgrove, Norman A. Graebner, Peter P. Hill, and Lawrence S. Kaplan, eds. *The Emerging Nation: A Documentary History of the Foreign Relations of the United States Under the Articles of Confederation, 1780–1789*. Vols. 1–3. Washington, DC: Government Printing Office, 1996.

Hamilton, Alexander, James Madison, and John Jay. *The Federalist Papers*. Mineola: Dover Publications, Inc., 2014.

Henderson, Dwight. *Courts for a New Nation*. Washington, DC: Public Affairs Press, 1971.

Historical Society of the New York Courts. "Crown v William Prendergast." Accessed May 10, 2018. http://www.nycourts.gov/history/legal-history-new-york/legal-history-eras-01/history-new-york-legal-eras-crown-predergast.html.

Historical Society of the Courts of the State of New York. "Duely & Constantly Kept." Accessed July 13, 2018. http://www.nycourts.gov/history/legal-history-new-york/documents/History_Supreme-Court-Duely-Constantly-Kept.pdf.

Historical Society of the New York Courts. "Robert Yates." Accessed September 19, 2018. http://www.nycourts.gov/history/legal-history-new-york/legal-history-eras-02/history-era-02-yates-r.html.

Historicalstatistics.org. "Historical Currency Converter." Accessed April 26, 2018. www.historicalstatistics.org/Currencyconverter.html.

Holt, Wythe. "'To Establish Justice': Politics, the Judiciary Act of 1789, and the Invention of the Federal Courts." 1989 *Duke Law Journal* 1421 (December 1989).

Hulsebosch, Daniel J. "A Civilized Nation: The Early American Constitution, the Law of Nations, and the Pursuit of International Recognition." 85 *New York Univ. Law Review* 932 (October 2010).

Hulsebosch, Daniel J. "Being Seen Like a State: How Americans (and Britons) Built the Constitutional Infrastructure of a Developing Nation." 59 *William & Mary Law Review* 1239 (March 2018).

Hulsebosch, Daniel J. "The Founders' Foreign Affairs Constitution: Improvising Among Empires." 53 *St. Louis University Law Journal* 209 (Fall 2008).

John Jay Homestead. "History." Accessed June 29, 2018. http://johnjayhomestead.org/about-us/history/.

John Jay Homestead. "The Life of John Jay." Accessed June 29, 2018. http://johnjayhomestead.org/about-john-jay/the-life-of-john-jay/.

Jay, William. *The Life of John Jay*. New York: J & J Harper, 1833.

Johnson, Herbert Alan. *John Jay: Colonial Lawyer*. Washington, DC: Beard Books, 2006.

Johnson, Herbert Alan. "John Jay: Lawyer in a Time of Transition." 126 *Univ. of Pennsylvania Law Review* 1764–1775, 1260 (May 1976).

Johnson, Herbert Alan. *John Jay 1745–1829*. Albany: New York State American Revolution Bicentennial Commission, 1976.

Joyce, Craig. "The Rise of the Supreme Court Reporter: An Institutional Perspective on Marshall Court Ascendancy." 83 *Michigan Law Review* 1291 (April 1985).

Kaye, Judith S. "Kaye on Jay: New York's First Chief the Family Man." 8 *Judicial Notice* 3 (Spring 2012).

Lahn, Jonathan. "The Demise of the Law-Finding Jury in America and the Birth of American Legal Science: History and Its Challenge for Contemporary Society." 57 *Cleveland State Law Review* 553 (2009).

Larsen, Timothy W. "West v Barnes: The First Supreme Court Decision." 59 *Rhode Island Bar Journal* 13 (July/August 2010).

Lash, Kurt T. "Leaving the Chisholm Trail: The Eleventh Amendment and the Principle of Strict Construction." 50 *William and Mary Law Review* 1579 (April 2009).

Laws.com. "Understanding the 11th Amendment." Accessed April 20, 2018. https://constitution.laws.com/american-history/constitution/constitutional-amendments/eleventh-amendment.

MacDonald, Joan Vos. "Fishkill and Its Role in the Revolution." *Hudson Valley Magazine* 19 (July 2018).

Main, Jackson Turner. *The Anti-federalists: Critics of the Constitution 1781–1788*. New York: W.W. Norton & Company, Inc., 1961.

Marcus, Maeva, ed. *The Documented History of the Supreme Court of the United States, 1789–1800*. Vols. 1–6 (referred to in footnotes as DHSC). New York: Columbia University Press, 1988.

Marcus, Maeva. "Is the Supreme Court a Political Institution?" 72 *George Washington Law Review* 95 (December 2003).

Marcus, Maeva. "The Effect (or Non-Effect) of Founders on the Supreme Court Bench." 80 *George Washington Law Review* 1794 (November 2012).

Marcus, Maeva, and Robert Teir. "Hayburn's Case: A Misinterpretation of Precedent." 1988 *Wisconsin Law Review* 527 (1988).

Mark, Irving, and Handlin, Oscar. "Land Cases in Colonial New York 1765–1767: The King v William Prendergast." 19 *N.Y.U. L.Q. Rev.* 165 (1941–1942).

Mazzone, Jason, and Carl Emery Woock. "Federalism as Docket Control." 94 *North Carolina Law Review* 7 (December 2015).

McCullough, David. *John Adams*. New York: Simon & Schuster, 2001.

Minnigerode, Meade. *Jefferson: Friend of France 1793*. New York: G.P. Putnam's Sons, 1928.

Monaghan, Frank. *John Jay*. New York: The Bobbs-Merrill Company, 1935.

Morris, Richard B. ed. *John Jay: The Making of a Revolutionary*. New York: Harper & Row Publishers, 1975.

Morris, Richard B. *John Jay: The Nation and the Court*. Boston: Boston University Press, 1967.

Morris, Richard B. *John Jay: The Winning of the Peace*. New York: Harper & Row Publishers, 1980.

Morris, Richard B. *The Peacemakers: The Great Powers & American Independence*. New York: Harper & Row Publishers, 1965.

Moscow, Henry. *The Street Book: An Encyclopedia of Manhattan's Street Names and Their Origins*. New York: Fordham University Press, 1990.

Mulligan, Mary Claire. "Jury Nullification: Its History and Practice." 33 *Colorado Lawyer* 71 (December 2004).

National Archives and Records Administration. "U.S. Electoral College, Historical Election Results." https://www.archives.gov/federal-register/electoral-college/scores.html#1796.

National Archives Founders Online. "The Recall of Edmond Charles Genet." https://founders.archives.gov/documents/Jefferson/01-26-02-0629-0001.

Nelson, William E. "The Province of the Jury." 37 *John Marshall Law Review* 325 (2004).

New York State Unified Court System. "9th Judicial District, History." Accessed December 26, 2018. https://www.nycourts.gov/courts/9jd/westchester/countyhistory.shtml.

North Carolina History Project. "Encyclopedia—James Iredell, Sr." Accessed September 8, 2018. http://northcarolinahistory.org/encyclopedia/james-iredell-sr-1751-1799/.

North, Louise V. "The 'Amiable' Children of John and Sarah Livingston Jay." Conference at Columbia University and The New York Historical Society, December 10, 2004. Accessed July 6, 2018. http://www.columbia.edu/cu/lweb/conferences/2004/john_jay/pdf/North.pdf.

Nycourts.gov. "History—Robert R. Livingston." Accessed September 19, 2018. http://www.nycourts.gov/history/legal-history-new-york/luminaries-court-chancery/livingston-robert.html.

O'Connor, John E. William Paterson: *Lawyer and Statesman, 1745–1806*. New Brunswick: Rutgers University Press, 1979.

PBA Galleries. "1st Complete Edition of the Federalist Papers in Book Form on May 31st." Accessed May 18, 2018. http://www.pbagalleries.com/content.

Pelletreau, William S. *History of Putnam County, New York, With Biographical Sketches of Its Prominent Men*. Philadelphia: W. W. Preston & Co., 1886.

Pellow, George. *John Jay: American Statesman*. Cambridge: Riverside Press, 1890.

Prendergast, Ken. "Prendergast's Rent War, a Colonial American Rebellion." Accessed August 19, 2018. http://prendergast-rent-war.blogspot.com/.

Pfander, James E. "Judicial Compensation and the Definition of Judicial Power in the Early Republic." 107 *Michigan Law Review* 1 (October 2008).

Powell, H. Jefferson. "The United States as an Idea: Constitutional Reflections." 49 *Loyola Univ. of Chicago Law Review* 705 (Summer 2018).

Puls, Mark. *Henry Knox: Visionary General of the American Revolution*. New York: St. Martin's Griffin, 2008.

Randolph County Commission. "History of Randolph County, WV." Accessed April 7, 2018. https://randolphcountycommissionwv.org/our-county/.

Regnier, Thomas. "Restoring The Founders' Ideal of the Independent Jury in Criminal Cases." 51 *Santa Clara Law Review* 775 (2011).

Rheingold, Paul D. "John Jay: Practicing Trial Lawyer for Seven Years." 15 *Judicial Notice* 31 (2020).

Reinstein, Robert J. "Executive Power and the Law of Nations in the Washington Administration." 46 *Univ. of Richmond Law Review* 373 (January 2012).

The Robinson Library. "Edmond Charles Genet." Accessed September 1, 2018. http://www.robinsonlibrary.com/america/unitedstates/1783/1789/1789/genet.htm.

Rodell, Fred. *Nine Men: A Political History of the Supreme Court of the United States from 1790 to 1955*. New York: Random House, Inc., 1955.

Shelfer, Lochlan F. "Special Juries in the Supreme Court." 123 *Yale Law Journal* 208 (2013).

Shepherd, Jack. *The Adams Chronicles: Four Generations of Greatness*. Boston: Little, Brown and Company, 1975.

Slavery in the North. "Emancipation in New York." Accessed July 12, 2018. http://slavenorth.com/nyemancip.htm.

Sloss, David. "Judicial Foreign Policy: Lessons From the 1790s." 53 *St. Louis University Law Journal* 145 (2008).

Smith, Charles Anthony. "Credible Commitments and the Early American Supreme Court." 42 *Law and Society Review* 75 (March 2008).

Spartacus Educational. "William Grenville (Lord Grenville)." Accessed July 31, 2018. www.spartacus-educational.com.

Stahr, Walter. "John Jay as New York's First Chief Justice." 5 *Judicial Notice* 1 (Autumn 2007).

Stahr, Walter. *John Jay: Founding Father*. New York: Diversion Books, 2005.

Sweeney, Joseph Modeste. "A Tort Only in Violation of the Law of Nations." 18 *Hastings International and Comparative Law Review* 445 (Spring 1995).

Sunderland, Edson R. "Verdicts, General and Special." 29 *Yale Law Journal* 253 (1920).

Supreme Court Historical Society. "Homes of the Court." Accessed May 28, 2019. https://supremecourthistory.org/history-of-the-court/home-of-the-court/.

Supreme Court Historical Society. "Timeline of the Justices." Accessed September 8, 2018. http://supremecourthistory.org/history_timeline.html.

Thomas, Charles Marion. *American Neutrality in 1793: A Study in Cabinet Government*. New York: AMS Press, Inc. 1967.

Town of Clinton. "About." Accessed September 19, 2018. http://www.townofclinton.com/about/.

Treanor, William Michael. "Judicial Review Before Marbury." 58 *Stanford Law Review* 455 (November 2005).

United States Census Bureau. "History: 1790." Accessed March 18, 2018. https://www.census.gov/history/www.through_the_decades/fast_facts/1790_fast_facts.html.

United States Census Bureau. "Census Bureau Predicts U.S. and World Populations on New Years' Day." Accessed March 18, 2018. https://www.census.gov/newsroom/press-releases/2017/new-years-2018.html.

United States Department of Justice. "Attorney General: William Bradford." Accessed July 16, 2018. https://www.justice.gov/ag/bio/bradford-william.

United States Department of Veteran's Affairs. "America's Wars." Accessed April 5, 2018. htpps://www.va.gov/opa/publications/factsheets/fs_americas_wars.pfd.

United States District Court, District of Rhode Island. "Henry Marchant." Accessed July 16, 2018. http://www.rid.uscourts.gov/judges/henry-marchant.

United States Senate. "George Clinton, 4th Vice President (1805–1812)." Accessed July 31, 2018. https://www.senate.gov/artandhistory/history/common/generic/VP_George_Clinton.htm.

University of Groningen. "Biographies." Accessed September 8, 2018. http://www.let.rug.nl/usa/biographies/.

UNC. "Timeline: The Revolutionary and Napoleonic Wars (1792–1815)." Accessed January 26, 2018. http://www.unc.edu/nbi/texte/NBITimeline.pdf.

University of Virginia Arthur J. Morris Law Library. "Biographical Information, Benjamin Kissam." Accessed July 8, 2018. http://archives.law.virginia.edu/person/benjamin-kissam.

Van Santvoord, George. *Sketches of the Lives and Judicial Services of the Chief Justices of the United States*. New York: Charles Scribner, 1854.

Warren, Charles. "Earliest Cases of Judicial Review of State Legislation by Federal Courts." 32 *Yale Law Journal* 15 (November 1922).

Webster, Phil. *Can a Chief Justice Love God?* New York: HarperCollins Publishers Inc., 2002.

Welch, Hon. Richard E., III. "Mr. Sullivan's Trunk: Constitutional Common Law and Federalism." 46 *New England Law Review* 275 (Winter 2012).

West, George M. *William West of Scituate, R.I.: Farmer, Soldier, Statesman*. St. Andrews, FL: Panama City Publishing, 1919.

Wexler, Natalie. "In the Beginning: The First Three Chief Justices." 154 *Univ. of Pennsylvania Law Review* 1373 (June 2006).

White, Casey. *John Jay: Diplomat of the American Experiment*. New York: Rosen Publishing Group, Inc., 2006.

William Paterson University. "About Us—Who We Are." Accessed September 8, 2018. https://www.wpunj.edu/university/history/WilliamPaterson_Bio.html.

Williams, Greg H. *The French Assault on American Shipping 1793–1813: A History and Comprehensive Record of Merchant Marine Losses*. Jefferson, NC: McFarland & Company, Inc., 2009.

Wilson, Woodrow. *Constitutional Government in the United States*. New Orleans: Quid Pro, LLC, 2011.

Wordpress.com. "Jay Street, West Tribeca, Manhattan." Accessed September 19, 2018. https://mediahistoryny.wordpress.com/jay-street/.

Theses and Dissertations

Glasson, William Henry. "History of Military Pension Legislation in the United States." PhD Thesis, Columbia University Department of Political Science (1900). Accessed April 6, 2018. https://www.archive.org/stream/historyofmilitar00glasrich/historyofmilitar00glasrich_djvu.txt.

Vanhorn, Kellie Michelle. "Eighteenth-Century Colonial Merchant Ship Construction." Master of Arts Thesis, Office of Graduate Studies of Texas A & M University (December 2004). Accessed March 18, 2018. http://nautarch.tamu.edu/pdf-files/VanHorn-MA2004.pdf.

Newspapers

Aurora General Advertiser (Philadelphia)
The Diary (New York)
Daily Advertiser (New York)
Federal Gazette (Philadelphia)
General Advertiser (Philadelphia)
Independent Gazetteer (Philadelphia)
Independent Journal (New York City)

Maryland Journal (Baltimore)
National Gazette (Philadelphia)
New York Daily Gazette (New York)
New York Journal (New York)
New York Packet, later renamed the *New York Gazetteer Packet* (New York)
Providence Gazette (Providence)
United States Chronicle (Providence)

Government/Legal Sources

United States Constitution
New York State Constitution (1777)
New York State Constitution (rev. 2014)

Treaties and Proclamations

Proclamation Declaring the Cessation of Arms, as Well by Sea as by Land, Agreed Upon Between the United States of America and His Britannic Majesty (1793)
The Definitive Treaty of Peace, Signed at Paris (Treaty of Paris) (1783)
Commerce and Consular Convention (1788)
Treaty of Amity, Commerce, and Navigation ("The Jay Treaty") (1794)
Treaty of Amity and Commerce Between the United States and France (1778)
Declaration of Paris (1856)

United States Statutes

Treaty of Amity and Commerce Between the United States and France, 8 Stat. 22 (1778)
Treaty of Paris of September 3, 1783, 8 Stat. 81 (ratified January 14, 1784)
Commerce and Consular Convention of 1788, Proclaimed by President Washington April 9, 1790
The Compensation Act, ch. 18, 1 Stat. 72 (1789)
The Judiciary Act of September 24, 1789, ch. 20, 1 Stat. 73 (1789)
The Naturalization Act of March 26, 1790, 1 Stat. 103 (1790)
Act Making Provision for the Payment of Debt of the United States, ch. 34, 1 Stat. 138 (1790)
Process and Compensation Act of March 23, 1792, ch. 11, 1 Stat. 243 (1792)
The Judiciary Act of April 13, 1792, ch. 21, 1 Stat. 252 (1792)

Invalid Pensions Act of March 23, 1792, ch. 17, 1 Stat. 243 (1792)
Invalid Pensions Act of February 28, 1793, ch. 17, 1 Stat 324 (1793)
Preliminary Articles of Peace Between the United States of America and His Britannic Majesty
Judiciary Act of March 2, 1793, ch. 22, sec. 1, 1 Stat. 333, 333–34 (1793)
Act of September 22, 1793, ch. 17, 1 Stat. 70 (1793)
Act of June 5, 1794, ch. 50, sec. 1, 1 Stat. 381 (1794)
The Jay Treaty, 8 Stat. 116 (ratified June 24, 1795)
The Sedition Act, Act of July 14, 1798, 1 Stat. 596, ch. 73 (1798)
An Act to provide for the more Convenient Organization of the Courts of the United States, ch. 4, 2 Stat. 89 (1801) ("The Midnight Judges Act")
Judiciary Act of 1802, ch. 8, 2 Stat. 136 (1802)
Act of June 26, 1812, ch. 107, 2 Stat. 759 (1812)
Judiciary Act of 1891, ch. 517, secs. 2 and 3, 26 Stat. 826 (1891)

United States Decisional Authorities

Alden v Maine, 527 U.S. 706, 119 S.Ct. 2240, 144 L.Ed. 636 (1999)
Bingham v Cabot, 3 U.S. 19, 3 Dall. 19, 1 L.Ed 491 (1795)
Champion v Casey (unreported opinion, C.C. D.R.I., 1792)
Chisholm, Ex'r. v Georgia, 2 U.S. 419, 2 Dall. 419, 1 L.Ed. 440 (1793)
Collet v Collet (discontinued at Supreme Court before opinion, 1792)
Ex Parte *Corbly, Lockery, Hamilton, Segwick* (unreported US Supreme Court opinion, 1795)
Deblois v Hawley (unreported opinion, C.C. D.Conn, 1791)
Del Col v Arnold, 3 U.S. 333, 3 Dall. 333, 1 L.Ed. 872 (1796)
The Den Onzekeren, 3 U.S. 285, 3 U.S. Dall. 285, 1 L.Ed. 605 (1796)
Elliot v Sage (unreported opinion, C.C. D.Conn, 1791)
Findlay v The William, 9 F.Cas. 57, 1 Pet. Adm. 12 (D. Pa. 1793)
Fitzpatrick v Bitzer, 427 U.S. 445, 96 S. Ct. 2666, 49 L.Ed.2d 614 (1976)
Fletcher v Peck, 10 U.S. 87, 6 Cranch 87, 3 L.Ed. 162 (1810)
Gibbons v Ogden, 22 U.S. 1, 9 Wheat. 1, 6 L.Ed. 23 (1824)
Glass v Sloop Betsey, 3 U.S. 6, 3 Dall. 6, 1 L.Ed. 485 (1794)
Hamilton v Eaton, 11 F.Cas. 336, 1 Hughes 249, 1 N.C. 641 (C.C. D.N.C., 1792)
Hans v Louisiana, 134 U.S. 1, 10 S.Ct. 504, 33 L.Ed. 842 (1890)
In Re *Hayburn*, 2 U.S. 408, 2 Dall. 408, 1 L.Ed. 436 (1792)
Henfield's Case, 11 F.Cas. 1099, Whart.St.Tr. 49 (C.C. D.Pa., 1793)
Hills v Ross, 3 U.S. 311, 3 Dall. 311, 1 L.Ed. 623 (1796)
Hollingsworth v Virginia, 3 U.S. 378, 3 Dall. 378, 1 L.Ed. 644 (1798)
Kingsley v Jenkins (unreported US Supreme Court opinion, 1793)
Marbury v Madison, 5 U.S. 137, 1 Cranch 137, 2 L.Ed. 60 (1803)

Ex Parte *Martin* (unreported US Supreme Court opinion, 1793)
Martins v Ballard, 16 F. Cas. 923, Bee 51 (D. S.C., 1794)
Meade v The Brigantine Catherine (unreported opinion, D. N.Y., 1793)
Monsanto Co. v Geerston Seed Farms, 561 U.S. 139, 130 S.Ct. 2743, 177 L.Ed. 461 (2010)
Moodie v The Ship Phoebe Anne, 3 U.S. 319, 3 Dall. 319, 1 L.Ed. 618 (1796)
Moxon v The Fanny, 17 F.Cas. 942, 2 Pet. Adm. 309 (D. Pa. 1793)
New York Times v Sullivan, 376 U.S. 254, 84 S.Ct. 710, 11 L.Ed.2d 686 (1964)
Oswald v New York, 2 U.S. 401, 2 Dall. 401, 1 L.Ed. 433 (1792)
Oswald v New York, 2 U.S. 402, 2 U.S. 402, 1 L.Ed. 433 (1792)
Oswald v New York, 2 U.S. 415, 2 Dall. 415, 1 L.Ed. 438 (1793)
Pagan v Hooper (unreported Supreme Court opinion denying proposed writ, 1793)
Penhallow's v Doane's Administrators, 3 U.S. 54, 3 Dall. 54, 1795 WL 821 (1795)
Skinner v May (unreported opinion, C.C. D.Mass., 1794)
Sparf v United States, 156 U.S. 51, 15 S.Ct. 273, 39 L.Ed. 343 (1895)
State of Georgia v Brailsford, 2 U.S. 402, 2 Dall. 402, 1 L.Ed. 433 (1792)
State of Georgia v Brailsford, 2 U.S. 415, 2 Dall. 415, 1 L. Ed 438 (1793)
State of Georgia v Brailsford, 3 U.S. 1, 3 Dall. 1, 1 L.Ed. 483 (1794)
Talbot v Jansen, 3 U.S. 133, 3 Dall. 133, 1 L. Ed 540 (1795)
United States v Ferreira, 54 U.S. 40, 13 How. 40, 14 L.Ed. 40 (1851)
United States v Hopkins (unreported Supreme Court opinion, 1794)
United States v Hudson, 11 U.S. 32, 7 Cranch 32, 3 L.Ed 259 (1812)
United States v Peters, 3 U.S. 121, 3 Dall. 121, 1 L. Ed 535 (1795)
United States v Todd (unreported US Supreme Court opinion, 1794), excerpted in *United States v Ferreira*, 54 U.S. 40, 13 How. 40, 14 L.Ed. 40 (1851)
Vanhorne's Lessee v Dorrance, 2 U.S. 304, 2 Dall. 304, 28 F.Cas. 1028 (C.C. D.Pa., 1795)
VanStophorst v State of Maryland, 2 U.S. 401, 2 Dall. 401, 1 L.Ed. 433 (1791)
Ware, Administrator of Jones v Hylton, 3 U.S. 199, 3 Dall. 199, 1 L.Ed. 568 (1796)
West v Barnes, 2 U.S. 401, 2 Dall. 401, 1 L.Ed. 433 (1791)

State Statutes

Rhode Island Sequestration Act (August 1786), suspended eff. September 19, 1789, repealed eff. October 12, 1789
Act Va. October 20, 1777
An Act for Confiscating the Estates of Certain Persons Commonly Called Absentees (April 30, 1779), Acts and Laws, Passed by the Great and General Court or Assembly of the State of the Massachusetts Bay, in New England [April 1779 session]
Georgia Sequestration Act of May 4, 1782

An Act for the Restraining the Taking of Excessive Usury, March 16, 1784, The First Laws of the Commonwealth of Massachusetts (March 16, 1784)
An Act for the Gradual Abolition of Slavery, March 29, 1799, Laws of New York State, 22nd Session Chap. 62, vol. 4, 388–89 (1799)
Gradual Emancipation Law, N.Y. Sess. Laws 1817, p. 137, § 6 (1817)
Laws of the State of New York. Vols. 1–5. Albany: Weed, Parsons (1886–87)
1 N.Y. Rev. Stat. c. 20, tit. 7, Part 1, as amended by Act 1841, c. 247 (1841)
Sess. of May 1784, 1784 Conn. Laws 283–84 (1984)

New York State Decisional Authorities

Anthony v Franklin (unreported)
Bloomer v Hinchman (unreported, High Court of Chancery)
Budd v Thompkins (unreported, Westchester County, New York 1770)
Canfield v Dickerson (unreported, Westchester County, New York 1771)
Crown v Prendergast (unreported, Dutchess County, New York)
Deane v Vernon (unreported, New York County 1772)
Doe, John ex dem. *Philip Verplanck v Griffin* (unreported)
Forsey v Cunningham (unreported)
Griffin v Potter, 14 Wend. 209 (1835)
King v Underhill (unreported, Westchester County, New York)
Leadbetter v Harison (unreported)
Quiet, Peter ex. dem. *Susannah Warren v Van Cortlandt* (unreported)
Rapalje v Brower (unreported)

Index

About the Author

Mark C. Dillon is an associate justice in the Appellate Division of the New York State Supreme Court, an Adjunct Professor of Law at Fordham University School of Law in New York City, an annual contributing author to McKinney's New York CPLR Practice Commentaries, and holds a special interest in legal history. He lives with family outside New York City, not far from the John Jay Homestead State Historic Site.

www.ingramcontent.com/pod-product-compliance
Lightning Source LLC
LaVergne TN
LVHW040200080826
844660LV00001B/50

* 9 7 8 1 4 3 8 4 8 7 8 5 4 *